Fourth Workshop on Speech and Language Processing for Assistive Technologies

(SLPAT 2013)

Grenoble, France
21-22 August 2013

ISBN: 978-1-62993-540-9

Printed from e-media with permission by:

Curran Associates, Inc.
57 Morehouse Lane
Red Hook, NY 12571

Some format issues inherent in the e-media version may also appear in this print version.

Printed by Curran Associates, Inc. (2014)

Association for Computational Linguistics
209 N. Eighth Street
Stroudsburg, Pennsylvania 18360

Phone: 1-570-476-8006
Fax: 1-570-476-0860

acl@aclweb.org

Additional copies of this publication are available from:

Curran Associates, Inc.
57 Morehouse Lane
Red Hook, NY 12571 USA
Phone: 845-758-0400
Fax: 845-758-2634
Email: curran@proceedings.com
Web: www.proceedings.com

Introduction

We are pleased to bring you the Proceedings of the Fourth Workshop on Speech and Language Processing for Assistive Technologies (SLPAT), held in Grenoble, France on the 21st and 22nd of August, 2013. We received 23 paper submissions, of which 12 were chosen for oral presentation and another 5 for poster presentation. In addition, two demo proposals were accepted. All 19 papers are included in this volume.

This workshop was intended to bring researchers from all areas of speech and language technology with a common interest in making everyday life more accessible for people with physical, cognitive, sensory, emotional or developmental disabilities. This workshop builds on three previous such workshops (co-located with NAACL HLT 2010, EMNLP in 2011, and NAACL HLT 2012) and includes a special topic, "Speech Interaction Technology for Ambient Assisted Living in the Home", which is a follow-up of two events (ILADI 2012 co-located with JEP-TALN-RECITAL 2012 and a special session in EUSIPCO 2012). The workshop provides an opportunity for individuals from research communities, and the individuals with whom they are working, to share research findings, and to discuss present and future challenges and the potential for collaboration and progress.

While Augmentative and Alternative Communication (AAC) is a particularly apt application area for speech and Natural Language Processing (NLP) technologies, we purposefully made the scope of the workshop broad enough to include assistive technologies (AT) as a whole, even those falling outside of AAC. While we encouraged work that validates methods with human experimental trials, we also accepted work on basic-level innovations and philosophy, inspired by AT/AAC related problems. Thus we have aimed at broad inclusivity, which is also manifest in the diversity of our Program Committee.

We are very delighted to have Prof. Mark Hawley from the University of Sheffield as invited speaker. In addition we continue our tradition of a panel of AAC users, who will speak on their experiences and perspectives as users of AAC technology. Finally, this year we also have a tour of the DOMUS "smart home" of the Laboratoire d'Informatique de Grenoble. Because of the many submissions and program points, we have for the first time extended the workshop to two full days.

We would like to thank all the people and institutions who contributed to the success of the SLPAT 2013 workshop: the authors, the members of the program committee, the member of the organising committee and the invited speaker Mark Hawley. Finally, we would like to thank the Universities of Grenoble for sponsoring and hosting the workshop in the Laboratoire d'Informatique de Grenoble premises.

Jan Alexandersson, Peter Ljunglöf, Kathleen F. McCoy, François Portet, Brian Roark, Frank Rudzicz and Michel Vacher

Co-organizers of SLPAT 2013

Organizing committee:

Jan Alexandersson, DFKI GmbH, Germany
Peter Ljunglöf, University of Gothenburg, Sweden
Kathleen F. McCoy, University of Delaware, USA
François Portet, Grenoble Institute of Technology/LIG, France
Brian Roark, Oregon Health & Science University, USA
Frank Rudzicz, Toronto Rehabilitation Institute and the University of Toronto, Canada
Michel Vacher, CNRS/LIG, France

Program committee:

Jean-Yves Antoine, Université François-Rabelais, France
John Arnott, University of Dundee, UK
Véronique Aubergé, CNRS/Laboratoire d'Informatique de Grenoble, France
Melanie Baljko, York University, Canada
Jan Bedrosian, Western Michigan University, USA
Yacine Bellik, Université Paris-Sud/LIMSI, France
Rolf Black, University of Dundee, UK
Jerome Boudy, Télécom SudParis, France
Annelies Braffort, CNRS/LIMSI, France
Torbjørg Breivik, Language Council of Norway
Corneliu Burileanu, University Politehnica of Bucharest, Romania
Heidi Christensen, University of Sheffield, UK
Ann Copestake, University of Cambridge, UK
Stuart Cunningham, University of Sheffield, UK
Rickard Domeij, Swedish Language Council, Sweden
Alistair Edwards, University of York, UK
Michael Elhadad, Ben-Gurion University, Israel
Alain Franco, Nice University Hospital, France
Corinne Fredouille, Université d'Avignon/LIA, France
Björn Granström, Royal Institute of Technology, Sweden
Phil Green, University of Sheffield, UK
Mark Hasegawa-Johnson, University of Illinois, USA
Jean-Paul Haton, Université Henri Poincaré/LORIA, France
Per-Olof Hedvall, Lund University, Sweden
Javier Hernando, Technical University of Catalonia, Spain
Linda Hoag, Kansas State University, USA
Matt Huenerfauth, CUNY, New York, USA
Dan Istrate, ESIGETEL, France
Sofie Johansson Kokkinakis, University of Gothenburg, Sweden
Simon Judge, Barnsley NHS & Sheffield University, UK
Per Ola Kristensson, University of St. Andrews, UK
Benjamin Lecouteux, Université Pierre Mendès-France/LIG, France
Greg Lesher, Dynavox Technologies Inc., USA

Eduardo Lleida, University of Zaragoza, Spain
Ornella Mich, Fondazione Bruno Kessler, Italy
Climent Nadeu, Technical University of Catalonia, Spain
Yael Netzer, Ben-Gurion University, Israel
Torbjørn Nordgård, Lingit A/S, Norway
Rupal Patel, Northeastern University, USA
Ehud Reiter, University of Aberdeen, UK
Bitte Rydeman, Lund University, Sweden
Horacio Saggion, Universitat Pompeu Fabra, Spain
Fraser Shein, Quillsoft Ltd., Toronto, Canada
Kumiko Tanaka-Ishii, Kyushu University, Japan
Nava Tintarev, University of Aberdeen, UK
Keith Vertanen, Montana Tech of The University of Montana, USA
Nadine Vigouroux, Université Paul Sabatier/IRIT, France
Ravichander Vipperla, Nuance Communications Ltd., UK
Tonio Wandmacher, SYSTRAN, Paris, France
Jan-Oliver Wülfing, Fraunhofer Centre Birlinghoven, Germany
Virginie Zampa, Université Stendhal – Grenoble 3/LIDILEM, France

Table of Contents

Workshop Program

Wednesday, 21 August, 2013

09:00–09:45 Registration

09:45–10:00 Opening ceremony

10:00–11:00 Invited talk by Mark Hawley

SLPAT in practice: lessons from translational research

11:00–11:30 Coffee break

11:30–12:30 Regular paper session

Towards Personalised Synthesised Voices for Individuals with Vocal Disabilities Voice Banking and Reconstruction

Improving Continuous Sign Language Recognition: Speech Recognition Techniques and System Design

12:30–14:00 Lunch break

14:00–15:00 Invited user panel

15:00–16:30 Poster and demo session, with coffee

The dramatic piece reader for the blind and visually impaired

Individuality-Preserving Voice Conversion for Articulation Disorders Using Locality-Constrained NMF

Sub-lexical Dialogue Act Classification in a Spoken Dialogue System Support for the Elderly with Cognitive Disabilities

Automatic Speech Recognition: A Shifted Role in Early Speech Intervention?

homeService Voice-enabled assistive technology in the home using cloud-based automatic speech recognition

Making Speech-Based Assistive Technology Work for a Real User

Visual Subtitles for Internet Videos

16:30–17:30 Regular paper session

Robust Feature Extraction to Utterance Fluctuation of Articulation Disorders Based on Random Projection

Comparing and combining classifiers for self-taught vocal interfaces

17:30–18:00 SIG-SLPAT business meeting

Thursday, 22 August, 2013

09:00–11:00	Special topic session: Ambient Assisted Living
	Experimental Evaluation of Speech Recognition Technologies for Voice-based Home Automation Control in a Smart Home
	Automatic Monitoring of Activities of Daily Living based on Real-life Acoustic Sensor Data a preliminary study
	Probabilistic Dialogue Modeling for Speech-Enabled Assistive Technology
	Analyzing the Performance of Automatic Speech Recognition for Ageing Voice Does it Correlate with Dependency Level?
11:00–11:30	Coffee break
11:30–12:30	Regular paper session
	Automating Speech Reception Threshold Measurements using Automatic Speech Recognition
	Automatic Speech Recognition in the Diagnosis of Primary Progressive Aphasia
12:30–14:00	Lunch break
14:00–15:00	Regular paper session
	A Self Learning Vocal Interface for Speech-impaired Users
	Word Recognition from Continuous Articulatory Movement Time-series Data using Symbolic Representations
15:00–15:30	Coffee break and closing ceremony
15:30–17:30	Smart home tour: "DOMUS" – The Smart Home of the Laboratoire d'Informatique de Grenoble
19:30–22:00	Joint gala dinner together with the co-located WASSS workshop at the restaurant "Le Téléférique"

SLPAT in practice: lessons from translational research

Mark Hawley

School of Health and Related Research, University of Sheffield, UK

mark.hawley@sheffield.ac.uk

Abstract

The talk will distil experience and results from several projects, over more than a decade, which have researched and developed the application of speech recognition as an input modality for assistive technology (AT). Current interfaces to AT for people with severe physical disabilities, such as switch-scanning, can be prohibitively slow and tiring to use. Many people with severe physical disabilities also have some speech, though many also have poor control of speech articulators, leading to dysarthria. Nonetheless, recognition of dysarthric speech can give people more control options than using body movement alone. Speech can therefore be an attractive option for AT input.

Techniques that have been developed for optimising the recognition of dysarthric speech will be described, resulting in recognition rates of greater than 80% for people with even the most severe dysarthria. Speech recognition has been applied as a means of controlling the home (via an environmental control system) and, probably for the first time, as a means of controlling a communication aid. The development of the Voice Input Voice Output Communication Aid (VICOCA) will be described and some early results of its evaluation presented.

The talk will discuss some of the lessons learnt from these projects, such as:

- The need to work in interdisciplinary teams including speech technologists, speech and language therapists, health researchers and assistive technologists.
- The value of user-centred design, involving users in defining their wants and needs and then working with them, in an iterative manner, to refine the AT such that it becomes usable and acceptable.
- The gap that exists between the results that can be achieved in the lab and those achievable in peoples homes under real usage conditions – something that is not often covered in research papers.
- The practical approaches that can be applied to optimising recognition for individuals. It is often possible to make significant improvements in recognition rates by altering the configuration of the AT set-up.

The talk will conclude by describing some of the future potential applications of speech technology that are being developed, or considered, for people with disabilities as well as for frail older people and people with long-term conditions.

Individuality-Preserving Voice Conversion for Articulation Disorders Using Locality-Constrained NMF

Ryo AIHARA, Tetsuya TAKIGUCHI, Yasuo ARIKI

Graduate School of System Informatics, Kobe University, Japan

aihara@me.cs.scitec.kobe-u.ac.jp
takigu@kobe-u.ac.jp, ariki@kobe-u.ac.jp

Abstract

We present in this paper a voice conversion (VC) method for a person with an articulation disorder resulting from athetoid cerebral palsy. The movements of such speakers are limited by their athetoid symptoms, and their consonants are often unstable or unclear, which makes it difficult for them to communicate. In this paper, exemplar-based spectral conversion using Non-negative Matrix Factorization (NMF) is applied to a voice with an articulation disorder. In order to preserve the speaker's individuality, we use a combined dictionary that was constructed from the source speaker's vowels and target speaker's consonants. Also, in order to avoid an unclear converted voice, which is constructed using the combined dictionary, we used locality-constrained NMF. The effectiveness of this method was confirmed by comparing its effectiveness with that of a conventional Gaussian Mixture Model (GMM)-based method.

Index Terms: Voice Conversion, NMF, Articulation Disorders, Assistive Technologies

1. Introduction

In this study, we propose assistive technology for people with speech impediments. There are 34,000 people with speech impediments associated with an articulation disorder in Japan alone. Articulation disorders are classified into three types. Functional articulation disorders exist in the absence of any apparent cause and are related to deficiencies in the relatively peripheral motor processes. Organic articulation disorders are articulation problems that are associated with structural abnormalities and known impairments, such as cleft lip and palate, tongue tie, hearing impairment, etc. Motor speech disorders involve problems with strength and control of the speech musculature. We propose a voice conversion system, which converts an articulation-disordered voice into a non-disordered voice, for people with motor speech disorders.

Cerebral palsy is one of the typical causes of motor speech disorders. About two babies in 1,000 are born with cerebral palsy [1]. Cerebral palsy results from damage to the central nervous system, and the damage causes movement disorders. Three general times are given for the onset of the disorder: before birth, at the time of delivery, and after birth. Cerebral palsy is classified into the following types: 1) spastic, 2) athetoid, 3) ataxic, 4) atonic, 5) rigid, and a mixture of these types [2].

In this study, we focused on a person with an articulation disorder resulting from the athetoid type of cerebral palsy. Athetoid symptoms develop in about 10-20% of cerebral palsy sufferers [1]. In the case of a person with this type of articulation disorder, his/her movements are sometimes more unstable than usual. Because of this symptom, their utterances (especially their consonants) are often unstable or unclear. Most people suffering from athetoid cerebral palsy cannot communicate by sign language, writing or voice synthesizer [3, 4, 5] because athetoid symptoms also restrict the movement of the sufferer's arms and legs. For this reason, there is a great need for a voice conversion (VC) system for such people.

Automatic speech recognition system for people with articulation disorders resulting from athetoid cerebral palsy has been studied. Matsumasa et al. [6] proposed robust feature extraction based on PCA (Principal Component Analysis) with more stable utterance data instead of DCT. Miyamoto et al. [7] used multiple acoustic frames (MAF) as an acoustic dynamic feature to improve the recognition rate of a person with an articulation disorder, especially in speech recognition using dynamic features only. In spite of these efforts, the recognition rate for articulation disorders is still lower than that of physically unimpaired persons. The recognition rate for people with articulation disorders using a speaker-independent model trained by non-disordered speech is 3.5%. This result implies that the speech of a person with an articulation disorder is difficult to understand for people who have not communicated with them before.

A GMM-based approach is widely used for VC because of its flexibility and good performance [8]. This approach has been applied to various tasks, such as speaker conversion [9], emotion conversion [10, 11], and so on. In the field of assistive technology, Nakamura et al. [12] proposed a GMM-based speaking aid system for electrolaryngeal speech. In this approach, the conversion function is interpreted as the expectation value of the target spectral envelope. The conversion parameters are evaluated using Minimum Mean-Square Error (MMSE) using a parallel training set. If the person with an articulation disorder is set as a source speaker and a physically unimpaired person is set as a target speaker, an articulation-disordered voice may be converted into a non-disordered voice. However, because the GMM-based approach has been developed mainly for speaker conversion [9], the source speaker's voice individuality is also converted into the target speaker's individuality.

In this paper, we propose a VC method for articulation disorders. There are two main benefits to our VC method. 1) We convert the speaker's voice into a non-disordered voice, thus preserving their voice individuality. People with articulation disorders wish to communicate by their own voice if they can therefore, this is important for VC as assistive technology. 2) Our method outputs a natural-sounding voice. Because our VC is exemplar-based and there is no statistical model, we can create a natural sounding voice.

In the research discussed in this paper, we conducted VC for articulation disorders using Non-negative Matrix Factorization (NMF) [13]. NMF is a well-known approach for source separation and speech enhancement. In these approaches, the observed signal is represented by a linear combination of a small number of elementary vectors, referred to as the basis, and its weights. In some approaches for source separation, the bases are grouped for each source, and the mixed signals are expressed with a sparse representation of these bases. Gemmeke et al. proposes an exemplar-based method for noise robust speech recognition [14].

In our study, we adopt the supervised NMF approach [15], with a focus on VC from poorly articulated speech resulting from articulation disorders into non-disordered articulation. The parallel exemplars (called the 'dictionary' in this paper), which consist of articulation-disordered exemplars and a non-disordered exemplars, are extracted from the parallel data. An input spectrum with an articulation disorder is represented by a linear combination of articulation-disordered exemplars using NMF. By replacing an articulation-disordered basis with a non-disordered basis, the original speech spectrum is replaced with a non-disordered spectrum.

In the voice of a person with an articulation disorder, their consonants are often unstable and that makes their voices unclear. Their vowels are relatively-stable compared to their consonants. Hence, by replacing the articulation-disordered basis of consonants only, a voice with an articulation disorder is converted into a non-disordered voice that preserves the individuality of the speaker's voice. In order to avoid a mixture of the source and target spectra in a converted phoneme which is constructed using the combined dictionary, we adopted locality-constraint to the supervised NMF.

The rest of this paper is organized as follows: In Section 2, NMF-based VC is described, the experimental data is evaluated in Section 3, and the final section is devoted to our conclusions.

2. Voice Conversion Based on NMF

2.1. Basic Approach of Exemplar-Based Voice Conversion

In the exemplar-based approach, the observed signal is represented by a linear combination of a small number of bases.

$$\mathbf{x}_l \approx \sum_{j=1}^{J} \mathbf{a}_j h_{j,l} = \mathbf{A}\mathbf{h}_l \tag{1}$$

$\mathbf{x}_l$ is the l-th frame of the observation. $\mathbf{a}_j$ and $h_{j,l}$ are the j-th basis and the weight, respectively. $\mathbf{A} = [\mathbf{a}_1 \dots \mathbf{a}_J]$ and $\mathbf{h}_l = [h_{1,l} \dots h_{J,l}]^T$ are the collection of the bases and the stack of weights. When the weight vector $\mathbf{h}_l$ is sparse, the observed signal can be represented by a linear combination of a small number of bases that have non-zero weights. In this paper, each basis denotes the exemplar of the spectrum, and the collection of exemplar $\mathbf{A}$ and the weight vector $\mathbf{h}_l$ are called 'dictionary' and 'activity', respectively.

Fig. 1 shows the basic approach of our exemplar-based VC using NMF. D, d, L, and J represent the number of dimensions of source features, dimensions of target features, frames of the dictionary, and basis of the dictionary, respectively. Our VC method needs two dictionaries that are phonemically parallel. One dictionary is a source dictionary, which is constructed from source features. Source features are constructed from an articulation-disordered spectrum and its segment features. The other dictionary is a target dictionary, which is constructed from target features. Target features are mainly constructed from a well-ordered spectrum. These two dictionaries consist of the same words and are aligned with dynamic time warping (DTW). Hence, these dictionaries have the same number of bases.

Input source features X^s, which consist of an articulation-disordered spectrum and its segment features, are decomposed into a linear combination of bases from the source dictionary A^s by NMF. The weights of the bases are estimated as an activity H^s. Therefore, the activity includes the weight information of input features for each basis. Then, the activity is multiplied by a target dictionary in order to obtain converted spectral features $\hat{X}^t$ which are represented by a linear combination of bases from the target dictionary. Because the source and target dictionary are parallel phonemically, the bases used in the converted features is phonemically the same as that of the source features.

Fig. 2 shows an example of the activity matrices estimated from a word "ikioi" ("vigor" in English). One is uttered by a person with an articulation disorder, and the other is uttered by a physically unimpaired person. To show an intelligible example, each dictionary was structured from just the one word "ikioi" and aligned with DTW. As shown in Fig. 2, these activities have high energies at similar elements. For this reason, when there are parallel dictionaries, the activity of the source features estimated with the source dictionary may be able to be substituted with that of the target features. Therefore, the target speech can be constructed using the target dictionary and the activity of the source signal as shown in Fig. 1.

Spectral envelopes extracted by STRAIGHT analysis [16] are used in the source and target features. The other features extracted by STRAIGHT analysis, such as F0 and the aperiodic components, are used to synthesize the converted signal without any conversion.

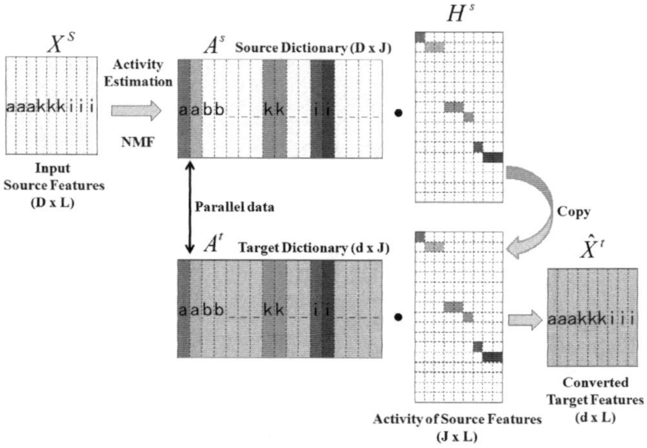

Figure 1: Basic approach of NMF-based voice conversion

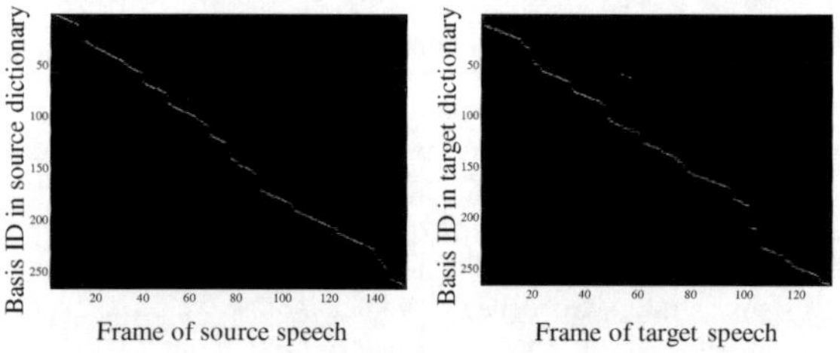

Figure 2: Activity matrices for the articulation-disordered utterance (left) and well-ordered utterance (right)

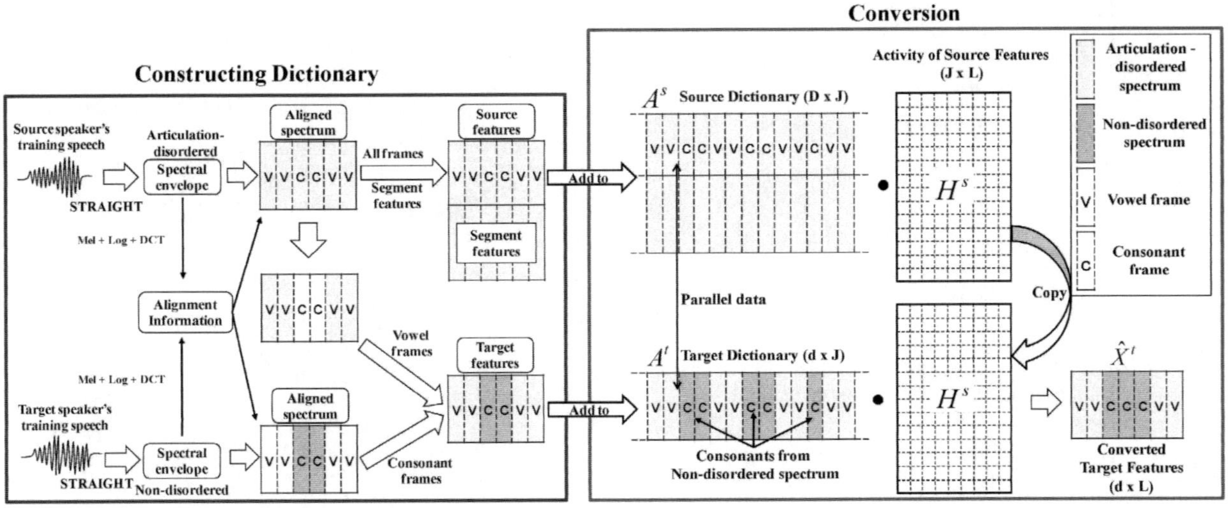

Figure 3: Individuality-preserving voice conversion

2.2. Constructing Dictionary to Preserve Individuality

In order to make a parallel dictionary, some pairs of parallel utterances are needed, where each pair consists of the same text. One is spoken by a person with an articulation disorder (source speaker), and the other is spoken by a physically unimpaired person (target speaker). The left side of Fig. 3 shows the process for constructing a parallel dictionary. STRAIGHT spectrum is extracted from parallel utterances. The extracted STRAIGHT spectra are phonemically aligned with DTW. The Mel-cepstral coefficient, which is converted from the STRAIGHT spectrum, is used to align. In order to estimate the activities of the source features precisely, segment features of source features, which consist of some consecutive frames, are constructed. Target features are constructed from consonant frames of the target's aligned spectrum and vowel frames of the source's aligned spectrum. Source and target dictionaries are constructed by lining up each of the features extracted from parallel utterances.

The right side of Fig. 3 shows how to preserve a source speaker's voice individuality in our VC method. Fig. 4 shows examples of the spectrogram for the word "ikioi" ("vigor" in English) of a person with an articulation disorder and a physically unimpaired person. The vowels of a person's voice strongly imply a speaker's individuality. On the other hand, the consonants of people with articulation disorders are often unstable. In Fig. 4, the area labeled "k" in the articulation-disordered spectrum is not clear, compared to that of the same region spoken by a physically unimpaired person. Therefore, by combining the source speaker's vowels and target speaker's consonants in the target dictionary, the individuality of the source speaker's voice can be preserved.

2.3. Estimation of Activity with Locality Constraint

In the NMF-based approach, the spectrum source signal at frame l is approximately expressed by a non-negative linear combination of the source dictionary and the activities.

$$\mathbf{x}_l = \mathbf{x}_l^s \approx \sum_{j=1}^{J} \mathbf{a}_j^s h_{j,l}^s \tag{2}$$

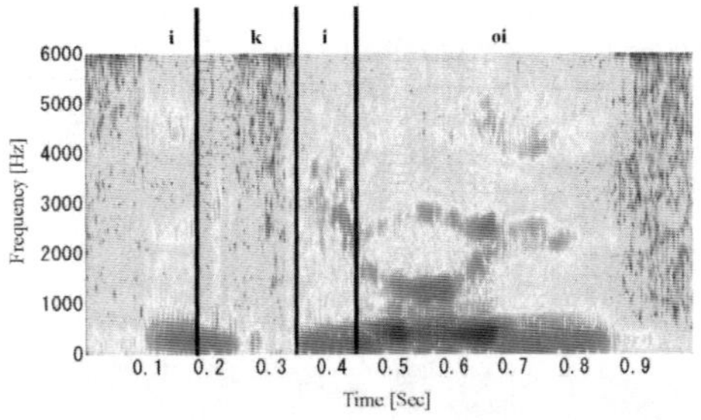

(a) Spoken by a person with an articulation disorder

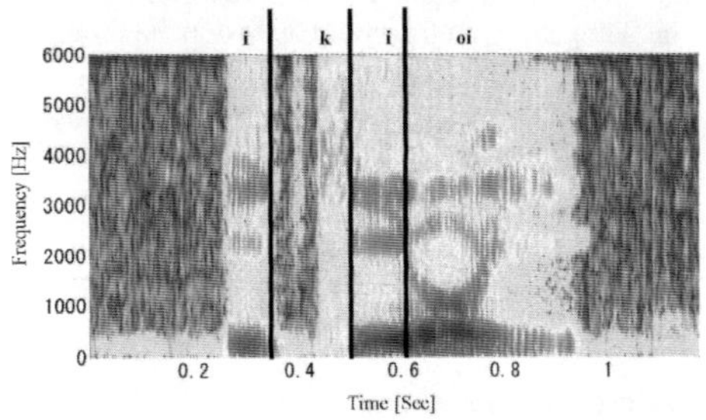

(b) Spoken by a physically unimpaired person

Figure 4: Examples of source and target spectrogram //i k i oi

$\mathbf{x}_l^s \in \mathbf{X}^s$ is the magnitude spectrum of the source signal.

Instead of using all bases, locality constraint is introduced.

$$\mathbf{\Delta}_{j,l} = \sqrt{(x_l^s - a_j^s)^2} \tag{3}$$

$\mathbf{\Delta}_l$ is a distance vector between $\mathbf{x}_l^s$ and $\mathbf{a}^s$. N nearest bases are chosen from all the bases.

$$\begin{aligned} \mathbf{S}_l^s &= \mathbf{nbest}_{\mathbf{\Delta}_l}(\mathbf{a}_1, \mathbf{a}_2, \ldots, \mathbf{a}_J) \\ &= \mathbf{nbest}_{\mathbf{\Delta}_l}(\mathbf{A}) \end{aligned} \tag{4}$$

$\mathbf{S}_l^s$ is a set of nearest bases of $\mathbf{x}_l^s$. The number of basis is defined by N. Eq. (2) can be written as follows:

$$\begin{aligned} \mathbf{x}_l &= \mathbf{x}_l^s \\ &\approx \sum_{j=1}^{N} \mathbf{s}_{l,j}^s h_{j,l}^s \\ &= \mathbf{S}_l \mathbf{h}_l \quad s.t. \quad \mathbf{h}_l \geq 0 \end{aligned} \tag{5}$$

$$\mathbf{X}^s \approx \mathbf{S}^s \mathbf{H}^s \quad s.t. \quad \mathbf{H}^s \geq 0 \tag{6}$$

The joint matrix $\mathbf{H}^s$ is estimated based on NMF with the sparse constraint that minimizes the following cost function.

$$d(\mathbf{X}^s, \mathbf{S}^s\mathbf{H}^s) + ||(\lambda \mathbf{1}^{1\times L}).*\mathbf{H}^s||_1 \quad s.t. \quad \mathbf{H}^s \geq 0 \tag{7}$$

$\mathbf{1}$ is an all-one matrix. The first term is the Kullback-Leibler (KL) divergence between $\mathbf{X}^s$ and $\mathbf{S}^s\mathbf{H}^s$. The second term is the sparse constraint with the L1-norm regularization term that causes $\mathbf{H}^s$ to be sparse. The weights of the sparsity constraints can be defined for each exemplar by defining $\lambda^T = [\lambda_1 \dots \lambda_J]$. In this paper, all elements in λ were set to 1. $\mathbf{H}^s$ minimizing Eq. (7) is estimated iteratively applying the following update rule [13]:

$$\begin{aligned} \mathbf{H}_{n+1}^s &= \mathbf{H}_n^s.*(\mathbf{S}^{sT}(\mathbf{X}^s./(\mathbf{S}^s\mathbf{H}_n^s))) \\ &\quad ./(\mathbf{S}^{sT}\mathbf{1}^{D\times L} + \lambda \mathbf{1}^{1\times L}) \end{aligned} \tag{8}$$

with $.*$ and $./$ denoting element-wise multiplication and division, respectively. To increase the sparseness of $\mathbf{H}^s$, elements of $\mathbf{H}^s$, which are less than threshold, are rounded to zero.

By using the activity and the set of target basis which is parallel to $\mathbf{S}^s$, the converted spectral features are constructed.

$$\hat{\mathbf{X}}^t = (\mathbf{S}^t\mathbf{H}^s) \tag{9}$$

3. Experimental Results

3.1. Experimental Conditions

The proposed method was evaluated on word-based VC for one person with an articulation disorder. We recorded 432 utterances (216 words, repeating each two times) included in the ATR Japanese speech database [17]. The speech signals were sampled at 12 kHz and windowed with a 25-msec Hamming window every 10 msec. A physically unimpaired Japanese male in the ATR Japanese speech database was chosen as a target speaker. Two hundred sixteen utterances were used for training, and the other 216 utterances were used for the test. The numbers of dimensions of source and target features are, 2,565 and 513. The number of bases of source and target dictionary is 64,467. We chose 10,000 nearest bases from dictionary by locality constraint.

We compared our NMF-based VC to conventional GMM-based VC. In GMM-based VC, the 1st through 24th cepstrum coefficients extracted by STRAIGHT were used as source and target features.

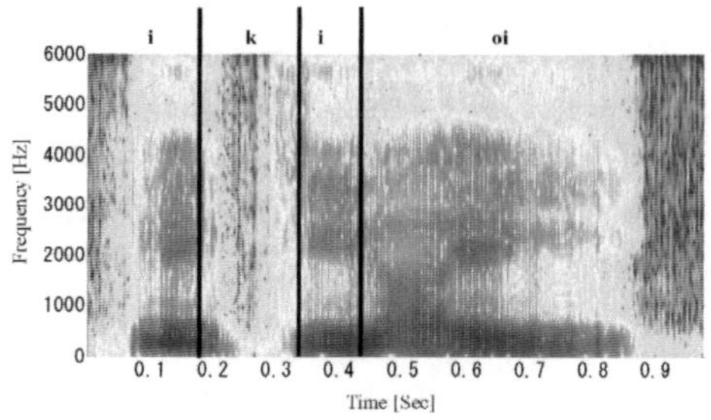

(a) Converted by GMM-based VC

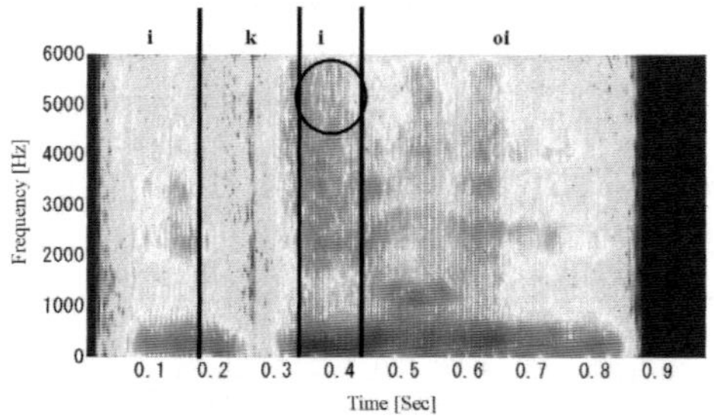

(b) Converted by NMF-based VC without locality

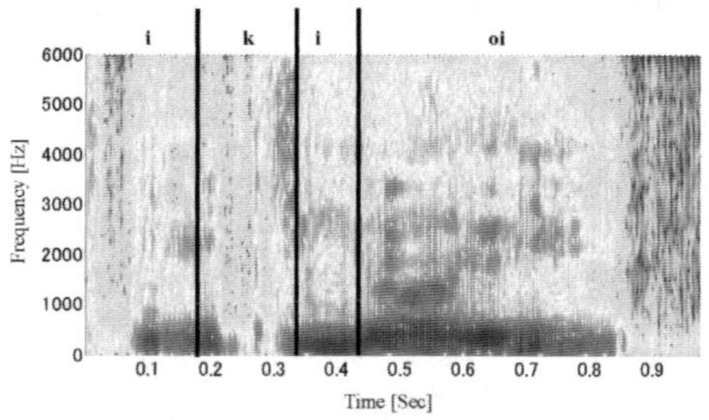

(c) Converted by NMF-based VC with 100 nearest bases

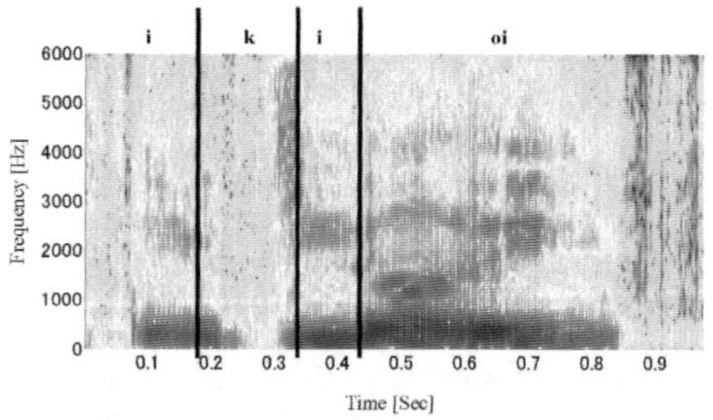

(d) Converted by NMF-based VC with 1,000 nearest bases

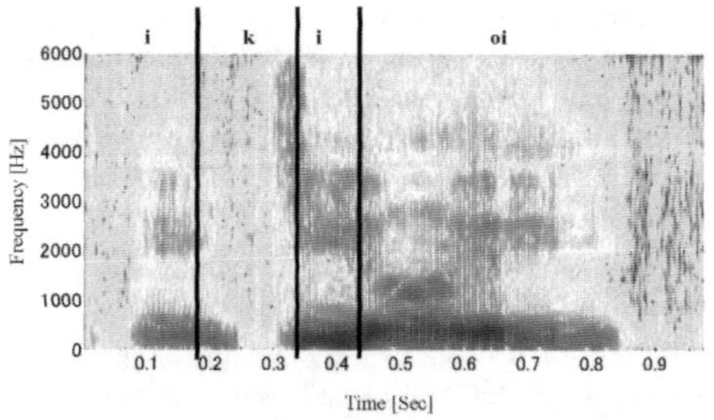

(e) Converted by NMF-based VC with 10,000 nearest bases

Figure 5: Examples of converted spectrograms for "i k i oi"

3.2. Subjective Evaluation

We conducted subjective evaluation on 3 topics. A total of 10 Japanese speakers took part in the test using headphones. For the "listening intelligibility" evaluation, we performed a MOS (Mean Opinion Score) test [18]. The opinion score was set to a 5-point scale (5: excellent, 4: good, 3: fair, 2: poor, 1: bad). Thirty-eight words, which are difficult for a person with an articulation disorder to utter, were evaluated. The subjects were asked about the listening intelligibility in the articulation-disordered voice, the NMF-based converted voice, and the GMM-based converted voice. Each voice uttered by a physically unimpaired person was presented as a reference of 5 points on the MOS test.

Fifty words were converted using NMF-based VC and GMM-based VC for the following evaluations. On the "similarity" evaluation, the XAB test was carried out. In the XAB test, each subject listened to the articulation disordered voice. Then the subject listened to the voice converted by the two methods and selected which sample sounded most similar to the articulation disordered voice. On the "naturalness" evaluation, a paired comparison test was carried out, where each subject listened to pairs of speech converted by the two methods and selected which sample sounded more natural.

3.3. Results and Discussion

Fig. 5 shows examples of converted spectrograms. Using GMM-based conversion, the area labeled "oi" becomes unclear compared to NMF-based conversion. This might be because unexpected mapping during the GMM-based VC degraded the conversion performance. Because NMF-based VC converts consonants only, the same area is relatively clear and similar to the labeled "oi" area in Fig. 4(a). In the spectrogram converted by NMF-based VC without locality, there are some misconversions in the black circled area. This is because there is some mixing of the vowel and consonant spectra. By using local constrained NMF, such misconversions are eliminated. Also, in comparison between (d) and (e) in Fig. 5, the converted voice using 10,000 nearest bases is more clear than that using 1,000 nearest bases, especially the areas labeled "i" and "oi". For this reason, locality-constraint is useful to the combined dictionary, however, using too few bases degrades conversion performance.

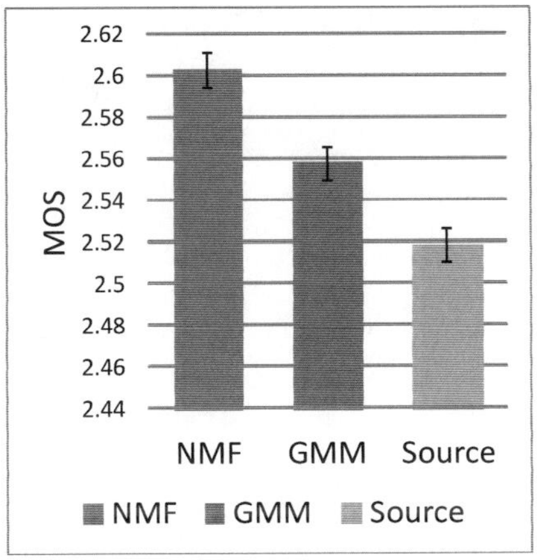

Figure 6: Results of MOS test on listening intelligibility

Fig. 6 shows the results of the MOS test for listening intelli-

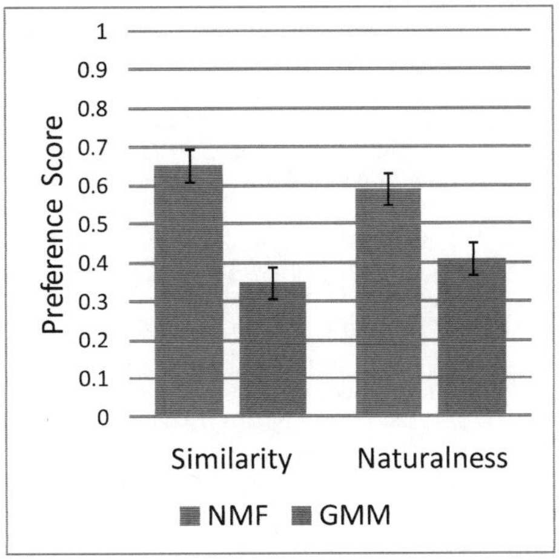

Figure 7: Preference scores for the similarity to the source speaker and naturalness

gibility. The error bars show a 95% confidence score. As shown in Fig. 6, NMF-based VC and GMM-based VC can improve listening intelligibility. NMF-based VC obtained a higher score than GMM-based VC. This is because GMM-based VC creates conversion noise. NMF-based VC also creates some conversion noise, but it is less than that created by GMM-based VC.

Fig. 7 shows the preference score on the similarity to the source speaker and naturalness of the converted voice. The error bars show a 95% confidence score. NMF-based VC got a higher score than GMM-based conversion on similarity because NMF-based conversion used a combined dictionary. NMF-based VC also got a higher score than GMM-based conversion on naturalness.

4. Conclusions

We proposed a spectral conversion method based on NMF for a voice with an articulation disorder. Experimental results demonstrated that our VC method can improve the listening intelligibility of words uttered by a person with an articulation disorder. Moreover, compared to conventional GMM-based VC, NMF-based VC can preserve the individuality of the source speaker's voice and the naturalness of the voice. In this study, there was only one subject person, so in future experiments, we will increase the number of subjects and further examine the effectiveness of our method.

5. References

[1] M. V. Hollegaard, K. Skogstrand, P. Thorsen, B. Norgaard-Pedersen, D. M. Hougaard, and J. Grove, "Joint analysis of SNPs and proteins identifies regulatory IL18 gene variations decreasing the chance of spastic cerebral palsy," *Human Mutation, Vol. 34, pp. 143-148*, 2013.

[2] S. T. Canale and W. C. Campbell, "Campbell's operative orthopaedics," Mosby-Year Book, Tech. Rep., 2002.

[3] C. Veaux, J. Yamagishi, and S. King, "Using HMM-based speech synthesis to reconstruct the voice of individuals with degenerative speech disorders," *Proc. Interspeech*, 2012.

[4] A. Kain and M. Macon, "Personalizing a speech synthesizer by voice adaption," *Proceedings of the Third ESCA/COCOSDA International Speech Synthesis Workshop, pp.225-230.*, 1998.

[5] C. Jreige, R. Patel, and H. T. Bunnell, "VocaliD: Personalizing text-to-speech synthesis for individuals," *in Proceedings of ASSETS'09, pp.259-260*, 2009.

[6] H. Matsumasa, T. Takiguchi, Y. Ariki, I. Li, and T. Nakabayashi, "Integration of metamodel and acoustic model for dysarthric speech recognition," *Journal of Multimedia, Volume 4, Issue 4, pp. 254-261*, 2009.

[7] C. Miyamoto, Y. Komai, T. Takiguchi, Y. Ariki, and I. Li, "Multimodal speech recognition of a person with articulation disorders using AAM and MAF," *IEEE International Workshop on Multimedia Signal Processing (MMSP'10), pp. 517-520*, 2010.

[8] Y. Stylianou, O. Cappe, and E. Moilines, "Continuous probabilistic transform for voice conversion," *IEEE Trans. Speech and Audio Processing, Vol. 6, No. 2, pp. 131-142*, 1998.

[9] T. Toda, A. Black, and K. Tokuda, "Voice conversion based on maximum likelihood estimation of spectral parameter trajectory," *IEEE Trans. Audio, Speech, Lang. Process., Vol. 15, No. 8, pp. 2222-2235*, 2007.

[10] Y. Iwami, T. Toda, H. Saruwatari, and K. Shikano, "GMM-based voice conversion applied to emotional speech synthesis," *IEEE Trans. Seech and Audio Proc., Vol. 7, pp. 2401-2404*, 1999.

[11] R. Aihara, R. Takashima, T. Takiguchi, and Y. Ariki, "GMM-based emotional voice conversion using spectrum and prosody features," *American Journal of Signal Processing, Vol. 2 No. 5*, 2012.

[12] K. Nakamura, T. Toda, H. Saruwatari, and K. Shikano, "Speaking-aid systems using GMM-based voice conversion for electrolaryngeal speech," *Speech Communication, Vol. 54, No. 1, pp. 134-146*, 2012.

[13] D. D. Lee and H. S. Seung, "Algorithms for non-negative matrix factorization," *in Proc. Neural Information Processing System, pp. 556-562*, 2001.

[14] J. F. Gemmeke and T. Virtanen, "Noise robust exemplar-based connected digit recognition," *ICASSP, pp. 4546-4549*, 2010.

[15] M. N. Schmidt and R. K. Olsson, "Single-channel speech separation using sparse non-negative matrix factorization," *INTERSPEECH*, 2006.

[16] H. Kawahara, I. Masuda-Katsuse, and A. Cheveigne, "Restructuring speech representations using a pitch-adaptive time-frequency smoothing and an instantaneous-frequencybased F0 extraction: possible role of a repetitive structure in sounds," *Speech Communication, Vol. 27, No. 3-4*, 1999.

[17] A. Kurematsu, K. Takeda, Y. Sagisaka, S. Katagiri, H. Kuwabara, and K. Shikano, "ATR japanese speech database as a tool of speech recognition and synthesis," *Speech Communication, Vol. 9, pp. 357-363*, 1990.

[18] INTERNATIONAL TELECOMMUNICATION UNION, "Methods for objective and subjective assessment of quality," *ITU-T Recommendation P.800*, 2003.

Analysing the Performance of Automatic Speech Recognition for Ageing Voice: Does it Correlate with Dependency Level?

Frédéric Aman, Michel Vacher, Solange Rossato and François Portet

LIG, UMR5217 UJF/CNRS/Grenoble-INP/UPMF, 38041 Grenoble, France

{frederic.Aman, Michel.Vacher, Solange.Rossato, Francois.Portet}@imag.fr

Abstract

Ambient Assisted Living aims at providing assistance by allowing people with special needs to perform tasks which they have increasing difficulty with and to provide reassurance through surveillance in order to detect distress and accidental falls. Aged people are among the ones who might benefit from advances in ICT to live as long as possible in their own home. Voice-base smart home is a promising way to provide AAL, but even mature technologies must be evaluated from the perspective of its potential beneficiaries. In this paper, we investigate which characteristics of the ageing voice that challenge a state of the art ASR system. Though in the literature, chronological age is retained as the sole factor predicting decrease in performance, we show that degree of loss of autonomy is even more correlated to ASR performance.

Index Terms: Ambient Assisted Living (AAL), Dependency, Elderly speech, Voice command

1. INTRODUCTION

With advances in medicine, life expectancy has increased. However, this phenomenon coupled with a low birthrate has led to an ageing population in industrialised countries. To help elderly people to live as long as possible in their home, solutions have been developed based on robotics, automation, cognitive science, and computer networks. These solutions are being developed to compensate their possible physical or mental decline to keep them with a good degree of autonomy. The aim is to provide assistance by allowing them to perform tasks which they have increasing difficulty with and to provide reassurance through surveillance in order to detect distress and accidental falls. Such a system must allow independence of elderly while facilitating social contact, with a major impact on well-being and health. In addition, it helps caregivers and reassure relatives. However, technological solutions must be able to adapt to the needs and the specific capacities of this population. Indeed, elderly are often confused by complex interfaces of devices. Therefore, the usual interfaces (remote controls, mice or keyboards) must be complemented by more accessible and natural interfaces such as a system of Automatic Speech Recognition (ASR) [1].

In this context, the CIRDO project[1] wherein the authors take part aims to promote autonomy and support of elderly people by caregivers through a social inclusion product. The objective of the project is to integrate an ASR system into this product to perform detection of distress situations, distress calls and voice commands. Such kind of voice based interaction is an emerging feature of many AAL related research projects [2, 3, 4, 5, 6] but this remains a very challenging area due to the atypical nature of the application (distant speech, aged people, noise, uncontrolled area, multi-speaker, etc.) [7].

One of the main challenges in this domain is to make sure that the ASR performance will be good enough to deliver a high quality voice order recognition system. This is a fear of the elderly population who are inclined to switch the system off if it has difficulties in understanding them. Most of the deployed ASR systems have reached a very good recognition rate in close, noise free talking, but their performances were rarely assessed with aged or children voice. A few studies compared ageing voice vs. non-ageing voice on ASR performance [8, 9, 10, 11], but their fields was quite far from our topic of home automation commands recognition. Moreover, an issue for our work was the non-existence of a speech corpus in French containing distress signals and automation commands.

The purpose of this study was to determine the impact of ageing voice on the ASR system performance and to find out which people characteristics might serve to predict ASR performance. The method we used is detailed in Section 3 after having discussed the related work in Section 2. Then the results of the evaluation are presented in Section 4 and an outlook on further work is given Section 5.

2. RELATED WORK

The perception of voice alteration with age has been the subject of many studies [12, 13, 14, 15, 16]. Elderly speakers are characterized by tremors, hesitations, imprecise production of consonants, broken voice, and slower articulation [13]. Regarding women, the changes seem partly due to an increase of the vocal cords mass due to some changing levels of certain hormones [17]. Regarding men, perception of gasp come from an incomplete closure of the vocal cords that would be compensated by an increasing tension in larynx [18]. From the anatomical point of view, some studies have shown age-related degeneration with atrophy of vocal cords, calcification of laryngeal cartilages, and changes in muscles of larynx [19, 20].

Some studies have shown a significant increase in the standard deviation measures of the fundamental frequency of elderly, both men and women [21, 16, 15]. Stability of the fundamental frequency (F0) is reduced in elderly voice [12] and is associated with variability in the peak-to-peak amplitude of speech signal. Hesitations and gasping in pathological voices have been associated with increased noise in the speech signal driven by an aperiodic vibration of the vocal cords [22, 23]. Some measures of the ratio between noise energy and harmonics have quantified this phenomenon by comparing older and younger speakers [21, 24]. Incomplete closure of vocal cords was observed during vocalisation [14]. The study cited above [12] confirms fundamental frequency instabilities and the increasing noise on both sexes for healthy people with an average

[1] http://liris.cnrs.fr/cirdo/

age of 70. These studies show that aged voice presents a much greater variability than typical voice. Ability of state-of-the-art ASR systems to handle this kind of population can thus be questioned.

A more general study of Gorham-Rowan and Laures-Gore [12] highlights the effects of ageing on the speech utterance and the consequences on the speech recognition. The experiments carried out in automatic speech recognition have shown performance degradation for "atypical" population such as children or elderly people [25, 10, 26] and have shown the interests of an adaptation to the target populations [27, 26]. Speech recognition adapted to the voice of elderly people is still an under-explored area. The relevant languages are mainly English [10] and Asian languages such as Japanese [8]. A very interesting study [10] used some recordings of speeches delivered in the Supreme Court of the United States over a decade. These recordings are particularly interesting because they were used to study the evolution of recognition performance on the same person depending on his age over 7-8 years. These studies show that the performance of recognition systems decreases steadily with age, and that a special adaptation to each speaker can get closer to the scores obtained from the youngest speakers without adaptation. The implicit consequence is that the recognition system is adapted to a single speaker. To make the system adapted to the person, Renouard et al. [28] proposed to use the recognized words to adapt online the recognition models. Proposed in the context of home assistance, this research does not appear to have been pursued.

From an applicative point of view in the smart home context, speech recognition has been mainly implemented marginally in the field of voice commands in English. Indeed, most current studies use conventional sensors (presence sensor, door contact, etc.) and tactile interfaces (remote controls, handset, touch-screens) more reliable but less natural, offering fewer opportunities for interaction and comfort (for example: need to walk to reach the remote device). Among the advances in the field of voice controlled devices, a study conducted by Anderson [27] showed that a voice interface which is adapted (models acquired on 300 elderly speakers) allows to make voice requests on computer with the same performance than a query typed at the keyboard. This study has also revealed that only 2 of the 37 participants preferred the keyboard compared to the voice interface. In the same field, Kumiko [29] proposed a computer voice command interface that takes into account the possible sources of error (duration, intensity, vocabulary) to improve performance and feedback. While Interactive Voice Response is a pervasive component of today's telephone communication, some of which take into account the different voice population [30], voice control in smart home is clearly in its infancy. A large number of issues, such as noisy environment, number of sound sources (for example: several people), vocabulary coverage, coverage of speakers, etc. still need to be addressed [7]. Recently, Moir and Filho [31] proposed a low-coverage system using adaptive filters for a good recognition of keywords. But this research remains still exploratory.

To the best of our knowledge, no application of voice control in smart home has explicitly considered the problem of voice recognition of French elderly speakers, even though major advances in terms of ergonomics, safety and data acquisition with high semantic value can be made by this modality. From this short literature review, it can be emphasized that no study had considered French aged voice in smart home condition. Moreover, most studies considered the chronological age as global explanatory factor while many other effects can also be responsible for ASR performance degradation as raised by [11]. There is thus no certainty that age can predict the reliability of a voice-based control system. That is why our study includes an evaluation from the dependence perspective.

3. METHOD

To assess the impact of the ageing voice on ASR performance, we started by acquiring a corpus targeted to the elderly population. From this corpus and a non-aged one, the first task was to identify the most problematic phonemes and to check whether standard adaptation can be employed to reduce the discrepancy between aged and non-aged speakers at phoneme level. Once adapted, the second task was to assess whether measures other than strictly chronological age can explain ASR performance degradation.

3.1. Corpus collection

The corpus collection was performed sporadically from 2009 to 2012 in collaboration with a rehabilitation centre, volunteers and a nursing home. Targeted speakers were persons aged of more than 60 years old, able to read and with no mental disorder or pathologies altering the voice. The recording was done with a single microphone positioned about 30 cm from the speaker's mouth. Most speakers were sat, but some were in a wheelchair or laying in a bed. The recording was done using a computer and a home made software to prompt sentences to be read by the speaker and to record the utterances using voice activity detection. Given the targeted application (in-home voice commands and distress calls) the participants were requested to read a list of short distress/home automation and casual sentences such as *Aidez-moi* (Help me) or *Il fait beau* (It's sunny). Based on [32], who interviewed elderly people in nursing homes to identify and describe what situations of distress they could have experienced, we created a list of home automation orders the person could utter during a distress situation to request for assistance. Ten samples of each kind are given in Table 1.

The non-aged corpus was previously recorded in our laboratory in 2004 and was complemented in 2013 with sentences based on [32]. The procedure was similar to the aged corpus acquisition.

This aged and non-aged corpus is called the AD corpus (Anodin-Détresse: *anodin* means colloquial and *détresse* means distress).

Finally, another aged corpus, the ERES38 corpus (Entretiens RESidences 38: *Entretiens* means interviews) was acquired for model adaptation purpose. This corpus was recorded in 2011 in the living place of the person. During the interviews, we requested each speaker to read a text but they were also asked to talk freely about their life. The text was an article about gardening created by the experimenters in order to target phoneme issues reported in [9, 33].

All the corpora were annotated at the sentence level using the Transcriber software.

3.2. ASR system

The ASR toolkit chosen in our study was Sphinx3 [34]. This decoder used a context-dependent acoustic model with 3-state left-to-right HMM. The acoustic vectors are composed of 13 MFCC coefficients, the delta and the delta delta of each coefficient. This HMM-based context-dependent acoustic model was trained on the BREF120 corpus [35] which is composed of about 100 hours of annotated speech from 120 non-elderly

Sample	Distress Sentence	Home Automation Order	Casual Sentence
1	Aidez-moi !	e-lio appelle le samu !	Bonjour madame !
2	Au secours !	e-lio appelle les pompiers !	Ça va très bien.
4	Je me sens mal !	e-lio appelle les secours !	Ce livre est intéressant.
5	Je suis tombé !	e-lio appelle un docteur !	Il fait soleil.
3	Du secours s'il vous plaît !	e-lio appelle une ambulance !	J'ai ouvert la porte.
6	Je ne peux plus bouger !	e-lio appelle une infirmière !	Je dois prendre mon médicament !
7	Je ne suis pas bien !	e-lio appelle ma fille !	J'allume la lumière !
8	Je suis blessé !	e-lio appelle mon fils !	Je me suis endormi tout de suite !
9	Je ne peux pas me relever !	e-lio tu peux téléphoner au samu ?	Le café est brûlant !
10	Ma jambe ne me porte plus !	e-lio il faut appeler les secours !	Où sont mes lunettes ?

Table 1: Examples of sentences of the AD corpus

French speakers. We called it the generic acoustic model.

3.3. Language model

A general language model (LM) was estimated from the French *Gigaword* corpus which is a archive of newswire text data that has been acquired over several years by the Linguistic Data Consortium (LDC) at the University of Pennsylvania[2]. It was 1-gram with 11018 words. Moreover, to reduce the linguistic variability, a 3-gram domain language model was learned from the sentences used during the corpus collection described in Section 3.1, with 88 1-gram, 193 2-gram and 223 3-gram models. Finally, the language model was a 3-gram-type which results from the combination of the general language model (with a 10% weight) and the domain one (with 90% weight). This combination has been shown as leading to the best WER for domain specific application [36]. The interest of such combination is to bias the recognition towards the domain LM but when the speaker deviates from the domain, the general LM makes it possible to correctly recognise the utterances.

3.4. Word error rate and phoneme matching

The simplest and most common way to evaluate ASR performances is to compute the Word Error Rate (WER). The WER is computed by first aligning the output (the decoded speech) with the reference (i.e., the ground truth) and then applying $WER = \frac{I+D+S}{N}$ where I, D and S is the number of insertions, deletion and substitution of words and N is the number of words in the reference.

Though this measure was used in many related studies [8, 10, 11], it does not indicate which specific phonemes play a role in the ASR performance degradation. To do so, the annotation should be performed at the phoneme level. However, this is a very laborious and time-consuming task which furthermore requires a good level of expert agreement. That is why we analysed the results of the forced alignments. The forced alignment algorithm that was used is the one of Sphinx3.

Forced alignment consists in finding the boundaries of phonemes in an utterance knowing the uttered sentence. This sentence is mapped in phoneme (using a dictionary) which is used to constrain an optimal alignment between the acoustic model and the speech utterance. The forced alignment scores are for each signal segment within a boundary, the likelihood of belonging to a phoneme model. This score can be interpreted as a proximity to the "standard" pronunciation, modelled by the generic acoustic model. The differences in scores of phoneme categories between the aged group and the non-aged group allow to identify which phonemes are the most difficult for the ASR system. We are not aware of any study having used such method to assess ASR performances.

Phonemes were grouped according to their highest level catgories as shown in table 2.

Unvoiced Plosive	p, t, k
Voiced Plosive	b, d, g
Nasal Consonant	m, n, ŋ, ɲ
Liquid Consonant	l
Unvoiced Fricative	f, s, ʃ
Voiced Fricative	v, z, ʒ, ɾ
Front Vowel	i, e, ɛ
Central Vowel	y, ø, œ, ə
Back Vowel	u, o, ɔ
Open Vowel	a, ɑ
Nasal Vowel	ẽ, ã, õ, œ̃
Semi-Vowel	ɥ, j, w

Table 2: Phoneme categories (IPA symbols)

3.5. Adaptation with MLLR

Once the phonemes are identified, the most common method to overcome the ASR limitation is to apply speaker adaptation. Speaker adaptation consists in generating a new acoustic model from a generic one and some new annotated speech in limited quantity. One of the most popular technique is to apply the Maximum Likelihood Linear Regression (MLLR) which is particularly adapted when a limited amount of data per class is available. MLLR is an adaptation technique that uses small amounts of data to train a linear transform which warps the Gaussian means so as to maximize the likelihood of the data. The principle is that acoustically close classes are grouped and transformed together.

3.6. Assessing the level of autonomy

Despite the acoustic adaptation, there might be a disparity between the WERs of the elderly group even in aged people of the same age category. Therefore, we investigated other criteria and focused on elderly dependence. As reference, we used a French national test which is daily used in assessing the degree of loss of autonomy: the AGGIR (Autonomie Gérontolo-

[2]http://www.ldc.upenn.edu/Catalog/CatalogEntry.jsp?catalogId=LDC2006T17

gie Groupes Iso-Ressources) grid[3]. The degree of autonomy loss is evaluated in terms of physical and cognitive decline. According to the result of this test, the person can receive financial support: the Personalized Allocation of Autonomy (APA). The evaluation is done using 17 variables. Ten variables refer to the loss of physical and cognitive autonomy: coherence, orientation, washing, feeding, disposal, transfers (to rise, to lie down, to sit down), internal displacement, external displacement and remote communication. Seven variables refer to the loss of domestic and social autonomy: personal management of budget and possessions, cooking, cleaning, transporting, purchasing, treatment monitoring and past time activities. Each variable is coded with A (independent), B (partially dependent) and C (totally dependent). The GIR (Iso-Ressources Group) score is computed from the variables to classify the person in one of the six groups: GIR 1 (total dependence) to GIR 6 (total autonomy).

4. RESULTS

4.1. Collected Corpus

4.1.1. The AD80 French test corpus

The AD corpus (cf. 3.1) was acquired from 95 speakers (36 men and 59 women) which are divided into two groups: the elderly group composed of 43 speakers (11 men and 32 women), 62 to 94 years old, with 2796 distress and home automation sentences for a duration of 1 hour 5 minutes, and 3006 casual sentences for a duration of 1 hour 6 minutes, and the non-elderly group composed of 52 speakers, 18 to 64 years old, with 3903 distress and home automation sentences for a duration of 1 hour 18 minutes, and 3897 casual sentences for a duration of 1 hour 12 minutes.

We fixed the limit of the non-aged group at 65 years old, but we recorded 2 people aged 62 and 63 years old with autonomy loss, looking very aged physically and living in nursing home. Thus we included this two persons, as exceptions, in the aged group.

For the 43 speakers of the aged AD corpus, a GIR score was obtained after clinicians filled the AGGIR grid.

Finally, the AD corpus is made up of 13,602 annotated sentences, with 4 hours and 42 minutes of recording.

4.1.2. Collection of the training ERES38 corpus

The ERES38 (cf. 3.1) corpus was acquired from 22 elderly people (14 women and 8 men) between 68 and 98 years old. The corpus included 48 minutes of read speeches (around 2 minutes per speaker) and 17 hours of interviews. The speakers lived in specialized institutes, such as nursing homes and were cognitively intact without severe disabilities.

4.2. Phoneme distance between aged and non-aged voice

When performing ASR using the generic acoustic model on the distress/home automation sentences of the AD corpus, we obtained an average WER of 9.07% for the non-elderly group, and an average WER of 43.47% for the elderly group. Thus, we observed a significant performance degradation of ASR for elderly speech, with an absolute difference of 34.40%. Figure 1 represents the WER according to the chronological age for both groups. It shows that the WER is globally higher for elderly group as previous studies showed [8, 10, 11]. However, it can also be seen that the variability between speakers also increases with the age. For instance, some 83 years old speakers have their WER ranging from 13.6% to 80.2%. Standard deviation is 6% for the non-elderly group and 17.27% for the elderly group. In other words, the WER is far less predictable in the elderly group than in the non-elderly group. Consequently, we have to deal with the fact that a speech recognition with such a system can work very well with some of the elderly speakers, and very badly with others.

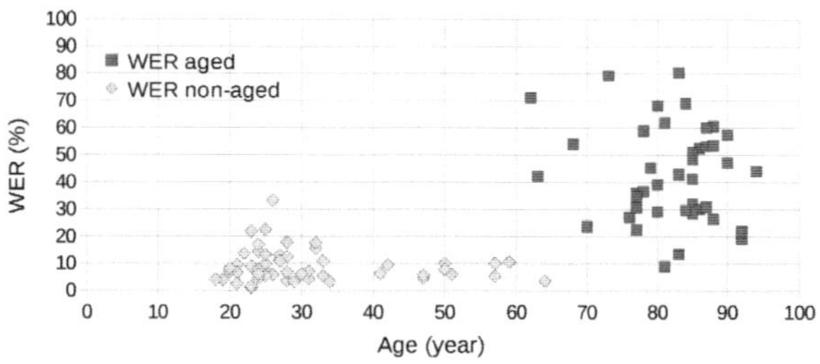

Figure 1: WER as a function of age for aged and non-aged groups

The forced alignment scores on both AD groups non-elderly and elderly with the generic acoustic model are presented in Figure 2 based on phonemic categories.

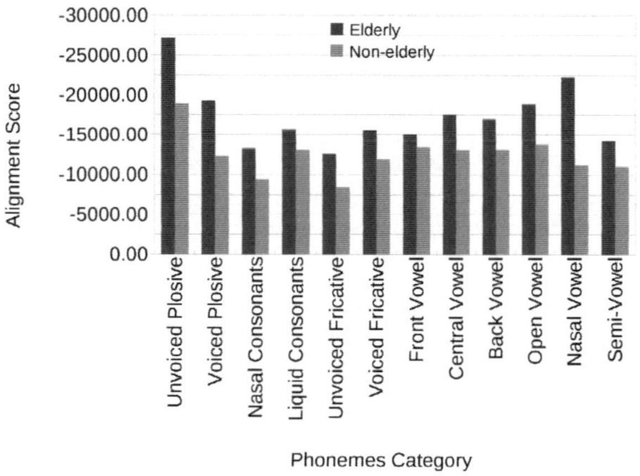

Figure 2: Forced alignment scores by phonemes categories before adaptation

The relative differences of forced alignment scores observed between both groups led to sort the phoneme categories in descending order of differences: nasal vowels (-100,34%), voiced plosives (-56,55%), unvoiced fricatives (-50,48%), unvoiced plosives (-44,05%), nasal consonants (-41,03%), open vowels (-37,12%), central vowels (-34,80%), voiced fricatives (-31,30%), back vowels (-29,26%), semi-vowels (-29,18%), liquids (-19,99%), and front vowels (-11,89%). The repartition of French phonemes inside the different groups are presented in Table 2.

For the elderly group, the alignment scores are lower than those obtained for the non-elderly group especially for plosives and nasal vowels. Based on the relative differences, the phoneme categories most affected for elderly group are nasal vowels, plosive consonants, unvoiced fricatives and nasal consonants.

[3]http://vosdroits.service-public.fr/F1229.xhtml

4.3. Impact of the acoustic adaptation on ASR performance with aged voice

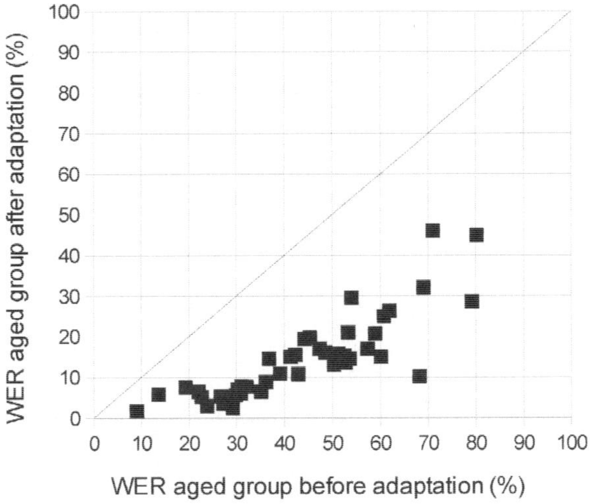

Figure 3: WER on aged group before and after adaptation

Figure 3 shows that using the MLLR adapted acoustic model was able to reduce the WER significantly for all speakers of the AD corpus. With the global MLLR adaptation using ERES38, the average WER was 14.52%. Compared to the 43.47% WER without adaptation (see Section 4.2), the absolute difference was -28.95%. Furthermore, the speaker with the worst performance had his error rate reduced from 80.2% to 44.9%, and the speaker with the best performance had his error rate reduced from 9% to 1.8%. Also, the standard deviation was reduced from 17.27% to 10.34%, showing a reduction of the variability between the speakers.

A comparison between the forced alignment scores obtained for non-elderly without adaptation and for elderly after adaptation using the ERES38 corpus is shown in Figure 4. On the whole, the scores for the elderly after adaptation are better than those of non-elderly with the generic acoustical model.

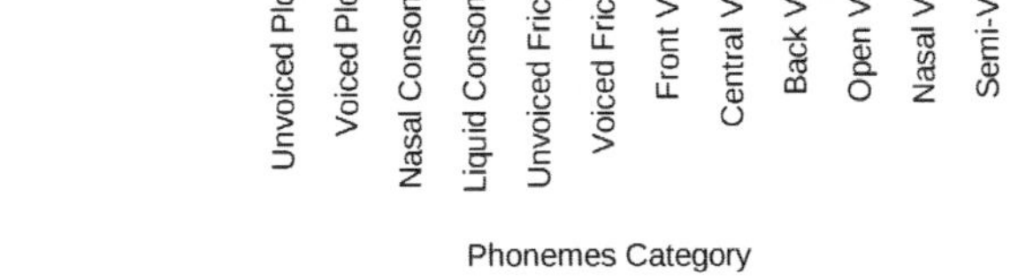

Figure 4: Forced alignment scores by phonemes categories for non-elderly with the generic acoustical model and for elderly after adaptation

Indeed, the use of an acoustical model adapted to elderly people reduces the mismatching of phonemes. The alignment scores of the adapted model presented in Figure 4 show that the average distance has reduced below the non-aged one for all phonemes except for unvoiced fricatives and nasal vowels.

From an applicative point of view, this test shows that we can use a database of elderly speech in MLLR adaptation with speakers which are different from the test database. Even though the size of the corpus is small, we have a significant improvement of WER. Furthermore, this demonstrates that the voices of ageing people have common characteristics.

4.4. Influence of elderly dependence on ASR system

Despite the acoustic adaptation, there is a great variability between the WERs of the elderly group. Therefore, we investigated to establish if the level of elderly dependence can be an indicator of the ASR performance for the elderly group. Figure 5 shows a box-and-whisker diagram of the WER from MLLR adaptation as a function of the elderly dependence. Four speakers were in GIR 2, two speakers were in GIR 3, 21 speakers were in GIR 4, one speaker was in GIR 5 and 15 speakers were in GIR 6. No speaker was represented in GIR 1. Due to the small number of speakers in GIR 2, GIR 3 and GIR 5, we merged GIR 2 with GIR 3 and GIR 4 with GIR 5.

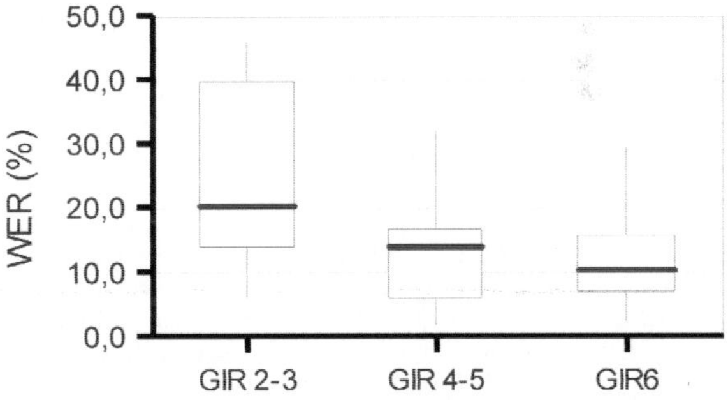

Figure 5: WER as a function of levels of dependence

From Figure 5 it can be seen that WERs are different according to the GIR category. Indeed, the WER averages for GIR 2-3, GIR 4-5 and GIR 6 are respectively 25.2%, 13.2% and 12.2%, and the WER standard deviations are respectively 16.8%, 8.4% and 7.6%. Then, we performed an ANOVA test on the groups GIR 2-3, GIR 4-5 and GIR 6. From this test, the GIR score have a significant effect on WER ($F(2, 40) = 4.3; p < 0.05\%$).

We conducted a Bonferroni post-hoc analysis to characterize which groups were significantly different from other groups. The post-hoc test highlighted that there was a significant difference between the GIR 2-3 group and both groups GIR 4-5 and GIR 6, while there is no significant difference between GIR 4-5 and GIR-6.

5. CONCLUSION

The paper presents our study on the behavior of an ASR system with elderly voices. Given the absence of a corpus containing the voice of elderly in French language usable for testing ASR system, we recorded the AD corpus. From this corpus, we observed an increase of the average WER of the ASR system for elderly people, with an absolute difference between non-elderly and elderly voice of 34.4%. With forced alignment, we analyzed which phonemes for elderly speech were posing the most problems to ASR systems. These results allowed us to proceed to the recording of the ERES38 corpus, allowing us to adapt the generic acoustic model to the voice of elderly people through the MLLR adaptation method. The global MLLR adaptation was interesting because with less than one hour of recordings from speakers different from the test speakers, we obtained a WER close to the case of recognition with the generic acoustic model on non-elderly group, with a WER of 14.53%, against 43.47% before adaptation. Moreover, we showed that inside the elderly group, the WER was not correlated with the age but could be correlated with the level of dependence due to a general physical degradation. The continuation of our work would be to show how the different parameters of the AGGIR grid are correlated to the WER. Therefore, predicting the ASR behavior would allow in facilitating the use of these new technologies in the daily life of the dependent elderly people.

6. ACKNOWLEDGMENT

This study was funded by the National Agency for Research under the project CIRDO - Industrial Research (ANR-2010-TECS-012). The authors would like to thank to Mrs Vézignol and Bonnefond-Jimenez, Mr Debrus, Mrs Aman, Bron, Lalande and Martins of the medical institutions SSR "Les Cadières" and EHPAD "Château de Labahou" for their help in corpus recording. Special thanks to R. Dugheanu, J. Le Grand and Y. Sasa for their active contribution, and to various elderly and caregivers who agreed to participate in the recordings.

7. References

[1] F. Portet, M. Vacher, C. Golanski, C. Roux, and B. Meillon, "Design and evaluation of a smart home voice interface for the elderly — Acceptability and objection aspects," *Personal and Ubiquitous Computing*, vol. 17, no. 1, pp. 127–144, 2013.

[2] J.-C. Wang, H.-P. Lee, J.-F. Wang, and C.-B. Lin, "Robust environmental sound recognition for home automation," *IEEE Transactions on Automation Science and Engineering*, vol. 5(1), p. 25–31, 2008.

[3] A. G. Jianmin Jiang and S. Zhang, "Hermes: a FP7 funded project towards computer aided memory management via intelligent computations," in *3rd Symposium of Ubiquitous Computing and Ambient Intelligence*, 2009, p. 249–253.

[4] O. Brdiczka, M. Langet, J. Maisonnasse, and J. Crowley, "Detecting human behaviour models from multimodal observation in a smart home," *IEEE Transactions on Automation Science and Engineering*, vol. 6(4), p. 588 –597, 2009.

[5] P. Milhorat, D. Istrate, J. Boudy, and G. Chollet, "Hands-free speech-sound interactions at home," in *20th European Signal Processing Conference (EUSIPCO)*, 2012, pp. 1678–1682.

[6] M. Vacher, F. Portet, B. Lecouteux, and C. Golanski, *Telhealthcare Computing and Engineering: Principles and Design*. CRC Press, Taylor and Francis Group, 2013, no. 21, ch. Speech Analysis for Ambient Assisted Living: Technical and User Design of a Vocal Order System, pp. 607–638, ISBN: ISBN-978-1-57808-802-7.

[7] M. Vacher, F. Portet, A. Fleury, and N. Noury, "Development of Audio Sensing Technology for Ambient Assisted Living: Applications and Challenges," *International Journal of E-Health and Medical Communications*, vol. 2, no. 1, pp. 35–54, 2011.

[8] A. Baba, S. Yoshizawa, M. Yamada, A. Lee, and K. Shikano, "Acoustic models of the elderly for large-vocabulary continuous speech recognition," *Electronics and Communications in Japan, Part 2*, vol. 87, pp. 49–57, 2004.

[9] R. Privat, N. Vigouroux, and P. Truillet, "Etude de l'effet du vieillissement sur les productions langagières et sur les performances en reconnaissance automatique de la parole," *Revue Parole*, vol. 31-32, pp. 281–318, 2004.

[10] R. Vipperla, S. Renals, and J. Frankel, "Longitudinal study of ASR performance on ageing voices," *Interspeech*, pp. 2550–2553, 2008.

[11] T. Pellegrini, I. Trancoso, A. Hämäläinen, A. Calado, M. S. Dias, and D. Braga, "Impact of Age in ASR for the Elderly: Preliminary Experiments in European Portuguese," in *Advances in Speech and Language Technologies for Iberian Languages - IberSPEECH 2012 Conference, Madrid, Spain, November 21-23, 2012. Proceedings*, 2012, pp. 139–147.

[12] M. Gorham-Rowan and J. Laures-Gore, "Acoustic-perceptual correlates of voice quality in elderly men and women," *Journal of Communication Disorders*, vol. 39, pp. 171–184, 2006.

[13] B. Benjamin, "Frequency variability in the aged voice," *Journal of Gerontechnology*, vol. 36, pp. 722–726, 1981.

[14] S. Linville and E. Korabic, "Elderly listeners' estimates of vocal age in adult females," *Journal of the Acoustical Society of America*, vol. 80, pp. 692–694, 1986.

[15] E. Morgan and M. Rastatter, "Variability of voice fundamental frequency in elderly female speakers," *Perceptual and Motor Skills*, vol. 63, pp. 215–218, 1986.

[16] R. Morris and W. Brown, "Age-related differences in speech variability among women," *Journal of Communication Disorders*, vol. 27, pp. 49–64, 1994.

[17] I. Honjo and N. Isshiki, "Laryngoscopic and voice characteristics of aged persons," *Archives of Otolaryngology*, vol. 106, pp. 149–150, 1980.

[18] W. Ryan and K. Burk, "Perceptual and acoustic correlates in the speech of males," *Jounal of Communication Disorders*, vol. 7, pp. 181–192, 1974.

[19] N. Takeda, G. Thomas, and C. Ludlow, "Aging effects on motor units in the human thyroarytenoid muscle," *Laryngoscope*, vol. 110, pp. 1018–1025, 2000.

[20] P. Mueller, R. Sweeney, and L. Baribeau, "Acoustic and morphologic study of the senescent voice," *Ear, Nose, and Throat Journal*, vol. 63, pp. 71–75, 1984.

[21] S. Xue and R. Deliyski, "Effect on aging on selected acoustic voice parameters: Preliminary normative data and educational implications," *Educational Gerontology*, vol. 27, pp. 159–168, 2001.

[22] L. Eskenazi, D. Childers, and D. Hicks, "Acoustic correlates of vocal quality," *Journal of Speech and Hearing Research*, vol. 33, pp. 298–306, 1990.

[23] J. Selby, H. Gilbert, and J. Lerman, "Perceptual and acoustic evaluation of individuals with laryngopharyngeal reflux pre- and post-treatment," *Journal of Voice*, vol. 17, pp. 557–570, 2003.

[24] C. Ferrand, "Harmonic-to-noise ratio: An index of vocal aging," *Journal of Voice*, vol. 16, pp. 480–487, 2002.

[25] J. Wilpon and C. Jacobsen, "A study of speech recognition for children and the elderly," in *IEEE International Conference on Acoustics, Speech, and Signal Processing*, vol. 1, 1996, pp. 349–352.

[26] M. Gerosa, Giuliani, and F. D., Brugnara, "Towards age-independent acoustic modeling," *Speech Communication*, vol. 51(6), pp. 499–509, 2009.

[27] S. Anderson, N. Liberman, E. Bernstein, S. Foster, E. Cate, B. Levin, and R. Hudson, "Recognition of elderly speech and voice-driven document retrieval," in *IEEE International Conference on Acoustics, Speech, and Signal Processing ICASSP '99*, vol. 1, 1999, pp. 145–148.

[28] S. Renouard, M. Charbit, and G. Chollet, *Independent Living for Persons with Disabilities*, 2003, ch. Vocal interface with a speech memory for dependent people, pp. 15–21.

[29] O. Kumiko, M. Mitsuhiro, E. Atsushi, S. Shohei, and T. Reio, "Input support for elderly people using speech recognition," IEIC Technical Report (Institute of Electronics, Information and Communication Engineers), Tech. Rep. 104(139), 2004.

[30] E. Pinto, D. Charlet, H. François, D. Mostefa, O. Boëffard, D. Fohr, O. Mella, F. Bimbot, K. Choukri, Y. Philip, and C. F., "Development of new telephone speech databases for french : the neologos project," in *4th International Conference on Language Resources and Evaluation*, 2004, pp. 1–4.

[31] T. Moir and G. Filho, "From science fiction to science fact: A smart-house interface using speech technology and a photo-realistic avatar," in *15th International Conference on Mechatronics and Machine Vision in Practice*, 2008, pp. 327–333.

[32] M.-E. B. Chaumon, B. Cuvillier, S. Bouakaz, and M. Vacher, "Démarche de développement de technologies ambiantes pour le maintien à domicile des personnes dépendantes : vers une triangulation des méthodes et des approches," in *Actes du 1er Congrès Européen de Stimulation Cognitive*, Dijon, France, 23-25 May 2012, pp. 121–122.

[33] F. Aman, M. Vacher, S. Rossato, R. Dugheanu, F. Portet, J. le Grand, and Y. Sasa, "Etude de la performance des modèles acoustiques pour des voix de personnes âgées en vue de l'adaptation des systèmes de RAP (Assessment of the acoustic models performance in the ageing voice case for ASR system adaptation) [in French]," in *Actes de la conférence conjointe JEP-TALN-RECITAL 2012, volume 1: JEP*, 2012, pp. 707–714.

[34] K. Seymore, C. Stanley, S. Doh, M. Eskenazi, E. Gouvea, B. Raj, M. Ravishankar, R. Rosenfeld, M. Siegler, R. Stern, and E. Thayer, "The 1997 CMU Sphinx-3 English broadcast news transcription system," in *DARPA Broadcast News Transcription and Understanding Workshop*, Lansdowne, VA, USA, 1998.

[35] L. Lamel, J. Gauvain, and M. EskEnazi, "BREF, a large vocabulary spoken corpus for french," in *Proceedings of EUROSPEECH 91*, vol. 2, Geneva, Switzerland, 1991, pp. 505–508.

[36] B. Lecouteux, M. Vacher, and F. Portet, "Distant Speech Recognition in a Smart Home: Comparison of Several Multisource ASRs in Realistic Conditions," in *Interspeech 2011*, Florence, Italy, 2011, p. 4p.

Visual Subtitles For Internet Videos

Chitralekha Bhat, Imran Ahmed, Vikram Saxena, Sunil Kumar Kopparapu

TCS Innovation Labs - Mumbai, Yantra Park, Thane (West), Maharashtra, INDIA

{bhat.chitralekha, ahmed.imran, vik.saxena, sunilkumar.kopparapu}@tcs.com

Abstract

We present a visual aid for the hearing impaired to enable access to internet videos. The visual tool is in the form of a time synchronized lip movement corresponding to the speech in the video which is embedded in the original internet video. Conventionally, access to the audio or speech, in a video, by the hearing impaired is provided by means of either text subtitles or sign language gestures by an interpreter. The proposed tool would be beneficial, especially in situations where such aids are not readily available or generating such aids is difficult. We have conducted a number experiments to determine the feasibility and usefulness of the proposed visual aid.

Index Terms: Lip movement synthesis, Phone recognition, resource deficient languages

1. Introduction

As per World Health Organization, over 360 million people which account for 5% of the world's total population suffer from hearing loss and a significant majority of them live in developing nations. Moreover, one third of people over the age of 65 years, especially from South Asia, Asia Pacific and Sub-Saharan Africa are affected by disabling hearing loss [1]. A person with hearing impairment, especially acquired deafness in adulthood, can with some training interpret spoken speech by observing lip movements corresponding to the spoken speech.

Lip reading, also known as speech-reading in literature, allows access to speech through visual reading of the movement of the lips, face and tongue in the absence of audible sound. Lip reading also makes use of the information associated with the context, the knowledge of the language, and also the residual hearing of the person [2]. Hearing impairment can prove to be a major handicap especially when a person wishes to understand an internet video while viewing it. Any tool that can make video assessible is useful for the hearing impaired. This motivates our work in developing a tool that allows for viewing a video without having to actually hear the audio track of the video.

Text based subtitles is one way by which a person with hearing loss interprets what is being spoken in a video. However, text subtitles are not always readily available; especially in a country like India where subtitling is not mandated by law unlike in some of the developed nations (example [3, 4]). Moreover, manual generation of subtitles is a long drawn, laborious and an expensive process [5]. An alternative is to automatically generate text subtitles using an Automatic Speech Recognition (ASR) engine, but non-availability of ASR engines for a resource deficient language [6] hinders generation of accurate subtitles, additionally, generating subtitles in the script of the spoken language would be another impediment.

IBM's SiSi (Say It, Sign It) is an automatic sign language generator for spoken audio. SiSi uses a speech recognition module that converts the spoken speech into text; the text is interpreted into gestures, that are used to animate an avatar which signs in British Sign Language [7]. SiSi largely depends on the accuracy of recognition of audio. eSign project was primarily designed to help interpret textual internet content using sign language. eSign synthesizes the signing gestures using Signing Gesture Markup Language (SiGML), along with information regarding speed and viewpoint [8]. However, there are about 200 different sign languages, each with a vocabulary of considerable size. Building an automated system that would generate sign language interpretation of audio would then be complex owing to not only the non-availability of an efficient ASR engine but also the difficulty associated in translation of generated text, to sign language gestures for resource deficient languages.

In this paper, we propose a tool for visual subtitling which is largely based on associating a visual lip movement corresponding to the audio track of the video. The essential idea is based on the fact that recognition accuracies of audio, even for resource deficient languages is higher in viseme space than in the phoneme space. The rest of the paper is organized as follows: We describe the process of generation of visemes in Section 2 and describe the experimental work and evaluation of the proposed tool in Section 3 and conclude in Section 4.

2. Generation of Viseme Sequence

Visual subtitles are essentially a time sequence of visemes corresponding to and in sync with the speech in a given video. Visual subtitles could be in lieu of or in addition to text subtitles, wherein the lip movement for a particular speech will be displayed. It is anticipated that, the user

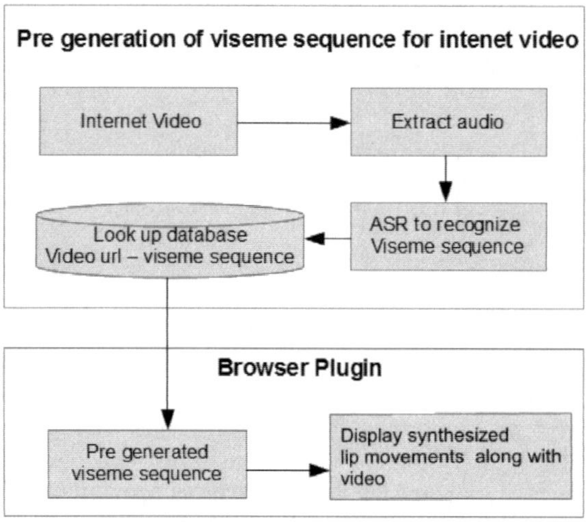

Figure 1: Overview of Visual Subtitling.

will be able to view the visual subtitles embedded with the original video. Figure 1 represents the proposed the tool. As seen in Figure 1 audio is first extracted from the video. The spoken speech is recognized using a phoneme recognizer and then mapped to the corresponding viseme. Visual subtitles are synthesized using MPEG-4 FAPs for mouth and tongue as defined in [9].

Note 1 *for the purpose of demonstration the videos chosen are predominantly speech audio content.*

2.1. Visemes and MPEG-4 FAPs

Viseme is the basic unit of mouth movement that represents a phoneme or a group of phonemes in the visual domain. We use the standard set of 22 visemes [10]. It is a many phonemes to one viseme mapping with several different phonemes mapped to the same viseme owing to the fact that the lip position for different phonemes is the same; for example the phones /k/ and /g/ correspond to the viseme k or the phonemes /p/, /b/ and /m/ correspond to the viseme p. We first created a mapping between the standard 22 visemes and the Hindi phoneme set as shown in 1 (shows the first 11 visemes only).

Note 2 *The mapping was done so as to include both Hindi and English phonemes to be able to cater to mixed language usage.*

It is desirable to have the lip movement as natural as possible for the user to be able to comfortably understand the audio. MPEG-4 FAPs for mouth and tongue for a given viseme are sufficient to visualize the spoken phoneme completely as can be seen in Figure 2. For each of the 22 visemes, the corresponding FAPs were computed in the form of (x, y) coordinates. For natural visualization of the lip movement, transition between two consequent visemes was simulated by means of a linear interpolation. So in some sense we had intermediate visemes generated.

Table 1: Phoneme to Viseme mapping rule.

Phoneme	Viseme
/sil/	Viseme0
/ae/, /ax/, /ah/, /E/, /EM/, /ai/, /a/	Viseme1
/aa/, /A/, /ah/, /AM/	Viseme2
/ao/, /O/, /au/	Viseme3
/ey/, /eh/, /uh/, /e/, /eh/	Viseme4
/er/, /axr/	Viseme5
/y/, /iy/, /ih/, /ix/, /I/, /IM/, /i/	Viseme6
/w/, /uw/, /U/, /UM, /ux/, /u/, /uh/	Viseme7
/ow/, /o/	Viseme8
/aw/	Viseme9
/oy/	Viseme10
/ay/	Viseme11

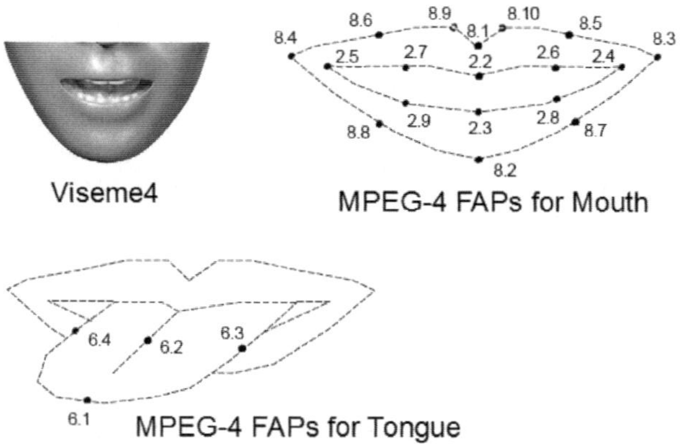

Figure 2: *Viseme and MPEG-4 FAPs for Mouth and Tongue.*

HTK 3.4 ASR [11] was used for phoneme recognition. The recognizer was trained on annotated Hindi data from 100 native speakers of Hindi; each of the speaker spoke 10 sentences each. The HTK 3.4 recognizer performed with 70% correctness on viseme classes when used in the free decoding mode.

Note 3 *The recognition improved by upward of* 10% *for viseme recognition compared to phoneme recognition.*

Manual verification of phone sequence and duration is done to ensure that the lip movement generated by the viseme sequence is a representation of the speech.

A visual subtitle browser plug-in allows the user to view the internet video along with the lip movements corresponding to the speech in the form of a viseme sequence. As stated earlier, given the context, a person with hearing loss would be able to understand the spoken speech from the lip movements, we believe that the video would set the context.

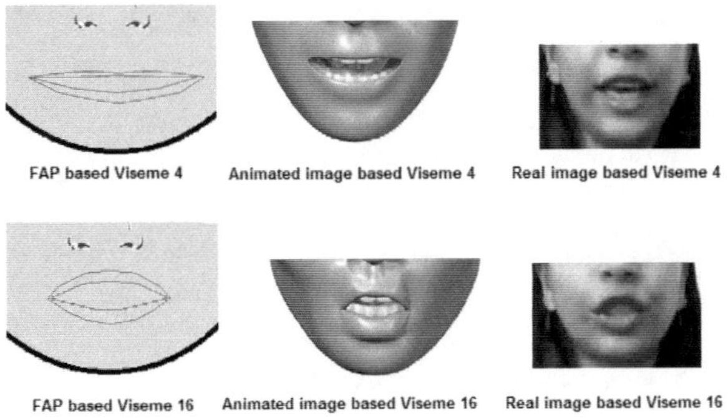

Figure 3: A snapshot of the FAP, animated image and real image based visemes.

Figure 4: Sample snapshot of a video with visual subtitle.

3. Experimental Results and Discussion

Figure 3. shows the snapshots of FAPs, animated viseme and real viseme that were used to generate the videos. Several videos available on the internet were selected and visual subtitles were generated [12] as mentioned in the earlier sections. While a mix of English and Hindi videos were selected and visual subtitles generated (a snapshot of the video with FAP is shown in Figure 4), the evaluation of the usefulness of the tool was tested on only the English videos because the subjects who evaluated the videos for visual titles were trained to lip read in English.

3.1. Evaluation

All the evaluation results are for English videos only because the subjects were trained in Indian English lip reading. We found access to people who are familiar with lip reading in a language other than English was hard to find. The participants were asked to lip read a video of ten naturally recorded sentences to establish a baseline. Only the mouth portion of the face was used in the baseline videos.

Evaluation was done under different experimental setups, namely,

- Visual subtitles generated using three different visual features, namely, (a) MPEG-4 FAPs, (b) animated viseme images and and (c) real viseme images.
- Visual subtitles with and without the context of video.
- Videos played at different rates, namely, played at their original speed and half the speed.
- Videos comprised of animated clip, classroom lecture, dias/conference lecture.

The participants' understanding based on visual observation of the visual subtitles was evaluated in terms of number of words correctly recognized. In summary, visual subtitles were better understood under the following conditions (a) with the context of video, (b) when played at half the original speed and (c) when generated with real viseme images

Note 4 *MPEG-4 standard does not define FAPs for teeth, which play a significant role in lip reading, hence this aspect needs to be considered during the generation of Visual subtitles using MPEG-4 FAPs.*

4. Conclusions

Visual subtitles are essentially the lip movements corresponding to the audio track in a video. Displaying visual subtitles along with the video would augment the understanding of the content of a video for a person with hearing impairment. Although text subtitles and sign language gesture display can be thought of as alternatives, generating them manually is a tedious task. Automatic generation of text subtitles and sign language gestures for a particular language using ASRs, would require robust ASRs with rich speech corpus. However, lip movements are less language specific, that is one can move from one language to another by modifying the phoneme-visemes mapping. Given these advantages, automatic generation of lip movement from audio emerges as an encouraging solution, especially for resource deficient languages like Hindi. However, automatic generation of lip movements will still be limited by the ASR performance under noisy and with background music. We are also experimenting with other methods like optical flows [13] for generation of transition between visemes.
Acknowledgements: We would like to express our sincere gratitude to all the participants whom we would not like to name. Our thanks are due to Mrs. Alpa Shah for participating and making possible the evaluation of visual subtitles.

5. References

[1] WHO, http://www.who.int/mediacentre/factsheets/fs300/en/, viewed July 2013.

[2] Wikipedia, "Speech reading," http://en.wikipedia.org/wiki/Speech_reading, viewed July 2013.

[3] CVVA, "U.S. Accessibility Regulations for Online Video Captions," http://dotsub.com/enterprise/laws, viewed July 2013.

[4] N. K. Aas, "Mandatory subtitling of films for the benefit of the deaf and hard of hearing," http://merlin.obs.coe.int/iris/2012/1/article34.en.html, viewed July 2013.

[5] Wikipedia, "Subtitle captioning," http://en.wikipedia.org/wiki/Subtitle_(captioning), viewed July 2013.

[6] I. Ahmed and S. K. Kopparapu, "Speech recognition for resource deficient languages using frugal speech corpus," in *Signal Processing, Communication and Computing (ICSPCC), 2012 IEEE International Conference on*, 2012, pp. 750–755.

[7] IBM, http://www-03.ibm.com/press/us/en/pressrelease/22316.wss, viewed July 2013.

[8] ISO, "MPEG-4 International Standards." ISO, Geneva, Switzerland, 1998, no. ISO 14496.

[9] J. R. Kennaway, J. R. W. Glauert, and I. Zwitserlood, "Providing signed content on the internet by synthesized animation," *ACM Trans. Comput.-Hum. Interact.*, vol. 14, no. 3, Sep. 2007. [Online]. Available: http://doi.acm.org/10.1145/1279700.1279705

[10] Aidreams, "Visemes for character animation," http://aidreams.co.uk/forum/index.php?page=Visemes-for_Character_Animation, viewed July 2013.

[11] S. J. Young, D. Kershaw, J. Odell, D. Ollason, V. Valtchev, and P. Woodland, *The HTK Book Version 3.4*. Cambridge University Press, 2006.

[12] B. Chitralekha, I. Ahmed, and S. K. Kopparapu, https://sites.google.com/site/awazyp/splat2013, viewed July 2013.

[13] T. A. Faruquie, C. Neti, N. Rajput, L. V. Subramaniam, and A. Verma, "Animating expressive faces to speak in indian languages," in *National Conference on Communications*, Bombay, 2002, pp. 355–362.

Comparing and combining classifiers for self-taught vocal interfaces

Lize Broekx, Katrien Dreesen, Jort F. Gemmeke, Hugo Van hamme

ESAT, KU Leuven, Leuven, Belgium

{katrien.dreesen, lize.broekxl}@student.kuleuven.be

{jort.gemmeke, hugo.vanhamme}@esat.kuleuven.be

Abstract

An attractive approach to enable the use of vocal interfaces by impaired users with dysarthric speech is the use of a system which learns from the end-user. To enable such technology, it is imperative that the learning is fast to reduce the time spent training the interface. In this paper we investigate to what extend various machine learning techniques are able to learn from only a single or a few spoken training samples. Additionally, we explore whether these techniques can be combined through boosting to improve the performance. Our evaluations on a small, but highly realistic home automation database reveal that non-negative matrix factorization seems best suited for fast learning and that some of the boosting approaches can indeed improve performance, especially for small amounts of training data.

Index Terms: vocal user interface, self-taught learning, machine learning, boosting

1. Introduction

Vocal user interfaces (VUIs) allow us to control a wide range of appliances and devices such as computers, smart phones, car navigation and other domestic devices and environments. While for most the use of a VUI is just a luxury, for individuals with a physical disability using a VUI can greatly improve their independence and quality of living, because for them operating and controlling devices would often require exhausting physical effort [1].

Conventional speech recognition systems employed in VUIs are trained by the developer using vast amounts of speech material. While offering impressive performances for users whose word choice, grammar and speech conforms to the training material used, performance suffers in the presence of accented, dialectical and disordered speech. A possible solution, adaptation of existing acoustic models, may not suffice for severe speech pathologies [2, 3, 4, 5, 6].

The goal of this research is to explore methods which allow training speech commands by the end-user himself. This way, the acoustic models of the VUI are maximally adapted to the end-user's speech while at the same time bringing development costs down. The challenge is to employ a learning strategy that can learn from only one or a few examples, in order to minimize the time the end-user spends on training the system. In this work, we will offer a comparison between multiple popular machine learning strategies to evaluate their effectiveness in developing a fast learning self-taught VUI.

In previous work, we obtained encouraging results on fast vocabulary acquisition [7] using non-negative matrix factorization (NMF). Although in that work the learning speed of acquiring acoustic models was investigated, it focused on larger amounts of training data than targeted in this work. Moreover, it considered a *multi-label* task in which spoken utterances were associated with multiple labels at once, which penalized other machine learning methods less suited for multi-label learning. In contrast, in this work we will focus on *speech classification*, labelling a spoken utterance with a single label.

Our contribution is twofold. First, we compare the performance of five machine learning techniques: Dynamic Time Warping (DTW), Gaussian Mixture Models (GMMs), Hidden Markov Models (HMMs), Support Vector Machines (SVMs) and Non-negative Matrix Factorization (NMF). Each of these techniques have their strengths and weaknesses; for example, while a HMM improves upon a GMM by being able to model temporal structure, it does require more parameters to be trained. When training with only one or a few training samples, this may lead to overfitting. Second, we investigate to what extent combining the aforementioned classification techniques, 'boosting', can improve results. We do this by comparing a number of combination rules operating at the class label posterior level [8].

The remainder of the paper is organised as follows. In Section 2 we give an overview of the speech classification methods that are investigated. In Section 3 we describe the various boosting approaches that will be considered. In Sections 4 and 5 we describe the experimental setup for evaluation on a small, but highly realistic home automation database collected in the ALADIN project [9]. The results of these experiments are presented in Section 6 and discussed in Section 7, and we conclude with our summary and thoughts for future work in Section 8.

2. Classification methods

In a speech classification problem an unlabelled speech signal X is assigned to one of the m possible commands $\{\omega_1, \ldots, \omega_m\}$. The classification methods Dynamic Time Warping (DTW), Gaussian Mixture Model (GMM) and Hidden Markov Model (HMM) use a spectrographic feature vector representation $\mathbf{X} = [\mathbf{x_1}, ..., \mathbf{x_T}]$ of a speech signal X, with T the number of frames. The number of rows of $\mathbf{X}$ is the dimension of the feature vector $\mathbf{x_t}$ for one frame.

The classification methods Non-negative Matrix Factorization (NMF) and Support Vector Machine (SVM) use a utterance based feature vector $\mathbf{x}$ of a speech signal X. The utterance based feature vector $\mathbf{x}$ is a column vector whose dimension N depends on the kind of feature vector. More information about the feature vectors used in this work for each of the techniques is given in Section 4.2.

A classification method evaluates how well the unlabelled speech signal X resembles speech signals associated with a command class ω_k. This similarity is expressed by the positive number $\Pi(\omega_k, X)$, which is method dependent. The larger $\Pi(\omega_k, X)$, the larger the similarity between X and the speech signals belonging to command ω_k. The speech signal X is assigned to the command ω_j with the highest similarity:

$$\text{assign } X \to \omega_j = \underset{\omega_k}{\text{argmax}}\, \Pi(\omega_k, X). \quad (1)$$

2.1. Dynamic Time Warping

Dynamic Time Warping (DTW) [10, 11, 12], is a method in which an unlabelled speech signal is compared with a large collection of labelled speech signals (exemplars) extracted from the training data. Since such a comparison needs to take different signal lengths and speech rate variations into account, DTW first finds an optimal alignment between each pair of utterances through non-linear time warping. The unlabelled speech signal is labelled with the command which is associated with the most similar exemplar.

As a learning method, DTW has the advantage that it makes optimal use of all the available labelled data, because all training samples can be used as an exemplar. A drawback of DTW is that the computational complexity of classification increases linearly with the number of training samples.

Formally, the similarity between the frames of the unlabelled speech signal X and the frames of each exemplar X_i is represented by a $T \times T_i$ matrix $\mathbf{D}_{X,X_i}$ containing the cosine distance between the spectrographic based feature vectors representations $\mathbf{X}$ and $\mathbf{X_i}$:

$$\mathbf{D}_{X,X_i} = \frac{\mathbf{X}'\mathbf{X_i}}{\|\mathbf{X}\|\|\mathbf{X_i}\|}. \quad (2)$$

The similarity between two speech signals is expressed as the score $\tilde{D}_{X,X_i}$ along the optimal path through the distance matrix $\mathbf{D}_{X,X_i}$. The optimal path, from the left upper corner to the right lower corner (Figure 1(a)), minimises the cumulative acoustic differences and the total number of steps. The optimal path is determined using a dynamical programming approach with the Needleman-Wunsch algorithm [13].

The unlabelled speech signal X is assigned to the command of the exemplar X_i with the highest similarity. The similarity between X and ω_k is expressed by the positive number

$$\Pi(\omega_k, X) = \max_{X_i \text{ of } \omega_k} \tilde{D}_{X,X_i}. \quad (3)$$

2.2. Gaussian Mixture Model

In a Gaussian Mixture Model (GMM), the probability density function is used to determine the acoustic likelihood of a command given the feature vectors of the unlabelled speech signal [14].

Using a GMM is attractive, because it is a parametric model in which the classification of an unlabelled speech signal takes the same time independent of the amount of training data. Another advantage is that the use of a parametric model typically allows better generalisation to unseen data, provided enough training data is available to accurately estimate the parameters.

Each command ω_k is represented by a weighted sum of multivariate Gaussian distributions

$$f_k(\mathbf{x_t}, \boldsymbol{\mu}, \boldsymbol{\Sigma}) = \sum_{i=1}^{M} w_i N(\mathbf{x_t}, \boldsymbol{\mu_i}, \boldsymbol{\Sigma_i}), \quad (4)$$

with $\boldsymbol{\mu_i}$ the mean spectrographic based feature vector, $\boldsymbol{\Sigma_i}$ the covariance matrix, w_i the weights for each multivariate Gaussian distribution in the GMM and M the number of multivariate Gaussian distributions in the GMM. The weighted sum of multivariate Gaussian distributions for each command ω_k is trained on the collection of speech signals $\{X^{(1)}, \ldots, X^{(N)}\}$ in the training data belonging to command ω_k. By applying the Expectation Maximization algorithm [15], the mean spectrographic based feature vector $\boldsymbol{\mu_i}$, the covariance matrix $\boldsymbol{\Sigma_i}$ and the weights w_i are obtained for each multivariate Gaussian distribution in the GMM. The similarity between X and ω_k is expressed by the positive number

$$\Pi(\omega_k, X) = \exp\left(\frac{1}{T}\sum_{t=1}^{T} \log\left(f_k(\mathbf{x_t}, \boldsymbol{\mu}, \boldsymbol{\Sigma})\right)\right). \quad (5)$$

2.3. Hidden Markov Model

A Hidden Markov Model (HMM), the de facto standard model in automatic speech recognition, augments the GMM by taking the temporal structure of the speech into account.While known to be a powerful model for speech given enough training data, it is not clear a priori whether it can perform better than a GMM if there is very little training data and when whole-word HMMs to model the spoken commands are used rather than sub=words HMMs.

In a HMM for speech classification, the commands ω_k are represented by a sequence Q of states q [16, 14]. For speech classification the order in the speech signal X is important, therefore a left-to-right (Bakis) HMM (Figure 1(b)) is used. A HMM $\lambda_k = (\boldsymbol{\Pi}_k, \mathbf{A}_k, \mathbf{B}_k)$ is characterized by the initial probabilities $\pi_i^{(k)}$, the transition probabilities $a_{ij}^{(k)}$ and the emissions $b_i^{(k)}(\mathbf{x_t})$, where i and j are the state indices. The emissions $\mathbf{B_k}$ are a GMM $f_k(\mathbf{x_t}, \boldsymbol{\mu}, \boldsymbol{\Sigma})$ for each state.

The HMM λ_k is trained on the collection of speech signals $\{X^{(1)}, \ldots, X^{(N)}\}$ in the training data belonging to command ω_k by the Baum-Welch algorithm.

For an unlabelled speech signal X the optimal state sequence $\tilde{Q}$ in each HMM λ_k is calculated as

$$\tilde{Q} = \arg\max_{Q} P(Q|\mathbf{X}, \lambda_k) = \arg\max_{Q} \frac{P(Q, \mathbf{X}|\lambda_k)}{P(\mathbf{X}|\lambda_k)}. \quad (6)$$

The similarity between X and ω_k, which is obtained by applying the Viterbi algorithm, is the positive number

$$\Pi(\omega_k, X) = P(\mathbf{X}, q, |\lambda_k). \quad (7)$$

2.4. Support Vector Machine

A Support Vector Machine is a linear classifier which is trained to be maximally discriminative between classes, possibly augmented by working in a high dimensional (kernalized) space [17]. SVMs are known to generalize well to unseen data, but it may be difficult to accurately train the hyperplane dividing classes with only few data points.

A SVM can be used for binary classification; to separate the m commands in our speech classification task we use the one-versus-one multi-label approach in this paper. For each pair of commands ω_k and ω_l, a binary classification problem is solved, which results in n_y binary classification problems with

$$n_y = \frac{m(m-1)}{2}. \quad (8)$$

The hyperplane of the linear classifier that separates two commands ω_k and ω_l can be formulated as

$$y_{\omega_k,\omega_l}(\mathbf{x}) = \mathbf{w}_{\omega_k,\omega_l}^T \mathbf{x} + b_{\omega_k,\omega_l} = \text{constant}, \quad (9)$$

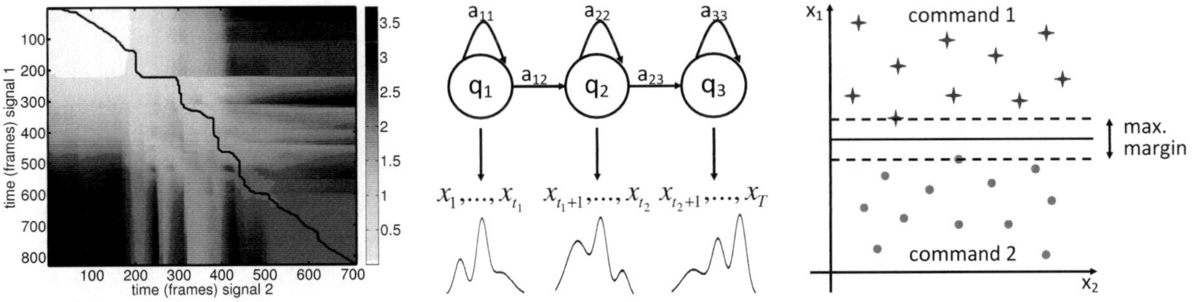

(a) *Example of the optimal path in the distance matrix* $\mathbf{D}$ *between two speech signals as found by DTW.*

(b) *Example of a left-to-right HMM with 3 states* q_i, *transition probabilities* a_{ij} *and emissions* $b_i(\mathbf{x_t})$.

(c) *Optimal hyperplane of the SVM classifier maximizing the margin dividing two classes.*

Figure 1: *Graphical representation of the classification methods DTW, HMM and SVM.*

with $\mathbf{w}_{\omega_k,\omega_l} \in \mathbb{R}^n$, $\mathbf{x} \in \mathbb{R}^n$, $b_{\omega_k,\omega_l} \in \mathbb{R}$, $y_{\omega_k,\omega_l} \in \mathbb{R}$. The unique hyperplane for a binary classification problem (Figure 1(c)) can be found by rescaling the problem such that the $\mathbf{x}$ closest to the hyperplane satisfy

$$|\mathbf{w}_{\omega_\mathbf{k},\omega_\mathbf{l}}{}^T \mathbf{x} + b_{\omega_k,\omega_l}| = 1. \tag{10}$$

The speech signal X is associated with label vector

$$\mathbf{y}(\mathbf{x}) = [y_{\omega_1,\omega_2}(\mathbf{x}), \ldots, y_{\omega_{m-1},\omega_m}(\mathbf{x})]^T, \tag{11}$$

with $\mathbf{x}$ the utterance based feature vector of X.

Each command ω_k is associated with a command label vector $\mathbf{y}^{(\mathbf{k})} \in \{-1,+1\}^{n_y}$. The similarity between the speech signal X and command ω_k is the positive number

$$\Pi(\omega_k, X) = \left(\mathbf{y}^{(\mathbf{k})} == \text{sign}(\mathbf{y}(\mathbf{x}))\right). \tag{12}$$

2.5. Non-negative Matrix Factorization

Non-negative Matrix Factorization is an approach which factorises the training data into a set of recurrent acoustic patterns and their activations. In a supervised setting, these acoustic patterns take on the distribution of the spoken commands, as well as the acoustic patterns of filler words which are shared between commands, e.g. the, and, please. As such, it can potentially leverage shared information between commands.

A scheme of the Non-negative Matrix Factorization (NMF) is given in Figure 2 [18]. The non-negative matrix $\mathbf{V}^{(\text{train})}$ consists of two parts, viz. $[\mathbf{V_0}^{(\text{train})}; \mathbf{V_1}^{(\text{train})}]$. Each of the m commands ω_k is represented by a vector representation $\mathbf{y}^{(\mathbf{k})}$, which is a zero m dimensional vector with a 1 on position k. The columns of the matrix $\mathbf{V_0}^{(\text{train})}$ contain the vector representation $\mathbf{y}^{(\mathbf{k})}$ of the command ω_k for each utterance in the training data, so $\mathbf{V_0}^{(\text{train})}$ is a matrix of dimension $m \times N_{\text{train}}$. The columns of the matrix $\mathbf{V_1}^{(\text{train})}$ contain the utterance based feature vector $\mathbf{x}$ for each utterance X in the training data, so $\mathbf{V_1}^{(\text{train})}$ is a matrix of dimension length$(\mathbf{x}) \times N_{\text{train}}$. A low rank representation for $\mathbf{V_1}^{(\text{train})}$ is obtained by factorizing $\mathbf{V}^{(\text{train})}$ as the product of two non-negative matrices $\mathbf{W}$ and $\mathbf{H}^{(\text{train})}$, viz.

$$\begin{bmatrix}\mathbf{V_0}^{(\text{train})} \\ \mathbf{V_1}^{(\text{train})}\end{bmatrix} \approx \begin{bmatrix}\mathbf{W_0} \\ \mathbf{W_1}\end{bmatrix} \mathbf{H}^{(\text{train})} = \mathbf{W}\mathbf{H}^{(\text{train})}. \tag{13}$$

The number of columns of $\mathbf{W}$, i.e. the number of acoustic patterns to extract from the training data, is fixed in advance. The matrices $\mathbf{W}$ and $\mathbf{H}^{(\text{train})}$ are obtained by iteratively minimizing the Kullback-Leibler divergence [19] between $\mathbf{V}^{(\text{train})}$ and $\mathbf{W}\mathbf{H}^{(\text{train})}$. After training, the matrix $\mathbf{W_1}$ contains as columns the acoustic patterns that exist in the training data. Element $\mathbf{W_0}(k,j)$ indicates if the acoustic pattern in column j of $\mathbf{W_1}$ is present in command ω_k. The element $\mathbf{H}^{(\text{train})}(i,j)$ indicates how much the acoustic pattern in column i of $\mathbf{W_1}$ is present in utterance $X^{(j)}$ of the training data (column j of $\mathbf{V_1}^{(\text{train})}$).

For speech classification with NMF, the utterance based feature vector $\mathbf{x}$ of speech signal X is used as vector $\mathbf{V_1}^{(\text{test})}$. By minimizing the Kullback-Leibler divergence between $\mathbf{V_1}^{(\text{test})}$ and $\mathbf{W_1}\mathbf{H}^{(\text{test})}$, the vector $\mathbf{H}^{(\text{test})}$ is calculated

$$\mathbf{V_1}^{(\text{test})} \approx \mathbf{W_1}\mathbf{H}^{(\text{test})}. \tag{14}$$

An approximation of $\mathbf{V_0}^{(\text{test})}$, containing the representation of the command for each utterance in the test data, is given by the activation vector $\mathbf{A}$

$$\mathbf{V_0}^{(\text{test})} \approx \mathbf{A} = \mathbf{W_0}\mathbf{H}^{(\text{test})}. \tag{15}$$

The similarity between speech signal X and command ω_k is given by the positive number

$$\Pi(\omega_k, X) = A(k). \tag{16}$$

3. Combining methods

Each classification method uses different mechanisms to assign an unlabelled speech signal X to the most probable command ω_j. As a result, not all classification methods assign an unlabelled speech signal to the same command, so the misclassifications differ. In this paper we investigate whether combining R different classification methods, i.e. boosting [8], might reduce the number of misclassifications. Each method r calculates a positive number $\Pi_r(\omega_k, X)$ for each command ω_k.

The numbers $\{\Pi_r(\omega_k, X)\}_{k=1}^M$ are normalized to construct a probability vector $\mathbf{p_r}$ for each method. The combination of the classification methods assigns the unlabelled speech signal X to the command ω_j with the highest a posteriori probability

$$\text{assign } X \rightarrow \omega_j = \underset{\omega_k}{\text{argmax}}\ P(\omega_k|\mathbf{p_1}, ..., \mathbf{p_R}). \tag{17}$$

Possible combination rules are the product rule, sum rule, maximum rule, minimum rule, median rule and majority rule. Table 1 gives the a posteriori probability for these rules.

Figure 2: *Scheme of Non-negative Matrix Factorization.*

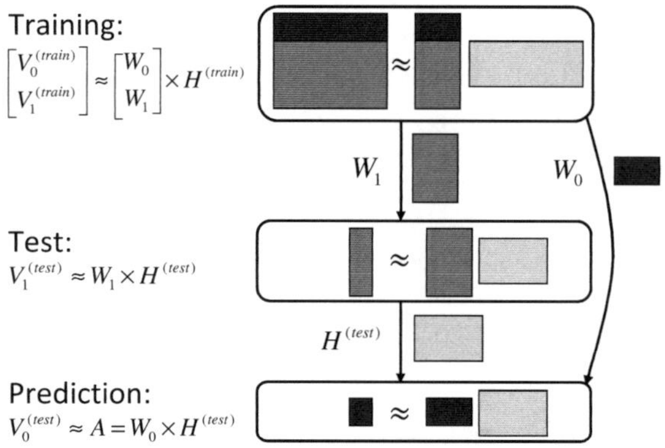

The combination rules in Table 1 make the assumption that each method assigns a speech signal to a command independently of the other methods, which results in

$$P(\mathbf{p_1}, ..., \mathbf{p_R}|\omega_k) = \prod_{i=1}^{R} P(\mathbf{p_i}|\omega_k). \tag{18}$$

In this paper the extra assumption of equal a priori probabilities is made for each rule. The a posteriori probability of the product rule is obtained by repeatedly applying Bayes' rule. In the sum rule the assumption is made that the a posteriori probabilities $P(\omega_k|\mathbf{p_i})$ calculated by the different methods do not significantly differ from the a priori probabilities $P(\omega_k)$. The maximum rule is obtained starting from the sum rule and using the relation

$$\frac{1}{R}\sum_{i=1}^{R} P(\omega_k|\mathbf{p_i}) \leq \max_i P(\omega_k|\mathbf{p_i}). \tag{19}$$

The minimum rule is obtained starting from the product rule and using the relation

$$\prod_{i=1}^{R} P(\omega_k|\mathbf{p_i}) \leq \min_i P(\omega_k|\mathbf{p_i}). \tag{20}$$

The a posteriori probability of the median rule is obtained by replacing the mean by the more robust median in the sum rule. In the majority rule the assumption is made that the a posteriori probabilities $P(\omega_k|\mathbf{p_i})$ calculated by the different methods do not significantly differ from the a priori probabilities $P(\omega_k)$.

4. Experimental setup

4.1. Dataset

The experiments are performed on the first home automation dataset (DOMOTICA-1) of the ALADIN project [9]. The dataset consists of non-pathological speech commands which were recorded in a realistic setting, i.e. a fully automated room using a wizard-of-oz device control. The commands were prompted using visual cues (a video) on a computer screen. In order to simulate situations with environmental noise, recordings were also made with a concurrent sound source. In addition to a close-talk microphone, multichannel audio recordings were made with multiple microphone arrays, placed near the user, on walls and near the optional noise source.

Table 1: *A posteriori probabilities for combination rules in assumption of equal a priori probabilities.*

rule	$P(\omega_k\|\mathbf{p_1}, ..., \mathbf{p_R})$
product	$\prod_{i=1}^{R} P(\omega_k\|\mathbf{p_i})$
sum	$\sum_{i=1}^{R} P(\omega_k\|\mathbf{p_i})$
maximum	$\max_i P(\omega_k\|\mathbf{p_i})$
minimum	$\min_i P(\omega_k\|\mathbf{p_i})$
median	$\operatorname{med}_i P(\omega_k\|\mathbf{p_i})$
majority	$\frac{1}{R}\sum_{i=1}^{R} \Delta_{k,i}$
	with $\Delta_{k,i} = \begin{cases} 1 & \text{if } \omega_k = \operatorname{argmax}_{\omega_l} P(\omega_l\|\mathbf{p_i}) \\ 0 & \text{otherwise} \end{cases}$

The noisy recordings were created by playing a radio in the background with a sound level of 60dB Sound Pressure Level, which is the sound level of average speech. It was ensured that the measured SNR to the nearest microphone remained above 15dB.

The dataset consists of 27 test subjects of which 20 are of the targeted user group. Each person was asked to go repeatedly through a list of 33 different actions, until a recording time of 30 minutes was reached, yielding a dataset of 1888 commands for the target group. In addition to this set, longer recording sessions with 7 non-target users were carried out, yielding 1699 spoken commands.

The experiments are performed on persons 5,7,20,22 and 26, on the noisy dataset recorded with the close-talk microphone. These speakers were selected because they were the only speakers with at least 3 spoken samples of each command. We will refer to them by these numbers to keep correspondence with other work on the same dataset.

4.2. Acoustic representation

In this paper two classes of feature vectors are used: spectrographic based feature vectors and utterance based feature vectors [20, 21]. The MFCC, MFCCDD and MIDA feature vectors are used as spectrographic based feature vectors. The GMM-supervector and the feature vector based on the histogram of acoustic occurrences and co-occurrences (sumHAC) are used as utterance based feature vector [18]. In this paper a Hamming window of size 30 ms is used with frame shifts of 15 ms. A pre-emphasis of 0.95 is used.

The MFCC feature vectors are obtained by applying an Inverse Discrete Cosine Transform (IDCT) to log-Mel spectra. In this paper, we use 12 MFCCs in each frame, in addition to the log energy, resulting in 13-dimensional feature vectors. To obtain the MFCCDD feature vectors, the 13-dimensional MFCC feature vectors are augmented with their first and second order differences (Δ- and $\Delta\Delta$-features), yielding a total of 39 coefficients per frame.

The Mutual Information Discriminant Analysis (MIDA) feature vectors are obtained with a linear transformation that maximizes the separability between different classes of input frames [22]. In this paper, we determine Δ- and $\Delta\Delta$-features on the 24 log-Mel spectral features, leading to 72-dimensional input vectors. On these representations we then perform the MIDA-transformation, separating the classes in the input space and at the same time reducing its dimensionality from 72 to 39.

The spectrographic based feature vectors are the starting point to construct the utterance based feature vectors. The GMM-supervector combines 60-dimensional MFCCDD spectrographic based feature vectors to one high-dimensional utterance based feature vector [21]. The construction of a GMM-supervector consists of three steps. The first step is training a Gaussian Mixture Model Universal Background Model (GMM UBM). To be more robust, a trained GMM UBM with 512 multivariate Gaussian distributions is used. The development data set used to train the UBM includes over 30,000 speech recordings and was sourced from NIST 2004-2006 SRE databases, LDC releases of Switchboard 2 phase III and Switchboard Cellular (parts 1 and 2) [23]. The second step in constructing a GMM-supervector is adapting the means of the multivariate Gaussian distributions of the GMM UBM according to the spectrographic based feature vectors of the speech signal. In the last step the 512 adapted means of dimension 60 are placed in a column vector, which gives the resulting 30720-dimensional GMM-supervector of the speech signal.

The utterance based feature vector based on the histogram of acoustic occurrences and co-occurrences (sumHAC) is constructed by applying a k-means clustering algorithm [16] to the MFCCDD spectrographic based feature vectors to obtain a codebook [18]. Each spectrographic based feature vector is assigned to a prototype vector in the codebook by means of an extension (softVQ) to vector quantization [24]. With softVQ a frame based feature vector characterized by its proximity to multiple prototypes is obtained. Proximity is measured as the posterior probability of a collection of Gaussians, much like in semi-continuous HMMs.

In this paper Voice Activity Detection (VAD) is used to improve the performance of a classification method [25]. By distinguishing speech and silence frames in the speech signal, both training and classification are only based on the speech frames. The distinction between speech and silence frames is made based on the energy in the frame.

4.3. Classification methods

Below, we detail the acoustic representations and parameter settings for each of the methods. To ensure a best-case scenario for each of the methods, we optimised the settings for each method individually.

DTW employs MFCC feature vectors. The use of MFCCDD and MIDA features was explored in a pilot experiment, but did not result in significant improvements.

Both the GMM and the HMM use the spectrographic MIDA feature vectors. The full-covariance GMM consists of 10 mixtures, while the GMM employed in the HMM uses 5 mixtures and a three state left-to-right HMM. The implementation uses the logarithm of the probabilities to obtain a numerically stable implementation [26].

The linear kernel SVM operates on GMM-supervectors, tuned using a cross-validation grid search. Finally, NMF is applied to the utterance based feature vector sumHAC, constructed starting from the spectrographic based feature vector MFCCDD and using the vector quantization method softVQ. In this paper codebooks of size 50 are used for softVQ and 36 acoustic patterns are extracted from the training data (columns of $\mathbf{W}$), where 3 are used for filler words.

Table 2 gives an overview of the setting for the different classification methods.

Table 2: *Settings for each classification method.*

method	setting
DTW	MFCC
GMM	MIDA, 10 mixtures
HMM	MIDA, 3 states, 5 mixtures
SVM	GMM-supervector (MFCCDD)
NMF	sumHAC (MFCCDD, softVQ)

5. Experiments

5.1. Comparing classifiers

For the experiment to determine the best classification method only 22 commands with 3 examples or more in the noisy recording scenario of person 5, 7, 20, 22 and 26 are considered. There is not enough data for the other persons in the data to investigate the influence of the number of examples for each command on the classification.

In a small dataset, the division of the commands in groups with cross-validation is more important than in larger datasets. Therefore an adaptation of cross-validation is used in the experiments. The commands are randomly divided in groups with the requirement that in each group there is exactly one speech signal belonging to each command. The least frequent command in the dataset determines the number of disjunct groups. The remaining speech signals are not used in the experiments.

To determine the accuracies of the different classification methods for k examples for each command, the classification methods are trained on k disjunct groups and tested on 1 disjunct group. All possible combinations of training groups and test group are considered. To minimize the influence of the division in groups, the experiments are repeated with 5 different random divisions in groups.

5.2. Combining classifiers

For the experiment to determine the influence of boosting on the accuracy only 22 commands with 3 examples or more in the noisy dataset of person 26 are considered. For each method $i \in \{\text{DTW, GMM, HMM, SVM, NMF}\}$ the 22×22 matrix $\mathbf{\Pi}_i$ is constructed with as (k, j) element the number $\Pi_i(\omega_k, X^{(j)})$ where ω_k is the considered command and $X^{(j)}$ a speech signal in the testdata. Each column in the matrix $\mathbf{\Pi}_i$ is scaled to a probability vector, resulting in the matrix $\mathbf{P}_i$. The adaptation of cross validation, as discussed in section 5.1, is used and the experiments are repeated with 5 different random divisions in groups to minimize the influence of the division in groups. The matrices $\mathbf{P}_i$ of the different combinations of test group and trainingsdata with 5 random divisions in groups are concatenated in the matrix $\mathbf{P}_{i,\text{TOT}}$ for n examples in the trainingsdata. The matrix $\mathbf{P}_{i,\text{TOT}}$ is of dimension $22 \times N_{\text{TOT}}$, where N_{TOT} is the product of the number of commands (22), the number of random divisions in groups (5), the number of test groups and the number of different trainingsdata for n examples in the trainingsdata.

The goal of boosting is to achieve an improvement in the accuracies with respect to the individual classification methods. In the boosting experiment, each method i is assigned a positive weight w_i, so $P(\omega_k|\mathbf{p_i})$ becomes $w_i P(\omega_k|\mathbf{p_i})$. For the

Table 3: *Accuracies obtained with classification methods in noisy recording scenario for person 5, 7, 20, 22 and 26.*

Person 5					
N_{EX}	DTW	GMM	HMM	SVM	NMF
1	48.6	30.5	17.9	5.3	**56.4**
2	56.1	72.4	56.1	6.7	**87.0**
Person 7					
N_{EX}	DTW	GMM	HMM	SVM	NMF
1	23.9	28.3	16.5	4.8	**42.4**
2	30.9	51.5	32.7	3.0	**62.7**
Person 20					
N_{EX}	DTW	GMM	HMM	SVM	NMF
1	45.0	47.3	29.2	10.8	**47.6**
2	54.8	71.2	55.8	30.6	**80.0**
Person 22					
N_{EX}	DTW	GMM	HMM	SVM	NMF
1	**67.0**	45.9	29.7	10.2	49.8
2	73.6	82.1	71.2	13.9	**86.7**
Person 26					
N_{EX}	DTW	GMM	HMM	SVM	NMF
1	**66.5**	45.5	34.0	23.9	63.4
2	75.8	69.3	66.0	53.1	**81.6**
3	80.2	78.4	79.2	69.0	**87.5**
4	83.5	83.3	84.7	77.8	**90.8**
5	85.6	85.9	88.2	81.5	**91.8**

majority rule the definition of $\Delta_{k,i}$ becomes

$$\Delta_{k,i} = \begin{cases} w_i & \text{if } \omega_k = \underset{\omega_l}{\text{argmax}}\ P(\omega_l|\mathbf{p_i}) \\ 0 & \text{otherwise.} \end{cases} \tag{21}$$

In this way a better classification method has a higher influence on the a posteriori probability.

The optimal weights w_i of the matrices $\mathbf{P}_{i,\text{TOT}}$ of the methods i in the boosting rules are obtained using grid search for 1 example for each command. The grid search of the weight w_i for each method i is between 0 and 1 with step size 1/4. Each possible combination of the weights $\mathbf{w} = [w_{\text{DTW}}, w_{\text{GMM}}, w_{\text{HMM}}, w_{\text{SVM}}, w_{\text{NMF}}]$ is scaled to one. For the combination rules, the weights $\mathbf{w} = [1/4, 1/4, 1/4, 1/4, 1/4]$ and $\mathbf{w} = [1, 1, 1, 1, 1]$ result in the same normalized weights $\mathbf{w} = [1/5, 1/5, 1/5, 1/5, 1/5]$. Only the unique normalized weights are considered. If there are multiple weights $\mathbf{w}$ which result in the highest accuracies, the first $\mathbf{w}$ is used as optimal weight.

6. Results

6.1. Comparing classifiers

Table 3 shows the accuracies with different N_{EX} examples for each command in the trainingsdata and for person 5, 7, 20, 22 and 26 with the settings of Table 2.

Table 3 shows that NMF gives the highest accuracies for each person, except for person 22 and 26 with one example for each command. The lowest accuracies are obtained with classification method SVM. The accuracies improve with an increasing number examples N_{EX} for each command, except for person 7 with SVM. The accuracies of person 7 are significantly lower than those of the other persons. For person 5 the second highest accuracies are obtained with DTW and NMF for 1 and 2 examples for each command respectively. For person 7 and 20 the second highest accuracies are obtained with GMM. The second highest accuracies for person 22 are obtained with NMF (1 example) and GMM (2 examples). For person 26 the second highest accuracies are obtained with NMF (1 example), DTW (2-3 examples) and HMM (4-5 examples). The accuracies of person 26 with GMM are initially higher than those of HMM (1-2 examples), but for more examples (3-5) the accuracies of HMM are higher.

Table 4: *Weights for person 26 with combination rules.*

rule	DTW	GMM	HMM	SVM	NMF
product	4/5	0	0	0	1/5
sum	4/5	0	0	0	1/5
maximum	4/5	0	0	0	1/5
minimum	1/17	4/17	4/17	4/17	4/17
median	1/6	4/6	0	0	1/6
majority	2/6	1/6	0	1/6	2/6

Table 5: *Accuracies for person 26 with combination rules.*

N_{EX}	product	sum	max	min	med	maj
1	**73.0**	70.6	70.7	23.9	66.7	70.2
2	**85.2**	83.8	83.5	52.7	79.3	83.4
3	**89.3**	88.8	87.8	68.7	84.4	88.3
4	**91.2**	91.0	90.6	77.5	88.2	90.8
5	**92.9**	92.0	91.1	81.2	90.5	91.7

6.2. Combining classifiers

In Table 4 the optimal weights are shown that are obtained by grid search with 1 example for each command in the training data.

Table 4 shows that the product rule, sum rule and maximum rule assign an unlabelled speech signal X based on the probability vectors $\mathbf{p_{DTW}}$ and $\mathbf{p_{NMF}}$. The median rule uses the probability vectors $\mathbf{p_{DTW}}$, $\mathbf{p_{GMM}}$ and $\mathbf{p_{NMF}}$. The majority rule uses all probability vectors except $\mathbf{p_{HMM}}$. The minimum rule bases the assignment on the probability vectors of all classification methods. The according non normalized weights in the grid search are $\mathbf{w} = [1/4, 1, 1, 1, 1]$. In the minimum rule the probability vector $\mathbf{p_{DTW}}$ gets the smallest weight. In Table 5 the accuracies obtained with the individual classification methods and the different boosting rules with weights as in Table 4 are shown.

Table 5 shows that the highest individual accuracies are obtained with the classification method DTW (1 example) and NMF (2-5 examples). The classification method SVM gives the lowest accuracies. The more examples for each command in the training data, the higher the accuracies of the individual classification methods are.

In Table 5 a significant improvement in the accuracies is observed for the product rule and sum rule with respect to the highest accuracies obtained with the individual classification methods. The maximum rule and majority rule give higher accuracies for 1 to 3 examples for each command in the training data with respect to the individual methods. For more examples for each command in the training data, the accuracies obtained with the maximum rule and majority rule are similar to those obtained with NMF. The accuracies obtained with median rule are lower than the accuracies obtained with the best individual classification method NMF, except for 1 example for each command. The median rule performs better than all individual classification methods except NMF. The minimum rule gives similar accuracies as the worst individual classification method SVM.

7. Discussion

7.1. comparing classifiers

When comparing the classifiers in Table 3, we observe a very large difference between classification methods. Since for speaker 26, the difference between methods becomes substantially smaller with increasing numbers of examples per command, we can indeed attribute most of these difference to the amount of training data used. Although it is difficult to set a target accuracy which suffices for practical applicability of these techniques, it is encouraging that for most speakers 2 examples suffice to achieve 80 to 90 % accuracy. The lower accuracies of speaker 7, although still at 62.7 % for NMF, are due to a speech impairment. Informal listening tests revealed that for this speaker, the spoken commands are difficult to understand even for humans.

As expected, DTW achieves good results when presented with only a single training sample, but is outperformed by models which learn their parameters as soon as there is more training data. It is interesting to observe that HMM is outperformed by the simpler GMM until at least 3 training samples are presented. It seems that even though the GMM employed by the HMM is smaller (5 vs 10 mixtures), the larger number of parameters that needs to be trained is still problematic for small training sizes.

Of all the methods, the SVM performs the worst, with results almost at chance level for some speakers. The results on speaker 26 indicate once again, that with more data the results become comparable. NMF, on the other hand, is able to perform well both with little and larger amounts of training data. Presumably, this is due to its capability to use some of its recurrent patterns to model phenomena such as filler words, which allows the recurrent patterns modelling commands to be more discriminative. Although these results do not allow us to investigate the accuracy when presented with much more data (hundreds of examples), but results in [7] do indicate that also in these regimes, NMF be adequate.

7.2. Combining classifiers

Unfortunately, the amount of data available did not allow us to explore methods which learn the boosting weights from the data. Our experiments therefore show an upper limit on the performance gains that can be expected using boosting. Additionally, the weights that are obtained allow us to judge which methods offer complementary information.

The product rule, sum rule and maximum rule only use the 2 classification methods DTW and NMF which have the highest accuracies for 1 example for each command. The weight w_{DTW} is higher than w_{NMF} because the accuracy of DTW is higher than that of NMF for 1 example for each command. Since these rules have the highest weight to the best classification method, the best accuracies are obtained for these rules in comparison with the other boosting rules. This effect is only visible for a few examples for each command. An explanation for this is that the best classification method DTW for 1 example gains little in comparison with the other classification methods when increasing the amount of examples for each command.

The accuracies obtained with the minimum rule are not more than the accuracies obtained with the worst classification method SVM. It is plausible that the minimum rule only gives good results if the entropy of the probabilities of the different commands for the classification methods is small (probabilities of different commands in one classification method are close together). This is not the case for the considered classification methods. In this experiment, the minimum rule has the opposite effect of what is expected of a boosting rule.

The median rule does not take the classification method HMM and SVM, which have the lowest accuracies for 1 example for each command. The obtained accuracies are similar to the accuracies obtained with NMF. This is achieved by giving the best classification methods NMF and DTW a weight such that their weighted probability vector is median.

The majority rule assigns a relative high weight to the 2 best classification methods DTW and NMF for 1 example for each command, as expected. GMM and SVM also get a non zero weight. HMM is assigned a zero weight, which is explained by the fact that HMM makes more and similar misclassifications than GMM, because of the lack of data for 1 example for each command.

The effect of boosting decreases when increasing the amount of examples for each command. This is explained by the weights are trained on 1 example for each command and the changing order of best classification methods. Some classification methods (HMM, SVM) need more data to obtain a higher accuracy, while DTW gains relatively little in accuracy when increasing the number of data.

8. Conclusions

In this paper the performance of the classification methods Dynamic Time Warping (DTW), Gaussian Mixture Model (GMM), Hidden Markov Model (HMM), Support Vector Machine (SVM) and Non-negative Matrix Factorization (NMF) are investigated on a speech classification task. Evaluations on a realistic home automation database show that NMF is best suited for speech classification with a small amount of data. Next, we investigated if combining different methods through boosting might improve the classification. Both the product rule and the sum rule give higher accuracies than the best individual classification method. The gain of combining classification methods is higher for a small amount of data. Future work will focus on exploring methods to learn the boosting weights on small amounts of training data.

9. Acknowledgements

The research of Jort F. Gemmeke is funded by IWT-SBO grant 100049.

10. References

[1] J. Noyes and C. Frankish, "Speech recognition technology for individuals with disabilities," *Augmentative and Alternative Communication*, vol. 8, no. 4, pp. 297–303, 1992.

[2] H. Christensen, S. Cunningham, C. Fox, P. Green, and T. Hain, "A comparative study of adaptive, automatic recognition of disordered speech," in *Proc Interspeech 2012*, Portland, Oregon, US, Sep 2012.

[3] K. T. Mengistu and F. Rudzicz, "Comparing humans and automatic speech recognition systems in recognizing dysarthric speech," in *Proceedings of the Canadian Conference on Artificial Intelligence*, 2011.

[4] H. V. Sharma and M. Hasegawa-Johnson, "State transition interpolation and map adaptation for hmm-based dysarthric speech recognition," in *HLT/NAACL Workshop on Speech and Language Processing for Assistive Technology (SLPAT)*, 2010, pp. 72–79.

[5] F. Rudzicz, "Acoustic transformations to improve the intelligibility of dysarthric speech," in *Proceedings of the Second Workshop on Speech and Language Processing for Assistive Technologies (SLPAT2011)*, 2011.

[6] M. S. Hawley, P. Enderby, P. Green, S. Cunningham, S. Brownsell, J. Carmichael, M. Parker, A. Hatzis, P. O'Neill, and R. Palmer, "A speech-controlled environmental control system for people with severe dysarthria," *Medical Engineering & Physics*, vol. 5, no. 29, pp. 586 – 593, 2007.

[7] J. Driesen, J. Gemmeke, and H. Van hamme, "Weakly supervised keyword learning using sparse representations of speech," in *Proceedings of the 36th International Conference on Acoustics, Speech and Signal Processing*, Kyoto, Japan, 2012.

[8] J. Kittler, M. Hatef, R. P. W. Duin, and J. Matas, "On combining classifiers," *Pattern Analysis and Machine Intelligence, IEEE Transactions on*, vol. 20, no. 3, pp. 226–239, 1998.

[9] ALADIN, "Adaptation and Learning for Assistive Domestic Vocal INterfaces," Project Page: http://www.esat.kuleuven.be/psi/spraak/projects/ALADIN.

[10] T. N. Sainath, B. Ramabhadran, D. Nahamoo, D. Kanevsky, D. V. Compernolle, K. Demuynck, J. F. Gemmeke, J. R. Bellegarda, and S. Sundaram, "Exemplar-based processing for speech recognition," *IEEE Signal Processing Magazine*, vol. 29, no. 6, pp. 98–113, 2012.

[11] D. Ellis, "Dynamic Time Warp (DTW) in Matlab," Web resource, available: http://www.ee.columbia.edu/ dpwe/resources/matlab/dtw/, 2003.

[12] M. De Wachter, M. Matton, K. Demuynck, P. Wambacq, R. Cools, and D. Van Compernolle, "Template-based continuous speech recognition," *Audio, Speech, and Language Processing, IEEE Transactions on*, vol. 15, no. 4, pp. 1377–1390, 2007.

[13] S. B. Needleman and C. D. Wunsch, "A general method applicable to the search for similarities in the amino acid sequence of two proteins," *Journal of molecular biology*, vol. 48, no. 3, pp. 443–453, 1970.

[14] D. Jurafsky and J. H. Martin, *Speech and language processing: an introduction to natural language processing, computational linguistics and speech recognition*, 2nd ed. Pearson International Edition, 2009.

[15] S. K. Ng, T. Krishnan, and G. J. McLachlan, "The EM algorithm," *Handbook of computational statistics*, vol. 1, pp. 137–168, 2004.

[16] X. Huang, A. Acero, H.-W. Hon *et al.*, *Spoken language processing*. Prentice Hall PTR New Jersey, 2001, vol. 15.

[17] J. A. K. Suykens, T. Van Gestel, J. De Brabanter, B. De Moor, and J. Vandewalle, *Least Squares Support Vector Machines*. World Scientific Publishing Co. Pte. Ltd., 2002.

[18] J. Driesen, "Discovering words in speech using matrix factorization," Ph.D. dissertation, Ph. D. dissertation, KU Leuven, ESAT, 2012.

[19] T. M. Cover and J. A. Thomas, *Elements of information theory*. Wiley-interscience, 2012.

[20] J. Driesen, J. F. Gemmeke, and H. Van hamme, "Data-driven speech representations for NMF-based word learning," in *Proc. SAPA-SCALE*, 2012, pp. 98–103.

[21] M. H. Bahari *et al.*, "Speaker age estimation using Hidden Markov Model weight supervectors," in *Information Science, Signal Processing and their Applications (ISSPA), 2012 11th International Conference on*. IEEE, 2012, pp. 517–521.

[22] K. Demuynck, J. Duchateau, and D. Van Compernolle, "Optimal feature sub-space selection based on discriminant analysis," in *Proc. Eurospeech*, vol. 3, 1999, pp. 1311–1314.

[23] M. H. Bahari, R. Saeidi, H. Van hamme, and D. van Leeuwen, "Accent recognition using i-vector, gaussian mean supervector and gaussian posterior probability supervector for spontaneous telephone speech," *Proceedings ICASSP 2013*, 2013.

[24] S. Meng and H. Van hamme, "Coding Methods for the NMF Approach to Speech Recognition and Vocabulary Acquisition," 2011.

[25] J. Ramirez, J. M. Górriz, and J. C. Segura, "Voice activity detection. fundamentals and speech recognition system robustness," *Robust Speech Recognition and Understanding*, pp. 1–22, 2007.

[26] T. P. Mann, "Numerically stable hidden Markov model implementation," *An HMM scaling tutorial*, pp. 1–8, 2006.

homeService: Voice-enabled assistive technology in the home using cloud-based automatic speech recognition

H. Christensen[1], *I. Casanuevo*[1], *S. Cunningham*[2], *P. Green*[1], *T. Hain*[1]

[1]Computer Science, University of Sheffield, Sheffield, United Kingdom
[2]Human Communication Sciences, University of Sheffield, Sheffield, United Kingdom

h.christensen@dcs.shef.ac.uk, i.casanueva@sheffield.ac.uk, s.cunningham@sheffield.ac.uk
p.green@dcs.shef.ac.uk , t.hain@dcs.shef.ac.uk

Abstract

We report on the development of a system which will bring personalised state-of-the-art automatic speech recognition into the homes of people who require voice-controlled assistive technology. The ASR will be sited remotely ('in-the-cloud') and run over a broadband link. This will enable us to adapt the system to the user's requirements and improv the accuracy and range of the system while it is in use. We outline a methodology for this: the 'Virtuous Circle'. A case study indicates that we can obtain acceptable performance by adapting speaker-independent recognisers with 10 examples of each word in a 30-word command-and-control vocabulary. We explain the idea of a PAL - a Personal Adaptive Listener - which we intend to develop out of this study.

Index Terms: dysarthric speech recognition, 'in-the-field' speech recognition, cloud-based speech recognition

1. Introduction

With an ageing population and the increasing acceptance of community-based care, there is a growing demand for electronic assistive technology (EAT). One of the major uses of EAT is to support independent living, particularly among the elderly and the physically impaired. Devices such as environmental control systems (ECSs) allow people to control many aspects of their home environment through a single control interface. Typically these systems will be operated using a switch-scanning interface which accommodates the limited motor control abilities of users who have physical disabilities.

A major drawback of switch-scanning interfaces is that they can be time-consuming and effortful to use. It is therefore appropriate to consider alternative input-methods for EAT that can accommodate users with limited physical abilities. The use of speech is an attractive alternative to switch-scanning interfaces. Indeed the prospect of using automatic speech recognition (ASR) as an alternative input-method for EAT has been discussed in the literature for more than thirty years [1, 2].

A significant proportion of people requiring EAT have dysarthria, a motor speech disorder associated with their physical disability [3]. As a result of the effect of dysarthria on speech production, inexperienced listeners find speech from people with dysarthria difficult to recognise [4]. Machine recognition of dysarthric speech is also considered a difficult problem.

Large vocabulary speaker adaptive recognition systems have been successfully used for people with mild and moderate dysarthria as a means of inputting text. These systems, however, have been shown to be less successful for people with severe dysarthria (e.g. [5, 6]). Specific modifications to speaker adaptive speech recognition algorithms with the aim of improving the recognition of dysarthric speech patterns have been described but they have not yet appeared in a widely available form [7, 8].

Speaker dependent speech recognition has often been thought to be more appropriate for users with severe dysarthria. This is because models can be trained directly with the speaker's utterances rather than assuming their speech is similar to the typical speech the models were originally trained with [9]. Speaker dependent recognisers have been shown to perform well for severely dysarthric users in several studies [10, 11]. In these examples however, the input vocabularies were quite small, which can limit the potential usefulness of the EAT system.

In recent years, new corpora of dysarthric speech have become available [12, 13]. These data sets have enabled researchers to conduct more systematic studies than before [14, 15], and open the possibility of comparing techniques using reference test sets. These corpora are however small compared to those used in modern, mainstream ASR. One reason for their relatively small size is the fact that prolonged speaking for people with severe dysarthria can be tiring. Therefore passive data collection from this population is likely to remain limited, unlike data collection for the typical speaking population. The only way to acquire substantial amounts of data is from a system which is being actively used.

Most voice-enabled EATs described in the literature have been systems that have been developed for relatively small scale studies and with the main focus being on the observed ASR performance. There are some real challenges to be solved when porting such systems and setups to more 'realistic' scenarios, especially because of the larger number of users involved, and the need for a large degree of automation whilst still accommodating the needs of the individual users for personalisation. This paper describes recent work on designing a real 'in-the-field' ASR-based EAT system where scalability and ease of initialisation has been at the forefront of the design from the onset. We have focused on two issues: how to most effectively setup an initial system for a given speaker (finding their optimal 'operating point') and how to use cloud-based ASR servers to allow the researcher free access to maintain and update ASR models.

We present the homeService system in which we are developing state-of-the-art ASR. homeService is part of the UK EPSRC Project in Natural Speech Technology project, a collaboration between the Universities of Edinburgh, Cambridge and Sheffield. homeService users are being provided with speech-driven ECS and eventually spoken access to other digital applications. We are in the process of recruiting around 10 users to a longitudinal study: each user will be engaged with homeService for at least 6 months.

From our experience in previous projects [10, 16], which included user requirement studies, we will continue to work with users in a collaborative way: the users effectively become part of the research team. As part of this process, users will inform the design and specification of the functionality of their personal system. In addition we will work with users to close what we have referred to as the 'virtuous circle'. By working with each user we will establish an initial 'operating point': a task which is sufficiently simple that we can expect good performance from the ASR and yet sufficiently useful that the user's interest is maintained. We deploy this system and provide software which enables the user to practice with it. Practice improves the user's pronunciation consistency and, crucially, provides more data for ASR training. The exercises provide the user with feedback, not based on the match to a standard pronunciation but on how well a new utterance fits the user's current model. When the performance of the system has improved sufficiently, we widen the vocabulary and range of target devices homeService controls. This process is iterated: the 'virtuous circle'. This is an example of Participatory Design [17].

As part of the ethical approval obtained for the study, the informed consent of users will enable us to collect examples of speech data from their interactions with the homeService system. These interactions will be stored and used to create a database which will become available to the research team but will not be made publicly available due to privacy issues. To further reduce any concern users might have about the system's ability to 'listen' to them, the interface will clearly indicate when the microphone is open - typically only a couple of seconds for each voice command. At any time participants will also be able to "opt-out" of the recording process, or even request recordings be deleted and not used in the database.

The ASR will run remotely 'in-the-cloud', and be connected to the homeService users' home by a dedicated broadband link. This is a novel approach for providing speech-driven EAT which will enable us to collect speech data, train new statistical models, experiment with adaptation algorithms, change vocabularies and so on without having to modify the equipment in the user's home. This will reduce the amount of researcher time spent travelling to visit users, but more importantly will enable us to modify the system rapidly. This means new models can be deployed when they are ready, and new data can be analysed as soon as it is collected. We explain the homeService setup in more detail in section 2.

The development of the 'in-the-cloud' recognition system is described in section 3. In section 5 our participatory design methodology is further developed. Some preliminary results of the speech recognition system are presented in section 4.

2. homeService setup

A schematic diagram of the homeService system is shown in figure 1. The system consists of two distinct parts: the atHome system and the atLab system. The atHome system will be deployed in a user's home and comprises a PC and a series of input and output devices to enable the system to receive spoken commands and interact with devices in the home environment, for example through the transmission of infrared signals. The atLab system resides at the university and comprises the main server which operates the ASR system and maintains the system state for each atHome system.

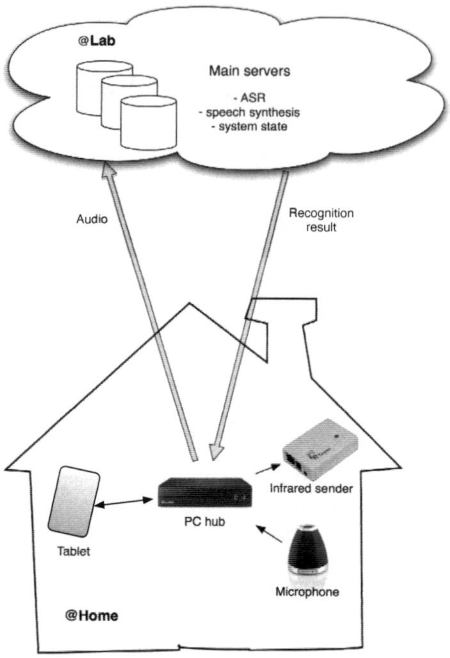

Figure 1: *Diagram of the homeService system with its two distinct parts: the atHome component in a user's home and the atLab 'in-the-cloud' part. For simplicity, only one user is drawn here but the cloud-based ASR server enables us to scale to many simultaneous users.*

The system hardware consists of 'off-the-shelf' items such as a microphone array, an Android tablet for display and an infrared transmitters, which reduces the overall cost of each installation, and means the system will not need to rely on specialist hardware. In the following sections the components of the system are described in detail.

2.1. Components

2.1.1. The PC

The atHome software is designed to run on a Linux-based PC. This PC will act as the main hub for the atHome system. It maintains the communication between the atLab part of the system and the peripherals in the atHome part of the system. The software controls the recording of audio from the system microphone, sends the audio back to the lab via a broadband link, provides feedback to the user, and controls the sending of infrared signals to various devices in the home. The software also sends updates to the screen of the tablet, and when appropriate, will play synthesised speech output.

Although, from an operational point of the view, the PC is at the heart of the atHome system, the design philosophy of the atHome system ensures that the PC is as unobtrusive as possible. Consequently, from the users' perspective the system microphone and the tablet PC are the key parts of the system.

The requirements for the PC are that it should to be relatively small, quiet and discrete, with a low energy consumption.

For this a Shuttle XH61v with a core i3 3220 was chosen (30.5 x 6.4 x 21.6 cm).

2.1.2. *Microphone*

For speech data capture, we use a high-quality USB microphone array (Dev-audio Microcone). It has a hexagonal design with 6 microphones placed in each of the six sectors, each covering approximately 60° of the surroundings. The Software Development Kit gives access to each of the 6 individual microphone channels as well as a stereo output of the beam-formed and noise-reduced signal, which will help us to reduce cross-talk from other speakers, the TV and so on. The Microcone also has a pleasing design, which is important as it will have to have a relatively prominent and very visible position in the users' homes throughout the full study.

2.1.3. *Infrared transmitter*

Remote control of the devices (such as TV, radio, lights etc.) is performed by an USB infrared (IR) emitter (IRtransWiFi IRDB). To make it personalised for each home, there is a configuration step where the emitter is trained with the IR commands from the original remote controls of the home devices. The researcher has to perform this step manually, using the software provided with the IR emitter. After this step is completed, the system is able to associate system actions (e.g. "turn on TV") to the specific IR commands for the devices it is controlling.

2.1.4. *Android tablet*

The Android tablet acts as a personalised, visual interface for the user. This has several advantages; during system operation it will

- display a representation of the system state,
- display the options available for the user (this directly corresponds to the current ASR vocabulary),
- act as a touch input if necessary.

In addition, the tablet will have an app which will enable the system to acquire additional training data from the user. Software for user practice exercises will run on the tablet.

The configuration of the display is loaded from a XML file, where the description of each device is written by the system developer. This permits the personalisation of the display.

2.1.5. *atLab Server*

The audio signal which is to be recognised is transferred across to the atLab part of the homeService system over the broadband link and subsequently passed on to the ASR server, also running at the university. When the recognition result is known it is 'acted' upon by the atLab software: for the environmental control system this means determining the next state of the system including possible infrared-codes which need transmitting and whether the tablet screen activity needs updating. All of the information concerning the state is then communicated back to the home of the user and acted upon. The two main communication links in the system (to the home and to the lab) are governed by individual APIs.

The atLab software runs on a dedicated server at the university. Apart from being the main interface to the individual users, it also handles the communication to and from a *bank* of ASR servers (one for each user) which will provide online speech recognition based on models and setups that are personalised to each user.

3. ASR

One of the main design aims was to base the system on 'in-the-cloud' ASR. This provides the research team with full control over the specifics of the ASR for each user; it is relatively straight-forward to change for example acoustic models, vocabularies and lexicons without disturbing the user unnecessarily. It also gives the researchers more scope for monitoring the state of the atHome systems, and crucially, for much more immediate trouble-shooting. Software components can easily be taken down and re-started. In the future, we also envisage having short remote chat-sessions with the users/carers to discuss any issues about the system.

It is important to bear in mind that this easy access design does impose constraints on the research team. For instance, given that data will be collected from the microphone for speech events while the system is in use, all users must be carefully briefed about how these recordings will be made and stored before they can provide informed consent to take part in the study. In the future it is envisaged that the system will be used in 'open mic' sessions when all the audio from the microphone will be gathered at agreed times of the day. Again, careful briefing of the users will be required as are procedures for users to retrospectively opt-out of these data collection sessions.

Each user has a dedicated ASR server which will be pre-loaded with personal acoustic and language models as well as grammars. To maximise performance we intend to use grammars which restrict the vocabulary according to the given state the system is in. For example, if the system is operating in the environmental control mode and the user has just turned on the guide on the TV, a state-dependent grammar would contain words needed for navigating the guide, e.g. 'up', 'down', 'left', 'right', 'ok' and 'exit' as well as certain *power* or *meta* words which would allow the user the change state, for example by saying 'home' or 'back'.

The ASR server's recognition technology is built around an in-house decoder based on weighted finite state transducers (WFSTs). This decoder was the winner in the NIST meeting recognition evaluations in 2007 and 2008. For details see [18, 19]. Every *recognition cycle* (consisting of audio being recorded, transferred across to the servers and subsequently recognised) will trigger the possibility of a change of state dependent on the current state and the newly recognised word. To further support this, the ASR server can dynamically load the next WFST from a set of pre-computed WFSTs matching all of the possible states of the system. We plan to expand this to enable online compilation of WFSTs.

4. Experimental setup

Recruitment of users is underway for the homeService study. In preparation for setting up dedicated ASR systems for each user, we have carried out a pilot-study using data from a potential user, which we recorded during previous studies. This user (F01) is a female, in her mid fifties at the time the recordings were made, who has cerebral palsy. Her speech is classified as spastic dysarthric of a severe nature. She has always been a very keen participant in our studies, and as such is a valued member of our extended research team.

We have chosen her as one of the first users in the homeService study as she has previously demonstrated that she is a highly motivated adopter of new technology; she is also a keen PC user.

She currently uses a switch mounted on the headrest of her

wheelchair to access her scanning-based environmental control system and as well as to control her PC via dedicated software.

4.1. Data

F01 has provided speech recordings for two research projects in the last decade, which is of interest here. These are all isolated words initially recorded with the aim of providing training material for whole word ASR models used in an an ECS system similar to the primary homeService task. The word lists consisted of isolated words such as "TV", "on", "off", "channel", etc. In total we have 1286 individual word recordings covering a vocabulary of 33 words (approximately 38 examples of each word).

In this study we wish to train tri-phone derived word models, and the ideal training data would be sets of phonetically rich words or sentences. However, given the nature of this data set of isolated words, it is possible to quickly create a realistic test set using examples drawn from the data set.

After a process of initial alignment to remove extraneous silences, around 40 minutes of data recorded from two different projects remained; project A provided 23 minutes of 8 kHz data (for the work here, this data has been up-sampled to 16 kHz) recorded using a headset microphone (SkyTronic Tie-Clip Microphone) onto a dedicated Arm-based embedded device (Balloon 3 board with a GEWA PROG III infrared micro chip). The remaining data from project B was recorded at 16 kHz on a laptop using a microphone array (the Acoustic Magic Voice Tracker array) [10].

4.2. Acoustic modelling

All hidden Markov models (HMMs) were trained using the maximum likelihood (ML) criterion. State-clustered, triphones having Gaussian mixture models with 16 components per state were used.

4.3. F01 case study

Although the amount of data we have available from speaker F01 is relatively small compared to what one would normally need to train a high-performance, personalised ASR system, it far exceeds what we could expect to be able to record from a new homeService user in a typical enrolment session. What it does do is enable us to explore the effect of having access to different amounts of data for e.g., adaptation purposes. The experiments presented here aim to investigate the relationship between the quantity of training and recognition performance. When recruiting new users for homeService this will be a useful indicator of how much enrolment data will need to be recorded to provide a good, initial *operating point.*

4.4. Results

First though, it is useful to assess F01's data in terms of baseline performance. Table 1 shows some baseline results for her, where we have tested all of her speech on high-performance models trained on typical speech meeting data and on good, speaker-independent models trained on the dysarthric UASpeech corpus [12]. The achieved accuracies of 8.9% and 13.5% are very low and indicate the severity of F01's speech impairment. The UASpeech result is in a range comparable to what has been reported for some of those speakers as well [20, 15].

Table 1 also shows the results from using some of F01's data to perform a *maximum a posteriori* (MAP) adaptation from the original, speaker-independent meeting models or UASpeech models [21]. As we have very limited data, the presented accuracy is the mean of the accuracies obtained from doing a round-robin style test using 10 folds of the complete dataset, each having a 90%/10% split into an adaptation set and a test set. The MAP-based systems performed best in precursor experiments reported in [15] and show large improvements over the baseline systems with accuracies of 74.7% and 75.5% respectively.

System	Accuracy
Meeting (SI)	8.9 %
Meeting+MAP (SD)	74.7 %
UASpeech (SI)	13.5 %
UASpeech+MAP (SD)	75.5 %

Table 1: *Word accuracy rates for baseline systems. Please see text for further explanation.*

It is important to note that these results were obtained using more than 1100 words from speaker F01, which is far beyond what would be reasonable and realistic to obtain from a prospective user. This is not only because prolonged periods of speaking can be tiring for these users, but also it would be a considerable undertaking to make that many recordings. In our experience it would take several weeks to collect this quantity of data.

For projects like homeService, there is a notable trade-off between not asking participants to endure lengthy enrolment sessions, whilst still ensuring we can deliver a sufficiently useful level of performance in the first system we deploy. Although all users will be aware that the systems are not perfect, if it becomes frustrating to use because of too many errors we run a real risk of the users rejecting the system (and the study), thereby breaking the foundations of the 'virtuous circle', where good systems will lead to increased use and data collection.

We therefore wished to investigate how much adaptation would be needed to get a particular level of performance. Figure 2 shows the results of increasing the amounts of data used for adapting from the speaker-independent UASpeech and meeting models respectively.

Both curves follow the same trend, and as expected the accuracy increases with increasing amounts of data (presented as number of words out of a total of 1158 words in each of the training/adaptation folds). For the lower number of words there is a dramatic increase in performance; this can be seen to taper off approximately at around 300 words. Given F01 here has a vocabulary of just over 30 words, this corresponds to approximately 10 instances of each word.

Interestingly, both the UASpeech based and the meeting model based systems converge on approximately the same, stable level after about 400 examples, but the initial curve ascends more slowly for the meeting models, so in situations where smaller amounts of adaptation data is available the closer models from UASpeech are a better starting point.

5. Longer-term plans

As the pool of homeService users grows we will continue to monitor the design choices surrounding the cloud-based setup including ease of use for the researcher as well as whether the users' feel comfortable with the idea of their system being monitored from outside of their home. It will also be interesting to

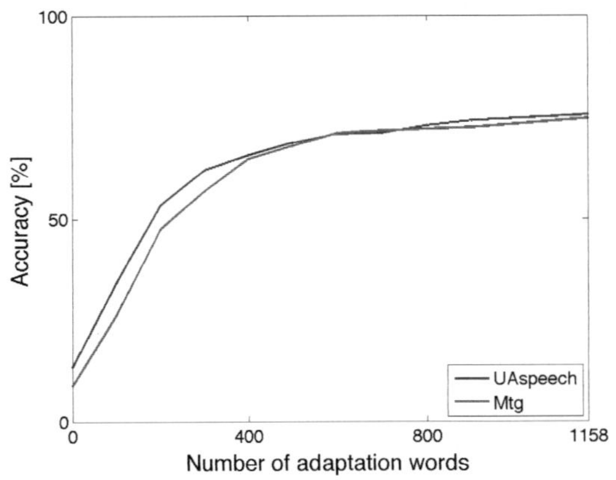

Figure 2: *Word accuracy as a function of increasing amount of data used for MAP adaptation of acoustic models; x-axis shows the number of utterances (each containing a single word) out of a possible 1158 used for adaptation.*

follow how the impact on the success of each individual user's virtuous circle.

We see the homeService systems as the first generation of PALs - Personal Adaptive Listeners. A PAL is a portable, perhaps wearable, device that belongs to an individual and adapts to the speech communication characteristics and preferences of its owner. Like human listeners, it does this whilst in use, does it quickly and extends its utility over time. A PAL is somewhat akin to a human valet: It understands its owner's needs, carries out their wishes and sometimes acts on their behalf. The technology adapts to its user, rather than the other way round. Crucially, The owner is able to teach the PAL through spoken dialogues, which develop differently for different owners. The owner-PAL relationship should be something like training a dog.

To make the step from homeService to PALs requires spoken dialogues between the owner and the device. Dialogue management techniques in commercial dialogue systems are usually hand-crafted, which makes them difficult to adapt. During the last decade it has become fashionable to approach the dialogue management problem statistically, modelling the dialogue as a Partially Observable Markov Decision Process (POMDP) and optimising the dialogue policy with Reinforcement Learning (RL) [22]. This framework provides robustness against speech understanding errors and automatic learning of dialogue policy. As the dialogue policy is learned with the data gathered from interaction with the user, it is optimised for its specific user, making it a personalised policy. RL permits online learning, so the system can also adapt its policy to changes in the user behaviour (e.g. when the user becomes more familiar with the system) and to the changes in the speech understanding system (e.g. when the ASR improves as more data is gathered). The user can also explicitly give a reward to the system after each interaction, 'teaching' the system.

The main problem with statistical dialogue management is its intractability, due to the size of the state space and to the impossibility of exact solving the POMDP, but it is possible to use approximate algorithms to build real sized dialogue systems. Another problem is the long time that takes to learn a suitable policy, but recent studies have been able to learn a policy for a non trivial tourist information system in less than 200 dialogues, which makes possible learning a policy directly from user interaction.

Adapting these techniques for PAL dialogues raises several interesting issues:

- 'teaching your PAL' should correspond to seeding the dialogue statistics.
- A PAL should not make the same mistake twice.
- The owner will know exactly what the PAL understands.

6. Acknowledgements

This research was supported by the EPSRC Programme Grant EP/I031022/1 (Natural Speech Technology).

7. References

[1] J. A. Clark and R. B. Roemer, "Voice controlled wheelchair," *Archives of Physical Medicine & Rehabilitation*, vol. 58, no. 4, pp. 169–75, 1977.

[2] A. Cohen and D. Graupe, "Speech recognition and control system for the severely disabled," *Journal of Biomedical Engineering*, vol. 2, no. 2, pp. 97–107, 1980.

[3] J. R. Duffy, *Motor Speech Disorders*, 3rd ed. London, UK: Mosby, 2013.

[4] S. A. Borrie, M. J. Mcauliffe, and J. M. Liss, "Perceptual learning of dysarthric speech : A review of experimental studies," *Journal of Speech, Language, and Hearing Research*, vol. 55, pp. 290–305, Feb 2012.

[5] M. S. Hawley, "Speech recognition as an input to electronic assistive technology," *British Journal of Occupational Therapy*, vol. 65, no. 1, pp. 15–20, 2002.

[6] N. Thomas-Stonell, A.-L. Kotler, H. A. Leeper, and C. Doyle, "Computerized speech recognition: influence of intelligibility and perceptual consistency on recognition accuracy," *Journal of Augmentative and Alternative Communication*, vol. 14, pp. 51–55, 1998.

[7] J. R. D. Jr, D. Hsu, and I. J. Ferrier, "On the use of hidden markov modelling for recognition of dysarthric speech," *Computer Methods & Programs in Biomedicine, 1991, 35(2), 125-139*, vol. 35, pp. 125–139, 1991.

[8] H. V. Sharma and M. Hasegawa-Johnson, "State transition interpolation and map adaptation for hmm-based dysarthric speech recognition," in *HLT/NAACL Workshop on Speech and Language Processing for Assistive Technology (SLPAT)*, 2010, pp. 72–79.

[9] K. Rosen and S. Yampolsky, "Automatic speech recognition and a review of its functioning with dysarthric speech," *Journal of Augmentative and Alternative Communication*, vol. 16, pp. 48–6, 2000.

[10] M. S. Hawley, P. Enderby, P. Green, S. Cunningham, S. Brownsell, J. Carmichael, M. Parker, A. Hatzis, P. O'Neill, and R. Palmer, "A speech-controlled environmental control system for people with severe dysarthria," *Medical Engineering & Physics*, vol. 5, no. 29, pp. 586 – 93, 2007.

[11] M. S. Hawley, S. P. Cunningham, F. Cardinaux, A. Coy, S. Seghal, and P. Enderby, "Challenges in developing a voice input voice output communication aid for people with severe dysarthria," in *Proceedings of the AAATE - Challenges for Assistive Technology*, 2007, pp. 363–367.

[12] H. Kim, M. Hasegawa-Johnson, A. Perlman, J. Gunderson, T. Huang, K. Watkin, and S. Frame, "Dysarthric speech database for universal access research," in *Proceedings of Interspeech*, Brisbane, Australia, 2008, pp. 22–26.

[13] F. Rudzicz, A. K. Namasivayam, and T. Wolff, "The TORGO database of acoustic and articulatory speech from speakers with dysarthria," *Language Resources and Evaluation.*, pp. 1–19, 2011.

[14] H. V. Sharma, M. Hasegawa-Johnson, J. Gunderson, and A. Perlman, "Universal access: Speech recognition for talkers with spastic dysarthria," in *Interspeech'09*, Brighton, UK, sep 2009.

[15] H. Christensen, S. Cunningham, C. Fox, P. Green, and T. Hain, "A comparative study of adaptive, automatic recognition of disordered speech," in *Proc Interspeech 2012*, Portland, Oregon, US, Sep 2012.

[16] H. Christensen, S. Siddharth, P. O'Neill, Z. Clarke, S. Judge, S. Cunningham, and M. Hawley, "SPECS - an embedded platform, speech-driven environmental control system evaluated in a virtuous circle framework," in *In proc. Workshop on Innovation and Applications in Speech Technology*, 2012.

[17] S. L., *Participatory Design: Principles and Practices.* N.J.: Lawrence Erlbaum, 1993, ch. Forward, p. viiix.

[18] T. Hain, L. Burget, J. Dines, G. Garau, M. Karafiat, M. Lincoln, D. van Leeuwen, and V. Wan, "The 2007 AMI(DA) system for meeting transcription. in NIST rich transcription 2007," *Lecture Notes in Computer Science*, pp. 414–428, 2008.

[19] J. G. Fiscus, J. Ajot, and J. S. Garofolo, "The rich transcription 2007 meeting recognition evaluation," in *Multimodal Technologies for Perception of Humans*, vol. 4625/2008. Springer Berlin/Heidelberg, 2008, pp. 373–389.

[20] H. V. Sharma and M. Hasegawa-Johnson, "Acoustic model adaptation using in-domain background models for dysarthric speech recognition," *Computer Speech and Language*, 2012.

[21] J.-L. Gauvain and C.-H. Lee, "Maximum a posteriori estimation for multivariate Gaussian mixture observations of Markov chains," *IEEE Transactions on Speech and Audio Processing*, vol. 2, no. 2, pp. 291–298, 1994.

[22] M. Gasic, M. Henderson, B. Thomson, P. Tsiakoulis, and S. Young, "Policy optimisation of pomdp-based dialogue systems without state space compression," in *Workshop on Spoken Language Technology (SLT)*, 2012, pp. 31–36.

Automating speech reception threshold measurements using automatic speech recognition

Hanne Deprez[1], *Emre Yılmaz*[1], *Stefan Lievens*[2], *Hugo Van hamme*[1]

[1] Dept. of Electrical Engineering (ESAT), KU Leuven, Leuven, Belgium
[2] Cochlear Technology Center Belgium, Schaliënhoevedreef 20i, Mechelen, Belgium

hanne.deprez@student.kuleuven.be, emre.yilmaz@esat.kuleuven.be,
slievens@cochlear.com, hugo.vanhamme@esat.kuleuven.be

Abstract

The speech reception threshold (SRT) is the noise level at which the speech recognition rate of a test person is 50%. SRT measurement is relevant for patient screening, psychoacoustic research and algorithm development in hearing aids and cochlear implants. In this paper, we report on our efforts to automate SRT measurement using an automatic speech recognizer. During a test, sentences are presented to the test subject at different SNR levels. The person under test repeats the sentence and the keywords it contains are scored by an audiologist. If all keywords are repeated correctly, the sentence is evaluated as correct. The SNR level of each sentence is adjusted based on the previous sentence's evaluation. Aiming for an objective and repeatable measurement, the audiologist's assessment is replaced by an automatic speech recognizer's evaluation. For this purpose, we investigate different finite state transducer structures to model the expected sentences as well as the impact of several speaker adaptation schemes on the keyword detection accuracy. A baseline recognizer using general acoustic models achieves a performance of 88.8% keyword detection rate. Speaker adapted acoustic models improve the performance yielding a keyword detection accuracy of up to 90.7%. Finally, the impact of recognition errors on the estimated SRT value is simulated showing a minimal impact on the SRT measurement process. Based on this analysis, it can be concluded that the proposed automatic evaluation scheme is a viable tool for speech reception threshold measurements.

Index Terms: keyword detection, speaker adaptation, cochlear implant, speech test, speech reception threshold

1. Introduction

Speech reception threshold (SRT) measurements have been used in a clinical setting for evaluating a person's hearing capabilities and to diagnose hearing loss. The obtained SRT value is a subjective measure for quantifying the hearing ability of patients with cochlear implants (CI) in order to adjust the CI parameters and analyze the impact of new developments in CI devices on the patient's hearing abilities [1, 2, 3]. Moreover, these measurements provide useful data for psychoacoustic research, e.g. to investigate how cognitive load influences speech recognition of individuals.

Several Dutch speech tests for determining a patient's speech recognition threshold have been proposed, e.g. NVA-tests [4] and LIST-tests [5]. During these tests, words or sentences which are embedded in different levels of noise are presented to patients and they are asked to repeat what they hear. The responses are evaluated by an audiologist who decides if patients properly repeat the presented word or sentence. LIST-tests consist of ten sentences that are presented to a patient at a certain noise level. For each sentence, two to five content words (called keywords henceforth) are defined. Each keyword in the patient's response is evaluated by the audiologist and if all keywords were reproduced correctly (incorrectly), the noise level in which the following sentence is embedded is increased (decreased) by 2 dB resulting in a more (less) challenging recognition task. After ten sentences, the SRT value is obtained by averaging the SNR levels at which the last six sentences are presented. This speech reception threshold corresponds to the point where 50% of the keywords are understood correctly by the patient.

At the outset of this study, the SRT test procedure was identified as one that was particularly apt for automation since it seems feasible to set up an automatic speech evaluation method that makes significantly fewer errors than the human under test, who operates around a 50% rate. Hence, errors introduced by the speech recognizer are expected not to affect the test outcome significantly. An automated test provides the additional benefit of an objective and repeatable measurement compared to an audiologist whose evaluation may be biased. Furthermore, automating this procedure saves a great amount of time in which audiologists could focus more on their core tasks: providing a better assistance to CI patients.

Automation of these tests was investigated in [6] by letting the patients type what they have heard while accounting for spelling errors. A rehabilitation tool for CI users using automatic speech recognition (ASR) is described in [7]. CI patients are encouraged to repeat spoken sentences upon which correctness feedback is provided using ASR. The proposed system for SRT tests is similar in recognition task, but differs in the language model constraints since the main task is to detect the keywords rather than recognition of the complete utterance. It also differs from traditional keyword spotting (KWS) [8, 9, 10] because the knowledge of the embedding sentence can be exploited while KWS is mainly used for unconstrained and spontaneous speech. As the expected utterances are known in the scope of this paper, the use of deterministic language models is feasible. The design procedure of these deterministic language models is presented further in this paper.

We have further investigated the impact of several speaker adaptation techniques on the keyword detection accuracy. In this scenario, the data of an earlier SRT measurement session with the same patient is reused to adapt his/her acoustic models. Several adaptation methods such as MLLR [11] and constrained and unconstrained linear mean and covariance transforms [12] are applied to the speaker independent acoustic models and the

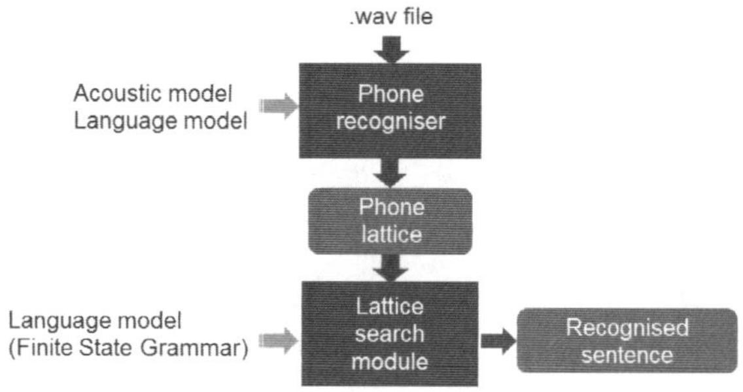

Figure 1: *Two layered speech recognition architecture.*

performances of the adapted models are compared.

The rest of the paper is organized as follows. Section 2 introduces the speech recognizer's architecture and discusses the design of deterministic language models and the speaker adaptation techniques that are applied in the experiments. The experimental setup is described in Section 3 and the results are presented in Section 4. Finally, the conclusions are discussed in Section 5.

2. Automatic Speech Evaluation Scheme

The proposed evaluation scheme uses an automatic speech recognizer that replaces the audiologist during the SRT measurements. The overview of the ASR that is used for this purpose is given in Section 2.1. As the expected utterances are known, deterministic language models with different structures are designed and used during recognition. Section 2.2 details the design procedure. Finally, several speaker adaptation techniques are applied to investigate the impact on the recognition accuracy which is the topic of Section 2.3.

2.1. ASR overview

A two layered HMM-based recognition system as illustrated in Figure 1 is used for obtaining the word-level recognition output. In the first layer, a phone recognizer generates a phone lattice using task-independent acoustic and language models. These models can be general models that are trained on the data of the target language. In the second layer, task-dependent information is provided in the form of a finite state transducer (FST) describing lexical and grammatical knowledge. The FST is composed of two levels, namely the word and garbage FSTs modeling the phone level information and the sentence FST containing multiple word and garbage FSTs to model the expected utterances. This structure comes with increased modularity as the generic phone recognizer can be used for any recognition task provided that the task-specific information is contained in the second stage [13]. Using the task-dependent information incorporated in the FSTs, the phone lattice obtained in the previous step is decoded into a word level recognition result which can further be processed to obtain the keywords that have been uttered.

2.2. Language model design

The basic FST structure models the expected sentence by allowing the correct utterances of the words in the order they appear in the prompt. Incorrect or irrelevant utterances are modeled by the garbage FST. However, due to the nature of SRT measurement tests, it is a requirement to have higher flexibility in the sentence FST as the patients can repeat the presented words in arbitrary order or they may skip some of the presented words. All FSTs consist of a number of nodes and arcs depending on the number of phones and words in the expected sentence. The start and end nodes are marked with <s> and </s> respectively. All other nodes are labeled with the keywords: visiting a state indicates the associated keyword was detected. State transitions occur upon a match between a word or phrase model (the edge's earmark) and a partial path in the phone lattice output by the first layer. Non-keywords (henceforth *filler words*), silence (marked with #) and garbage (marked with GBG) cause a self-transition. Garbage models any unanticipated speech allowing any phone sequence. To keep it from being preferred over other edges, it is penalized with a *garbage model cost* that is incurred once upon entry. Based on this principle, three different FSTs are designed modeling the expected patient's response, each of which handles the filler words differently.

In the first model, named the KWandFILLER model, each filler word is accepted as an input with an arc linked to the node of the preceding keyword. This model is illustrated with an example for the Dutch sentence "MAMA vertelt ons elke AVOND een kort VERHAAL" (MOM reads us a short STORY every NIGHT) in Figure 2, where keywords are written in uppercase characters.

In the KWandLONGFILLER model, only filler words of sufficient length are added to the model in order to limit the number of falsely detected filler words. This model is expected to reduce the false alarms due to short filler words.

The third design, the KWandFILLERSEQ model, contains a single arc that is associated with all filler words that appear between two keywords. In this model, the canonical order of the filler words is taken into account. This could have the advantage that the filler words are recognized in the correct order and should prevent (especially short) fillers from erroneously modeling keywords.

2.3. Speaker adaptation techniques

Speaker adaptation is implemented by linearly transforming the means and possibly also the covariances of the Gaussians of a speaker independent (SI) acoustic model. This transform is obtained by maximizing the likelihood of a selection of adaptation data as described in [11] and [12].

Three different adaptation techniques, namely a linear mean transform (MLLR), constrained mean and covariance transform (CMLLR) and unconstrained mean and covariance transform (UMLLR), are investigated. For MLLR, the means (μ) of the Gaussians of the SI acoustic models are linearly transformed with a transformation matrix W: $\hat{\mu} = W\xi$ with $\xi = [1\ \mu]$. For UMLLR, the transformation matrix W of the means (μ) and the transformation matrix H of the covariances (Σ) are separate: $\hat{\mu} = W\xi$ and $\hat{\Sigma} = H\Sigma H^T$. In the case of CMLLR, the transformation A' applied to the variances (Σ) must correspond to the transformation A' applied to the means (μ): $\hat{\mu} = A'\mu - b'$ and $\hat{\Sigma} = A'\Sigma A'^T$. These transforms are obtained by maximizing the likelihood of the adaptation data, details of which are given in [11] and [12].

In each of these adaptation schemes, the states that are present in the adaptation data should be provided. This information is captured in a state segmentation which is generated from a transcription of the utterance. This transcription is acquired by manual annotation of the data. To avoid this manual

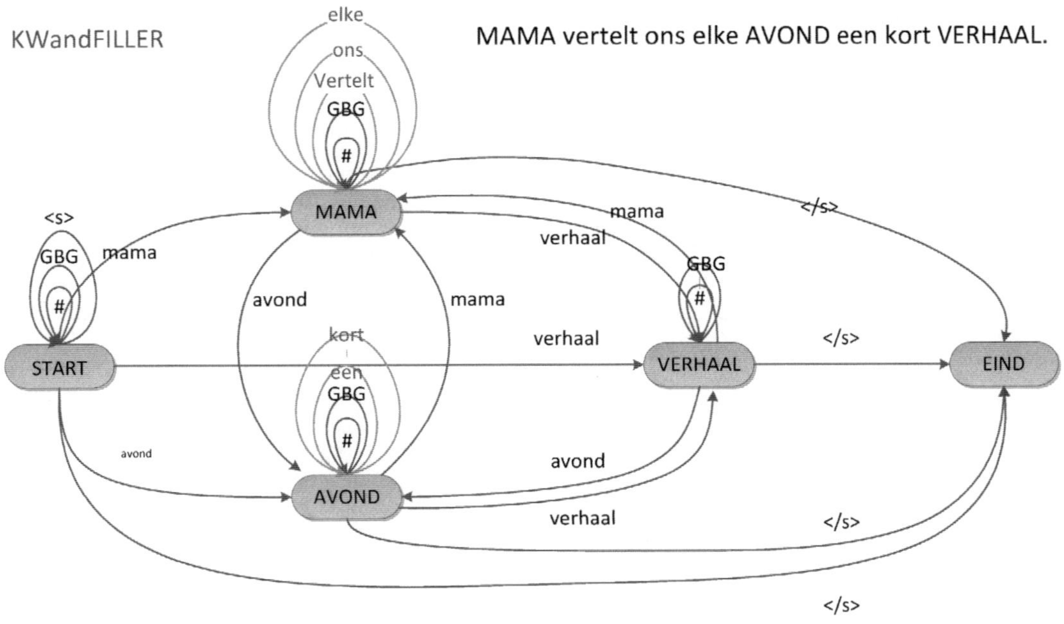

Figure 2: *Example of the KWandFILLER FST model.*

intervention, unsupervised adaptation is also considered, where only sentences that were assessed as correct by the system are retained as adaptation data.

3. Experimental setup

3.1. Speech data and baseline recognizer

The performance of the baseline system with the presented FST models and of the system with the adapted acoustic models was evaluated on recordings that contain the patient's responses to LIST-tests performed by normal hearing persons. Utterances from 17 speakers two of which are non-native Dutch speakers are captured in a recording cabin used for SRT measurements. In total, 79 lists are evaluated resulting in 4.64 lists per person on average. For the speakers with enough recorded lists, speaker adaptation was applied and performance of the speaker adapted system is evaluated using cross validation to obtain statistically significant results.

The acoustic models were trained based on the CoGen database ([14]) which contains 7 hours of read speech. The speaker independent acoustic models are semicontinuous HMMs with tied Gaussians consisting of 576 states and 10635 Gaussians. The task-independent language model consists of a trigram phoneme sequence model derived from a Dutch database with correctly read sentences [15]. The preprocessing is based on Mel-spectrum analysis and includes cepstral mean subtraction and discriminant analysis (MIDA) [15] [16].

3.2. Evaluation metrics

When evaluating the quality of the automated CI test, there are two important errors to consider: not detecting correct sentences on the one hand and classifying a sentence that is incorrect as correct on the other hand. Two performance criteria have been defined: keyword detection rate (KDR) quantifying the former and false alarm rate (FAR) quantifying the latter. Both of these metrics are defined at the sentence level, since the SNR is adapted based on the evaluation of an *entire* sentence. A sentence is correct if all keywords are repeated correctly by the patient and incorrect if the patient missed at least one keyword.

$$\mathrm{KDR} = \frac{\#\text{ of correctly detected sentences}}{\#\text{ of correct sentences}} \tag{1}$$

$$\mathrm{FAR} = \frac{\#\text{ of sentences incorrectly classified as correct}}{\#\text{ of incorrect sentences}} \tag{2}$$

4. Results and discussion

4.1. Baseline system

The FSG models presented above are evaluated according to their performance by means of a KDR-FAR plot in Figure 3. There are three different operating points obtained by manipulating the phone lattice density. The equal error rate points are marked with $\diamond$. The KWandLONGFILLER model provides the worst performance, whereas the other two models perform similarly. The reason for the bad performance of the KWandLONGFILLER model is that it has to use the garbage model to model the short filler words. The performance of the model is thus very dependent on the choice of the garbage model cost. If the garbage model cost is very high, keywords might be detected at the instants where short filler words are uttered. On the other hand, if the garbage model cost is too low, the garbage model is often used to explain the utterance resulting in an increased number of keyword deletions. The performance of the KWandFILLER and KWandFILLERSEQ model are comparable. The KWandFILLER model is the most flexible of the two allowing patients not to say filler words or repeat them in any order, though such deviations do not occur often in our data. Since it is expected that the KWandFILLER model would per-

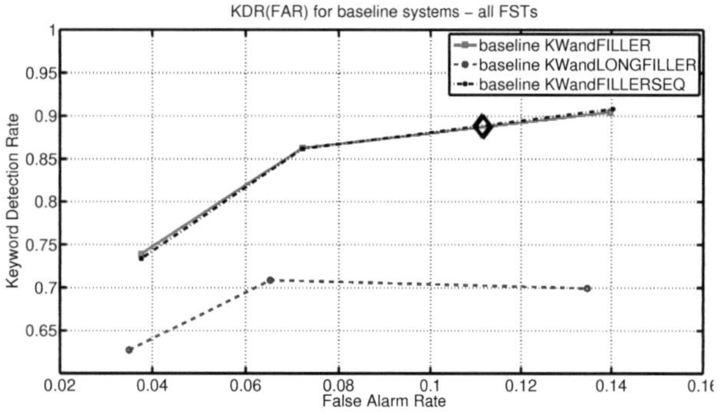

Figure 3: *Comparison of different FST models for the baseline system.*

form better in case a patient would deviate from the canonical word order, the KWandFILLER model is the best choice for practical applications. The equal error rate point is at a FAR of 11.2% and a KDR of 88.8% as indicated in Figure 3.

4.2. Speaker adapted system

The three adaptation techniques described above are implemented and the obtained KDR-FAR curves are illustrated in Figure 4. The adapted systems perform better than the baseline at most of the operating points. The equal error rate point is obtained at a false alarm rate of 9.7% for MLLR, 9.85% for UMLLR and 9.3% for CMLLR as indicated in the figure.

These adapted models are obtained using the manually annotated adaptation data from two LIST-tests (20 sentences). The adapted models for a certain speaker were tested on the other recorded lists for that speaker. To obtain enough statistical relevance, cross-validation is applied.

In the case of unsupervised adaptation, only sentences which were evaluated as correct by the baseline recognizer are included as adaptation data. When considering two lists per person, only a limited number of adaptation sentences could be included. It was not possible however to consider more lists, because of the limited number of recorded lists per speaker. Here, the expected utterance is used as the transcription. In Figure 5 the KDR-FAR curves for baseline, supervised and unsupervised adapted systems are plotted. The adaptation technique that was applied here is MLLR. The unsupervised adapted system performs worse than the baseline at some operating points. This is because not enough adaptation data could be included, due to the limited number of recordings per person. The equal error rate point for the unsupervised adapted system is obtained at a false alarm rate of 10.75%, compared to the 9.7% FAR for the supervised adapted system.

4.3. Theoretical impact of the recognition error on the measured SRT-value

A LIST test consists of ten sentences, the first of which is presented at a very low SNR. This sentence is repeated until it is evaluated as correct. Then, we advance to the next sentence adapting the SNR at which the sentence is presented according to the evaluation of the previous sentence. In the end, the mean of the SNR at which the last six sentences were presented is taken as the measured SRT-value.

Since the recognizer makes errors by not detecting correct

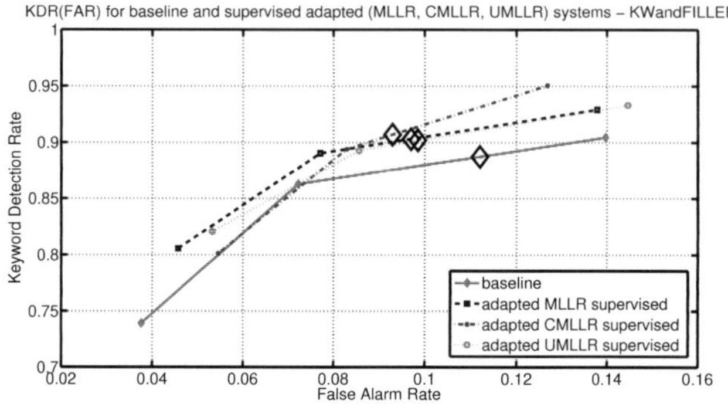

Figure 4: *Comparison of the adapted system performance (MLLR, CMLLR and UMLLR) with baseline system using the KWandFILLER model.*

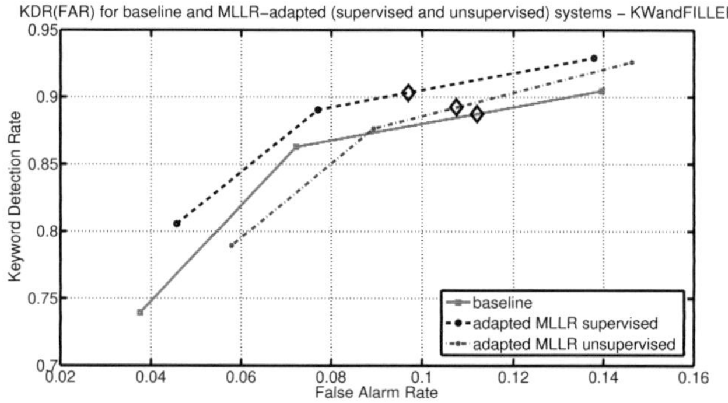

Figure 5: *Comparison of the MLLR-adapted system performance (supervised and unsupervised) with baseline system using the KWandFILLER model.*

sentences and falsely evaluating incorrect sentences as correct, the measured SRT using the automatic procedure will deviate from the manually obtained value. The effect of the recognizer error on the final SRT is modeled using performance intensity functions. These performance intensity functions model the patient's score as a function of the SNR at which the sentence is presented. An example of a performance intensity curve is given in Figure 6. Based on the input SNR, the probability of a patient understanding the sentence correctly is determined. A binomial variable with this probability is drawn indicating the patient's evaluation of the sentence. A recognition error is introduced by the speech recognizer which may flip this evaluation adjusting the SNR in the wrong way. Based on the recognizer's evaluation, the next SNR is calculated. By simulating a large number of lists, we obtain the distribution of the measured SRT-value with and without a recognizer error. Without introducing the recognizer error, the mean measured SRT over 300 lists is found to be -7.8 dB with a standard deviation of 1.2 dB. With a recognizer error of 10 %, the mean measured SRT becomes -8.0 dB with a standard deviation of 1.8 dB. The evolution of the mean and standard deviation of the measured SRT in function of the ASR's error rate are presented in Figure 7 and 8 respectively. It can be seen that the mean measured SRT value deviates further from the initial value of -7.8 dB for normal hearing persons as the recognizer error increases. The standard deviation on the

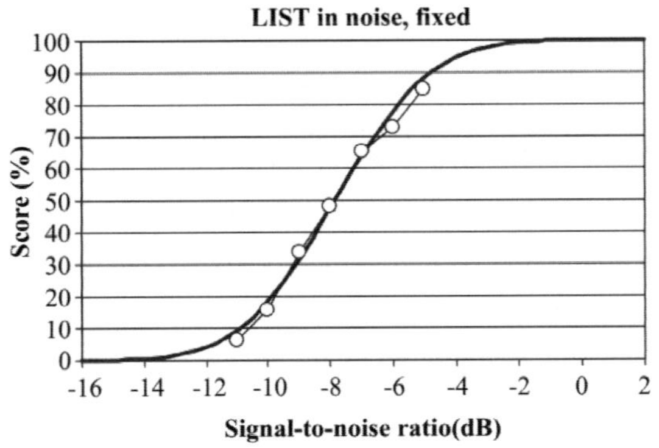

Figure 6: *Performance intensity curve for a LIST sentence presented at a certain SNR. (Taken from [5]).*

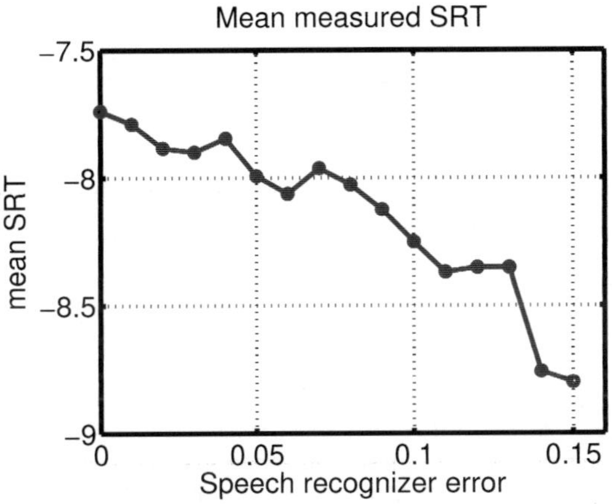

Figure 7: *The mean of the measured SRT as a function of the speech recognition error.*

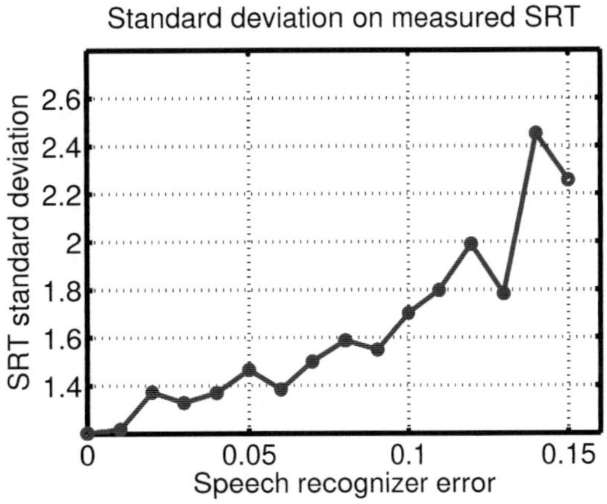

Figure 8: *The standard deviation on the measured SRT as a function of the speech recognition error.*

measured SRT also increases with an increase in the recognizer error.

When new CI techniques are assessed, a comparative measurement before and after activation of the new component is performed. In this case, the bias on the measurement observed when comparing the manual and the automatic test results is of minor importance. It is important however that measurements can be conducted with significant accuracy. If desired, the standard deviation on the measured SRT can be reduced using more sentences per LIST-test. Using 20 instead of 10 sentences per LIST, reduces the standard deviation on the measured SRT to $1.13\ dB$, for a recognizer error of 10%.

Another use of LIST-tests is to assess the hearing of patients based on their SRT score. In this task, an absolute SRT value is obtained and hence a bias might lead to inaccurate estimations. However, when assessing whether a person has normal hearing or needs some treatment, the differences in SRT scores are so large that this bias will not lead to a different evaluation.

5. Conclusions

A Dutch CI speech reception threshold test (LIST) has been automated using automatic speech recognition. The LIST consists of ten sentences played at different SNR levels depending on the evaluation of the previous sentence. The speech reception threshold is estimated as the mean of the last six SNR levels.

A speaker independent speech recognizer can work at an operating point with a false alarm rate of 11.2% and keyword detection rate of 88.8% which are both defined at the sentence level. Speaker adaptation improves the results to 9.3% false alarm rate and 90.7% keyword detection rate. The results are obtained at the equilibrium point on the keyword detection rate-false alarm rate curve which reduces the impact of recognition errors on the measured SRT value.

Furthermore, a simulation of the impact of recognizer error on the SRT estimate is provided. In comparison to a manually performed test, there is a bias of 0.2 dB on the SRT measured with the automatic procedure. The standard deviation also increases from 1.2 dB to 1.8 dB. We conclude that these results are sufficiently small for using the automated test in practice.

6. Acknowledgements

The authors would like to thank the participants of the recording sessions of the LIST-tests.

7. References

[1] P. C. Loizou, O. Poroy, and M. Dorman, "The effect of parametric variations of cochlear implant processors on speech understanding," *The Journal of the Acoustical Society of America*, vol. 108, p. 790, 2000.

[2] J. Müller, F. Schon, and J. Helms, "Speech understanding in quiet and noise in bilateral users of the MED-EL COMBI 40/40+ cochlear implant system," *Ear and Hearing*, vol. 23, no. 3, pp. 198–206, 2002.

[3] M. F. Dorman, P. C. Loizou, and D. Rainey, "Simulating the effect of cochlear-implant electrode insertion depth on speech understanding," *The Journal of the Acoustical Society of America*, vol. 102, p. 2993, 1997.

[4] J. Wouters, W. Damman, and A. J. Bosman, "Vlaamse opname van woordenlijsten voor spraakaudiometrie," *Logopedie: informatiemedium van de Vlaamse vereniging voor logopedisten*, vol. 7, no. 6, pp. 28–34, 1994.

[5] A. Van Wieringen and J. Wouters, "LIST and LINT: Sentences and numbers for quantifying speech understanding in severely impaired listeners for Flanders and the Netherlands," *International journal of audiology*, vol. 47, no. 6, pp. 348–355, 2008.

[6] T. Francart, M. Moonen, and J. Wouters, "Automatic testing of speech recognition," *International Journal of Audiology*, vol. 48, no. 2, pp. 80–90, 2009.

[7] W. Nogueira, F. Vanpoucke, P. Dykmans, L. De Raeve, H. Van Hamme, and J. Roelens, "Speech recognition technology in CI rehabilitation," *Cochlear Implants International*, vol. 11, no. Supplement 1, pp. 449–453, 2010.

[8] R. C. Rose and D. B. Paul, "A hidden Markov model based keyword recognition system," in *Acoustics, Speech, and Signal Processing, 1990. ICASSP-90., 1990 International Conference on*. IEEE, 1990, pp. 129–132.

[9] H. Bourlard, B. D'hoore, and J.-M. Boite, "Optimizing recognition and rejection performance in wordspotting systems," in *Acoustics, Speech, and Signal Processing, 1994. ICASSP-94., 1994 IEEE International Conference on*, vol. 1. IEEE, 1994, pp. I–373.

[10] R. C. Rose, "Keyword detection in conversational speech utterances using hidden Markov model based continuous speech recognition," *Computer Speech & Language*, vol. 9, no. 4, pp. 309–333, 1995.

[11] C. J. Leggetter and P. C. Woodland, "Maximum likelihood linear regression for speaker adaptation of continuous density hidden Markov models," *Computer speech and language*, vol. 9, no. 2, p. 171, 1995.

[12] M. J. F. Gales, "Maximum likelihood linear transformations for HMM-based speech recognition," *Computer speech and language*, vol. 12, no. 2, 1998.

[13] J. Duchateau, M. Wigham, K. Demuynck, and H. Van hamme, "A flexible recognizer architecture in a reading tutor for children," in *Proc. of the ITRW on Speech Recognition and Intrinsic Variation*, Toulouse, France, May 2006, pp. 330–331.

[14] K. Demuynck, D. Van Compernolle, C. Van Hove, and J.-P. Martens, "CoGen een corpus gesproken Nederlands voor spraaktechnologisch onderzoek - eindverslag," *Tech. Rep. K.U. Leuven - ESAT & Universiteit Gent*, 1997.

[15] J. Duchateau, Y. O. Kong, L. Cleuren, L. Latacz, J. Roelens, A. Samir, K. Demuynck, P. Ghesquière, W. Verhelst *et al.*, "Developing a reading tutor: Design and evaluation of dedicated speech recognition and synthesis modules," *Speech Communication*, vol. 51, no. 10, pp. 985–994, 2009.

[16] K. Demuynck, J. Duchateau, and D. Van Compernolle, "Optimal feature sub-space selection based on discriminant analysis," in *Proc. Eurospeech*, vol. 3, 1999, pp. 1311–1314.

Improving Continuous Sign Language Recognition: Speech Recognition Techniques and System Design

Jens Forster, Oscar Koller, Christian Oberdörfer, Yannick Gweth, Hermann Ney

Human Language Technology and Pattern Recognition Group
Computer Science Department
RWTH Aachen University
Aachen, Germany
{surname}@cs.rwth-aachen.de

Abstract

Automatic sign language recognition (ASLR) is a special case of automatic speech recognition (ASR) and computer vision (CV) and is currently evolving from using artificial lab-generated data to using 'real-life' data. Although ASLR still struggles with feature extraction, it can benefit from techniques developed for ASR. We present a large-vocabulary ASLR system that is able to recognize sentences in continuous sign language and uses features extracted from standard single-view video cameras without using additional equipment. ASR techniques such as the multi-layer-perceptron (MLP) tandem approach, speaker adaptation, pronunciation modelling, and parallel hidden Markov models are investigated. We evaluate the influence of each system component on the recognition performance. On two publicly available large vocabulary databases representing lab-data (25 signer, 455 sign vocabulary, 19k sentence) and unconstrained 'real-life' sign language (1 signer, 266 sign vocabulary, 351 sentences) we can achieve 22.1% respectively 38.6% WER.

Index Terms: Continuous Sign Language Recognition, Large Vocabulary, ASR, Computer Vision, Recognition System

1. Introduction

Sign languages are natural languages that develop in communities of deaf people around the world and vary from region to region. A sign consists of manual and non-manual components that partly occur in parallel but are not perfectly synchronous [1]. Manual components comprise hand configuration, place of articulation, hand movement and hand orientation while non-manual components include body pose and facial expression. ASLR is a subfield of CV and ASR allowing methods of both worlds to be deployed but it also inherits their respective challenges. Large inter-/intra-personal signing variability, strong coarticulation effects, context dependent classifier gestures, no agreed written form or phoneme-like definition in conjunction with partly parallel information streams, high signing speed inducing motion blur, missing features and the need for automatic hand and face tracking make video-based ASLR a notoriously challenging research field.

Although ASLR is starting to tackle 'real-life' data, the majority of work in the community still focusses on the recognition of isolated signs, particularly in the context of gesture recognition. Deng and Tsui [2] and Wang et al. [3] use parallel HMMs to recognize isolated signs in American Sign Language or Chinese Sign Language, respectively, achieving recognition accuracies over 90%. Ong et al. [4] use boosted sequential pattern trees to recognize isolated signs in British sign language (BSL) allowing to combine partly parallel, not perfectly synchronous, automatically mined phoneme-like units in the recognition process. Pitsikalis et al. [5] extract subunit definitions from linguistic annotation in HamNoSys [6], whereas Koller et al. [7] employ an open SignWriting [8] dictionary to produce and align linguistically meaningful subunits to signs in German sign language (GSL).

However, in real tasks ASLR is more likely to face continuous signing, that is what this work focusses on. In this context, Cooper et al. [9] compare boosted sequential pattern trees to HMMs using linguistically inspired subunits and 3D tracking information finding that the trees outperform HMMs for BSL. Forster et al. [10] investigate techniques to combine not perfectly synchronous information streams within an HMM-based ASLR system finding that synchronization just at word boundaries improves the recognition performance. Recognizing a sign language sentence by spotting individual signs has been investigated by several authors [11, 12, 13, 14] reporting promising results. Finally Yang et al. [15] use a nested dynamic programming approach to handle coarticulation movements between signs.

Given the cited work and the works described in the survey on sign language recognition by Ong and Ranganath[16], two approaches to ASLR are observable. On the one hand, ASLR is viewed as a pure CV problem neglecting the natural language processing nature of the task and focussing on developing tailor-made solutions for gestures. However, we believe to be soon able to tackle real-world problems, ASLR should much more be seen as application of ASR, exploiting previous knowledge gained in that area. Following that track, we provide systematically gathered knowledge on how to create a large vocabulary ASLR system for continuous SL evaluating which techniques from ASR are applicable. Specifically, we investigate the impact of CV and ASR techniques on the recognition performance. Among others, the impact of the performance of automatic hand tracking on the recognition performance is investigated. Tackling the question of suitable features for non-rigid objects such as the hands, HoG3D [17] features proposed in the area of action recognition, appearance based features and learned MLP features used in ASR are investigated. Addressing inter signer variability, the technique of automatic signer adaptation is adopted from ASR (speaker adaptation) and tested within our proposed large-vocabulary, HMM-based sign language recognition system. Additionally, techniques to combine

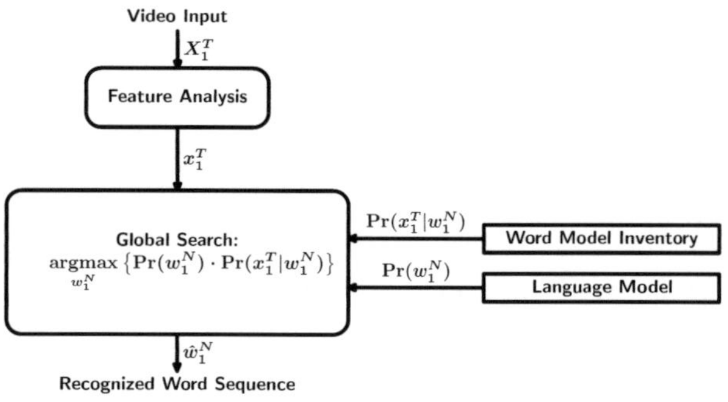

Figure 1: Bayes' decision rule used in ASLR.

partly parallel information streams/modalities are presented and evaluated. The system and its components are tested in the context of continuous ASLR for two publicly available, large-vocabulary databases. One database represents lab-data created for pattern recognition purposes and one database represents 'real-life' data recorded from German public TV. Comparing findings on lab-data and 'real-life' data we investigate which findings on lab-data generalize to 'real-life' scenarios.

2. System overview and features

The ASLR system described here follows the system design proposed in [18] and is based on Bayes's decision rule but differs in several aspects. Specifically, features adapted from action recognition, learned features, a number of techniques to combine different modalities within the system, class-based language models, gap/noise models and signer adaptation techniques for multi-signer data are employed.

The recognition result of the system is the sequence of words that best fits the trained word models and the language model (see Figure 1). One has to note that linguistically this represents a major simplification but the use of gloss annotations (see Section 2.1 for a short definition) is a common practice within the recognition community to deal with the non-availability of a common writing system for sign languages. While linguistically motivated writing notations such as HamNoSys[6] or SignWriting [8] cover information about different modalities used within sign languages, they are still a weak labeling scheme for signs because they do not give an annotation of the movement, facial expression, etc. per time frame. Furthermore, using glosses as target classes and annotation scheme allows for faster annotation of large amounts sign language data which is needed for a automatic statistical recognition approach.

Finally, the proposed recognition system has been tested on the two publicly available databases SIGNUM [19] and RWTH-PHOENIX-Weather (PHOENIX) [20] for GSL which are among the biggest datasets available for continuous ASLR.

2.1. Visual modeling

Albeit the cited work on automatic subunit extraction from sign language videos, it is still unclear how signs can be split into subunits. Furthermore, the majority of sign language corpora including those used in this work (see Section 3) is annotated using *glosses* effectively labeling the meaning of a sign rather than its appearance. Therefore, the proposed system is based on whole-word models. The visual model (VM) of a sign consists of a left-to-right HMM in Bakis topology [21] where each segment of the model (each pair of consecutive states) is modelled by a separate Gaussian mixture model (GMM) with globally pooled covariance matrix. The number of segments per model is estimated from manually annotated sign boundaries on the training data. Due to strong visual pronunciation variances (3 different signs for Sunday exist in GSL), the effect of explicit visual pronunciation modelling is investigated in Section 3.

2.2. Language models

Language models (LMs) play a crucial role in state-of-the-art ASR and ASLR systems. Dreuw et al. [18] showed that the impact of the well-known LM scale on the recognition performance of an ASLR system is in the same order of magnitude as in an ASR system. Therefore, the LM scale is optimized for all experiments presented in this work.

In contrast to ASR where it is possible to obtain language-specific almost arbitrarily large text collections for every language and domain, here the LM can only be trained on the transcribed training data of any given database for ASLR inheriting the problem of singletons and infrequent signs which often make up more than 40% of the available vocabulary of typically 200 to 500 signs. Inspired by the idea of class and topic LMs in ASR [22, 23, 24] and statistical sign language translation [25], we propose to use classes of visually and contextual similar signs within the LM. Class selection is based on the analysis of errors of a baseline system without LM classes. In this work, all LMs are trained using the SRILM toolkit [26] with modified Kneser-Ney discounting with interpolation [27].

2.3. Manual and non-manual features

GSL conveys information through manual and non-manual parameters. Manual parameters comprise both hands' shape, their orientation and position. There are two-handed, as well as single-handed signs. Single-handed signs are usually signed using the dominant hand which in the databases used in this work corresponds to the right hand for all subjects in PHOENIX and all but two in the SIGNUM database.

Manual features: For full coverage of a sign, manual features of both hands are used as well as non-manual features of the face and upper-body. To extract hand features, tracking is performed for both hands separately using a robust tracking algorithm with decision back-tracing originally proposed in [28]. Four different kinds of manual features are extracted. The first one are colored image patches cut out around the tracked positions of the dominant hand with a size of 32×32 Pixel for SIGNUM and 53×65 Pixel for PHOENIX. As second feature, histograms of oriented image gradients in 3D space (HoG3D) [17] are extracted using a non-dense spatio-temporal grid from video volumes of ± 4 cropped patches. Third, the movement trajectory of the right hand is extracted, represented by the position relative to the nose and the eigenvectors and eigenvalues of the movement within a time window of $2\delta + 1$ frames. Fourth, MLP features have been successfully used in ASR [29] and optical character recognition [30]. Here a feed-forward network with one hidden layer of 2000 nodes is trained using frame alignments from a previously trained HMM system as labels and PCA reduced hand patches in case of SIGNUM and HoG3D and trajectory features in case of PHOENIX. The training of the MLP has been performed on the training set of the HMM system. Cross validation is used to adjust the learning rate and to avoid over-fitting.

Non-manual features: Face patches are extracted using the same tracking approach as described above. Furthermore, a position and orientation invariant active appearance model (POIAAM) [31] is fitted to each frame obtaining a 109 dimensional shape descriptor, including shape model parameters, head rotation in space, mouth and eye openings and degrees of eyebrow raise. Finally, every frame of a video sequence is scaled down to 32×32 and 53×65 respectively to get a simple upper body feature as originally proposed in [18].

For all features, temporal context is included by stacking ± 4 video frames for SIGNUM and ± 2 frames for PHOENIX. Since the resulting feature dimension is too high to robustly estimate HMM parameters, PCA is applied. All features but the movement trajectory are reduced to 200 dimensions. In case of the colored hand and face patches PCA is applied to each color channel (red, green, blue) separately, yielding a final feature dimension of 210. The movement trajectory feature itself has only limited discriminative power and is therefore combined with the HoG3D features of the right hand.

2.4. Signer adaptation and modality combination

Sign languages use partly parallel, but not perfectly synchronous information streams/modalities to convey meaning. These modalities must be handled in the recognition process but it is an open question how to incorporate different modalities within such a system. A similar situation exists in audio-visual speech recognition (AVSR) where acoustic features and visual features of the mouth are combined. Following the work in AVSR, we investigated feature combination (concatenation), system combination using (i)ROVER [32] as well as combination between HMMs on state level (synchronous combination) and at word boundaries (asynchronous combination). Experimental results show that the first two types of combination are not effective for current ASLR because either the resulting feature space dimension is too high or the systems make too similar recognition errors [10]. Here, only results for synchronous and asynchronous combination are presented.

Signer adaptation: ASR systems trained on different speakers have to address the speakers' voice and speech patterns to achieve good recognition performance. A common approach is to use speaker adaptive training (SAT) and learn speaker dependent feature transformation matrices using constraint maximum likelihood linear regression (CMLLR). Analogous to ASR, ASLR has to tackle signing styles. Therefore, SAT/CMLLR is evaluated in the context of ASLR for 25 signers.

3. Experimental results

The SIGNUM database [19] contains lab recordings of 25 signers wearing black long-sleeve clothes in front of a dark blue background signing predefined sentences. Videos are recorded at 780×580 Pixel and 30 frames per second (fps). Each signer signs the 603 unique training and 177 testing sentences once, whereas they are signed thrice in the single signer setup. 3.6% of the glosses are out of vocabulary (OOV). Table 1 shows statistics of the single signer setup only. The multi signer setup has the same vocabulary and OOV rate but 15k sentences (92k running glosses) for training and 4.4k sentences (23k running glosses) for testing. If not stated explicitly otherwise, all presented SIGNUM results refer to the single signer setup.

The PHOENIX [20] database contains 'real-life' sign language footage recorded from weather-forecasts aired by the public German TV-station PHOENIX. 'Real-life' is meant from a computer vision point of view, where the signers were not artificially restricted in any sense in their signing (sentence structure, choice of vocabulary, size and intensity of signs, ...) and where the recording conditions have a much larger variance than on other signing corpora (lighting, camera-signer position, ...). The video footage has not been created for pattern recognition purposes or linguistic research. From a linguistic point of view the employed language has to be classified as non-native, as the signer is a hearing interpreter, whose parents are deaf. The videos (210×260 Pixel, 25 fps interlaced) show the interpreter wearing dark clothes in front of an artificial gray gradient background and pose a strong challenge to CV and ASLR due to high signing speed (majority of signs spans less than 10 frames), strong coarticulation effects and more than 30% of the vocabulary being singletons. Statistics of both databases are shown in Table 1.

Table 1: Statistics for SIGNUM single signer and PHOENIX

	SIGNUM		PHOENIX	
	Train	Test	Train	Test
# sentences	1809	531	304	47
# running glosses	11,109	2805	3309	487
vocabulary size	455	-	266	-
# singletons	0	-	90	-
# OOV [%]	-	3.6	-	1.6
perplexity (3-gram)	17.8	72.2	15.9	34.9

The system is trained using maximum likelihood and the EM-algorithm. The number of Gaussian densities and the LM-scale are optimized. For PHOENIX, the system uses 1433 emission distributions with a total of 4k Gaussians and a globally pooled covariance matrix. The same applies to SIGNUM, but the numbers are 1366 emission distributions with 24k Gaussians for single signer and 198k for multi-signer. Recognition uses word-conditioned tree search and Viterbi approximation.

Basic Features: In order to build a well performing ASLR system, the feature selection plays a crucial role. The full video images can be seen as a global descriptor of manual and non-manual parameters and are, thus, a good starting point. As the hands are known to carry the most information in signing, tracked and cut out hand patches have often been preferred [18] over full frames. Comparing both features, hand patches outperform full images on both databases (see Table 2, Row 1).

Model length estimation: In ASR, the HMM model of a word is formed by the linked models of the word's subunit HMMs. Thereby, the typical temporal length of a word is modelled. This approach is not yet possible in ASLR because the definition and extraction of subunits is still an open research question. PHOENIX includes word boundary annotations from which the number of segments for each gloss HMM can been estimated by choosing the median of the lengths minus 20% and adjusting the length in case the adapted median is shorter than the shortest utterance of the gloss. The hand patch baseline presented above uses this approach. Using uniform length for all glosses, the recognition result is 60.8% instead of 55.0% WER. 'Bootstrapping' the initial system alignment using the word boundary ground truth, we achieve 57.5% WER.

No word boundary ground truth is available for SIGNUM. Model length estimation is performed using statistics on the

Table 2: WERs for competing features (Rows 1.-6.), WERs without and with specific techniques (Rows 7.-11.). '+' denotes a synchronous, asynchronous or feature combination. Please see corresponding text parts for explanations. HoG3D uses tracked hand locations. For PHOENIX, in rows 3.-5., manual ground truth annotation has been used instead.

Competing Features		PHOENIX		SIGNUM	
1. Full image	Hand patch	80.1	55.0	31.6	16.0
2. Hand patch	HoG3D	55.0	49.7	16.0	12.5
3. HoG3D	+Traj	45.2	42.1	12.5	14.2
4. HoG3D+Traj	+Face	42.1	41.9	14.2	14.2
5. HoG3D	+Full	45.2	45.2	12.5	10.7
Impact of Techniques		WER [%]		WER [%]	
6. Model Length Estimation		60.8	55.0	16.0	17.5
7. Temporal Context		51.3	49.7	12.7	12.4
8. MLP		39.8	43.3	16.0	13.0
9. Manual Tracking Annotation		55.0	48.3	–	–
10. Gap Models		42.1	39.8	–	–
11. Class LM		39.8	38.6	–	–

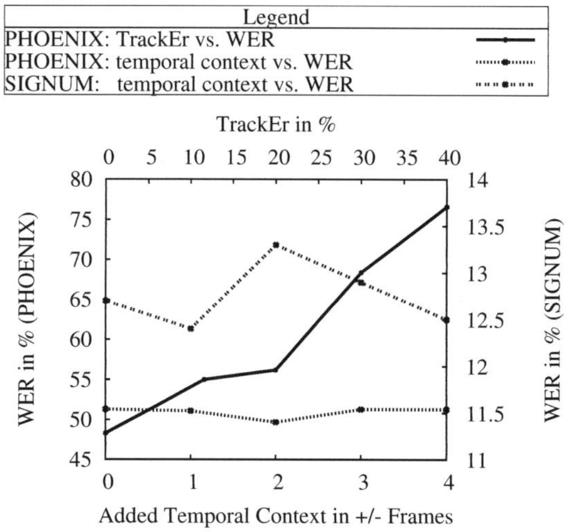

Figure 2: Solid Black: Influence of tracking performance in TrackEr on WER for PHOENIX using right hand patches features (read top x-axis vs. left y-axis). Dotted: Impact of temporal context using HoG3D (right hand) on WER for PHOENIX (read bottom x-axis vs. left y-axis). Dashed: Impact of temporal context using HoG3D (right hand) on WER for SIGNUM (read bottom x-axis vs. right y-axis)

frame alignment of an HMM system with uniform length. No improvement over uniform length is observed due to the estimation on the frame alignment having limited accuracy and the signs in the video already sharing a similar length.

Visual pronunciation variants: Sign languages exhibit strong pronunciation variation which manifest in visual sign variants. Visual variants are not explicitly labeled in PHOENIX or SIGNUM. While in SIGNUM no variants exist because of the artificial nature of the database, PHOENIX shows high variability within signs annotated by the same gloss. This arises mainly from the interpreter mixing different dialects.

We have manually annotated the variants with regard to the visual appearance and the motion of the hand yielding on average 2.7 variants per gloss and a total of 711 different variants. Using these annotations, each variant is modelled by a distinct HMM with model length estimation achieving 56.5% WER in contrast to the baseline of 55.0%. Further, both systems outperform the 62.2% WER of a 'nearest-neighbor' style system where each gloss occurrence is modelled independently. Apparently, increasing the number of dedicated HMMs per gloss worsens recognition. Coherent manual definition of variants is likely to be a problematic factor, as well as the HMMs not generalizing well over unseen data because of the reduction in training data per HMM and strong coarticulation effects.

Tracking Influence: The presented hand patch baselines rely on tracking to localize the hands of the signer. Tracking is not perfect and errors propagate through the recognition system. Figure 2 shows the impact of tracking quality measured in tracking error rate (TrackEr) [28] counting a tracked position as wrong if it differs by more than 20 Pixel from ground truth on ASLR for PHOENIX. The TrackEr of 0 at 48.3% WER refers to using ground truth tracking annotation (see Table 2, Row 9).

HoG3D: HoG3D features encode the shape and its change over time of a tracked hand. The latter aspect is not covered by hand patch features. Further, HoG3D features are more compact than hand patches, and robust against local illumination changes. Comparing to the hand patch baselines, recognition results are improved from 55.0% to 49.7% WER for PHOENIX and from 16.0% to 12.5% WER for SIGNUM. The result on PHOENIX is almost as good as using ground truth tracking information for the hand patches.

Temporal Context: The temporal context of a feature includes information that cannot easily be learned by an HMM system but has been shown to improve results in ASR [33].

Although HoG3D features already incorporate temporal context, we find that including additional context benefits the recognition, as can be seen in Figure 2. More context than ± 2 frames degrades recognition accuracy on PHOENIX, capturing too much information of the following glosses. On SIGNUM, we observe only marginal recognition improvement indicating that the context included in HoG3D is sufficient. The chosen system defaults are at ± 2 frames for PHOENIX and ± 4 frames for SIGNUM and are, thus, well chosen for both cases.

Modalities: In addition to the body pose (full image) and the right hand (HoG3D), we evaluate the performance using facial expressions (POIAAM), the left hand (HoG3D) and the movement of the right hand (Traj). For both databases, the left hand tracking quality is worse than the right hand. Henceforth ground truth tracking annotations are used for PHOENIX to avoid tracking bias. Thus, the HoG3D baseline improves to 45.2% WER. Using left hand features 63.9% respectively 51.0% WER are achieved for PHOENIX and SIGNUM. The stronger recognition degradation for PHOENIX reflects the difficulty of the database. With facial features, the recognition result is 62.6% respectively 89.3% WER for PHOENIX and SIGNUM. The high WER for SIGNUM is due to the fact that hardly any facial expressions are present here. Concatenating movement trajectory and right hand HoG3D, results are improved for PHOENIX but not for SIGNUM (Table 2, Row 3).

Using synchronous (Table 2, Row 4) and asynchronous (Table 2, Row 5) modality combination techniques, recognition results for both databases are improved if the respectively best single modalities are combined. For a full overview of modality combination techniques and results refer to [10].

Gap Models: The SIGNUM database is designed to contain only one-handed signs and no switching of the hand. Contrarily, in PHOENIX signers partly switch hands and use the left hand for signing while holding the right. This effect introduces missing features in the information stream of the right and left hand. One way to remedy this problem is to borrow the idea of noise models from ASR and to augment the system's vocabulary by two such models. One model subsuming signs performed by the left hand only and one for long gaps between signs of more than five frames that are part of the sentence but do not belong to either neighboring sign. The training data annotation is automatically augmented by labels for both aspects using ground truth annotation. Using these gap models, the WER is improved from 42.1% to 39.8% on PHOENIX, due to the models only being populated with clean and complete data. Further, we observe an improved feature to HMM state alignment (measured as distance to the ground truth annotation).

MLP-tandem: The MLP-tandem approach was evaluated for SIGNUM and PHOENIX. For SIGNUM the MLP is trained on hand patch features resulting in 13.0% WER that outperforms the baseline by 3%. This result is comparable to the 12.5% obtained using HoG3D features. For PHOENIX, the MLP is trained on concatenated HoG3D with Trajectory features. The recognition result is with 43.3% WER (at $\pm$ 1 frame temporal context) 3.5% worse than the baseline of 39.8% obtained by the HoG3D+Traj features alone. Including more temporal context does not help because it is already included in the MLP posterior estimates. Two aspects feature into the performance of the MLP features on PHOENIX. On the one hand, it is not clear if the MLP can reliably extract the relevant information from the HoG3D+Traj features although following the ASR praxis of using the best feature available. On the other hand, the MLPs for PHOENIX and SIGNUM have about the same number of parameters but the MLP on SIGNUM is trained using ten times the data of PHOENIX. Anyhow, the results show that MLP features as used in ASR achieve comparable results to specialized features from CV although requiring training themselves.

Class LM: With regard to PHOENIX the analysis of the recognition errors showed that 3.8% absolute of all errors are due to misclassified numbers and 2.2% absolute are due to orientations such as *north*. Further, both classes appear in a specific context such as a number before the gloss TEMPERATURE which is not adequately captured by sign-level LMs. Additionally, numbers have a low frequency in the LM training data appearing on average less than ten times. Augmenting the LM for PHOENIX with a class for numbers, the perplexity (PPL) on the test data is reduced from 34.9 to 29.3. Orientations reduce PPL to 31.2 and using both classes PPL is reduced to 25.7.

Table 3 shows that using the orientation category the recognition performance is only marginally improved but using the number category alone improves the overall recognition result by 1.2% WER. Other categories as used in sign language translation [25] did not improve results. For SIGNUM, class LMs have not been used because of the special and artificial structure of the sentences.

Table 3: Class LM results for PHOENIX. Error rates in %.

Class	del/ins	WER
None	20.7/4.5	39.8
Orientation	18.1/5.3	39.2
Numbers	19.3/4.1	38.8
+ Orientation	16.2/6.2	**38.6**

Signer adaptation: Applying the findings on SIGNUM single signer to the case of 25 signers and using tracked hand patches of the right hand as features, the system achieves 23.6% WER.

In ASR SAT is used to adapt the features to better fit the learned models. In the same fashion, we use SAT to adapt the baseline system to the signers sign patterns. In a second training pass, signer specific feature transformation matrices are estimated using CMLLR. In SIGNUM the signer ids are annotated and hence no signer clustering is performed.

Using the signer ids of the test data, it is possible to evaluate what is the maximal achievable improvement in terms of WER using SAT/CMLLR on the given test data. In the typical recognition setup the ids of the signers in the test data are not known and the resulting improvement is lower due to errors in the clustering process. Adapting the proposed recognition system build for the SIGNUM multi-signer database using SAT/CMLLR, the WER of 23.6% is improved to 22.1% showing that the standard approach from ASR is applicable to ASLR without any modifications.

4. Summary and conclusion

In this work, a large-vocabulary ASLR system for continuous sign language using single-view videos as well as the process of feature selection, technology transfer from ASR and CV and system design have been presented. Techniques from ASR and CV have been evaluated in the context for ASLR for challenging 'real-life' data and data designed for pattern recognition.

Some aspects were found to generalize over both data sets: HoG3D alone outperforms all other tested features with MLPs being a close second. The combination of the two best single performing modalities achieves the best combination result and the system benefits from including temporal context in features.

Other findings are related to particularities of the given corpora: On PHOENIX, gap models improve results but use specific annotations not necessarily available in other corpora. The improvement by class LMs exploits domain-specific knowledge and model length estimation relies on accurate sign boundaries.

To sum up, the WER on 'real life' data has been reduced from over 80% to 38.6% and on lab data from over 30% to 10.7% for single signer and to 22.1% for multi signer. Although this might sound very high compared to the state-of-the-art in ASR, this is one of the first times that recognition results have been published on 'real-life' data. We believe that our work helps pushing ASLR towards more realistic application scenarios, which come along with challenges most of the current sign language data sets ignore. This goes especially for the use of single-view video material in contrast to using special hardware such as bulky cyber gloves, or stereo cameras.

Future work will investigate sub units and coarticulation effects.

5. Acknowledgements

This work has been partly funded by the European Community's Seventh Framework Programme FP7-ICT-2007-3, grant agreement 231424 - SignSpeak project and the Janggen-Pöhn-Stiftung. Special thanks to Thomas Hoyoux (Technical University Innsbruck) and Yvan Richard (Centre de Recerca i Innovacio de Catalunya (CRIC)) for providing AAM and HoG3D features.

6. References

[1] C. Vogler and D. Metaxas, "A framework for recognizing the simultaneous aspects of american sign language," *Computer Vision and Image Understanding*, vol. 81, no. 3, pp. 358–384, 2001.

[2] J. Deng and H. T. Tsui, "A Two-step Approach based on PaHMM for the Recognition of ASL," in *ACCV*, Jan 2002.

[3] C. Wang, X. Chen, and W. Gao, "Expanding Training Set for Chinese Sign Language Recognition," in *FG*, 2006.

[4] E.-J. Ong, H. Cooper, N. Pugeault, and R. Bowden, "Sign language recognition using sequential pattern trees," in *CVPR*, Jun. 16 – 21 2012, pp. 2200 – 2207.

[5] V. Pitsikalis, S. Theodorakis, C. Vogler, and P. Maragos, "Advances in phonetics-based sub-unit modeling for transcription alignment and sign language recognition," in *CVPR*, 2011, pp. 1 – 6.

[6] T. Hanke, "HamNoSys - representing sign language data in language resources and language processing contexts," in *LREC 2004, Workshop proceedings : Representation and processing of sign languages*, 2004, pp. 1 – 6.

[7] O. Koller, H. Ney, and R. Bowden, "May the force be with you: Force-aligned signwriting for automatic subunit annotation of corpora," in *FG*, Apr. 2013.

[8] V. Sutton and Writing, Deaf Action Committee for Sign, *Sign writing*. Deaf Action Committee (DAC), 2000.

[9] H. Cooper, E.-J. Ong, N. Pugeault, and R. Bowden, "Sign language recognition using sub-units," *JMLR*, vol. 13, pp. 2205–2231, Jul 2012.

[10] J. Forster, C. Oberdörfer, O. Koller, and H. Ney, "Modality combination techniques for continuous sign language recognition," in *IbPRIA*, Jun. 2013.

[11] P. Buehler, M. Everingham, and A. Zisserman, "Learning sign language by watching TV (using weakly aligned subtitles)," in *CVPR*, 2009.

[12] H. Cooper and R. Bowden, "Learning signs from subtitles: A weakly supervised approach to signlanguage recognition," in *CVPR*, Jun 2009, pp. 2568 – 2574.

[13] H.-D. Yang, S. Sclaroff, and S.-W. Lee, "Sign language spotting with a threshold model based on conditional random fields," *PAMI*, vol. 31, no. 7, pp. 1264–1277, July 2009.

[14] S. Najak, K. Duncan, S. Sarkar, and B. Loeding, "Finding recurrent patterns from continuous sign language sentences for automated extraction of signs," *JMLR*, vol. 13, pp. 2589 – 2615, Dec 2012.

[15] R. Yang, S. Sarkar, and B. Loeding, "Handling movement epenthesis and hand segmentation ambiguities in continuous sign language recognition using nested dynamic programming," *PAMI*, vol. 32, no. 3, pp. 462–477, Mar 2010.

[16] S. Ong and S. Ranganath, "Automatic sign language analysis: a survey and the future beyond lexical meaning," *IEEE Transactions on Pattern Analysis and Machine Intelligence*, vol. 27, no. 6, pp. 873–891, 2005.

[17] A. Kläser, M. Marszałek, and C. Schmid, "A spatio-temporal descriptor based on 3d-gradients," in *BMVC*, Sep 2008, pp. 995–1004.

[18] P. Dreuw, D. Rybach, T. Deselaers, M. Zahedi, and H. Ney, "Speech recognition techniques for a sign language recognition system," in *Interspeech*, Aug. 2007, pp. 2513–2516, iSCA best student paper award.

[19] U. von Agris, M. Knorr, and K.-F. Kraiss, "The significance of facial features for automatic sign language recognition," in *FG*, Sep 2008, pp. 1–6.

[20] J. Forster, C. Schmidt, T. Hoyoux, O. Koller, U. Zelle, J. Piater, and H. Ney, "Rwth-phoenix-weather: A large vocabulary sign language recognition and translation corpus," in *LREC*, May 2012.

[21] R. Bakis, "Continuous speech word recognition via centisecond acoustic states," in *91st Meeting of the Acoustical Society of America (ASA)*, Washington, DC, USA, April 1976.

[22] A. Emami and S. Chen, "Multi-class model m," in *ICASSP*, May 2011, pp. 5516–5519.

[23] S. F. Chen and S. M. Chu, "Enhanced word classing for model m," in *Interspeech*, 2010, pp. 1037–1040.

[24] W. Naptali, M. Tsuchiya, and S. Nakagawa, "Topic-dependent-class-based n-gram language model," *ASL*, vol. 20, no. 5, pp. 1513–1525, 2012.

[25] D. Stein, C. Schmidt, and H. Ney, "Analysis, preparation, and optimization of statistical sign language machine translation," *Machine Translation*, vol. 26, no. 4, pp. 325–357, Dec. 2012.

[26] A. Stolcke, J. Zheng, W. Wang, and V. Abrash, "SRILM at Sixteen: Update and outlook," in *ASRU*, Waikoloa, Hawaii, December 2011.

[27] S. F. Chen and J. Goodman, "An empirical study of smoothing techniques for language modeling," *Computer Speech & Language*, vol. 13, no. 4, pp. 359–393, 1999.

[28] P. Dreuw, T. Deselaers, D. Rybach, D. Keysers, and H. Ney, "Tracking using dynamic programming for appearance-based sign language recognition," in *FG*, 2006, pp. 293–298.

[29] Z. Tüske, M. Sundermeyer, R. Schlüter, and H. Ney, "Context-dependent mlps for lvcsr: Tandem, hybrid or both?" in *Interspeech*, Portland, OR, USA, Sep. 2012.

[30] G. R. J. Schenk, "Novel hybrid nn/hmm modelling techniques for on-line handwriting recognition," in *IWFHR*, Oct 2006, pp. 619 – 623.

[31] J. Piater, T. Hoyoux, and W. Du, "Video Analysis for Continuous Sign Language Recognition," in *4th Workshop on the Representation and Processing of Sign Languages: Corpora and Sign Language Technologies*, May 2010, lREC.

[32] B. Hoffmeister, R. Schlüter, and H. Ney, "icnc and irover: The limits of improving system combination with classification?" in *Interspeech*, Sep. 2008, pp. 232–235.

[33] A. Zolnay, R. Schlüter, and H. Ney, "Acoustic feature combination for robust speech recognition," in *ICASSP*, 2005.

Automatic speech recognition in the diagnosis of primary progressive aphasia

Kathleen Fraser[1], *Frank Rudzicz*[1,2], *Naida Graham*[2,3], *Elizabeth Rochon*[2,3]

[1]Department of Computer Science, University of Toronto; [2]Toronto Rehabilitation Institute
[3]Department of Speech-Language Pathology, University of Toronto

kfraser@cs.toronto.edu, frank@cs.toronto.edu,
naida.graham@utoronto.ca, elizabeth.rochon@utoronto.ca

Abstract

Narrative speech can provide a valuable source of information about an individual's linguistic abilities across lexical, syntactic, and pragmatic levels. However, analysis of narrative speech is typically done by hand, and is therefore extremely time-consuming. Use of automatic speech recognition (ASR) software could make this type of analysis more efficient and widely available. In this paper, we present the results of an initial attempt to use ASR technology to generate transcripts of spoken narratives from participants with semantic dementia (SD), progressive nonfluent aphasia (PNFA), and healthy controls. We extract text features from the transcripts and use these features, alone and in combination with acoustic features from the speech signals, to classify transcripts as patient versus control, and SD versus PNFA. Additionally, we generate artificially noisy transcripts by applying insertions, substitutions, and deletions to manually-transcribed data, allowing experiments to be conducted across a wider range of noise levels than are produced by a tuned ASR system. We find that reasonably good classification accuracies can be achieved by selecting appropriate features from the noisy transcripts. We also find that the choice of using ASR data or manually transcribed data as the training set can have a strong effect on the accuracy of the classifiers.

Index Terms: automatic speech recognition, classification, progressive aphasia

1. Introduction

Primary progressive aphasia (PPA) is a neurodegenerative disorder in which language is the most affected aspect of cognitive functioning. There are two main variants of PPA: progressive nonfluent aphasia (PNFA), in which speech is hesitant and effortful, and semantic dementia (SD), in which speech is fluent but with severe word findings difficulties [1]. A third subtype, logopenic progressive aphasia, has been identified in recent years but is not considered here.

The features of narrative speech in each variant of PPA have been characterized to some extent, but they are not yet fully understood. Evaluation of spoken output is an important part of diagnosis of PPA and in identification of the variant. From a clinical perspective, analysis of narrative speech has the advantage that it can provide a lot of information from a relatively brief assessment. A narrative speech sample can contain rich information about the speaker's ability to choose appropriate content and function words, construct sentences, and convey meaning. Systematic analysis of narrative speech is typically done manually, which is time-consuming and may be prohibitively expensive. The automated approach evaluated here has several advantages. For example, this method enables simultaneous consideration of multiple aspects of speech. Also, it should ultimately provide greater sensitivity to changes occurring in the earliest stages of disease, thereby facilitating early diagnosis. Similarly, it should provide objective measures of changes over time in language production, thereby enabling more accurate assessment of disease progression; this is important for patients and their families, as well as for evaluation of efficacy in drug trials (as potentially disease modifying drugs become available).

Fully automated analysis of narrative speech will require automatic speech recognition (ASR) in order to extract lexical and syntactic features from acoustic signals. Despite major improvements in ASR technology over the past few decades, accuracy for unrestricted (i.e., 'dictation-style') speech remains decidedly imperfect, as described in the next section. In order to estimate how effective a classifier of PPA and its subtypes might be when given textual transcripts derived from ASR, a wide range of potential system performances must be considered, to account for real-world variation. This research approximates various levels of ASR performance by randomly corrupting human transcripts according to pre-defined levels of error and compares these results against actual output from a leading commercial dictation system. Error levels are quantified by word-error rate (WER), which is the total number of erroneous insertions, deletions, and substitutions of words in an ASR transcript, divided by the total number of words in a reference transcript[1]. Simulated ASR errors have been used in various contexts, such as training dialogue systems [2] and for testing the safety of dictation systems for use in automobiles [3].

2. Related Work

In general, the accuracy of ASR systems on elderly voices tends to decrease with the age of the speaker [4]. Elderly voices typically have increased breathiness, jitter, shimmer, and a decreased rate of speech [4]. Older speakers may also exhibit articulation difficulties, changes in fundamental frequency, and decreased voice intensity [5]. These factors can result in speech that is less intelligible to both human listeners and ASR systems. For example, Hakkani-Tur *et al.* [6] found that in automatic scoring of a speech-based cognitive test, their ASR system had a higher WER for healthy speakers over the age of 70 than for those under the age of 70, with WERs between 26.3% and 34.1% for the elderly speakers, depending on the task and the gender of the speaker, while the error rates ranged between 21.1% and 28.2% for the younger speakers.

[1]If the number of insertions is large, it can overwhelm the total number of words in the reference transcript, therefore allowing for WERs above 100%.

Effective speech recognition can be further challenged by the presence of linguistic impairments such as those occurring in PPA. To our knowledge, there has only been one previous study on automatic speech recognition of PPA speakers. Peintner et al. [7] analyzed speech from patients with PNFA and SD as well as patients with a dementia affecting behavior and deportment, but not language. They achieved a WER of 37% for SD and 61% for PNFA. They also tested a control group, who had an average WER of 20%.

In this study, we use speech recognition as the input to a system that can analyze a spoken narrative and predict whether the speaker is cognitively normal or has a subtype of PPA. Peintner et al. [7] also attempted this task, although they did not report how the high error rates affected the lexical features studied or their classification accuracy. Other studies in this area have used manually transcribed transcripts [8]. One strategy which combines ASR technology with manual transcripts is to use forced-alignment with manual transcripts to measure acoustic features such as rate of speech and length of pauses [9, 10]. However, for a speech analysis system to be available online or as part of an in-home continuous monitoring system, there must be no reliance on manual transcriptions at the word-level, which forced-alignment requires.

3. Data

3.1. Narrative samples

Our data set comprises speech samples from 24 patients with PPA and 16 age- and education-matched controls. Of the 24 PPA patients, 14 were diagnosed with PNFA and 10 with SD. The speech samples were collected as part of a longitudinal study on language impairment in PPA in the Department of Speech-Language Pathology at the University of Toronto. See Table 1 for demographic information about the participants.

Narrative speech samples were elicited following the procedure described by Saffran et al. [11]. Participants were given a wordless picture book of the well-known fairy tale "Cinderella", and were asked to look through the book. The book was then removed, and participants were asked to tell the story in their own words.

The narrative samples were recorded on a digital audio recorder, and transcribed by trained research assistants. The manual transcriptions include filled pauses, repetitions, and false starts. Sentence boundaries were marked according to semantic, syntactic, and prosodic cues. The SD patients produced an average of 380 words and 20 sentences, the PNFA patients produced an average of 302 words and 16 sentences, and the control group produced an average of 403 words and 16 sentences.

	SD ($n = 10$)	PNFA ($n = 14$)	Controls ($n = 16$)
Age	65.6 (7.4)	64.9 (10.1)	67.8 (8.2)
Years of education	17.5 (6.1)	14.3 (3.6)	16.8 (4.3)
Sex	3 F	6 F	7 F

Table 1: Demographic information for each participant group. Averages (and standard deviations) are given for age and years of education.

3.2. Features

Two types of features are extracted for each participant individually, namely textual transcripts and acoustic samples. From these, we derive 31 lexical/syntactic features from the text transcripts and 23 features from the acoustics, giving a total of 54 available features, described below.

3.2.1. *Text features*

A number of features can be extracted from the text transcripts. Some of our features are based on the part-of-speech (POS) tags assigned by the Stanford tagger [12]. SD patients have been observed to produce proportionally fewer nouns and more verbs and pronouns, while PNFA patients tend to produce more nouns and fewer verbs [13, 14, 15]. PNFA patients also tend to omit function words, such as determiners or auxiliaries [13, 16].

We look up the frequency of each word in the SUBTL norms, which are derived from a large corpus of subtitles from film and television [17]. We calculate the average frequency over all words as well as specically for nouns and verbs. Similarly, we calculate the average familiarity, imageability, and age of acquisition of the words in each transcript using the combined Bristol norms and Gilhooly-Logie norms [18, 19]. Each word in these psycholinguistic databases has been ranked according to human perception of how familiar the word is, how easily the word evokes an image in the mind, and the approximate age at which a word is learned. Frequency, familiarity, imageability, and age of acquisition have all been found to influence speech production in aphasia [14, 20, 21, 22, 23]. The coverage of these norms on our data is variable. The frequency norms have excellent coverage – between 0.92 and 0.95 across the three groups on the manually transcribed data. The coverage for the familiarity, imageability, and age of acquisition norms is not as good, possibly due to the fact that the authors of the norms specifically excluded high frequency words [18]. The coverage for those norms ranges from 0.25 to 0.31 for all content words across the three groups for the manual transcripts.

From the transcripts we also measure such quantities as the average length of the words and the type-token ratio, as well as measures of fluency such as the number of filled pauses produced. We measure the combined occurrence of all filled pauses, as well as the individual counts for "um" and "uh", since it has been suggested that they may indicate different types of hesitation [24].

In previous work using manual transcripts, researchers have also examined measures which can be derived from parse trees, such as Yngve depth, or the number and length of different syntactic constructions [8, 9]. However, such parse trees will depend on the location of the sentence boundaries in the transcript, the placement of which can be a difficult task for ASR systems [25]. Indeed, the Nuance system used here does not place punctuation except by explicit command. For the purposes of this preliminary study, we avoid using features which depend on accurate sentence boundaries.

3.2.2. *Acoustic features*

We follow the work of Pakhomov et al. [10] and measure pause-to-word ratio (i.e., the ratio of non-silent segments to silent segments longer than 150 ms), mean fundamental frequency (F0) and variance, total duration of speech, long pause count (> 0.4 ms), and short pause count (> 0.15 ms and < 0.4 ms). To this we add mean pause duration and phonation rate (the amount of the recording spent in voiced speech) [9], as well as the mean and variance for the first 3 formants ($F1$, $F2$, $F3$), mean instantaneous power, mean and maximum first autocorrelation function, skewness, kurtosis, zero-crossing rate, mean recurrence period density entropy (a method for measuring the periodicity of a signal, which has been applied to pathological speech generally [26]), jitter [27], and shimmer.

Slow, effortful speech is one of the core symptoms of PNFA, and apraxia of speech can be an early feature [1]. PNFA patients may make speech sound errors and exhibit disordered prosody [1, 28]. Similarly, typical F0 range and variance have been shown to be indicative of articulatory neuropathologies within the context of speech recognition [29, 30]. In contrast, speech production is generally spared in SD, although SD patients may produce long pauses as they search for words [13].

4. Methods

4.1. ASR and simulated errors

We use two methods to produce errorful textual transcripts. The first method represents the current leader in commercial dictation software, Nuance Dragon NaturallySpeaking Premium; here, audio files are transcribed by Nuance's desktop dictation software. The second method corrupts human-produced transcripts according to pre-defined levels of WER; this method allows for an indirect approximation of the performance given a wide range of potential alternative ASR systems.

The Nuance Dragon NaturallySpeaking 12.5 Premium for 64-bit Windows dictation system (hereafter, 'Nuance') is based on traditional hidden Markov modeling of acoustics and, historically, on trigram language modeling [31]. This system is initialized with the default 'older voice' model suitable for individuals 65 years of age and older. The default vocabulary consists of 150,478 words, plus additional control phrases for use during normal desktop dictation (e.g., "*new paragraph*", "*end of sentence*"); this feature cannot be deactivated. The core vocabulary, however, can be changed. In order to get a more restricted vocabulary, all words used in our manually transcribed Cinderella data set plus all words used in a selection of 9 stories about Cinderella from the Gutenberg project (totalling 22,168 word tokens) were combined to form a reduced vocabulary of 2633 word types. Restricted vocabularies, by their nature, have higher random baselines and less phonemically confusable word pairs, usually resulting in proportionally higher accuracies in ASR. The Nuance system scales the language model to the reduced vocabulary.

For the simulated ASR transcripts, each word in the manual transcript is modified with a probability equal to the desired WER. In this set of experiments, we use a language model obtained from the Gigaword corpus [32], since the Nuance language model is proprietary and not accessible to the user. A word w can be modified in one of three ways:

- Substitution – w is replaced with a new word w_S.
- Insertion – w is followed be a new word w_I.
- Deletion – w is removed.

In the case of insertion, the word to be inserted is chosen randomly according to the bigram distribution of the language model. That is, words that frequently occur after w are more likely to be chosen as w_I. If w is not found in the Gigaword vocabulary, then w_I is chosen randomly according to the unigram distribution of the language model. In the case of substitution, the new word is randomly chosen from a ranked list of words with minimal phonemic edit distance from the given word, as computed by the Levenshtein algorithm.

Once it has been determined that a word will be modified, it is assigned one of the above modifications according to a predefined distribution. Different ASR systems may tend towards different distributions of insertion errors (IE), substitution errors (SE), and deletion errors (DE). We create data noise according to three distributions, each of which favours one type of error over the others: [60% IE, 20% SE, 20% DE], [20% IE, 60% SE, 20% DE], and [20% IE, 20% SE, 60% DE]. We then also adjust these proportions according to proportions observed in Nuance output, as described in Section 5.

4.2. Classification

We use stratified leave-one-out cross-validation to test our diagnostic classifiers. For each fold, one transcript is removed as test data. We then apply a simple feature selection algorithm to the remaining transcripts: we calculate a Welch's t-test for each feature individually and determine the significance of the difference between the groups on that feature. We then rank each feature by increasing p-value, and include as input to the classifier only the top ten most significant features in the list. For each fold, different training data is used and therefore different features may be prioritized in this manner. Similar methods for feature selection have been used in previous studies on the classification of dementia subtypes [7, 9, 33].

Once the features have been selected, we train three types of classifier: naïve Bayes (NB), support vector machine with sequential minimal optimization (SVM), and random forests (RF). The classifiers are then tested with the same subset of features derived from the held-out transcript. This procedure is repeated for every transcript in the data set, and the average accuracy is computed.

We consider two classification tasks, PPA-vs.-control and SD-vs.-PNFA, since these binary tasks allow for less confusion than a trinary classification task and can be cascaded. For each task, there are two possible feature sets: text features only, or a combination of text and acoustic features. There are also two possible training sets for each task: i) the classifiers can be trained on the human-transcribed data and tested on the ASR data[2], and ii) the classifiers are both trained and tested on the noisy ASR (or simulated ASR) data. We test our classifiers on each combination of these variables.

5. Results

5.1. Features and feature selection

First, we examine whether the feature selection method selects different types of features depending on the WER. It might be expected that as the WER increases, the text features will become less significant. Figure 1 shows the p-values, averaged across folds, for the text and acoustic features selected at each WER for each noise distribution. Note that the values of the acoustic features do not change with the noise levels, but the average p-value will change as different features are selected in each case, depending on the values of the text features. For the case of PPA versus controls, a mix of text and acoustic features are chosen, and the features tend to be significant at $p < 0.05$, even when the error rate is high. A combination of text and acoustic features are also selected for SD versus PNFA at all

[2] This represents the scenario in which researchers have access to a corpus of manual transcriptions for training purposes

noise levels; however in this case the mean p-values are often not significant, suggesting that the features are not as discriminative between these groups. This effect is reflected in the lower classification accuracies for the SD versus PNFA task reported below. So, Figure 1 does not support the hypothesis that text features become irrelevant at the highest noise levels, but rather suggests that the transcripts still contain some information which is at least as valuable as the acoustic information in the speech signal.

	p-value	PPA mean	Control mean
Nuance default vocabulary			
verb imageability	0.0006	401	354
noun frequency	0.002	3.51	3.26
noun familiarity	0.04	575	558
Nuance reduced vocabulary			
average word length	0.003	5.44	6.21
noun frequency	0.006	3.13	2.77
noun imageability	0.01	487	554
noun familiarity	0.02	558	531
frequency	0.04	3.60	3.20

Table 2: Significant text features ($p < 0.05$) for PPA vs. Controls using the Nuance system with default and reduced vocabularies.

	p-value	SD mean	PNFA mean
Nuance default vocabulary			
noun familiarity	0.002	596	560
familiarity	0.002	594	568
Nuance reduced vocabulary			
None	N/A	N/A	N/A

Table 3: Significant text features ($p < 0.05$) for SD vs. PNFA using the Nuance system with default and reduced vocabularies.

Some text features are still significant in the Nuance data as well, despite the high WER. Table 2 shows the text features that were significant ($p < 0.05$) when comparing PPA and controls using the two Nuance models. As before, since the feature set changes with each fold in the cross-validation, the p-value is an average across folds. The means for the two groups are also shown to indicate the direction of the difference. Using the default vocabulary, there are three significant text features: verb imageability, noun frequency, and noun familiarity. These three features are all significant in the manually-transcribed data as well, and with the same direction. For the system trained on the reduced vocabulary, there are five significant text features, as indicated, only one of which (noun imageability) is not significant in the manual transcripts. All five features show differences in the same direction. Table 3 shows that only noun familiarity and overall familiarity are significant in the SD vs. PNFA case using the default vocabulary system, as they are in the manually transcribed data, with the difference in the same direction. There are no significant text features using the reduced vocabulary system.

The significant acoustic features for each classification task are shown in Tables 4 and 5. These features remain the same regardless of the transcription method. For a complete discussion of the acoustic features of this data set, see [33].

	p-value	PPA mean	Control mean
phonation rate	0.0000006	0.733	0.920
mean duration of pauses	0.00002	37 800	14 500
mean recurrence period density entropy	0.00002	0.549	0.477
long pause count	0.0006	34.7	10.6
skewness	0.0006	-0.0733	-0.532
mean instantaneous power	0.0003	-26.1	-22.1
short pause count	0.002	49.9	22.1
kurtosis	0.005	20.4	14.1
shimmer	0.05	0.00560	0.00748

Table 4: Significant acoustic features ($p < 0.05$) for PPA vs. Controls.

	p-value	SD mean	PNFA mean
mean first autocorrelation function	0.02	0.848	0.730

Table 5: Significant acoustic features ($p < 0.05$) for SD vs. PNFA.

5.2. Recognizing PPA speech

Table 6 shows the WER of the Nuance system across populations and vocabularies. Somewhat surprisingly, using the reduced vocabulary reduces accuracy considerably, despite all words in the test set being present in the vocabulary. A possible explanation may be found in the distribution of error types across the uses of both vocabularies, which is shown in table 7. In particular, when using the reduced vocabulary, Nuance makes significantly more deletion errors, which may be attributed to a lower confidence assigned to its word sequence hypotheses which in turn may be attributed to a language model that is not adapted to non-default vocabularies. A general language model may assign a high lexical probability to a series of words that are phonemically similar to an utterance but if those words are not in the reduced vocabulary, a more domain-specific sequence of words may be assigned a low lexical probability and therefore a low confidence. When confidence in a hypothesis is below some threshold, that hypothesis may not be returned, resulting in an increase in deletion errors. Not having access to these internals of the Nuance engine prohibits modification at this level.

Another point to highlight is that, given Nuance's default vocabulary, there is no significant difference between the WER obtained with the control and PNFA groups ($t(26.78) = -0.62, p = 0.54, CI = [-0.16, 0.08]$), nor with the con-

	Default Vocabulary	Reduced Vocabulary
SD	73.1	98.1
PNFA	67.7	97.3
Control	64.0	97.1
All	67.5	97.5

Table 6: Mean word error rates for the Nuance systems on each of the participant groups.

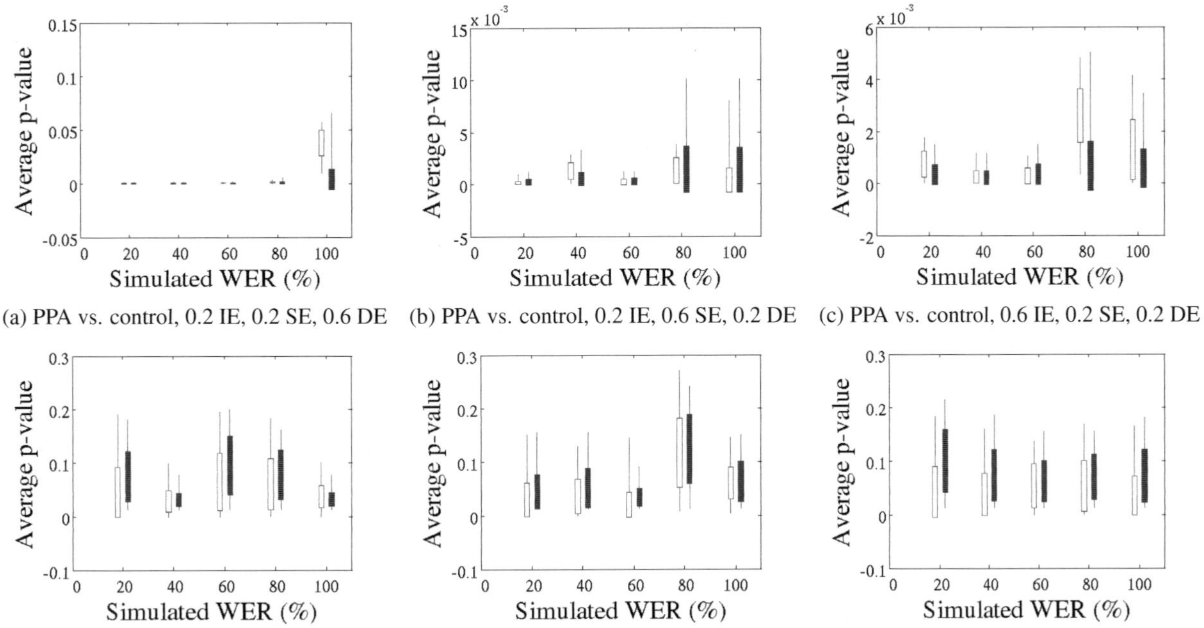

(a) PPA vs. control, 0.2 IE, 0.2 SE, 0.6 DE (b) PPA vs. control, 0.2 IE, 0.6 SE, 0.2 DE (c) PPA vs. control, 0.6 IE, 0.2 SE, 0.2 DE

(d) SD vs. PNFA, 0.2 IE, 0.2 SE, 0.6 DE (e) SD vs. PNFA, 0.2 IE, 0.6 SE, 0.2 DE (f) SD vs. PNFA, 0.6 IE, 0.2 SE, 0.2 DE

Figure 1: Acoustic features (filled bars) and text features (empty bars) selected for the feature sets at each WER for each distribution of insertion errors (IE), substitution errors (SE), and deletion errors (DE). Each bar represents one standard deviation from the mean, and the lines indicate the minimum and maximum values.

	Default Vocabulary	Reduced Vocabulary
Insertion errors	0.00602	0.00008
Substitution errors	0.39999	0.11186
Deletion errors	0.59398	0.88804

Table 7: Distribution of error types for the Nuance systems.

trol and SD groups ($t(23.77) = -1.47, p = 0.16, CI = [-0.22, 0.04]$), although the differences in Table 7 might seem large.

5.3. Diagnosing PPA and its subtypes

We evaluate the accuracy of diagnosing PPA and its subtypes based on the selected features across the three classification methods using the simulated ASR method. In practice, classification models might be trained on data that have been manually transcribed by humans (clinicians or otherwise). However, as the amount of data increases, this becomes less practical and it may become necessary to train these models from transcripts that were automatically generated from ASR. We replicate our experiments once on data that have been manually transcribed and once on the same data, but with transcripts corrupted by synthetic word errors (in which case the training data and test data have the same WER). Classifiers trained on human-produced transcripts have an average accuracy of 65.71% ($\sigma = 12.42$) and those trained on 'noisy' transcripts have an average accuracy of 70.72% ($\sigma = 13.89$), which is significant at heteroscedastic $t(543) = -4.47, p < 0.00001, CI = [-0.072, -0.028]$. These differences can be observed in Figure 2. Interestingly, the classifiers trained with 'noisy' transcripts outperform those trained with 'clean' transcripts fairly consistently in the PPA vs. control task, but this is far less pronounced (and to some extent reversed) in the SD vs. PNFA task. This may be partially explained by a significant three-way interaction between WER, the task (i.e., the participant groups), and the training set (i.e., 'noisy' vs. 'clean') on a followup ANOVA ($F(6) = 2.43, p < 0.05$).

This trend is also apparent when the classifiers are tested using the Nuance transcripts. Figure 3 shows the classification accuracies for each classifier on each diagnostic task using the data generated using the default and reduced vocabularies. When classifiying PPA versus controls, training on the 'noisy' Nuance data always leads to equal or greater accuracies than training on the 'clean' (human-transcribed) data. For SD versus PNFA, the results are mixed, although the results from the reduced vocabulary suggest the opposite trend.

We compare the diagnostic accuracies across all classifiers given transcripts from Nuance using the reduced vocabulary with the accuracies of the synthetic WER method using the nearest WER (100%) and the associated error type distribution (i.e., 10% substitutions, 90% deletions, over all errors). We find no difference between results obtained with Nuance data and those obtained with the synthetic method ($t(44.25) = 1.1072, p = 0.27, CI = [-0.04, 0.13]$). We repeat this analysis with the default Nuance vocabulary and its equivalent synthetic WER (70%) and distribution (i.e., 40% substitution, 60% deletion) and again find no significant difference ($t(44.61) = 1.46, p = 0.15, CI = [-0.02, 0.11]$). Here, distributions of WER are approximately Gaussian over the various parameterizations of the systems. The lack of apparent difference in diagnosis when using the Nuance ASR and the synthetic method supports the use of the latter in these experi-

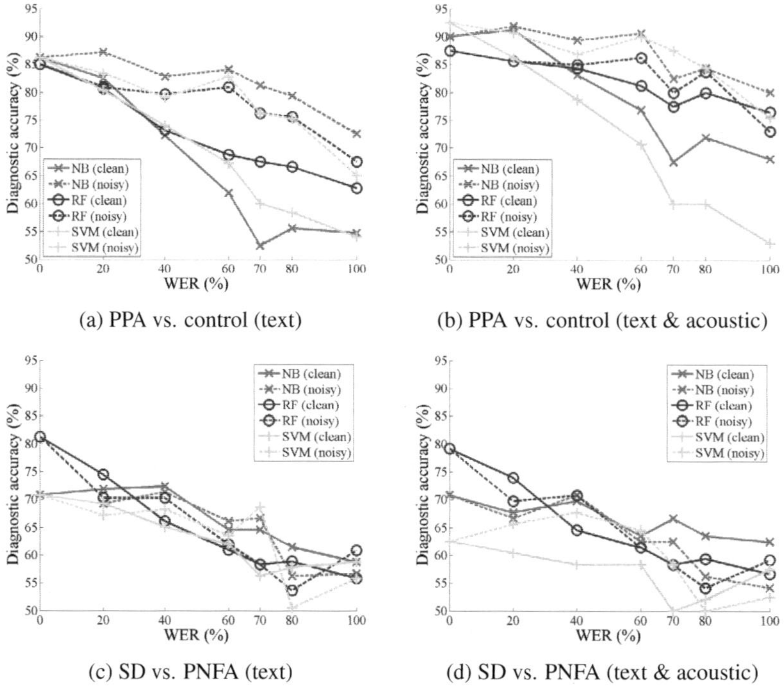

(a) PPA vs. control (text)

(b) PPA vs. control (text & acoustic)

(c) SD vs. PNFA (text)

(d) SD vs. PNFA (text & acoustic)

Figure 2: Accuracy in diagnosing the indicated classes given features derived from potentially error-full textual transcriptions alone and in combination with features derived directly from the acoustics. Lines marked with x's, circles, and pluses indicate the use of the naïve Bayes, random forest, and support vector machine classifiers. Solid lines indicate those trained with human-transcribed (clean) data and dashed lines indicate those trained with corrupted data.

ments.

Among the simulated ASR data, an n-ary ANOVA reveals significant main effects for each of the classification problems (PPA-vs.-control or PNFA-vs.-SD; $F(1) = 124.19, p = 0$), WER ($F(5) = 31.69, p = 0$), error distribution (proportions of IE, SE, and DE; $F(4) = 6.32, p < 0.0005$), and training set ('noisy' or 'clean'; $F(1) = 35.41, p = 0$) on the accuracy of classification; there is no effect of the classifier, however ($F(2) = 2.27, p = 0.1039$). There were significant interaction effects between WER and the classification problem ($F(5) = 5.18, p < 0.0005$), error distribution ($F(12) = 2.2, p < 0.05$), and the training set ($F(5) = 4.95, p < 0.0005$), but not with the data subset (text or text with acoustics; $F(5) = 1.42, p = 0.2146$), or the classifier ($F(10) = 0.49, p = 0.8993$).

6. Discussion

Our goal is to provide assistive technologies, including diagnostic software, to various populations with pathological speech and language, including those with PPA. This study represents an initial step towards ASR for this population. One main result of this research is that fairly accurate diagnosis of PPA and of its subtypes can remain relatively accurate, even at very high levels of WER, by selecting appropriate features from the data at training time. Acoustic features are valuable, as they remain constant as the WER increases. However, our data suggest that some features from the text can still be informative, even when the transcripts are very noisy.

One important direction for future work is to improve ASR for clinical populations. Clearly, modern speech recognition has greater difficulty in recognizing PPA speech relative to speech the general elderly population, especially for individuals with SD. While more appropriate acoustic models built for older-adult voices will be important (based on available data), a focus on improving language modeling and the pruning of the lattices produced by hidden Markov models may be more fruitful if the cause of the pathology is semantic or lexical.

Another limitation of our approach is that the t-test method for feature selection does not consider interactions between features. In the future we would like to examine these interactions, particularly between text and acoustic features.

In this study we did not take into account any syntactic features, although agrammatism and/or syntactic simplification are characteristic of PNFA. Presumably, including information of this type could increase the classification accuracy. One approach would be to apply a sentence boundary detection algorithm to the ASR transcripts and extract traditional syntactic complexity measures (e.g. Yngve depth). Another approach would be to explore localized complexity metrics which do not depend on full sentence parses.

7. Acknowledgements

This work was supported by the Canadian Institutes of Health Research (CIHR), Grant #MOP-82744, and the Natural Sciences and Engineering Research Council of Canada (NSERC).

8. References

[1] M. L. Gorno-Tempini, A. E. Hillis, S. Weintraub, A. Kertesz, M. Mendez, S. F. Cappa, J. M. Ogar, J. D. Rohrer, S. Black, B. F.

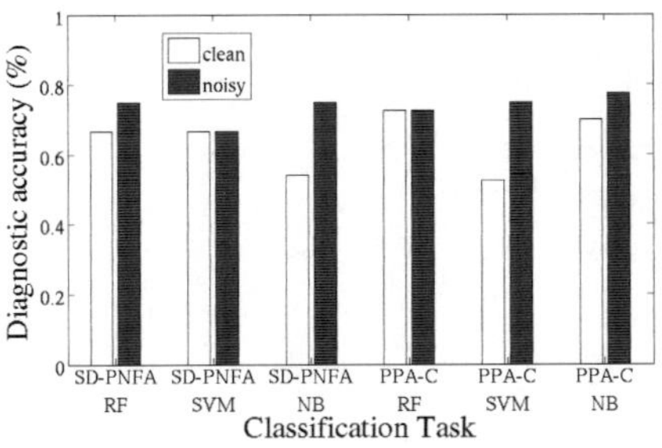

(a) Text features, default vocabulary

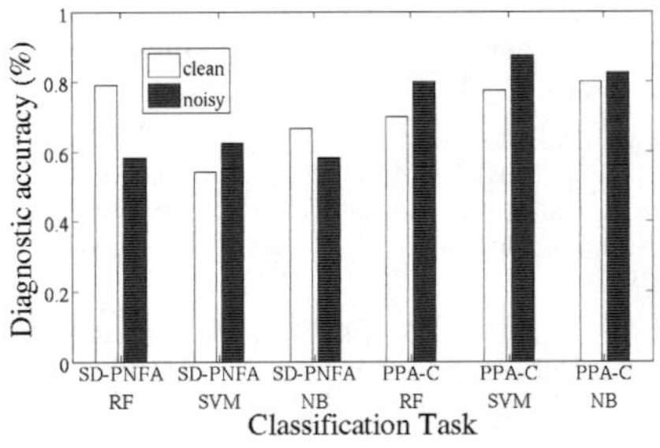

(b) Text and acoustic features, default vocabulary

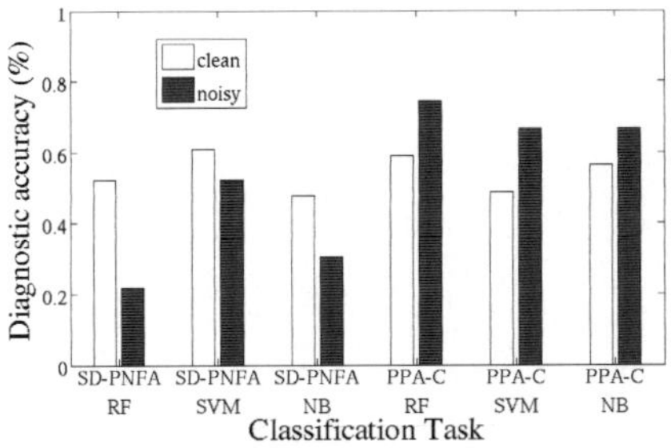

(c) Text features, reduced vocabulary

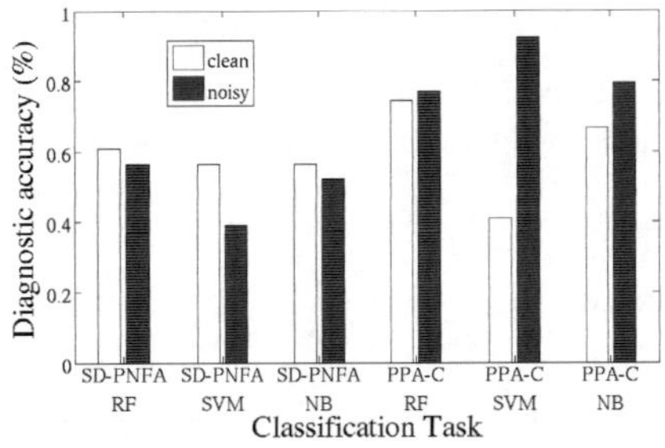

(d) Text and acoustic features, reduced vocabulary

Figure 3: Classification accuracies using transcripts from the Nuance system with the default and reduced vocabularies, for random forest (RF), support vector machine (SVM), and naïve Bayes (NB) classifiers. Empty bars indicate the accuracy achieved when training on the clean, human-transcribed data, while filled bars indicate the accuracy when training on the noisy ASR data.

Boeve, F. Manes, N. F. Dronkers, R. Vandenberghe, K. Rascovsky, K. Patterson, B. L. Miller, D. S. Knopman, J. R. Hodges, M. M. Mesulam, and M. Grossman, "Classification of primary progressive aphasia and its variants," *Neurology*, vol. 76, pp. 1006–1014, 2011.

[2] J. Schatzmann, B. Thomson, and S. Young, "Error simulation for training statistical dialogue systems," in *Automatic Speech Recognition & Understanding, 2007. ASRU. IEEE Workshop on.* IEEE, 2007, pp. 526–531.

[3] M. Labský, J. Cuřín, T. Macek, J. Kleindienst, L. Kunc, H. Young, A. Thyme-Gobbel, and H. Quast, "Impact of word error rate on driving performance while dictating short texts," in *Proceedings of the 4th International Conference on Automotive User Interfaces and Interactive Vehicular Applications*, ser. AutomotiveUI '12. ACM, 2012, pp. 179–182.

[4] R. Vipperla, S. Renals, and J. Frankel, "Longitudinal study of ASR performance on ageing voices," in *Proceedings of INTERSPEECH*, 2008, pp. 2550–2553.

[5] V. Young and A. Mihailidis, "Difficulties in automatic speech recognition of dysarthric speakers and implications for speech-based applications used by the elderly: A literature review," *Assistive Technology*, vol. 22, no. 2, pp. 99–112, 2010.

[6] D. Hakkani-Tur, D. Vergyri, and G. Tur, "Speech-based automated cognitive status assessment," in *Proceedings of INTERSPEECH*, 2010, pp. 258–261.

[7] B. Peintner, W. Jarrold, D. Vergyri, C. Richey, M. L. G. Tempini, and J. Ogar, "Learning diagnostic models using speech and language measures," in *Engineering in Medicine and Biology Society, 2008. EMBS 2008. 30th Annual International Conference of the IEEE*, 2008, pp. 4648–4651.

[8] K. C. Fraser, J. A. Meltzer, N. L. Graham, C. Leonard, G. Hirst, S. E. Black, and E. Rochon, "Automated classification of primary progressive aphasia subtypes from narrative speech transcripts," *Cortex*, 2013.

[9] B. Roark, M. Mitchell, J.-P. Hosom, K. Hollingshead, and J. Kaye, "Spoken language derived measures for detecting mild cognitive impairment," *IEEE Transactions on Audio, Speech, and Language Processing*, vol. 19, no. 7, pp. 2081–2090, 2011.

[10] S. V. Pakhomov, G. E. Smith, D. Chacon, Y. Feliciano, N. Graff-Radford, R. Caselli, and D. S. Knopman, "Computerized analysis of speech and language to identify psycholinguistic correlates of frontotemporal lobar degeneration," *Cognitive and Behavioral Neurology*, vol. 23, pp. 165–177, 2010.

[11] E. M. Saffran, R. S. Berndt, and M. F. Schwartz, "The quantitative analysis of agrammatic production: procedure and data," *Brain and Language*, vol. 37, pp. 440–479, 1989.

[12] K. Toutanova, D. Klein, C. Manning, and Y. Singer, "Feature-rich part-of-speech tagging with a cyclic dependency network," in *Proceedings of the 2003 Conference of the North American Chapter of the Association for Computational Linguistics: Human Language Technologies*, 2003, pp. 252–259.

[13] S. M. Wilson, M. L. Henry, M. Besbris, J. M. Ogar, N. F. Dronkers, W. Jarrold, B. L. Miller, and M. L. Gorno-Tempini, "Connected speech production in three variants of primary progressive aphasia," *Brain*, vol. 133, pp. 2069–2088, 2010.

[14] H. Bird, M. A. Lambon Ralph, K. Patterson, and J. R. Hodges, "The rise and fall of frequency and imageability: Noun and verb production in semantic dementia," *Brain and Language*, vol. 73, pp. 17–49, 2000.

[15] L. Meteyard and K. Patterson, "The relation between content and structure in language production: an analysis of speech errors in semantic dementia," *Brain and Language*, vol. 110, no. 3, pp. 121–134, 2009.

[16] S. Ash, P. Moore, L. Vesely, D. Gunawardena, C. McMillan, C. Anderson, B. Avants, and M. Grossman, "Non-fluent speech in frontotemporal lobar degeneration," *Journal of Neurolinguistics*, vol. 22, no. 4, pp. 370–383, 2009.

[17] M. Brysbaert and B. New, "Moving beyond Kučera and Francis: A critical evaluation of current word frequency norms and the introduction of a new and improved word frequency measure for American English," *Behavior Research Methods*, vol. 41, no. 4, pp. 977–990, 2009.

[18] H. Stadthagen-Gonzalez and C. J. Davis, "The Bristol norms for age of acquisition, imageability, and familiarity," *Behavior Research Methods*, vol. 38, no. 4, pp. 598–605, 2006.

[19] K. Gilhooly and R. Logie, "Age-of-acquisition, imagery, concreteness, familiarity, and ambiguity measures for 1,944 words," *Behavior Research Methods*, vol. 12, pp. 395–427, 1980.

[20] P. Hoffman, R. W. Jones, and A. Lambon Ralph, Matthew, "Be concrete to be comprehended: Consistent imageability effects in semantic dementia for nouns, verbs, synonyms and associates," *Cortex*, vol. 49, no. 5, pp. 1206–1218, 2013.

[21] D. Crepaldi, C. Ingignoli, R. Verga, A. Contardi, C. Semenza, and C. Luzzatti, "On nouns, verbs, lexemes, and lemmas: Evidence from the spontaneous speech of seven aphasic patients," *Aphasiology*, vol. 25, no. 1, pp. 71–92, 2011.

[22] F. Cuetos, C. Rosci, M. Laiacona, and E. Capitani, "Different variables predict anomia in different subjects: A longitudinal study of two Alzheimer's patients," *Neuropsychologia*, vol. 46, no. 1, pp. 249–260, 2008.

[23] M. A. Lambon Ralph, K. S. Graham, A. W. Ellis, and J. R. Hodges, "Naming in semantic dementia – What matters?" *Neuropsychologia*, vol. 36, no. 8, pp. 775–784, 1998.

[24] H. H. Clark and J. E. Fox Tree, "Using uh and um in spontaneous speaking," *Cognition*, vol. 84, no. 1, pp. 73–111, 2002.

[25] Y. Liu, E. Shriberg, A. Stolcke, D. Hillard, M. Ostendorf, and M. Harper, "Enriching speech recognition with automatic detection of sentence boundaries and disfluencies," *Audio, Speech, and Language Processing, IEEE Transactions on*, vol. 14, no. 5, pp. 1526–1540, 2006.

[26] M. Little, P. McSharry, I. Moroz, and S. Roberts, "Nonlinear, biophysically-informed speech pathology detection," in *Proceedings of ICASSP 2006*, Toulouse, France, 2006, pp. 1080–1083.

[27] D. G. Silva, L. C. Oliveira, and M. Andrea, "Jitter estimation algorithms for detection of pathological voices," *EURASIP Journal on Advances in Signal Processing*, vol. 2009, pp. 1–9, 2009.

[28] M. Grossman, "Primary progressive aphasia: clinicopathological correlations," *Nature Reviews Neurology*, vol. 6, pp. 88–97, 2010.

[29] K. Mengistu, F. Rudzicz, and T. Falk, "Using acoustic measures to predict automatic speech recognition performance for dysarthric speakers," in *Proceedings of the 7th International Workshop on Models and Analysis of Vocal Emissions for Biomedical Applications at INTERSPEECH 2011*, Firenze Italy, August 2011.

[30] R. D. Kent and Y.-J. Kim, "Toward an acoustic typology of motor speech disorders," *Clinical linguistics & phonetics*, vol. 17, no. 6, pp. 427–445, 2003.

[31] K. Francois, "The comprehensive dragon naturallyspeaking guide," in *Inclusive Learning Technologies Conference*, 2008.

[32] D. Graff and C. Cieri, *English Gigaword Corpus*. Linguistic Data Consortium, 2003.

[33] K. C. Fraser, F. Rudzicz, and E. Rochon, "Using text and acoustic features to diagnose progressive aphasia and its subtypes," in *Proceedings of Interspeech*, 2013.

Automatic Speech Recognition: A Shifted Role in Early Speech Intervention?

Foad Hamidi, Melanie Baljko

Department of Electrical Engineering and Computer Science,
Lassonde School of Engineering, York University, Toronto, Ontario, Canada
{fhamidi,mb}@cse.yokru.ca

Abstract

Although *automatic speech recognition* (ASR) has been used in several systems that support speech training for children, this particular design domain poses on-going challenges: an input domain of non-standard speech and a user population for which meaningful, consistent, and well designed automatically-derived feedback is imperative. In this design analysis, we focus on and analyze the differences between the tasks of speech *recognition* and speech *assessment*, and identify the latter as a central issue for work in the speech-training domain. Our analysis is based on empirical results from fieldwork with Speech-Language Pathologists concerning the design requirements analysis for tangible toys intended for speech intervention with primary-school aged children. This analysis leads us to advocate for the use of only rudimentary ASR feedback.

Index Terms: speech intervention, automatic speech recognition

1. Introduction

In the context of *control* systems, *automatic speech recognition* (ASR) refers to a series of techniques combining signal processing, statistical modeling, and machine learning to interpret human speech typically by deciphering input acoustic signals into phones or other linguistic elements such as syllables, words or phrases [1]. Speech, as a mode of input, has been taken up in many ASR-based applications in the disability community, such as for speech-to-text communication technologies and for command interpretation systems for hands-free computer use [2]. However, there are key differences between these speech-based *control* systems and those system for *speech training*.

Speech training for children, as conducted in face-to-face sessions led by a *speech language pathologist* (SLP), involves eliciting speech that includes the problematic segment that has been targeted for intervention. The child is provided with corrective feedback (best practices from clinicians adopt a feedback approach at word-level or even coarser granularity). The SLP draws upon a repertoire of techniques for speech elicitation and feedback.

The potential of ASR to support computer-based tools to improve the efficacy of the traditional face-to-face clinician-client dyad and the potential to provide new modes of intervention, outside of face-to-face sessions with an SLP has been recognized previously [3]. Despite the recognized benefits, relatively few computer intervention systems that incorporate ASR have been developed and thoroughly evaluated. A recognized obstacle for the use of ASR in speech intervention systems has been that this technology oftentimes does not perform well for non-standard pronunciations and can lead to inconsistent feedback [4]. Other systems focus on the use of multimedia instructions (i.e., animation and audio) to aid parents and SLPs communicate feedback to children in the course of speech exercises, but do not use ASR (e.g., [5]). In our design analysis, we discuss these systems with a view to clarify and reposition the design objective for this particular design domain.

Many language learning and practice applications have been developed in recent years for smartphones and tablets [6]. Many of these applications are digital versions of flashcards and pictures to help SLPs in intervention (e.g., Phonics Studio). A few of these applications record speech and provide data gathering (e.g., Articulate It!). The potential benefits of these applications for speech training and intervention are clear, and the field looks forward to systematic usability and efficacy evaluation.

Our design analysis focuses on the theoretically oriented question of what is the feasibility of automatic corrective speech feedback for children? Having clear answers to this and other foundational questions are prerequisites for good applications. We provide a literature review of previous computer speech intervention systems that incorporate ASR, with view of identifying challenges and techniques to address them. A goal is to contribute toward the design of new-generation speech intervention system and to yield novel insights. To this end, we have conducted fieldwork with five clinic-based SLPs who work with pediatric populations, with a particular focus on the designs of tangible toys intended for use as part of and in support of speech intervention protocols.

2. Analysis

2.1. Challenges in Repurposing

Prior speech intervention systems have either incorporated extant ASR engines or have developed specific ASR engines for their projects (such as [7] and [8]). Reuse, in general, is often a good strategy, since it has the advantage of repurposing a large amount of work and effort gone into the original design of the ASR. However, this reuse has introduced a number of issues. The first issue concerns the nature of the ASR output. Speech intervention systems require the *analysis* of input speech that is relative to a given target. The required output needs to provide useful information about the differences between the elicited and the targeted speech unit, which is necessary in order to provide corrective feedback. Traditional conceptions of ASR systems provision for the *identification* of words within speech, where the content of that input speech is not known *a priori*. The *recognition result* from the ASR module is provided in the form of a lexicographical interpretation for some particular input acoustic signal. Thus, one can recognize a misalignment between what ASR module provides and the design requirements. A key challenge in this design domain is the alignment and extraction of information that will be useful for corrective feedback, whereas a main challenge for ASR (more generally) is identification in the face of deviation from the training pronunciation.

Extant, general ASR modules (e.g., *Dragon Naturally Speaking* [9]) are mostly developed for speakers with clear speech. These modules are derived from human speech samples and are trained on clear "standard" speech. When the input speech differs from the modeled speech, due to reasons such as when the input speech is produced by a speaker with an accent or speech impairment, the performance of the ASR module degrades [2, 10]. The performance further degrades when speech is affected by environmental noise, distortion and sound quality change [11].

An *error,* in this context, can be understood as either a *recognition error,* where input is "correct" but the system fails to recognize it, or a *speech error,* where input speech significantly deviates from a standard model. Despite rapid improvements in ASR technology, some researchers believe that because sound and specifically speech is a noisy input channel, errors are an inevitable part of ASR technologies [1]. In the presence of non-standard speech, ASR modules produce low confidence scores for predicted candidates, reflecting the high possibility of recognition errors. In response, several research initiatives have focused on ASR specifically for dysarthric speech (e.g., [12, 13]) and/or the speech of children (e.g., [14]).

2.2. Prototype Systems

Kewley-Port et al.'s early system was developed using recorded templates of the child's best production, which were then used as standards against which to measure the acceptability of new utterances [15]. The researchers conjectured that recognition error rates as high as 20%, a rate within the capabilities of a small vocabulary speaker-dependent system, would be acceptable for articulation training. A more detailed assessment of the degree of success of the system was not provided. Adoption of this approach has been limited, however: training is required for each individual, and target words and phrases that consist of segments not producible by the child are not possible (thereby obviating application for speech intervention).

Speech intervention mediated by the *Speech Training, Assessment, and Remediation* (STAR) system, a system designed to distinguish between the segments /r/ and /w/, was achieved through a role-playing game with the premise that "aliens" need to understand the child's speech [16]. Evaluation was conducted in which likelihood ratios, as calculated automatically by the ASR module, were compared with perceptual quality ratings, as provided by human judges. The results showed high correlation between the two measures for substitution errors. In other words, the system worked well when /r/ and /w/ were misarticulated. However, the ASR module produced many false positives (i.e., the results correlated poorly for correctly articulated examples).

2.3. Box of Tricks

Vicsi et al. developed a speech intervention system, *Box of Tricks,* for children with hearing impairment [8]. *Box of Tricks* uses ASR to detect and to provide feedback about speech mistakes and was originally devised to support Hungarian, and has subsequently been expanded to also support English, Swedish and Slovenian. *Box of Tricks* is designed to train for vowels and also fricatives.

The goal of *Box of Tricks* is to teach children to modify their speech on the basis of visualizations of their speech signals. Picture-like images of energy, change in time, fundamental frequency, voiced or unvoiced detection, intonation, spectrum, spectrogram (cochleogram) and spectrogram differences were used for the visualization.

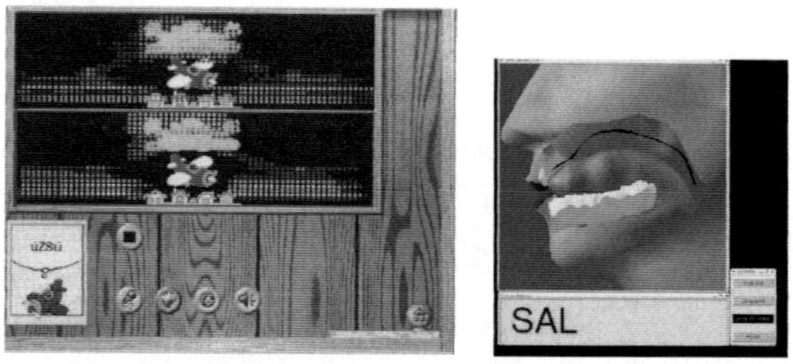

Figure 1: *Feedback from two systems designed for children: Box of Tricks (left) [8] and ARTUR (right) [7]*

For the visualizations, a filter was developed and applied that produces a representation based on inner ear processing rather than FFT spectra. The researchers hypothesized that the visualization generated by this filter would be a more intuitive representation of speech for their users than other types of visualizations. The representation of elicited pronunciation was shown in alignment with a representation of a target pronunciation. Parts of the representation were highlighted to signal more important features of the speech: to draw the children's attention to these parts that were highlighted by amusing background pictures. These visualizations, especially combined with gaming elements, would be more stimulating than numerical scores.

Box of Tricks did not provide overt instruction to the children about how to correct their speech, however. Although the users were provided with feedback that indicated, in some fashion, the differences between their input speech and the desired, target speech, they were not provided with clear instruction for how this difference might be decreased. The researchers conjectured that this approach provides meaningful feedback to children and allows them to use the system by themselves. It was not clearly demonstrated that, in the absence of such corrective feedback, the children were able to incorporate the information into their motor learning, but neither was the conjecture disproved.

2.4. ARTUR

Bälter et al. developed a prototype of a computer system for speech intervention for children with hearing impairments to be used in the absence of SLPs [7]. The system aims to identify problematic pronunciations and provide corrective feedback. A computer-animated head with exposed internal parts of the face and mouth, referred to as the *Articulation TUtoR* (ARTUR), was constructed. ARTUR was utilized to provide feedback based on the input (albeit not synchronously with the elicitation). The researchers hypothesized that, for children with hearing problems, the visualization of the movement of vocal tract is more useful than acoustic signal visualization. A knowledge base of mappings was constructed: for each possible error, an appropriate corrective response was developed (some corrective responses were reused). The feedback, in the form of spoken commands and corresponding animation, was drawn from this knowledge base. The researchers conjectured that showing the hidden parts of vocal tract would be key to effective speech intervention. In the final implementation of the system, audio input is to be supplemented with video footage of the user for more accurate categorization of pronunciation error.

The system was tested with two groups of children in a Wizard-of-Oz study. The children in the first group were six years old and the ones in the second group were between nine and eleven years old. In addition to children, an adult with English as second language also used the program and provided feedback.

The empirical qualitative data demonstrated that the children, especially the older group, liked the idea of playing with a computer and being given explicit feedback. However, while they (and especially the older group) liked the program in general, they found the visual feedback confusing and unhelpful. This was found of both the image representation of speech organs and the accompanying animation. The children suggested that adding more game-like features, such as goals and rewards, to make it more engaging. Also, they found the user interface of the program, as well as the anatomy of the vocal tract (e.g. the hard palate), unclear. When compared to interaction with the SLP, older children described the interaction as more relaxed. In more recent work, ARTUR's interface was assessed for use in second language pronunciation training for adults and children [17].

In a study of the pedagogy of feedback conducted to inform an application of the system for second language training, Engwall and Bälter demonstrated that, even given the availability of accurate information for feedback, many interaction decisions such as when and how to deliver feedback need to be built into the design of a given application [17, 18]. The study was done in the context of second language learning but the results are still relevant to pronunciation training.

2.5. Speech Viewer II

A commercial (but no longer in distribution) speech therapy system, *Speech Viewer II,* was developed to help adults with speech impairments improve their speech [19]. This system visualized speech signals and waveforms. Figure 2 shows speech visualization produced by this system.

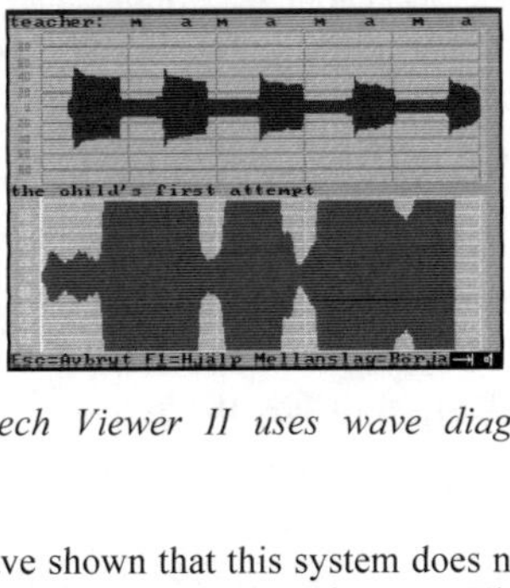

Figure 2: *Speech Viewer II uses wave diagrams as feedback [18].*

Two studies have shown that this system does not work well for use by children with hearing impairments. The first study showed that the program did not have any advantages over traditional speech therapy for vowel training for children with profound hearing impairments [20]. The second study tested a vowel accuracy feedback with children with hearing impairments and showed that the system produced modest gains but exhibited inaccuracies and inconsistencies in feedback [21].

When the use of *Speech Viewer* was restricted to the improvement of prosodic features of speech for children with hearing impairments, better results were produced. Öster conducted a study with two deaf children who were trained using the program for ten minutes twice weekly over an eight week period [22]. For each child, a different skill was targeted: a fifteen-year-old boy who had difficulty with producing durational contrast between phonologically long and short vowels, and a thirteen-year-old girl who had difficulties producing voicing contrasts between voiced and voiceless velar stops. Both children were reported to have improvements in the areas targeted. Öster also conducted a study with a five-year-old deaf boy who had difficulty controlling the loudness and pitch of his speech [19]. While detailed information about the amount of training, methodology and the results of the intervention is not provided, the researcher reported that use of the program, and specifically its graphical interface, allowed the SLP to communicate better with the child, resulting in improved loudness and pitch.

2.6. OPTACIA

Öster et al. have conducted initial experiments with the OPTACIA system, which is similar to Speech Viewer, and produces visual maps for training Swedish sibilant fricatives, fricatives with higher-frequency and acoustic energy than non-sibilant fricatives, to hearing-impaired users [23]. The system is designed to supplement speech intervention. The user is provided with a visual representation of his or her speech that is shown in relation to a visualization of a target pronunciation. The researchers hypothesize that having this feedback will help increase the frequency of correct pronunciations. In this system, the produced diagrams will be described by the SLP and used as a tool during therapy to visualize specific components of speech.

The speech of three severely hearing-impaired children when pronouncing the fricatives was recorded and mapped against the created maps and it was found that the visualizations corresponded well with the speech produced.

While this system shows it is possible to create visualizations that correspond with non-standard input speech, it did not discuss the usefulness of this approach for children. The input data was restricted to sibilant-vowel combinations rather than words, and the visualizations were shown in terms of time and frequency, an unintuitive approach for children. The project was in its initial phase and no user studies were conducted.

2.7. visiBabble and VocSyl

The visiBabble system, manifested either as a tangible toy or as a software application, processes infant vocalizations in real-time and produces brightly colored animations, intended to provide positive reinforcement of the production of syllabic utterances, intended as an early speech intervention and support for later language and cognitive development [24, 25].

In a similar vein, the VocSyl system also used speech and vocalization analysis and visualization to engage children's speech [26, 27, 28] using a software application. VocSyl uses a suite of audio visualizations to represent different audio features of speech (pitch, loudness, duration and syllables) in abstract visual representations that are presented to children in real-time.

visiBabble and VocSyl are intended to encourage children with speech delays. VocSyl was originally designed for motivating children with *Autism Spectrum Disorder* (ASD) to encourage speech vocalizations [28]. An initial study of VocSyl with 5 children with ASD showed that audio and visual stimulation increase the rate and duration of speech like vocalizations. Hailpern et al. found that each of the children responded to at least one form of feedback and that only some participants responded to visual stimuli whereas others responded to auditory stimuli or a combination of visual and auditory stimuli. They also found that it is likely that visualizations should be customized to some extent for each person [28].

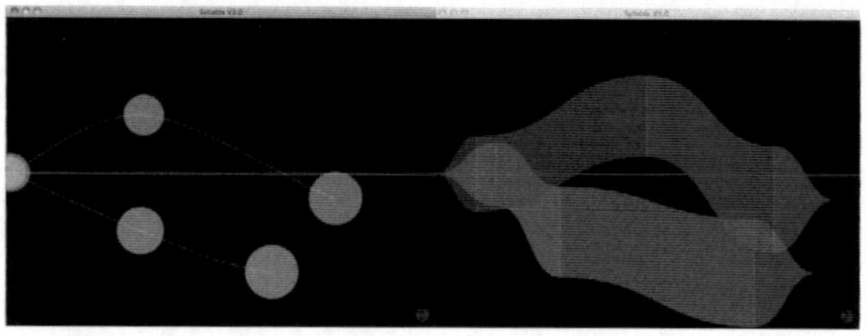

Figure 3: *VocSyl visualizations to illustrate multisyllable words [27]*

A more recent application of the VocSyl system supports the production of multi-syllabic speech production in children with autism speech apraxia and speech delays. One of the goals is to provide children with a persistent visual representation of their speech that would facilitate reflection and a new experience of language skills. The goal is to use visualizations to illustrate differences in utterances and help with the ability to combine syllables both as word combinations and in single multisyllabic words [26, 27].

Figure 3 shows the interface of *VocSyl.* Syllables are represented by discreet elements (left screenshot) or regions in continuous visualizations (rights screenshot) and emphasis, pitch change and pacing are represented by the diameter of the graphical element and position on the y-axis and x-axis, respectively. The researchers involved two children with ASD, two children with SPD and four children without disabilities in the design of the system.

While the system does not currently provide corrective feedback, it focuses on engagement and motivation and, also, provides the visualizations as a communication aid to help SLPs demonstrate specific aspects (i.e., syllable location and volume) of the vocalizations. It is apparent that if corrective feedback were given in the absence of SLPs or parents to facilitate their interpretation, the children would not have been as motivated to continue using their speech.

2.8. Field Interviews

Like Fell et al. [24, 25], we are also interested in the development of tangible interactive toys for the support of speech intervention [29]. To this end, we conducted open-ended interviews with five SLPs who work with children (our target user population is ages 4-7). We reached these SLPs by direct contact.

All the interviewed SLPs felt that a toy that focuses on speech elicitation would be useful. Three of the SLPs already use props such as dolls and physical toys, as well as, images and flash cards to engage children. These toys allow for the development of narrative and the engagement of the children's attention. They stressed that it is useful to have toys that when working with small children (ages 4-7) can be touched and grasped and are also durable.

Two of the SLPs who were interviewed used iPads to play games that involve speech. Surprisingly, they preferred games that encourage speech through stories and play but are not specifically developed for speech intervention and have simple interfaces, (e.g., My PlayHome). One SLP commented that she prefers to use non-computational material during intervention because too much technology can be distracting for the children.

It was noted that, sometimes, initial engagement of children is difficult and it takes a long time to establish a relationship with them to the point where they start using their speech more freely. It was also noted that capturing the child's natural speech (i.e., speech spoken in the absence of the SLP) would be helpful in assessing intervention needs. One SLP records samples of her client's speech during some of her sessions. She uses these samples for future comparison of intervention outcomes, analysis of speech in the absence of the client.

All SLPs indicated that having no or little feedback that is consistent and accurate is better than inconsistent or incorrect feedback, especially in the absence of the SLP who can mediate between the technology and the child. However, they mentioned that some measure of progress is necessary so that not all speech is rewarded equally. Additionally, the SLPs suggested that automatic tracking and record keeping of exercises are useful functions that a computational toy could provide.

Three of the interviewed SLPs discussed the context of multilingual communities. Working with children who are multilingual is quite common in Toronto, and in Canada more generally, due to the presence of many new immigrants. These SLPs noted that many immigrant children whose first language is not English face difficulties when moving to a new country where English is the main language and noted this condition as a contributor to speech delays. The issue is complex, as the home language is often not English, the parents and caregivers are not fluent and are not in a position to assist with speech exercises at home. Additionally, as the children grow up, they are faced with the challenge of switching between English and their home language. These challenges can place stress on interfamily relations and cause disconnect between children and their parents. These SLPs highlighted the particular need for a toy that is able to switch between languages and that supports communication between children and parents in languages other than English. School board policies oftentimes specifically encourage parents to speak and read with their children in the home language, as a support for language development.

3. Discussion

3.1. The challenges of feedback

As indicated previously and reinforced by our SLP interviews, the provision of meaningful and consistent feedback to children is a key priority. The feedback must not only be evaluative (i.e., indicating whether a given speech target was reached or not), but must also provide corrective analytic feedback (i.e., analyze and semantically interpret degrees of deviation between elicited speech and a given speech target). Analyses even from a decade ago identified that ASR technology is not able to provide corrective analytic feedback and can only provide evaluative feedback [30].

For an ASR module operating in a speech intervention context, if it is unable to produce a lexicographic candidate for a given speech input, then the system must decide whether this error is an instance of speech error due to poor speech or a recognition error due to poor system performance. In this situation, the system may exploit additional information in the form of information about the expected input.

Researchers have determined that systems, such as those reviewed in prior sections, which rely on abstract visualizations as feedback do not seem to work well for children. Neri et al. have identified a major problem with providing comparable waveforms, a popular form of feedback (e.g., *Speech Viewer II*), to the user [31]. Although showing target and input waveforms in alignment can be motivating for the user (i.e., to try to emulate the target waveform by modifying their pronunciation), it does not necessarily lead to behavior modification (i.e., correction of articulation). Moreover, Neri et al. argue that such alignments may be misleading, since it is possible for two articulations to both be "on target" and yet have waveforms that are very different from each other; they argue that even a trained phonetician cannot extract information needed to correct pronunciation from this feedback, let alone a user who does not have any training in interpreting this form of feedback [31].

3.2. Shifting from analysis to elicitation motivation

Although ASR is challenged by certain requirements of this design domain (namely the need for corrective analytic feedback), it supports admirably well another requirement: that the system be engaging, interactive and motivates repeated speech productions by the child. A key observation here is that incorporating ASR can make the computer system responsive to speech even if it does not provide detailed feedback. In the context of speech intervention, even rudimentary feedback can be of value, since it can motivate children to try multiple repetitions of words and phrases. This approach has been used in a remarkable study by Mitra et al., in the context of accent reduction, which found that even rudimentary feedback was helpful [32].

In this study, sixteen children between the ages of twelve and sixteen were chosen from an Indian English median school, where English was the primary medium of teaching but was spoken with a strong accent. They were grouped into four groups and given access to a computer for three hours a week. The children were provided with "Ellis", an English language learning program with no ASR support, four classic English-language films that they could choose to watch during their time at the computer and the previously mentioned *Dragon Naturally Speaking* program. The children were given the objective of making their speech understood by the *Dragon Naturally Speaking* program that either accepted or rejected input speech and did not provide corrective feedback. No further instructions were provided following an initial demonstration of the resources. Rather surprisingly, the approach was effective. To measure improvements in speech and whether they carry to real-life situations, four human judges were provided with video clips of children speaking at different evaluation points. A measure of the percentage of words correctly recognized was calculated. Significant improvements over a five-month period were observed. Furthermore, the word recognition rates by the ASR module were correlated with the human judges' assessments of pronunciation accuracy (e.g., an improvement of 117% was observed, as assessed by the human judges and of 79%, as assessed to the ASR module).

In another study of second language training, class observations and teacher interviews, revealed that in practice very little feedback is given to the students [17]. Reasons for limiting feedback were to maintain a positive atmosphere and communicative flow. A study of literature on the pedagogy of feedback shows that according to many theories (e.g., [33]), the *encouragement* of speech and communication is as important as its correction.

Scientific researchers in this domain may quickly conclude that the need for high-quality corrective analytic feedback clearly motivates the need for further work into automated speech analysis. And such work is ongoing. For instance, efforts in the area of *acoustic training*, which entails to the process of recording representative speech samples from a user to create or to augment an acoustic database [2]. In particular, Rudzicz has recently developed and validated a highly specialized ASR module for dysarthric speech [12]. Another project, the *Universal Access* (UA) dysarthria speech database has gathered a collection of speech samples from individuals with speech dysarthria that can be used to incorporate knowledge about dysarthric speech into an ASR application [13]. The other approach from the Assistive Technology domain to increase effectiveness of ASR for users with non-standard speech, *input restriction,* may also been seen as providing a useful avenue for speech intervention, since the approach relies on simplifying the recognition task by restricting the input to a limited number of isolated words, rather than continuous speech. This approach has been used widely, and improves accuracy rates (e.g., Rosengren et al. showed that adapting the vocabulary for each user improved accuracy rates from 28% to 62% [34]), and has been employed in some of the previously described systems (e.g., [19, 23]).

But in a parallel stream to the specific ASR research and development work underway, one may consider the broader design parameters of the application domain: a designer may see this situation not so much as an obstacle, but rather an occasion or opportunity to contemplate more generally the role of ASR in speech intervention systems, systems which are needed for the here and now, for deployment on a time-scale that is not hinged to the outcomes of medium- and long-term automated speech analysis research projects, and for contexts in which an SLP is already present and mediating the speech intervention session (who is trained and experienced with the design of corrective feedback).

Although it would seem unintuitive, we conjecture that rudimentary feedback provides more value than other more detailed types of corrective feedback. Rudimentary feedback preserves a main point of "value" of ASR, which is as the main driver for motivating, interactive technology-mediated experiences. These encounters motivate the elicitation of multiple and repeated speech productions over a sustained period of days or weeks. Engwall et al. [17, 18] correctly identified the need for nuanced and carefully designed strategies to deliver corrective feedback. We argue that the same care and attention is needed for the motivation strategy for eliciting productions. And though these two aspects are clearly intertwined, we are currently pursuing "low-tech" strategies in which there is a radical rethinking of the role of ASR in a speech intervention system. We recognize the limitation of ASR to analyze non-standard speech and instead use it to facilitate and motivate the use of speech as an input mode. The task of providing detailed feedback can be left to the SLP (the "human agent") and the use of ASR, and the computational media more generally, can be recruited for user engagement, motivation and the elicitation of speech productions.

A point that needs mention is that the findings discussed here is based on an assumption about the lexical unit being short and the language having a relative low ratio of morphemes to words (e.g., as in English); we expect the results to generalize to other moderately analytic languages, but may not generalize more broadly, for example to synthetic languages (e.g., Greek).

4. Conclusion

In this paper, we have reviewed a number of systems that employ ASR for speech or pre-speech intervention. We discuss how ASR technology as of present often provides unreliable and approximate feedback in the presence of ambiguous or erroneous speech, which results in unintuitive and inconsistent feedback that can be confusing and ineffective to users.

Extant intervention systems that use ASR face the main challenge of designing effective feedback. There remains a misalignment between the original design goal of ASR modules (i.e., recognition of speech) and their repurposed role in computer speech intervention systems (i.e., analysis and assessment of speech). Research demonstrates that abstract representations such as waveforms and closeness scores are unintuitive for children and have not been helpful in correcting speech. Our fieldwork shows that SLPs themselves highly value ASR and computational media more generally for its effect in motivating users and eliciting repeated speech productions.

While *input restriction,* a method used previously in systems developed for users with dysarthric speech and strong accents can be employed to improve the performance of ASR modules, based on reported interview results with SLPs and the literature review, a more radical shift in the role of the ASR module is suggested. This method involves using ASR to engage rather than evaluate speech, given the goal of facilitating sustained practice through the elicitation of multiple repetitions of target words and phrases. As demonstrated by Mitra et al., it can be effective to subordinate the accuracy of ASR to its use as a facilitator and "encourager" of interaction [32].

5. Acknowledgements

We would like to thank the SLPs who took time and provided us with useful information through the interviews. This research is supported by the Natural Sciences and Engineering Research Council of Canada Discovery Grant, "Embodied Interaction Design for Articulation Elicitation and Feedback".

6. References

[1] Danis, C. and Karat, J., "Technology-driven design of speech information systems", Proc. of DIS'95, ACM, 17-24, 1995.

[2] Hawley, M. S. "Speech recognition as an input to electronic assistive technology", British Journal of Occupational Therapy, 65(1): 15-20, 2002.

[3] Zhao, Y., "Speech technology and its potential for special education", Journal of Special Education Technology, 22(3): 35-41, 2007.

[4] Hsiao, M. L., Li, P. T., Lin, P. Y., Tang, S. T., Lee, T. C., and Young, S. T. "A computer based software for hearing impaired children's speech training and learning between teacher and parents in Taiwan", In Engineering in Medicine and Biology Society, Proc. of the 23rd Annual International Conference of the IEEE (Vol. 2, pp. 1457-1459). IEEE. 2001.

[5] Menzel, W., Herron, D., Bonaventura, P., and Morton, R. "Automatic detection and correction of nonnative English pronunciation", In Proceedings of Workshop Intergrating Speech Technology in the (Language) Learning and Assistive Interface, InStil , 49–56, 2000.

[6] Teachers with Apps. "31 Speech And Language Apps For iPad", Retrieved from: http://www.teachthought.com/literacy-2/31-speech-and-language-apps-for-ipad/. 2013.

[7] Bälter, O., Engwall, O., Öster, A., and Kjellström, H., "Wizard-of-Oz test of ARTUR: A computer-based speech training system with articulation correction", In Proceedings of ASSETS'05, ACM, 36-43, 2005.

[8] Vicsi, K., Roach, P., Öster, A. M., Kacic, Z., Barczikay, and Tantoa, A., Csatári F., Bakcsi Zs. and Sfakianaki A., "A multimedia, multilingual teaching and training system for children with speech disorders", International Journal of Speech technology, 3, 289-300, 2001.

[9] Dragon Systems, "Dragon NaturallySpeaking SDK, C++ and SAPI Guide and Reference", Dragon Systems, 1999.

[10] Teixeira, C., Trancoso, I. and Serralheiro, A., "Recognition of non-native accents", In Proceedings of EUROSPEECH-1997, 2375-2378, 1997.

[11] Huang, X., Acero, A., and Hon, H. W., "Spoken Language Processing: A Guide to Theory, Algorithm, and System Development", Prentice Hall, 2001.

[12] Rudzicz, F. "Using articulatory likelihoods in the recognition of dysarthric speech. Speech Communication", 54:430–444, 2012.

[13] Kim, H., Hasegawa-Johnson, M., Perlman, A., Gunderson, J., Huang, T. S., Watkin, K., and Frame, S., "Dysarthric speech database for universal access research", In Interspeech, 1741-1744, 2008.

[14] Potamianos, A., Narayanan, S., and Lee, S. "Automatic speech recognition for children. In Eurospeech, 97, 2371-2374, 1997.

[15] Kewley-Port, D., Watson, C.S., Elbert, M., Maki, D., and Reed, D., "The Indiana speech training aid (ISTRA) II: Training curriculum and selected case studies", Clinical Linguistics and Phonetics, 5(1): 13-38, 1991.

[16] Bunnell, H.T. Yarrington, D.M. and Polikoff, J.B., "STAR: Articulation training for young children", In Proceedings of InterSpeech'00, 4, 85-88, 2000.

[17] Engwall, O. Analysis of and feedback on phonetic features in pronunciation training with a virtual teacher. Computer Assisted Language Learning, 25(1): 37–64, 2012.

[18] Engwall, O. and Bälter, O. Pronunciation feedback from real and virtual language teachers. Computer Assisted Language Learning, 20(3): 235–262, 2007.

[19] Öster, A-M. "Teaching speech skills to deaf children by computer-based speech training", In Proceedings of the 18th International Congress on Education of the Deaf, 1995.

[20] Ryalls, J., Michallet, B, and Le-Dorze, G., "A preliminary evaluation of the clinical effectiveness of vowel training for hearing-impaired children on IBM's Speech Viewer", Volta Review, 96, 19–30, 1994.

[21] Pratt, S, Heintzelman, A., and Deming, S., "The efficacy of using the IBM Speech Viewer vowel accuracy module to treat young children with hearing impairment", Journal of Speech and Hearing Research, 36, 1063–1074, 1993.

[22] Öster, A-M. "Applications and experiences of computer-based speech training", STL-QPSR, 1, 59-62, 1989.

[23] Öster, A-M. House D., Green P., "Testing a new method for training fricatives using visual maps in the Ortho-Logo-Pedia project (OLP)", Phonum 9- Fonetik, 89-92, 2003.

[24] Fell, H. J., MacAuslan, J., Gong, J., Cress, C. and Salvo, T. "visiBabble for pre-speech feedback", CHI Extended Abstracts, 767-772, 2006.
[25] Fell, H. J., Cress, C., MacAuslan, J., Ferrier, L., J. "visiBabble for reinforcement of early vocalization", ASSETS 2004: 161-168, 2004.
[26] Hailpern, J., Harris, A., La Botz, R., Birman, B., and Karahalios, K. "Designing visualizations to facilitate multisyllabic speech with children with autism and speech delays", In Proceedings of the Designing Interactive Systems Conference, 126-135, 2012.
[27] Hailpern, J., Karahalios, K., DeThorne, L., and Halle, J. "Vocsyl: Visualizing syllable production for children with ASD and speech delays", In Proceedings of the Assets 12th international ACM SIGACCESS conference on Computers and accessibility, 297-298, 2010.
[28] Hailpern, J., Karahalios, K., and Halle, J. "Creating a spoken impact: encouraging vocalization through audio visual feedback in children with ASD", In Proceedings of the SIGCHI Conference on Human Factors in Computing Systems, 453-462, 2009.
[29] Hamidi, F. "Using interactive objects for speech intervention", SIGACCESS Access. Comput. 96, 28-31, 2010.
[30] Hincks, R., "Speech recognition for language teaching and evaluating: A study of existing commercial products", In Proceedings of ICSLP'02, 733-736, 2002.
[31] Neri, A., Cucchiarini, C., and Strik, W., "Automatic speech recognition for second language learning: How and why it actually works", In Proceedings of ICPhS'03, 257–1160, 2003.
[32] Mitra, S., Tooley, J., Inamdar, P. and Dixon, P., "Improving English pronunciation - an automated instructional approach", *Information Technologies and International Development,* 1(1): 75-84, MIT Press, 2003.
[33] Morley J. "The pronunciation component in teaching English to speakers of other languages", TESOL Quarterly, 25:481–520, 1991.
[34] Rosengren, E., Raghavendra, P., and Hunnicutt, S., "How does automatic speech recognition handle severely dysarthric speech?" in I. Placencia Porrero and P. de la Bellacas [Eds], In Proceedings of the 2nd TIDE Congress, IOS Press, 336–339, 1995.

Making Speech-Based Assistive Technology Work for a Real User

William Li[1], *Don Fredette*[2], *Alexander Burnham*[2], *Bob Lamoureux*[2], *Marva Serotkin*[2], *Seth Teller*[1]

[1] EECS/CSAIL, Massachusetts of Institute of Technology, Cambridge, USA
[2] The Boston Home, Boston, USA

wli@csail.mit.edu, dfredette@thebostonhome.org, aburnham@thebostonhome.org, bob@lamoureux.com, mserotkin@thebostonhome.org, teller@mit.edu

Abstract

We present a customized speech-activated email system that is the product of efforts focused on a single target user with high speech recognition error rates. The system, which includes off-the-shelf and custom hardware and software, allows the user to use speech to send emails with recorded audio attachments. Over the past 16 months, our target user has sent and received hundreds of emails and has integrated the system into his daily life. Key factors contributing to the long-term adoption of the device include our extended efforts to understand the target user over multiple years, iterative design, and the collaboration of our multidisciplinary team of assistive technology (AT) designers, clinicians, software developers, and researchers. Overall, we ask: if we set our sights on developing and supporting a technology that someone will actually use daily, what can we learn? We share our approach, system design, user observation and findings, with implications for speech-based AT research and development.

Index Terms: speech interfaces, usability, assistive technology

1. Introduction

Functional access to computers and other devices can help people with physical impairments stay connected with others, access information, or control the environment. For many individuals who cannot use touch-based interfaces like keyboards and mice, automatic speech recognition (ASR) could be a viable alternative access method. However, ASR systems can be challenging to use for individuals who have speech difficulties, since such systems are typically not trained on, or designed to be used by, people in these relatively small populations. These technical challenges mean that ASR-based assistive technology (AT) often falls short of its potential as an access equalizer for people with disabilities [Young2010].

The present paper describes a system that has enabled a single individual, an adult wheelchair user with advanced secondary progressive multiple sclerosis (SPMS), to send emails without assistance on a regular basis. We offer details on the multi-year process required to design and implement speech-based email system that has made a positive impact in his daily life. Where commercial off-the-shelf components existed and were appropriate, we tried and incorporated them. Our work has involved rehabilitation technology staff, clinicians, family members, and researchers who worked to understand his context, needs, and preferences in order to develop an appropriate, long-lasting AT intervention.

Our approach differs from most academic research on speech recognition for individuals with disabilities, which often prioritizes novel algorithms, new models, or superiority over baselines in short-term user studies. While we certainly do not dismiss these contributions – we follow these research paradigms most of the time ourselves – our deviation is deliberate. Specifically, in this work, we ask: What is required to *actually* deploy speech-based assistive technology and have tangible impact on a user's life? What can we learn from this implementation process?

This paper goes beyond describing an end product – we also discuss the target user's context and our design process. We introduce the target user (Section 2) and his past AT usage (Section 3), then describe the speech-based email system (Section 4). We provide details on how staff and clinicians, family and friends, students in a design-based assistive technology course, researchers, and, most importantly, our target user himself were involved in identifying the shortcomings and utility of various AT interventions. Section 5 discusses our findings: our target user's actual email usage over a 16-month period. We discuss our insights and their implications for researchers and practitioners in Section 6.

2. User and design constraints

Our work occurred at The Boston Home (TBH), a residence and center for care for adults with multiple sclerosis and other progressive neurological conditions. The 96 residents at TBH receive nursing, medical, physical therapy, speech-language pathology, and assistive technology services on site, in addition to an array of social, artistic, and residential activities.

2.1. Description of target user

Our target user is a middle-aged male living with advanced SPMS. He is a power wheelchair user, has minimal control of his arms and no active movement in his legs due to spastic quadriplegia, and vision challenges due to SPMS-associated optic neuritis. Meanwhile, he has high cognitive function, good working memory, and generally an eagerness to try new AT.

Given these limitations, ASR could be a promising access channel. However, our target user's speech is not recognized accurately by existing, large-vocabulary speech recognizers. Challenges include abnormally strained vocal quality, reduced respiratory support for duration and intensity of phonation, variable pitch control (vocal fry) over the course of a single utterance, and dialectical variation from standard American English, which he acquired as a second language in adulthood. Our target user's successes and difficulties of using ASR-based AT is discussed in Section 3.

2.2. Goal: Computer and email access

Our target user seeks greater independence. Any device that allows him to rely less on other individuals can have a positive impact. Our current goal is to enable independent (and thus private) computer access, particularly to email, which would help him better stay in touch with friends and family.

Our close interaction with our target user allowed us to define some key characteristics of our eventual system. The need for system training by the user and adjustment by outside experts should be minimized, even though his abilities can fluctuate over time. Meanwhile, the appearance and user interface of any solution is very important, particularly those that require mounting hardware on the target user's wheelchair, body, or living space.

3. Other assistive technology usage

Our team is intimately familiar with our target user's past and current AT. This knowledge helped us understand what might work for email access. We describe both speech and non-speech devices to illustrate where ASR has been used and where other channels were more appropriate.

Wheelchair control: Our target user operates a power wheelchair using proximity switches embedded in his headrest. He has independent control of driving, adjusting speed, tilting the chair, and changing modes. The headrest proximity switches have proven to be a robust access pathway for the target user's wheelchair. By using switches to operate in different modes and by activating combinations of switches to perform different functions, he can control dozens of wheelchair functions independently.

Television control: Our target user has an InVoca 3.0 Voice Activated Remote Control for controlling his television. This commercially available device allows users to program custom keywords that are transmitted as infrared signals, similar to any conventional TV remote control. It rests in a custom-built wooden stand on our target user's wheelchair tray, and he can instruct a caregiver to place the remote control in its recharge cradle (which is not on the wheelchair) at night.

The InVoca has worked well, even in environments with television or other ambient noise. Its major limitation is that it can only handle approximately 20 words or phrases. In addition, fluctuations in our target user's voice (even the common cold) can present significant challenges.

Telephone control: The target user has a voice-activated telephone system. Typically, a caregiver helps him don a headset connected to his landline telephone. From that point onwards, he uses a breath-activated switch to cycle through a preset list of telephone numbers. One of these preset numbers is tied to a commercially available voice recognition virtual assistant service, which contains an extended address book. This setup allows him to dial more than 50 contacts.

Our target user has had considerable success with this system and continues to use it for telephone calls, but the need for outside assistance reduces its convenience and his privacy. Furthermore, since our target user likes to communicate with family and friends in different time zones, it is not always feasible to coordinate mutually agreeable phone scheduling. An asynchronous communication medium like email could be useful for staying in touch with these contacts.

Spoken dialogue system: Our target user participated in a study that evaluated an assistive probabilistic dialogue system. This work hypothesized that that using confirmation questions to clarify the user's intent would help improve dialogue success rates for high-error speakers (the concept error rate of our target user in this study was 56.7%). As described in [4], the system helped the user complete more dialogues successfully in a supervised experimental setting, compared to a simpler baseline. While promising, the dialogue system would need to be deployed in a longer study to determine whether it is sufficiently useful for our target user.

3.1. Computer access

Our target user has tried numerous devices for desktop computer access with mixed success. While each of these technologies had drawbacks, they contributed to our insight into the user's preferences and abilities.

First, despite training commercial speech recognition software (Nuance Dragon NaturallySpeaking 7.0, and later, 10.0) with our target user's speech and adjusting the settings to the best of our ability, such software packages were too unreliable to allow him to use a desktop computer effectively. Our target user would often have to resort to time-consuming, lower-level mouse-scrolling commands instead of faster shortcut commands. Moreover, some software programs, such as browser-based Google Gmail, were not optimized for speech-based access, thereby increasing the failure rate.

We also tested non-speech access channels. Our target user tried using a head mouse, in which an infrared camera follows an infrared-reflecting sticker controlled by head movements, combined with an onscreen keyboard like Dasher [2]. Despite his use of headrest proximity switches, this method proved challenging: he experienced rapid onset of fatigue, double vision, and exacerbation of facial pain from SPMS-associated trigeminal neuralgia from the head and neck movements required to operate the headmouse successfully.

To address these speech-recognition and user-interface challenges, a team of undergraduate students in a semester-long course called Principles and Practice of Assistive Technology (PPAT) focused on how to make a desktop-computer setup more usable for our target user [3]. They evaluated different microphone stands, computer setups, and speech recognition software in our target user's bedroom. By working closely with the target user, the team determined that a desktop computer with the target user's large television set as a display would be a workable solution. Their work contributed to the groundwork for our current solution, which we describe next.

4. Email system description

The current system is situated in our target user's bedroom and allows him to keep in touch with friends and family through emails. Our customized email client has two components that make it effective for the target user: first, the user interface is optimized for speech-based access, with the ability to skip down to the desired message, open messages, reply, and delete messages with single voice commands. Second, to overcome speech recognition limitations, the emails are in the form of 20, 30 or 45-second *audio messages,* not transcribed text, that are sent as an attachment. Figure 1 shows a schematic of the entire user, hardware, and software setup, while Figure 2 shows the actual setup in his bedroom at TBH.

4.1. Hardware: Computer, screen, and audio capture

A large, flat-screen television serves as the display for a Windows 7-based computer. The target user also watches television on this screen, so he is comfortable viewing it for extended time periods.

Voice input occurs through two audio capture devices: First, we use the aforementioned InVoca device to switch between the cable television services and computer display inputs. As before, this device sits on the target user's wheelchair tray. Second, to record audio email messages, we use a Microsoft Kinect device which includes an array microphone. Although a close-talking microphone or headset could result in a clearer voice signal, these alternatives would require more precise positioning and outside assistance. We found that the Kinect's built-in mechanisms to improve speech capture (such as sound localization and beamforming) worked well for the target user's needs.

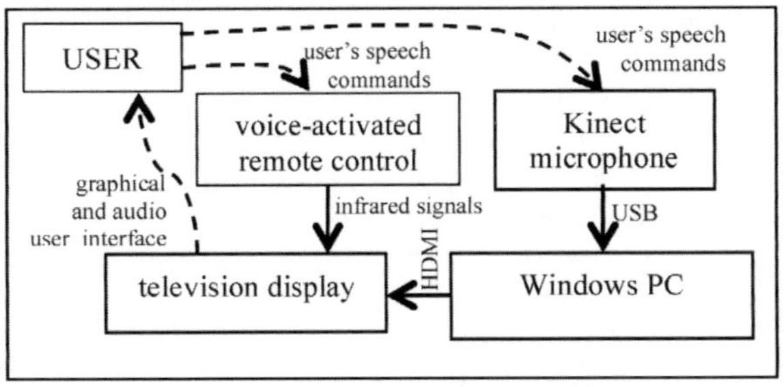

Figure 1: *Schematic of speech-based email client.*

Figure 2: *Actual bedroom setup with 1) television, 2) Kinect, 3) computer, and 4) wheelchair with voice activated remote control*

4.2. Speech recognition and customized email client

Our system uses Windows Speech Recognition, which has well-supported Kinect application programming interfaces (APIs) to process the Kinect's audio stream. Based on the current mode of the software (browsing or composing messages), a small set of custom grammar files are dynamically loaded. Setting this constraint dramatically improves the recognition rate since the grammar is targeted to the task at hand. The grammar is set to recognize vocabulary for one of about 45 pre-determined phrases required for the custom email software to function.

We developed a customized email client for our target user. As shown in Figure 3, the user interface shows a green square to indicate that the speech recognizer is active; a text box displaying the currently recognized speech (which is "Go" in Figure 3), and the "From" and "Subject" headers for several email messages. At the end of an utterance, the email client parses the recognized speech and also shows a percentage confidence score for the utterance in large text.

The target user can move the active message (highlighted in light blue with a triangle on the left side) with commands such as "Move down #" (where "#" is between 1 and 10) to skip to the desired message. He can then say "Open message" to view the message body, and "What does it say" in order to activate the Windows 7 voice synthesizer, which reads the emails to him when he is too tired or his eyes are not focusing clearly. The system reads the subject, sender and body of the message and recognizes when to stop reading the message body when the signature or quoted text is reached. Finally, he can reply to messages or choose from a pre-determined address book of contacts, all with further voice commands.

The email client automatically scans all attachments and includes them directly inline when displaying the message. This makes it easier for the user to view picture attachments without having to click or double click as with traditional email readers. It also detects links to sites such as YouTube and places large icons on the toolbar, allowing the user to easily navigate off to these external sites from the email client. New contacts are automatically added to the contact list simply when emails are received from a new individual. The system also automatically archives all picture attachments into a folder hierarchy so that the target user can replay slideshows of all these photos whenever he wants.

5. Results: Current usage

The speech-based email system has been used continuously by our target user since February 2012. Between February 2012 and June 2013, the system has handled 460 received messages and 210 sent messages. In peak weeks, he has sent 10 to 20 emails to his contacts. These usage statistics are noteworthy because our target user had *never sent emails without assistance before the creation of this system.* While the system is not perfect and the speech recognition sometimes falters, the benefits of email communication have made this system acceptable for our target user.

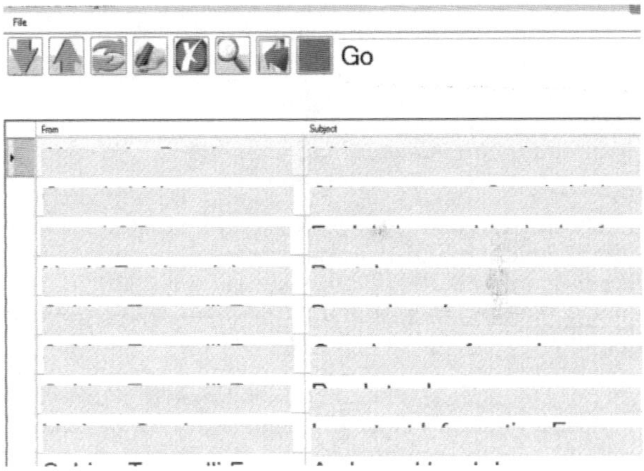

Figure 3: *Screenshot of user interface.*

5.1. Observations on Usage

Through long-term user observations and unstructured interviews, we have learned about how our target user interacts with the system. Typically, he does not reply to every message, but rather replies once to every few messages from a given person so that the sender knows he has read the emails. This behavior is feasible because the user has a small group of contacts who appear to be sending him emails regularly.

It is worth noting that our target user still uses the telephone because it enables immediate, two-way communication. While we have not done formal monitoring, it appears that the email system has augmented, not replaced, his telephone usage. He especially values messages with photo attachments of friends and family, which cannot be transmitted by telephone. He also receives many emails containing comic strips, jokes, and YouTube video links.

The target user has become adept at interpreting the user interface's visual cues and using these cues to adapt his behavior accordingly. For example, the hypothesized utterance and the large percentage confidence score are both displayed on the television screen. These cues allow him to see whether he needs to speak differently, adjust the microphone, reduce background noise, or report a bug.

6. Discussion

The process of developing the email system has yielded significant insights into developing customized speech-based assistive technology.

6.1. Factors for success

We believe that there were three main reasons why our target user has adopted the email system:

6.1.1. Design for a single user

Our approach focused intensely on our target user. Our success metric – and our singular goal while developing the system – was to enable him to communicate more frequently with friends and family. As a result, our work was tailored very specifically to the target user's abilities, preferences, environment, and feedback. Instead of focusing on an innovation that could potentially generalize across many users, our work deliberately was driven by our sole target user. Interestingly, it may be that some elements of system could be useful to other people, meaning that, in the process of seeking measurable impact on our target user, we have identified some generalizable components or ideas.

6.1.2. Multidisciplinary collaboration

Our team of authors has backgrounds in AT research, rehabilitation technology, speech-language pathology, speech recognition, and software development. In addition, some of our team members are staff or clinicians in the residential-care setting itself, which helped ensure that necessary issues or adjustments could be dealt with in a timely manner. The time and skills of each of these individuals were essential to the success of this project. The project would not have succeeded without any of the hardware and software components, readily available onsite support and physical care, and extensive speech therapy and training.

6.1.3. Frequent and long-term interaction with the user

The current system is the product of many years of interacting with our target user and learning from his AT usage patterns. For example, it is clear why the InVoca voice-activated remote control continues to be used: it is robust, requires little outside assistance or intervention to be operated, and enables him to watch television independently. In contrast, steep learning curves, reliability issues, and interface challenges made other speech technologies less appropriate. We considered these experiences as we developed the current system.

Perhaps more importantly, working with our target user over several years has allowed us to develop a working relationship that extends beyond simply being a research subject for new technologies. Whenever possible, we strived to incorporate his motivations, ideas, and direction, and we based our design decisions on in-home user observation. Such an approach may bear intrinsic value when working with people with disabilities, who often find mismatches between their abilities and existing technology. More directly, frequent communication and design iteration has helped us understand the subtleties that separate AT non-use from AT adoption.

6.2. Limitations

The purpose of this paper is to document the process leading to the development of a usable speech-based email client for our single target user. Our goal was not to develop a system that would necessarily work for other users. It may be the case that other users would find the limitations of our system unacceptable, or that their speech recognition error rates would be too high to use it successfully. Answering this question would only be possible with a study involving more users.

Clearly, the current system has limited functionality. The features that we did prioritize, though, made it possible for our target user to communicate with friends and family. Interestingly, through his extended usage, he has suggested feature ideas, including the ability to place pre-defined sets of sentences into emails for simple messages or pre-downloading attachments while he is sleeping so that emails load faster during the day. As a next step, our target user is interested in adding video calling capabilities. A separate grammar for Skype functions should make it possible to implement this feature without compromising speech recognition accuracy.

While actually deploying useful AT can be time-consuming and difficult, our efforts have helped us remain connected to the realities of users. Our work suggests relevant areas of inquiry for this user population, including the need to adapt acoustic models to speakers who may not be able to access a close-talking microphone, speech recognition that is robust to environmental noise in healthcare settings, and graphical user interfaces tailored to people who may have co-occurring vision or other impairments.

7. Conclusions

We described the implementation of a system that uses speech recognition to allow a single user to communicate via email with friends and family. The process of developing this assistive technology was made possible by embracing the target user's goals, focusing on a practical solution, learning from past devices and technologies, and drawing from our diverse professional backgrounds and skills. Building real-world, actual implementations of working assistive devices could help define worthwhile research efforts and illuminate the characteristics of successful assistive technology.

8. References

[1] V. Young and A. Mihailidis, "Difficulties in automatic speech recognition of dysarthric speakers and implications for speech-based applications used by the elderly: A literature review," *Assistive Technology*, vol. 22, no. 2, pp. 99-112, 2010.

[2] D.J. Ward et al, "Dasher – a data entry interface using continuous gestures and language models," in Proc. UIST, 2000, pp. 129-137.

[3] Principles and Practice of Assistive Technology (PPAT), Fall 2011. http://courses.csail.mit.edu/PPAT/fall2011.

[4] W. Li et al, "Probabilistic dialogue modeling for speech-enabled assistive technology," in Proc. SLPAT, 2013.

Probabilistic Dialogue Modeling for Speech-Enabled Assistive Technology

William Li, Jim Glass, Nicholas Roy, Seth Teller

MIT Computer Science and Artificial Intelligence Laboratory, Cambridge, MA 02139, U.S.A.

{wli, glass, nickroy, teller}@csail.mit.edu

Abstract

People with motor disabilities often face substantial challenges using interfaces designed for manual interaction. Although such obstacles might be partially alleviated by automatic speech recognition, these individuals may also have co-occurring speech-language challenges that result in high recognition error rates. In this paper, we investigate how augmenting speech applications with dialogue interaction can improve system performance among such users. We construct an end-to-end spoken dialogue system for our target users, adult wheelchair users with multiple sclerosis and other progressive neurological conditions in a specialized-care residence, to access information and communication services through speech. We use boosting to discriminatively learn meaningful confidence scores and ask confirmation questions within a partially observable Markov decision process (POMDP) framework. Among our target users, the POMDP dialogue manager significantly increased the number of successfully completed dialogues (out of 20 dialogue tasks) compared to a baseline threshold-based strategy ($p = 0.02$). The reduction in dialogue completion times was more pronounced among speakers with higher error rates, illustrating the benefits of probabilistic dialogue modeling for our target population.

Index Terms: spoken dialogue systems, speech interfaces, POMDPs

1. Introduction

People with mobility or physical impairments may have difficulty with touch-based user interfaces. Automatic speech recognition (ASR) potentially offers an alternative, natural means of device access, but such systems can still be challenging to use for individuals who have speech impediments or disorders. For example, mismatches may exist between their speech and that of trained ASR systems. These technical challenges mean that ASR often fall short of its potential as an access equalizer for people with disabilities [1].

Current approaches to recognizing speakers with disabilities often use speaker adaptation techniques [2, 3]. Such training, however, may be costly, tiring, and difficult for the speaker. As well, in some real-world systems, it may not be possible to access or adapt the underlying acoustic models. Meanwhile, in many assistive technology applications, such as device control or information access, the success metric may not be the word error rate, but rather whether the system successfully understands the user's intent and ultimately responds correctly. Motivated by this abstraction, and faced with highly challenging speech, we seek to construct a system that optimizes performance at the user intent level.

The present paper describes the use of probabilistic dialogue modeling for a population of speakers with high recognition error rates. Specifically, we developed an assistive spoken dialogue system in a partially observable Markov decision process (POMDP) framework, in which the the dialogue system seeks to infer the user's intent and handles speech recognition uncertainty by asking confirmation questions. We learn models of: 1) how speech recognition hypotheses map to user intents and 2) meaningful confidence scores from ASR features so that our dialogue manager can make better response decisions. Our work draws on modeling techniques from work in spoken dialogue system POMDPs (e.g., [4, 5, 6]) and is inspired by other POMDP-based assistive technologies for handwashing (e.g., [7]) and intelligent wheelchair navigation (e.g., [8, 9, 10]), all of which model the user's intent as a hidden state to be inferred from observations.

Our work has two main contributions. First, we defined and modeled our problem as a spoken dialogue system POMDP by understanding our users and the design constraints. We collected data specifically for this application, trained the probabilistic models that are part of the dialogue system, and made design decisions appropriate to our application, all of which we describe in this paper. Second, we conducted experiments involving speakers with disabilities that demonstrated the effectiveness of the POMDP framework under high-error conditions. As illustrated in our results, handling uncertainty with the POMDP-based dialogue manager led to higher dialogue completion rates and shorter dialogue times, particularly for users with high speech recognition error rates.

This paper is structured as follows: We describe our assistive technology application domain and our target user population (Section 2), the formulation of our POMDP-based spoken dialogue system (SDS-POMDP) (Section 3), our model-building efforts (Section 4), and the experiments designed to test the effectiveness of our end-to-end system (Section 5). We conclude with insights on using dialogue interaction for assistive technology.

2. Problem Domain

Our target population is the residents at The Boston Home (TBH), a specialized-care residence in Boston, Massachusetts, USA for adults with multiple sclerosis (MS) and other progressive neurological conditions, and our goal is to develop speech-enabled assistive technology that can be bedside or wheelchair accessible. One example physical setup for a resident is shown in Figure 1. MS and other related neurological conditions are often associated with co-occurring speech pathologies, including rapid fatigue, voice weakness, very slow speaking style, or mild to severe dysarthria [11]. In addition, cognitive impairments associated with MS can also lead to language disorders [12], which could challenge conventional ASR language models.

Table 1 illustrates the performance of our ASR system on on 30 utterances for members of our target population. All of

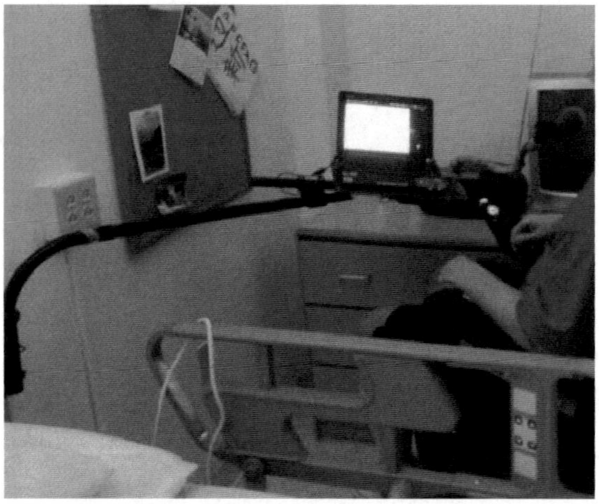

Figure 1: Example bedside setup of speech interface in resident room at TBH.

the utterances were processed by the MIT SUMMIT speech recognizer [13] using the same set of acoustic and language models. Our target users were seven adult residents at TBH (5 male, 2 female, ages 45 to 70), all of whom use wheelchairs and expressed an interest in using a speech recognition-based system. More precisely, our metric of interest is whether the speech recognition hypothesis maps to the user's intent — an utterance is labeled "correct" if its top hypothesis and its ground-truth label map to the same intent in our dialogue system. For example, if the utterance "what is monday's lunch menu" is hypothesized as "what is monday the lunch", this utterance would be marked as correct because both the hypothesis and the label correspond to the intent `(lunch monday)`.

Table 1 also shows the performance of the speech recognizer for a control group of seven students (6 male, 1 female, ages 21 to 32) without speech impairments of any kind. The target and control users are not paired in any way; our main reason for showing the system performance with these control users is to provide a quantitative sense of how the speech of our target users is handled conventional ASR systems. In addition, by evaluating our system with both target and control users in our dialogue system, as we show in Section 5, we can compare the value of using dialogue among high- and low-error speakers.

Table 1: Concept error rates (30 utterances) for target and control populations

Speaker (Target)	Intent Error Rate		Speaker (Control)	Intent Error Rate
target01	13.3%		control01	3.3%
target02	3.3%		control02	10.0%
target03	33.3%		control03	6.7%
target04	56.7%		control04	13.3%
target05	26.7%		control05	3.3%
target06	9.4%		control06	3.3%
target07	6.6%		control07	0.0%
mean	21.4%		mean	7.5%
std. dev.	18.9%		std. dev.	4.3%

Clearly, the target group of users has a much higher error rate, meaning that a system that simply parses the top hypothesis would be unusable for many target users. This research hypothesizes that dialog strategies that consider the uncertainty associated with user utterances can enable higher task completion rates, particularly for speakers with high speech recognition error rates. The system should handle ASR errors robustly, with the aim of deciphering the user's intent in order to respond appropriately.

3. Partially Observable Markov Decision Processes (POMDPs) for Spoken Dialog

Substantial research exists on modeling spoken dialogue as a partially observable Markov decision process (POMDP) [4, 5, 6]. Briefly, a POMDP is specified as a tuple $\{S, A, Z, T, \Omega, R, \gamma\}$ and is a sequential decision model that handles uncertainty in the environment in a principled way. A POMDP spoken dialogue system (SDS-POMDP) treats speech recognition results as noisy observations of the user's intent: it encodes the user's intent as a hidden state, $s \in S$; automatic speech recognition hypotheses as observations, $z \in Z$, of that state; and system responses as actions, $a \in A$. The transition model $T = P(s'|s, a)$ gives the probability that the user's intent will change to s' given the previous intent s and the system action a; the observation model $\Omega = P(z|s, a)$ describes the probability of ASR observation z for a given intent s and action a; and $R(s, a)$ specifies the immediate reward associated with each system action a and user intent s. The discount factor γ is a parameter ($0 \leq \gamma \leq 1$) that weighs the value of future rewards to immediate rewards.

Bayesian filtering is used to infer a distribution over the user's state at each time step t from the history of actions and observations, $p(s_t|a_{0:t}, z_{0:t})$ [14]. This distribution is usually referred to as the belief, b. The SDS-POMDP maintains the belief distribution, b, over the user's possible intents and chooses actions based on a policy, $\Pi(b)$, that maps every possible belief to an action, a, in order to maximize the expected discounted reward, $\sum_t \gamma^{-t} R(s, a)$. We describe the key elements of the SDS-POMDP in the context of the system that we developed for our experiments below.

3.1. SDS-POMDP System Implementation

User Goals (States, S) and System Responses (Actions, A): When a user interacts with the dialogue manager, we assume that he or she has a goal, $s \in S$. The purpose of the dialogue manager is to choose an action, $a \in A$, that satisfies the user's goal. More precisely, the dialogue manager seeks to infer which goal the user is trying to achieve and take an appropriate action.

For our system, we identified the following areas of interest to residents at TBH:

- Time and date;
- Recreational activities schedules;
- Breakfast, lunch, and dinner menus;
- Making phone calls.

Our SDS-POMDP has 62 states, corresponding to each of the possible user goals. For example, `(weather today)` or `(make phone call)` are two different states.

The definition of the action space, A, follows from the set of states. For every state, there are two corresponding action: one that asks the user for confirmation, and the other "executes" that goal in the SDS-POMDP's user interface. For example, the state `(weather today)` has two corresponding actions: `(confirm, (weather today))` and `(show, (weather today))`. In addition, the SDS-POMDP can greet the user or ask the user to repeat, for a set of 126 system actions.

ASR Outputs (Observations, Z): The SDS-POMDP uses the aforementioned MIT SUMMIT speech recognizer [13]. Each spoken utterance is processed into a ten-best list of hypotheses with acoustic and language model scores. We then extract keywords to deterministically map the top hypothesis into one of 65 concepts: observations corresponding to each of the 62 goals (such as `( weather today )` and `(lunch monday)`), a `( yes )` and `( no )` command, and a `( null )` command if there is no successful parse. Meanwhile, the text of the ten hypotheses for each utterance, along with the acoustic and language scores for each utterance computed by the speech recognizer, are used as features to assign a confidence score to the hypothesis, as detailed in Section 4. An observation z in the SDS-POMDP, therefore, consist of a discrete part, z_d (one of 65 possible parses) and a continuous confidence score, z_c (where $0 \leq z_c \leq 1$).

Observation Model (Ω): $\Omega = P(z|s,a)$ is our model, learned from data, of recognition hypotheses given the user's intent, s, and the system's response, a. As described above, our observations consist of a discrete (z_d) and a continuous (z_c) part, meaning that we need to learn the model $P(z_d, z_c|s,a)$. We factor the observation function into two parts as per Equation 1 using the chain rule:

$$\Omega = P(z_d, z_c|s,a) = P(z_d|s,a)P(z_c|s,a,z_d) \quad (1)$$

The first term, $P(z_d|s,a)$ is estimated from our labeled data using maximum likelihood; for each discrete observation z_d^*, the value $P(z_d^*|s,a)$ is computed as follows:

$$P(z_d^*|s,a) = \frac{c(z_d^*, s, a)}{\sum_{z_d} c(z_d, s, a)} \quad (2)$$

Meanwhile, for the term $P(z_c|s,a,z_d)$, data sparsity makes it challenging to directly learn the model of confidence score for every (s,a,z_d)-triple. To mitigate this issue, we use an approximation similar to the one used by [15], where we learn two models: 1) the distribution of confidence scores when the utterance hypothesis is correct ($P(z_c|\text{correct observation})$), and 2) the distribution of confidence scores when there is an error ($P(z_c|\text{incorrect observation})$). The motivation for this approach is that correctly recognized utterances should have a different distribution of confidence scores than incorrectly recognized utterances. In addition, an equivalent statement to the observation being correct is that that z_d *corresponds to* s (denoted below as $z_d \mapsto s$). As a result, for all possible user goals s and discrete observations z_d, we can approximate $P(z_c|s,a,z_d)$ as follows:

$$P(z_c|s,a,z_d) = \begin{cases} P(z_c|\text{correct observation}) & \text{if } z_d \mapsto s \\ P(z_c|\text{incorrect observation}) & \text{otherwise} \end{cases} \quad (3)$$

We describe our efforts to learn the confidence score model from our data in Section 4. Figure 3 illustrates that, indeed, the distributions of $P(z_c|\text{correct observation})$ and $P(z_c|\text{incorrect observation})$ are different in our dataset. These two models capture the insight that the confidence score contains information about whether the utterance has been correctly or incorrectly recognized. By assuming that the distribution of confidence scores for correct and incorrect observations are the same for every concept, our approach helps overcome data sparsity issues.

Transition Model, T: For our prototype system, our transition function $T = P(s'|s,a)$ is simple: we assume that that the user's goal does not change over the course of a single dialog, meaning that the transition function equals 1 if $s_{n+1} = s_n$ and 0 otherwise.

Reward Function, R: The reward function specifies a positive or negative reward for each state-action pair in the SDS-POMDP; as a result, it is described by as $R(S,A)$. We handcrafted a reward function that has positive rewards for "correct" actions (e.g. showing the user the weather if the user's goal was to know the weather), large negative rewards for "incorrect actions" (e.g. making a phone call if the user's goal was to know the lunch menu), and small negative rewards for information-gathering confirmation questions. The reward for confirmation questions that do not correspond to the user's goal is slightly more negative than for the "correct" confirmation question.

Belief Updates: Over the course of a dialog, our SDS-POMDP updates the belief distribution, b, from the observed hypothesis, the observed confidence score, and the transition function, $T = P(s'|s,a)$. At time step $n+1$, the SDS-POMDP uses these models and the prior belief, b_n, to compute b_{n+1}:

$$b_{n+1}(s') \propto P(z_d|s',a)P(z_c|s',a,z_d)\sum_s P(s'|s,a)b_n(s) \quad (4)$$

During runtime, the SDS-POMDP does not have access to the ground-truth label of the user's utterance. For each state s', the terms $P(z_d|s',a)$ and $P(z_c|s',a,z_d)$ are chosen from the appropriate conditional probability distribution in Equations 2 and 3, respectively.

Computing the Policy, Π: The policy, which maps beliefs to actions, is computed offline from the specified models in the SDS-POMDP. Given how we incorporate the continuous confidence score z_c into the observation function Ω, conventional methods of computing the POMDP policy are computationally expensive. We chose the QMDP approximation to compute the policy for the SDS-POMDP. While QMDP is a greedy heuristic, as opposed to an optimal POMDP solution, we hypothesized that it could produce an effective dialogue policy in our work. Specifically, the QMDP algorithm computes a function Q for each state-action pair,

$$Q(s_i,a) = R(s_i,a) + \sum_{j=1}^{N} \hat{V}(s_i)P(s_j|s_i,a) \quad (5)$$

where $\hat{V}$ is the converged value function of the SDS-POMDP's underlying Markov decision process (MDP) [16]. Then, for a belief state $b = (p_1, p_2, ...p_N)$, where p_i corresponds to the probability mass in state i, the policy is simply

$$\Pi(b) = \arg\max_a \sum_{i=1}^{N} p_i Q(s_i,a) \quad (6)$$

It is impractical to describe the policy's prescribed action for every possible b in our system, but a few representative belief points and corresponding actions are:

1. if b is uniform, then the dialogue system asks the user to repeat;
2. if b has very high probability in one state, s^*, and the remainder of the probability mass is uniformly distributed in the other states, then the dialogue system takes the terminal action corresponding to that state;

3. between situations 1 and 2, i.e. if the probability mass in s^* is not high enough for the system to perform the terminal action, then it will ask a confirmation question corresponding to s^*.

User Interface: Finally, the user interface for the SDS-POMDP is presented to the user on a netbook computer. In our current implementation, the speech recognizer is run locally. A screenshot of the interface is shown in Figure 2.

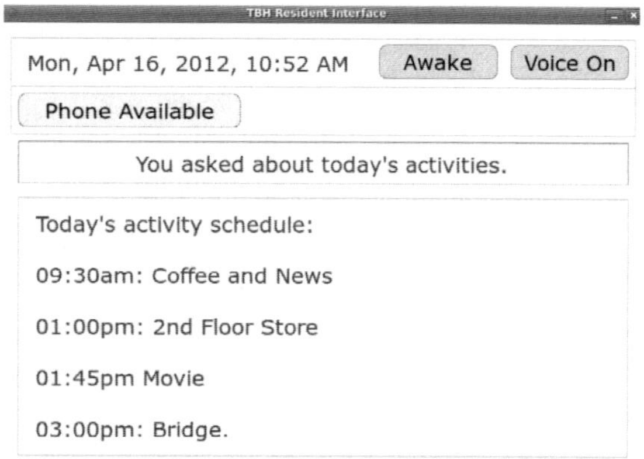

Figure 2: Graphical user interface of assistive spoken dialogue system, with indicators of time, system state ("Awake"), and speech synthesizer state ("Voice On").

4. Model Training and Confidence Scoring

Data Collection: A total of 2701 utterances were collected and manually transcribed from volunteers in our research lab and at TBH. Participants were prompted with possible goals and asked to speak a natural-language command corresponding to the goal, prefaced by an activation keyword like "chair" or "wheelchair." Because our target population has difficulty using buttons or other physical access devices, a speech-activity detector based on the measured spectral power of the audio signal was used instead of a push-to-talk activation method typical in many speech applications. This corpus of utterances was used to estimate the discrete and continuous parts of the observation model Ω, as summarized in Equations 2 and 3.

Learning the Confidence Score: To learn the confidence score, z_c, each of the 2701 utterances was labeled as "correct" $(+1)$ if the parse of the top hypothesis matched the parse of the transcription and "incorrect" (-1) otherwise. We then extracted features from each utterance's 10-best list and trained a classifier on 90% of the utterances using AdaBoost [17]. At each iteration, AdaBoost chooses a feature with the lowest weighted error, and re-weighs training data points by assigning more weight to misclassified examples; some of the features that it selected are shown in Table 2. Using this weighted set of features, the classification error rate on a held-out test set (10% of the utterances) was 6.9%.

Next, we fit a logistic regression curve to AdaBoost's weighted sum of features to interpret the AdaBoost classifier's result as a confidence score. The resulting distribution of confidence scores for correctly and incorrectly recognized utterances is shown in Figure 3. For a given confidence score z_c, we can compute the necessary quantities in Equation 3 from these two histograms. These two distributions reveal that the confidence score contains important information about whether the observed concept is correct or incorrect. During the belief update step of the SDS-POMDP, we draw from the "correct observation" distribution for the state corresponding to the observation concept and from the "incorrect observation" distribution for all other states. For example, the hypothesis `(lunch, today)` paired with a high confidence score could shift the belief distribution sharply toward the corresponding `(lunch, today)` state; in contrast, a low confidence score could actually cause the probability mass to shift away to other states.

Table 2: Features selected by AdaBoost classifier

Feature Category	Examples
Concept-level	parse success; category of concept
ASR scores	acoustic, language, and total model scores; difference between top score and second-highest hypothesis score
Word-/sentence-level	fraction of stop words; presence of multiple concepts; presence of highly misrecognized words or often merged/split word pairs
n-best list	concept entropy of n-best list; fraction of total acoustic or language model scores

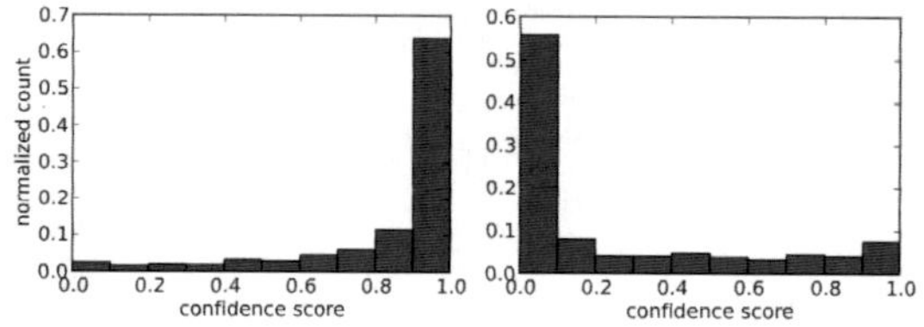

Figure 3: Distribution of confidence scores for correct ($P(z_c|\text{correct observation})$) *(left)* and incorrect ($P(z_c|\text{incorrect observation})$) *(right)* utterances.

5. SDS-POMDP Experiments

5.1. Experimental Design

We conducted a within-subjects study that compared our SDS-POMDP dialogue manager to a baseline threshold-based dialogue manager. In the SDS-POMDP, each dialogue began with a uniform distribution over states, the belief was updated according to Equation 4, and the system response was selected using the learned policy. In the threshold-based model, the confidence threshold was set at 0.75, where the system would ask the user to repeat if the threshold was not achieved.

The 14 individuals listed in Table 1 (seven "target" users and seven "control" users) participated in our experiments, which consisted of a single session for each user. In the session, the user was required to complete 40 dialogues. The 40 dialogues consisted of 20 goals, each presented once with the SDS-POMDP and once with the threshold-based dialogues manager. We randomized the ordering of the dialogues so that either the POMDP or baseline dialogue manager would be presented for a particular goal first. In addition, the same goal did not appear in consecutive dialogue tasks. Users were not told which dialogue manager was in operation for a given task.

Although a threshold-based, memory-less baseline dialogue manager is simple, we chose it as our point of comparison because it represents the current approach used by many existing speech-enabled assistive technologies. Such a system could potentially have advantages over the SDS-POMDP; for instance, there is no risk that belief probability mass would accumulate in incorrect states and require the user to speak additional utterances to correct errors. Meanwhile, it might have been useful to try to learn a optimal threshold, conduct experiments with different threshold-based dialogue managers, or evaluate the POMDP-based system with dialogue management strategies. However, because 40 dialogues already took substantial effort for some of our target users to complete, we did not perform these additional points of comparison.

Each of the dialogue tasks was presented with a text prompt on our graphical user interface, similar to the one shown in Figure 2. Our evaluation metrics were 1) the total number of dialogues (out of 20) completed within 60 seconds and 2) the total duration of the dialog, from the start of the user's first utterance until the system executed the correct response.

5.2. Results

All seven control users were able to complete all 20 dialogues successfully within 60 seconds. In contrast, as shown in Table 3, the seven target users completed an average of 17.4 out of 20 dialogues successfully with the SDS-POMDP and 13.1 with the threshold-based dialogue manager. A one-way repeated-measures ANOVA indicates a significant effect of the SDS-POMDP on the number of dialogues completed within sixty seconds ($F(1,6)=10.23$, $p=.02$), compared to the threshold-based model.

Table 3: Number of completed dialogues by target population users by dialogue manager

User	SDS-POMDP (/20)	Threshold (/20)
target01	18	13
target02	17	16
target03	20	20
target04	19	18
target05	13	5
target06	18	10
target07	17	10
average	17.4 ± 0.9	13.1 ± 0.9

In terms of dialogue completion times, the performance of the threshold-based and POMDP-based dialogue managers for all 14 participants is shown in Figure 4. In the case of unsuccessful dialogues, we assume that the total time elapsed was 60 seconds to compute the values in Figure 4.

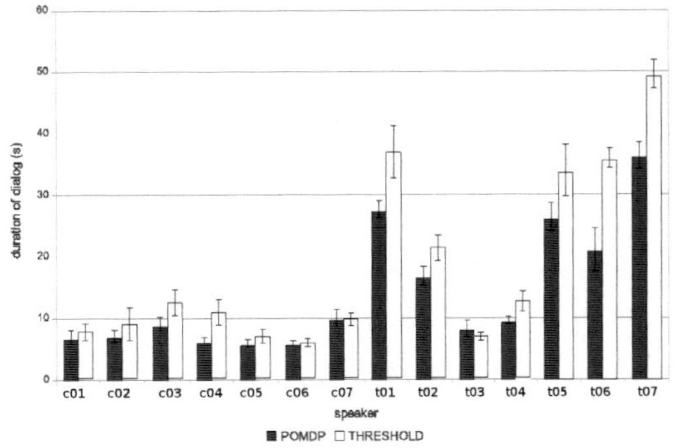

Figure 4: Dialog durations for POMDP- and threshold-based dialogue systems for control (c01-c07) and target (t01-t07) users. Error bars show standard error of the mean.

6. Discussion

6.1. Analysis of Results

The results in Table 3 show that the target population users benefited considerably from the POMDP-based dialogue manager. In general, this improvement was due to users being able to achieve the dialogue goal after a few low-confidence utterances in the SDS-POMDP; in contrast, they were unable to generate a correct utterance above the confidence threshold in the required time.

Figure 4 illustrates that the largest improvements, in terms of time saved, were among users with the highest completion times with the baseline system. These users were able to complete dialogues in less time using the SDS-POMDP. This trend underscores the benefit of probabilistic dialog management in handling noisy speech recognition inputs: the SDS-POMDP performs just as well as simpler, threshold-based methods for speakers with low ASR error rates (*i.e.* the control participants), but as the uncertainty increases among users with more ASR errors, the SDS-POMDP becomes superior.

The key advantage of the SDS-POMDP over the baseline was that it acquired information about the user's intent from every utterance. The top recognition hypothesis and the confidence score updated the SDS-POMDP's belief. In cases where there was a speech recognition error, it was likely that some probability mass was allocated to the user's actual goal. As well, utterances with speech recognition errors were more likely to have lower confidence scores, resulting in less "peaked" updates to the belief. This behavior meant that probability mass was not incorrectly allocated to the goal corresponding to the incorrect hypothesis. For these reasons, over the course of multiple dialogues, the SDS-POMDP's belief update operation made it superior to the threshold-based dialogue manager.

7. Conclusion

This paper offers empirical evidence that probabilistic dialog modeling, particularly the use of confidence scoring and confirmation questions in a POMDP framework, could enhance the effectiveness of spoken dialogue systems among users with high ASR error rates. By asking confirmation questions, a system can become more confident about taking the right action or avoid taking incorrect actions. Such methods could be useful for deploying speech-enabled assistive technology among users with challenging speech characteristics or in other situations where error-prone speech recognition is expected.

8. Acknowledgments

We thank Don Fredette and Alexander Burnham for their advice and guidance at The Boston Home.

9. References

[1] V. Young and A. Mihailidis, "Difficulties in automatic speech recognition of dysarthric speakers and implications for speech-

based applications used by the elderly: A literature review," *Assistive Technology*, vol. 22, no. 2, pp. 99–112, 2010.

[2] F. Rudzicz, "Comparing speaker-dependent and speaker-adaptive acoustic models for recognizing dysarthric speech," in *Proceedings of the 9th international ACM SIGACCESS conference on Computers and accessibility*. ACM, 2007, pp. 255–256.

[3] H. V. Sharma and M. Hasegawa-Johnson, "Acoustic model adaptation using in-domain background models for dysarthric speech recognition," *Computer Speech & Language*, 2012.

[4] N. Roy, J. Pineau, and S. Thrun, "Spoken dialogue management using probabilistic reasoning," in *Proceedings of the 38th Annual Meeting on Association for Computational Linguistics*. Association for Computational Linguistics, 2000, pp. 93–100.

[5] J. Williams and S. Young, "Partially observable markov decision processes for spoken dialog systems," *Computer Speech and Language*, vol. 21, no. 2, pp. 393 – 422, 2007.

[6] S. Young, M. Gašić, S. Keizer, F. Mairesse, J. Schatzmann, B. Thomson, and K. Yu, "The hidden information state model: A practical framework for pomdp-based spoken dialogue management," *Computer Speech & Language*, vol. 24, no. 2, pp. 150–174, 2010.

[7] J. Hoey, A. Von Bertoldi, P. Poupart, and A. Mihailidis, "Assisting persons with dementia during handwashing using a partially observable markov decision process," in *Proc. Int. Conf. on Vision Systems*, vol. 65, 2007, p. 66.

[8] J. Pineau and A. Atrash, "Smartwheeler: A robotic wheelchair test-bed for investigating new models of human-robot interaction," in *AAAI spring symposium on multidisciplinary collaboration for socially assistive robotics*, 2007, pp. 59–64.

[9] T. Taha, J. V. Miró, and G. Dissanayake, "Pomdp-based long-term user intention prediction for wheelchair navigation," in *Robotics and Automation, 2008. ICRA 2008. IEEE International Conference on*. IEEE, 2008, pp. 3920–3925.

[10] P. Viswanathan, J. J. Little, A. K. Mackworth, and A. Mihailidis, "Navigation and obstacle avoidance help (noah) for older adults with cognitive impairment: a pilot study," in *The proceedings of the 13th international ACM SIGACCESS conference on Computers and accessibility*. ACM, 2011, pp. 43–50.

[11] L. Hartelius, B. r. Runmarker, and O. Andersen, "Prevalence and characteristics of dysarthria in a multiple-sclerosis incidence cohort: relation to neurological data," *Folia phoniatrica et logopaedica*, vol. 52, no. 4, pp. 160–177, 2000.

[12] G. Arrondo, J. Sepulcre, B. Duque, J. Toledo, and P. Villoslada, "Narrative speech is impaired in multiple sclerosis," *European Neurological Journal*, vol. 2, no. 1, pp. 11–8, 2010.

[13] J. Glass, "A probabilistic framework for segment-based speech recognition," *Computer Speech and Language*, vol. 17, no. 2-3, pp. 137–152, 2003.

[14] L. R. Rabiner, "A tutorial on hidden markov models and selected applications in speech recognition," *Proceedings of the IEEE*, vol. 77, no. 2, pp. 257–286, 1989.

[15] J. Williams, "Partially observable markov decision processes with continuous observations for dialogue management," in *Computer Speech and Language*, 2005, pp. 393–422.

[16] M. Littman, A. Cassandra, and L. Kaelbling, "Learning policies for partially observable environments: Scaling up," *Proceedings of the Twelfth International Conference on Machine Learning*, pp. 362–370, 1995.

[17] Y. Freund and R. Schapire, "A decision-theoretic generalization of on-line learning and an application to boosting," in *Proceedings of the Second European Conference on Computational Learning Theory (EuroCOLT)*. London, UK: Springer-Verlag, 1995, pp. 23–37.

A Self Learning Vocal Interface for Speech-impaired Users

Bart Ons[1], *Netsanet Tessema*[1], *Janneke van de Loo*[2], *Jort F. Gemmeke*[1], *Guy De Pauw*[2], *Walter Daelemans*[2], *Hugo Van hamme*[1]

[1]ESAT, KU Leuven, Leuven, Belgium
[2]CLiPS - Computational Linguistics Group, University of Antwerp, Antwerp, Belgium

jort.gemmeke@esat.kuleuven.be

Abstract

In this work we describe research aimed at developing an assistive vocal interface for users with a speech impairment. In contrast to existing approaches, the vocal interface is self-learning, which means it is maximally adapted to the end-user and can be used with any language, dialect, vocabulary and grammar. The paper describes the overall learning framework and the vocabulary acquisition technique, and proposes a novel grammar induction technique based on weakly supervised hidden Markov model learning. We evaluate early implementations of these vocabulary and grammar learning components on two datasets: recorded sessions of a vocally guided card game by non-impaired speakers and speech-impaired users engaging in a home automation task.

Index Terms: vocal user interface, self-taught learning, dysarthric speech, non negative matrix factorization, hidden Markov models

1. Introduction

These days, vocal user interfaces (VUIs) allow us to control computers, smart phones, car navigation systems and domestic devices by voice. While still generally perceived as a luxury, assistive technology employing a VUI can make a prominent difference in the lives of individuals with a physical disability for whom operating and controlling devices would require exhaustive physical effort [1].

Unfortunately, even state-of-the-art speech recognition systems offer little, if any, robustness to dialectic or dysarthric speech (often encountered with disabled users), and are often restricted in their vocabulary and grammar. In practice, it is not feasible to design speech interfaces featuring custom acoustic and language models that cater to the dialectic and/or pathological speech of individual users, and adaptation of existing acoustic models is limited to only very mild speech pathologies [2, 3, 4, 5, 6]. Moreover, the user's voice may change over time due to progressive speech impairments.

Our aim is to build a VUI that is trained by the end-user himself, which means that it is maximally adapted to the — possibly dysarthric — speech of the user, and can be used with any vocabulary and grammar. The challenge is to learn both acoustics and grammar from a small number of examples, with as only supervisory information coarse annotation in the form of associated actions. For example, the annotation of the command "Turn on the television please", accompanied by a button press, would only be annotated at the utterance level with a device label (television) and an action label (turn on).

Our learning approach consists of two components that interact. Vocabulary acquisition first builds recurrent acoustic patterns representing words or parts of spoken commands, while grammar induction attempts to model the relationships between these patterns. For vocabulary acquisition, we build on existing work on child language learning modeling with non-negative matrix factorisation (NMF) [7]. For grammar induction, we propose the use of a weakly supervised Hidden Markov Model (HMM).

In short, we first use NMF to find recurrent acoustic patterns by mining utterance-level acoustic representations, supervised with relevant information about the action that was performed, such as a 'television' device and a 'turn on' action. Building on these, we then use the temporal occurrence of these patterns in the training data as observation features to train a multi-label version of a discrete HMM [8, 9]. In the HMM, the hidden states represent the collection of possible values in the data structures (devices and actions in the example). By mining the temporal occurrence of the NMF-based observations and the commonalities and differences across commands, the HMM is able to discover temporal structure in the commands, related to the data structures representing the actions.

The goals of our work are similar to those of [10, 11] in that we aim to discover acoustic patterns that recur in utterances and *ground* these by linking them to other modalities. However, to accommodate pathological voices, our work does not rely on pre-trained models, but they are learned from the speaker-specific acoustic data. In that sense, it shows similarities to the work in [12], but we learn form continuous speech and do not model low-level acoustics with an HMM. In terms of grammar learning, our task approaches unsupervised grammar induction [13, 14], but on a restricted domain with a small vocabulary.

We evaluate our learning framework on two databases: PATCOR, recorded sessions of a vocally guided card game by non-impaired speakers, and DOMOTICA-2, speech-impaired users engaging in a home automation task. The users were free to choose their own words and grammatical constructs to address the systems during the recording sessions.

The remainder of the paper is organised as follows. In section 2, we present an overview of the learning framework, describe the acoustic representations and introduce the NMF and HMM learning approaches. In section 3, the experimental setup is explained and in sections 4 and 5 the experimental results are presented and discussed. We conclude with our conclusions and thoughts for future work in section 6.

2. Architecture

2.1. Semantic frame representation of an utterance

A semantic *frame* is a data structure that contains all the relevant information (semantic concepts) associated with the ac-

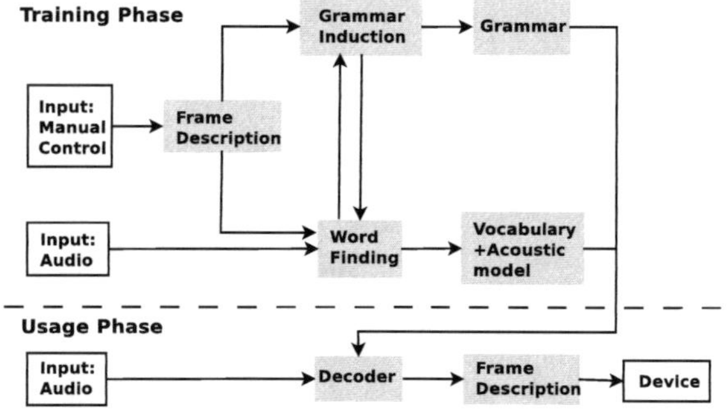

Figure 1: Overview of the vocal interface framework. The white boxes indicate events or systems outside the learning framework. The top panel shows the training phase and the bottom panel indicates the usage phase.

tion that is expressed in the spoken command. Semantic frames have been used in many spoken language processing applications [15]. A *frame* contains at least one *slot* representing a specific aspect of the *action*. Each *slot* in a frame can only be filled with a single *value*. A *frame description* of an *action* on the other hand, identifies a single frame out of the possible *frames* where the *action* is specified by the actual *slot values*.

2.2. The learning framework

The framework (Figure 1) is designed so it can learn from user interaction examples, i.e. a spoken command accompanied by an action on the device's user interface. For instance, users might say " Turn on the light" while pressing the button to switch on the light themselves or through the help of a care taker. The action performed on the device is translated into a *frame description*, which constitutes an abstraction layer making the learning algorithms application independent.

During the training phase, the word finding module looks for word-sized recurring acoustic patterns in the audio input that correlate well with the *frame description*. The *frame description* acts as a weak form of supervision in finding the recurring acoustic patterns. Here the term *weak supervision* is used because the supervision does not provide explicit information about the sequence of words within the spoken utterance.

The *grammar induction* module learns the relation between the different parts of a command. Given the frame description and the output of the word finding module, the grammar induction module learns the structure within commands, as well as the relation with the frame description during the training phase. During the usage phase, when only audio input is available, the grammar constrains the decoding process [16] and allows to propose a frame description of the spoken command. This frame description is then mapped onto an actual action on the device.

2.3. Audio representation

The word finding module in the training phase as well as the decoder in the usage phase need a suitable representation for the input speech. Both learning and recognition are based on NMF (section 2.4.1), which requires that the audio representation of an utterance be the sum of the representations of individual words. Therefore, and unlike main-stream ASR systems, an utterance is mapped to a vector of fixed size in three steps which are described below.

2.3.1. Spectral Representation

The first step of the audio processing chain extracts a 12-dimensional Mel Frequency Cepstral Coefficient (MFCC) representation of the short-term spectrum from speech segments of 25 ms with 10 ms overlap. The 12-dimensional MFCC is augmented with the log energy and the Δ and $\Delta\Delta$ features are appended, forming a 39 dimensional *spectral feature* stream.

2.3.2. Intermediate representations

The obtained MFCC spectral representations are further processed to form posteriorgrams from which the final representations described in section 2.3.3, are obtained. Two different forms of posteriorgrams are considered here: a *spectral feature* vector is either transformed into a vector of posterior probabilities of Gaussians forming a code book (soft VQ), or it is transformed to the posterior probability of phone classes.

In Soft Vector Quantisation, each *spectral feature* vector is softly assigned to all clusters in a code book. Each cluster is characterized by a Gaussian with full covariance. The degree of assignment is measured by the posterior probability of a Gaussian given the *spectral feature* vector.
The code book training starts off from a single cluster describing all training data. It is then split along the dominant eigenvector of its covariance matrix into two subclusters. The centres are refined with k-means iterations after which each subcluster is characterised by a full covariance Gaussian. This process is repeated, each time splitting the cluster with the largest volume as measured by the determinant of the covariance matrix. This process is either stopped when the desired number of clusters are obtained [17], which we will refer to by *Soft VQ*, or when the number of *spectral feature* vectors assigned to a cluster falls below a threshold, *minimum-number of frames*, which is referred to as *Adaptive Soft VQ*, because the number of clusters will depend on the amount of training data.

Phone posteriorgrams are constructed from 50 monophone HMMs (including a model for silence), each modeled by three states with GMM emission densities, connected in a strict left-to-right topology. The utterance is first transcribed into a phone lattice without using a phone-level language model. The acoustic likelihoods associated with the arcs are subsequently renormalised to posterior probabilities, which allows us to compute a posterior probability for each phone at any time.

A major difference with *Soft VQ* is that phone posteriorgrams exploit prior knowledge about the phone inventory that the user can produce.

2.3.3. Utterance-level HAC representation

The posteriorgrams of spectral feature clusters or of phone classes are not suitable to model directly with an NMF. To be able to discover recurring patterns in utterances, they need to be mapped to a representation of fixed dimension in which linearity holds, i.e. that the utterance-level speech representation is approximately equal to the sum of the speech representations of the acoustic patterns it contains [18, 19]. A mapping that exhibits this property is the so-called histogram of acoustic co-occurrences (HAC) [19]. The HAC of a speech segment is the posterior joint probability of two *acoustic events* happening at a predefined time lag τ, accumulated over the entire segment. An acoustic event is the observation of a spectral feature vector from a particular cluster in the case of soft VQ, or the observation of a phone in the case of phone posteriorgrams. Since the HAC representation considers event pairs, its dimensionality is the square of the number of acoustic event classes. In this paper, we stack HAC vectors computed for multiple values of the time lag $\tau = 20, 50, 90$ and 200 ms into a single *augmented HAC vector* to characterise an utterance. When multiple (training) utterances are available, their augmented HAC representations are arranged as columns of a matrix $\mathbf{V}_a$.

2.4. Non-negative matrix factorisation

NMF uses non-negativity constraints for decomposing a matrix into its components [20, 21, 22, 23], i.e given a non-negative matrix $\mathbf{V}$ of size $[M\text{x}N]$, NMF approximately decomposes it into its non-negative components $\mathbf{W}$ of size $[M\text{x}R]$ and $\mathbf{H}$ of size $[R\text{x}N]$. Under the right conditions, NMF is able to find parts in data. In ASR, NMF is used to discover recurring acoustic patterns (word units) through some grounding information [24, 25, 26].

In this paper, we use the Kullback-Leibler divergence to quantify the approximation quality of the NMF as expressed in Eq 1.

$$(\mathbf{H}, \mathbf{W}) = \arg \min_{(\mathbf{H},\mathbf{W})} D_{KL}(\ \mathbf{V}\ ||[\mathbf{WH}]) \tag{1}$$

Finding the $\mathbf{W}$ and $\mathbf{H}$ that minimize this approximation metric for a given data matrix $\mathbf{V}$ is achieved using multiplicative update rules[20].

2.4.1. Supervised NMF word learning

To employ NMF for word learning, we use a weak form of supervision represented by $\mathbf{V}_g$, which is used together with the augmented HAC acoustic representation of all the training utterances stacked into a matrix $\mathbf{V}_a$. The supervision information links the discovered acoustic patterns to *slot values* and also helps NMF to avoid local optima of the Kullback-Leibler divergence. The supervision $\mathbf{V}_g$ is a label matrix where each column represents an utterance and each row represents a *slot value*. The presence of a *slot value* in an utterance is represented in the label matrix with a '1' and its absence with a '0'.

Through the factorization of the composite matrix constructed by vertical concatenation of $\mathbf{V}_g$ and $\mathbf{V}_a$, NMF discovers latent *slot value* representations in each column of $\mathbf{W}_a$. The columns of W_g link the learned acoustic patterns in columns of $\mathbf{W_a}$ to the *slot values* represented by the rows of $\mathbf{V}_g$. Furthermore, some extra columns of $\mathbf{W_a}$ and $\mathbf{W_g}$ are used to represent *filler words* (words which are present in the utterance but are not related to any *slot value*). The columns of $\mathbf{H}$ matrix indicate which columns of $\mathbf{W}_a$ and $\mathbf{W}_g$ are combined to reconstruct $\mathbf{V}_a$ and $\mathbf{V}_g$ respectively. The learned acoustic patterns in $\mathbf{W}_a$ and labeling information in $\mathbf{W}_g$ as given in Eq. 2 will be used in the testing phase to detect the learned acoustic units within unseen test utterances.

$$\begin{bmatrix} \mathbf{V}_g \\ \mathbf{V}_a \end{bmatrix} \approx \begin{bmatrix} \mathbf{W}_g \\ \mathbf{W}_a \end{bmatrix} \mathbf{H} \tag{2}$$

2.4.2. NMF in the usage phase

The learned NMF model is applied in two different approaches to decoding. Both decoders apply the learned NMF model to word-sized segments of speech in a *sliding window* analysis. A sliding window of a width of 300 ms and a shift of 100 ms is used to produce an *augmented HAC vector* at 100 ms intervals across an utterance. As a result, an utterance is represented by a matrix $\mathbf{V}_s$, containing one column per window position. By employing the NMF factorization Eq. 3, which is called the *local* NMF, the corresponding *slot value activations* are calculated.

$$\mathbf{H}_s = \arg \min_{\mathbf{H}_s} D_{KL}(\mathbf{V}_s||\mathbf{W}_a\mathbf{H}_s) \tag{3}$$

This is followed by the calculation of the activation matrix $\mathbf{A}_s$. Each column of the activation matrix contains labeling information of all *slot values* for a particular window position.

$$\mathbf{A}_s = \mathbf{W}_g\mathbf{H}_s \tag{4}$$

In the simplest form of decoding, called *NMF decoding*, the slot values are inferred directly from the local (sliding window) NMF. The activations for all slot values are accumulated over all window positions, i.e. over the complete utterance. Since each slot can have at most one value assigned, only the value hypothesis with the largest accumulated activation is kept per slot. The slot value is considered to be detected, only if the accumulated activation exceeds a threshold. The order in which the acoustic patterns related to the slot values occur in the utterance is therefore ignored. Since this procedure may result in multiple possible frames, we select the frame with the highest average probability mass.

In a refinement, called *HMM decoding*, the local NMF model generates a data stream which is modeled by an HMM. The HMM captures the relation between word usage – including word order – and frame descriptions of actions. Since the HMM models the sequential aspects of the utterance (such as word order), we consider the learning of this HMM a form of *grammar induction*. The details of this approach are explained in the next section.

2.5. Grammar induction

Identical or similar words (e.g. numbers) may refer to different slots, so slot-value pairs can only be assigned correctly from spoken input if grammar is taken into account. *HMM decoding* fixes the major shortcoming of *NMF decoding*, i.e. that the order in which slot values occur, is ignored. The local NMF stream is then modeled by an HMM, which is learned from the user interaction examples.

2.5.1. HMM learning

The activation sequence is modeled by a multi-labeling HMM [9]. Like in discrete-density HMMs, each state q is characterized by probabilities $b_j(q)$ over observations j. In this framework, the observation is characterized by a probability distribution derived from NMF atom activations, obtained as $\mathbf{H}_s$, normalized to sum to unity. The state probability is then the inner product of this distribution with the state distribution.

Applied to this problem, each *semantic frame* is modeled by an HMM in which each *slot value* is assigned an HMM state referred to as *slot value state*. States are fully connected, with two exceptions. First, within slot transitions are prohibited, since each slot needs to be assigned only one value. Second, states can only transition to slot-value states within the same semantic frame, since each spoken command can only correspond to a single semantic frame. To limit the number of transition probabilities to be estimated, all transitions from states associated with a particular slot, to all states associated with another slot, share the same transition probability. The HMM will hence learn the sequence of slots in the user's utterances, but not the sequence of individual words. All the states can be initial or final states.

HMM training is done using the Baum-Welch algorithm [27]. Supervision information provided by the labeling matrix $\mathbf{V}_g$, is used to only assign non-zero state posteriors to *slot values* that are present in the *frame description* of an utterance. All non-zero entries of the state-transition matrix are initialised to (properly normalised) random values. The emission matrix is initialised by $\mathbf{W}_g$.

2.5.2. HMM decoding

During decoding, the maximum likelihood state sequence is obtained using the Viterbi algorithm for the given observation sequence $\mathbf{H}_s$. Visiting a state in an HMM corresponding to a semantic frame implies the corresponding *slot value* is detected. Since states representing slot values can only transition to states within the same semantic frame, the Viterbi search implicitly selects the most likely frame.

3. Experimental Setup

In this section, we give a description of the databases used for evaluation, the evaluation procedure and metrics.

3.1. Databases

3.1.1. PATCOR

The database PATCOR contains recordings of subjects playing a card game called "Patience" using spoken commands. The database contains 8 speakers with in total more than two thousand commands. The data was collected from unimpaired subjects with non-pathological speech, speaking Belgian Dutch. The users were free to choose their vocabulary and grammar, although in practice the vocabulary was limited indirectly by the number of cards, card positions and functionality.

A typical utterance in PATCOR is *"Put the four of clubs on the five of hearts"*. In this type of utterance, the order of the words plays a key role in discovering the utterance's meaning. The gold-standard frame descriptions of the utterances were created manually. In Table 1 an overview of the total number of frames, slots and slot values used is given. Since not all possible slot values occur for all speakers, Table 7 gives the actual number of slot values for each speaker. For a more detailed description of the frame descriptions that were used, as well as the slot values used for each speaker, we refer the reader to the technical report [28].

Table 1: *parameters of the speech databases*

Database	PATCOR	DOMOTICA
number of speakers	8	20
number of *frames*	2	4
number of *slots*	9	7
number of *slot values*	58	27
number of blocks	8	6

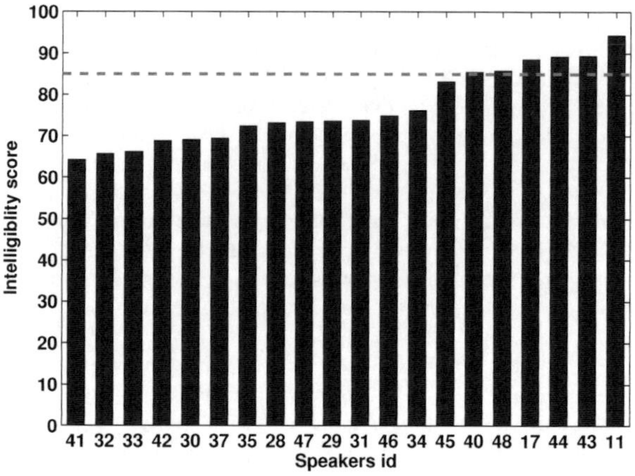

Figure 2: Speech intelligibility measurements of the speakers in DOMOTICA-2. The speakers are order by intelligibility score. Generally speaking, a score higher than 85% is non-pathological (see the dashed line).

3.1.2. DOMOTICA-2

The DOMOTICA-2 database contains recordings of impaired, dysarthric speakers controlling a home automation system. A typical DOMOTICA-2 utterance would look like *"Turn on the kitchen light"*.

Since collecting a large number of realistic, spontaneous spoken commands is difficult due to the targeted users getting tired quickly, a two-phase data collection method was used. In the first phase, 9 users were asked to control 31 different appliances in a 3D environment [28], guided by a visualised scenario in order to ensure an unbiased choice of words and grammar. In the second phase, these command lists were read back repeatedly by 21 test users. Of these 21, 8 speakers were selected based on their increased risk for degenerate voice rather than currently having a pathological voice.

For all speakers, speech intelligibility scores were obtained by analysing their recorded speech using an automated tool [29]. These scores are shown in Fig. 2. Table 1 gives an overview of the total number of frames, slots and slot values. For some speakers some slot values were not used, since some commands were not spoken enough times to allow a meaningful evaluation; Table 7 gives the actual number of slot values for each speaker. For a more detailed description of the slot values used for each speaker we refer the reader to the technical report [28].

3.2. Methodology

The goal of the experiments is to evaluate the performance as a function of the amount of training data used. However, since this means the amount of training data can be very small, a form of cross validation is needed to obtain statistically meaningful scores.

First, we divide the spoken commands (utterances) of each speaker into equal or nearly equal parts called *blocks*. The k blocks are created by minimising the Jensen-Shannon divergence (JSD) between the slot value distributions of all blocks. This optimisation is performed in an iterative process starting by dividing all utterances randomly into k blocks and then swapping at each iteration those two utterances that minimise the JSD the most from one block to the other one. The process stops when the JSD is minimised, i.e. when there are no swaps left that can lower the JSD. The slot values are then approximately evenly distributed throughout the blocks. Under the constraint that each slot value should occur at least once in each block, some slot values are excluded from the frame structure, meaning that the spoken words corresponding to these slot values, become filler words: they are not supervised and they are not scored anymore. Such adaptation to the supervision is speaker dependent and the number of slot values used for each speaker can be found in [28]. Utterances without any slot values were removed from the training and test sets.

To evaluate the learning speed of our framework, we created a $k \times k$ latin square in which each block occurs exactly once in each row and in each column. We selected five rows of the latin square to create a five-fold cross-validation experiment in which the train and test sets respectively increase and decrease in size. In each fold, we start with an experiment where only one block is used for training while the remaining $k-1$ blocks are used for testing. We incrementally increase the number of blocks n used for training in the subsequent experiments and the last experiment will be performed with $n = k - 1$ training blocks and one test block. Throughout the folds, the train and test sets are always composed of different blocks allowing for a more reliable scoring.

3.3. Parameters

The number of frames needed to have a reliable estimation of the cluster centres, depends on the dimensionality of the feature vectors. The minimum number of frames used for adaptive codebook training is chosen to be 78, two times the dimensionality of the MFCC feature vectors. For PATCOR, the resulting VQ codebook sizes typically ranged from 40 for the smallest training set to 145 for the largest training set. For DOMOTICA-2, the resulting codebook sizes typically ranged from 36 for the smallest training set to 118 for the largest training set.

For both databases, phone posteriorgrams were obtained using a free phone recognizer using a unigram language model. The phone recognizer was trained on a dataset containing recordings of selected radio and television news broadcasts in the same language as the collected databases. Phones are modeled with 3-state HMMs and in total 48845 tied Gaussians are used in the acoustic model. The phonetic alphabet includes one noise unit and one silence unit in addition to 48 phones.

For the utterance-based HAC representations, from both VQ and phone posteriorgrams, only the top-three largest indices at each time frame were retained.

3.4. Evaluation

For each utterance in the databases, we have a manually constructed gold standard frame description, which is used as a reference for system evaluation. In this reference frame description, the slot values that are expressed in the utterance, are filled in. The system was evaluated by comparing the automatically induced frame descriptions to the gold standard reference frames. The used metric is the *slot* $F_{\beta=1}$*-score*, which is the harmonic mean of the slot precision and the slot recall. These metrics are commonly used for the evaluation of frame-based systems for spoken language understanding [15]. The following formulas were used for calculation:

$$\text{slot precision} = \frac{\#\text{ correctly filled slots}}{\#\text{ total filled slots in induced frame}} \quad (5)$$

$$\text{slot recall} = \frac{\#\text{ correctly filled slots}}{\#\text{ total filled slots in reference frame}} \quad (6)$$

$$\text{slot F}_{\beta=1}\text{-score} = 2 \cdot \frac{\text{slot precision} \cdot \text{slot recall}}{\text{slot precision} + \text{slot recall}} \quad (7)$$

This means that only slots that are filled with a *correct* value are rewarded, and both slots that are falsely filled and slots that are falsely left empty are penalised. When an induced frame is of another type than the corresponding reference frame, the filled slots in the induced frame and in the reference frame are consequently different, which automatically results in a relatively large drop in the slot F-score. It should be noted that the reported F-scores aggregate slot counts over all five folds.

4. Results

In Fig. 3, F-scores for eight speakers per database are depicted as a function of the average number of utterances in the training set. The F-scores against increasing train set sizes provides some insight into the self-learning aspect of the framework. For each database, there are two graphs, one graph depicting NMF learning of slot value representations and one graph depicting HMM-based grammar induction.

For visibility, Fig. 3 does not contain all speakers from DOMOTICA-2. For this dataset, all F-scores for the NMF-based word finding module are presented in Table 2 and all scores for the HMM-based grammar induction module are presented in Table 3. There is one column for each speaker and the rows indicate the number of blocks in the training sets.

4.1. PATCOR

When we compare the respective F-scores for each speaker and for each training set size, we find a significant difference between the scores of the word finding module and the grammar induction module using a paired student's t-test, $t(55) = 5,11$, $p < 0.001$. On average, the grammar induction module improves the F-score with 5%, but the improvement varies between speakers. For some speakers, the induced grammar provides a considerable improvement, for instance for speaker 3, The improvement is 16% on average, $t(6) = 33,16$, $p < 0.001$. However, for instance, for speaker 5, we don't find a substantial improvement using the grammar induction module. In any case, using grammar induction does not seem to degrade the performance for any user in PATCOR.

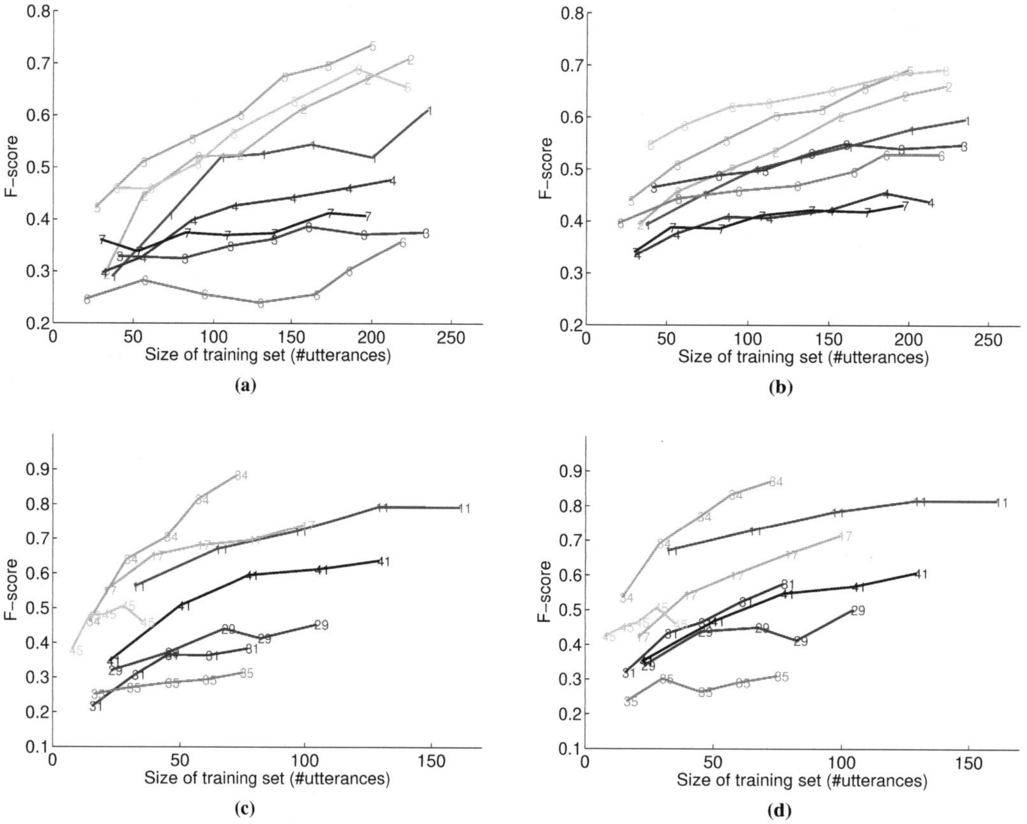

Figure 3: The F-scores per speaker against the averaged number of utterances in the respective training sets. In Panel (a), the NMF-based results of the word finding module for the PATCOR database are depicted. In Panel (b), the results of the word finding module augmented with the HMM-based grammar induction tool are displayed. Panel (c) and Panel (d) display the same results as Panel (a) and Panel (b), respectively, for eight selected speakers in the DOMOTICA-2 database.

Table 2: *F-scores for NMF word learning for all speakers of* DOMOTICA-2 *and all training set sizes*

speaker	11	17	28	29	30	31	32	33	34	35	37	40	41	42	43	44	45	46	47	48
1 block	0.56	0.55	0.30	0.32	0.27	0.22	0.22	0.27	0.46	0.25	0.24	0.36	0.35	0.28	0.34	0.31	0.38	0.16	0.17	0.36
2 blocks	0.67	0.65	0.36	0.37	0.32	0.31	0.26	0.31	0.64	0.27	0.30	0.44	0.51	0.29	0.37	0.46	0.48	0.16	0.17	0.29
3 blocks	0.72	0.68	0.41	0.44	0.40	0.37	0.33	0.32	0.71	0.28	0.36	0.50	0.60	0.32	0.39	0.53	0.48	0.20	0.15	0.33
4 blocks	0.79	0.70	0.50	0.41	0.41	0.36	0.32	0.32	0.81	0.29	0.36	0.48	0.61	0.41	0.38	0.61	0.51	0.17	0.14	0.29
5 blocks	0.79	0.74	0.48	0.45	0.43	0.38	0.38	0.40	0.88	0.31	0.44	0.53	0.64	0.45	0.44	0.63	0.46	0.22	0.13	0.26

Table 3: *F-scores for HMM grammar induction for all speakers of* DOMOTICA-2 *and all training set sizes*

speaker	11	17	28	29	30	31	32	33	34	35	37	40	41	42	43	44	45	46	47	48
1 block	0.67	0.42	0.32	0.34	0.26	0.32	0.21	0.18	0.54	0.24	0.27	0.33	0.35	0.21	0.32	0.43	0.42	0.20	0.18	0.40
2 blocks	0.73	0.54	0.36	0.44	0.36	0.43	0.24	0.31	0.69	0.30	0.28	0.45	0.47	0.26	0.44	0.55	0.45	0.23	0.19	0.46
3 blocks	0.78	0.60	0.43	0.45	0.46	0.46	0.25	0.29	0.77	0.26	0.45	0.58	0.55	0.33	0.41	0.58	0.46	0.25	0.16	0.48
4 blocks	0.82	0.66	0.49	0.41	0.50	0.52	0.31	0.32	0.83	0.29	0.37	0.59	0.57	0.31	0.32	0.66	0.51	0.22	0.19	0.58
5 blocks	0.82	0.71	0.48	0.50	0.43	0.58	0.29	0.35	0.87	0.31	0.50	0.60	0.61	0.28	0.59	0.70	0.46	0.24	0.19	0.61

Results are in the same range as the reported word finding results in [25], however, there are some speaker dependent differences in performance due to different experimental settings. The major discrepancies in settings are scoring and grammar discovery. While we report F-scores and investigate automatically induced grammar structures in this study, slot value recall scores are reported in [25] and frame decoding is guided by a handcrafted grammar. Additionally, the feature representations are also different between the two studies. While we combine phone posteriorgrams and adaptive softVQ for building the acoustic feature representations, the feature representation is based on softVQ using more larger codebooks in [25].

4.2. Domotica-2

For DOMOTICA-2, we find a small but significant improvement using a paired student's t-test when comparing the F-scores between the word finding module and the grammar induction module for each speaker and training set size (see Fig. 3c and Fig. 3d), $t(99) = 3,24$, $p < 0.01$. On average the grammar induction module cause an increase in F-scores of about 3%. For some speakers, the F-score improvements were more pronounced than for others. For instance, F-scores for speaker 31 improved on average with a decimal of 0.14, $t(4) = 7,6$, $p < 0.05$ while the F-scores for speaker 17 decreased with 8%, $t(4) = -3.77, p < 0.05$.

The differences between speakers is related to the intelligibility scores. We found a significant Kandall's tau rank correlation equal to $0.41, p < 0.05$ for the average F-score per speaker and their respective intelligibility score. There are trend lines in Fig. 3c and Fig. 3d that are rather short because the amount of data was limited, such as the graphs for speaker 35, resulting from early fatigue for some speakers in the recording phase of the DOMOTICA-2 corpus.

5. Discussion

In the word finding module, we aim to find the acoustic representation of the words corresponding to slot values in a semantic frame. In the grammar induction tool, the temporal structure in the commands is discovered and related to the semantic frame structure of the spoken commands. Positive scores necessitate a positive evaluation on both aspects, that is the correct recognition of the spoken words and the correct allocation of the recognised words to the slots in the semantic frame structure. The second aspect is not a trivial issue for the utterances used in the PATCOR database. For instance, in the utterance "Put the four of clubs on the five of hearts", words like "four" and "clubs" are related to the moving card while the same words are sometimes used to define the destination of the move. Some speakers specify the moving card first while others may specify the destination card first. Although spoken words are sometimes identical, different slot value labels specify different meanings. It can be seen in Fig 3b that the VUI gradually succeeds to distinguish these slots corresponding to the moved card and the destination card for at least some speakers, such as speaker $2, 5$ and 8. Scores above 0.5 are only possible when the correct slots are recognized, such as the slots related to the moving card versus the slots related to the destination card in PATCOR.

The NMF-based word finding module is able to learn more than words, as some context information of the words is incorporated in the slot value representations. The features used in NMF learning consist of the co-occurrence of acoustic events over multiple delays, up to $\tau = 200$ ms, allowing for learning context over spoken word boundaries. Moreover, the learned context of a word also involves the co-occurrence of acoustic events with the frame slot events of the demonstrated commands. The learned context is helpful in identifying the words but also the frame slots for some speakers as can be seen in Fig 3a and Fig 3c. However, context learning in NMF over word boundaries is only possible in a local time context because co-occurrence of acoustic events over longer time delays are more divergent. Useful time delays might be extended by using probabilistic time delays instead of fixed ones used here. The use of longer time delays in learning the co-occurrence of events poses a challenge for future research.

Although the frame structure is acquired for some speakers without using the grammar induction module, not all speakers display good scores without grammar induction, such as speakers $3, 6$ and 7 in PATCOR. The HMM-based grammar induction tool improves the learning of the frame structure, especially for those speakers for which the NMF word finding module demonstrates insufficiencies. The results demonstrated in Fig. 3 and Table 3 are encouraging in the sense that the graphs of all speakers in Fig. 3 tend to rise by increasing training set sizes, demonstrating the self-learning ability of the investigated framework. Further directions of research includes the acceleration of the learning plots for normal and dysarthric speech. Accelerating the speed of learning is especially important for speech-impaired users, because they have to make more effort to utter commands and train the system. Besides accelerating the speed of learning, it remains an open issue at which level the scores tend to level off. Obviously, all scores presented in the graphs of Fig. 3b and Fig. 3d are not at levelling off for the largest training set, as the training data is too scarce for the self learning VUI to reach maximal performance. More data is needed to find out the maximal performance of the system and the relation between maximal scores and intelligibility of the users. We could help this issue by gathering more data or by sharing the emission probabilities for particular slot values sharing identical words similar to the sharing of the transition probabilities explained in Section 2.5.1.

There are some differences in performance between databases. Our framework performs best for intelligible speech. The speakers with higher F-scores for the DOMOTICA-2 database are the speakers with the higher intelligibility scores close to 85%. The performance of our framework for different speakers in DOMOTICA-2 demonstrates a larger variability and more spurious trajectories in Fig.3d than for normal speakers in PATCOR. Low scores are corresponding to a low number of slot values which in turn is corresponding to a limited number of recorded utterances due to early fatigue. However, the scores between the two databases are difficult to compare since the complexities of the categorical decisions are different from each other. For instance, there are more frame slot values per slot in PATCOR than in DOMOTICA-2 and there is more hierarchical structure in the PATCOR-commands compared to the DOMOTICA-2-commands, making the recognition of PATCOR-commands much more difficult. In future research, we will evaluate our framework on more databases allowing us to compare the strengths and weaknesses of our system with other small-vocabulary, speaker-dependent systems, such as those described in [2, 6].

6. Conclusion

In this work we described research aimed at developing an assistive vocal interface for people with a speech impairment.

In contrast to existing approaches, the vocal interface is self-learning which means it is maximally adapted to the end-user and can be used with any language, dialect, vocabulary and grammar. We proposed a novel grammar induction technique, based on weakly supervised HMM learning, and we evaluated early implementations of these vocabulary and grammar learning components on two datasets: recorded sessions of a vocally guided card game by non-impaired speakers, and speech-impaired users engaging in a home automation task.

While the performance varied widely between speakers, both for impaired and non-impaired speakers, performance did improve even with relatively small amounts of additional training data. This demonstrates the potential of the self-learning vocal interface. Additionally, the proposed HMM approach to weakly supervised grammar induction did improve the results for all but a few speakers, indicating that a limited form of grammar induction is not only feasible, but also beneficial to distinguish between commands. Future work will focus not only on a detailed analysis of the obtained results, such as the grammars that were inferred and the relation between speech pathology and performance, but also on improvements such as more advanced acoustic modelling techniques, hierarchical approaches of HMM learning, and integrating grammar induction and vocabulary acquisition in a single probabilistic framework.

7. Appendix

Table 4: *number of* slot values *and maximum codebook size*

PATCOR		
speaker id	**number of** ***slot values***	**maximum codebook size**
1	29	117
2	37	145
3	23	152
4	27	78
5	25	151
6	18	189
7	27	165
8	19	142

DOMOTICA-2		
speaker id	**number of** ***slot values***	**maximum codebook size**
11	22	149
17	18	81
28	18	115
29	9	138
30	14	94
31	12	52
32	17	200
33	11	93
34	6	59
35	13	187
37	13	94
40	18	126
41	18	169
42	17	87
43	4	62
44	18	78
45	3	63
46	19	164
47	17	135
48	5	79

8. Acknowledgements

The research in this work is funded by IWT-SBO grant 100049.

9. References

[1] J. Noyes and C. Frankish, "Speech recognition technology for individuals with disabilities," *Augmentative and Alternative Communication*, vol. 8, no. 4, pp. 297–303, 1992.

[2] H. Christensen, S. Cunningham, C. Fox, P. Green, and T. Hain, "A comparative study of adaptive, automatic recognition of disordered speech," in *Proc Interspeech 2012*, Portland, Oregon, US, Sep 2012.

[3] K. T. Mengistu and F. Rudzicz, "Comparing humans and automatic speech recognition systems in recognizing dysarthric speech," in *Proceedings of the Canadian Conference on Artificial Intelligence*, 2011.

[4] H. V. Sharma and M. Hasegawa-Johnson, "State transition interpolation and map adaptation for hmm-based dysarthric speech recognition," in *HLT/NAACL Workshop on Speech and Language Processing for Assistive Technology (SLPAT)*, 2010, pp. 72–79.

[5] F. Rudzicz, "Acoustic transformations to improve the intelligibility of dysarthric speech," in *Proceedings of the Second Workshop on Speech and Language Processing for Assistive Technologies (SLPAT2011)*, 2011.

[6] M. S. Hawley, P. Enderby, P. Green, S. Cunningham, S. Brownsell, J. Carmichael, M. Parker, A. Hatzis, P. O'Neill, and R. Palmer, "A speech-controlled environmental control system for people with severe dysarthria," *Medical Engineering & Physics*, vol. 5, no. 29, pp. 586 – 593, 2007.

[7] J. Driesen, J. Gemmeke, and H. Van hamme, "Weakly supervised keyword learning using sparse representations of speech," in *Proceedings of the 36th International Conference on Acoustics, Speech and Signal Processing*, Kyoto, Japan, 2012.

[8] M. Nishimura and K. Toshioka, "Hmm-based speech recognition using multi-dimensional multi-labeling," in *Acoustics, Speech, and Signal Processing, IEEE International Conference on ICASSP '87.*, vol. 12, 1987, pp. 1163–1166.

[9] J. Hernando, I.B. Maririo, A. Moreno, and C. Nadeu, "Multiple multilabeling applied to hmm-based noisy speech recognition," in *Proc. ICSP '93*, 1993.

[10] R. Taguchi, N. Iwahashi, K. Funakoshi, M. Nakano, T. Nose, and T. Nitta, *Human Machine Interaction - Getting Closer*. InTech, 2012, ch. Learning Physically Grounded Lexicons from Spoken Utterances.

[11] D. Roy, "Grounded spoken language acquisition: Experiments in word learning," *IEEE Transactions on Multimedia*, vol. 5(2), pp. 197–209, 2003.

[12] I. Ayllon Clemente, M. Heckmann, and B. Wrede, "Incremental word learning: Efficient hmm initialization and large margin discriminative adaptation," *Speech Communication*, vol. 54, pp. 1029–1048, Nov. 2012.

[13] R. Collobert, J. Weston, L. Bottou, M. Karlen, K. Kavukcuoglu, and P. Kuksa, "Natural language processing (almost) from scratch," *Journal of Machine Learning Research*, vol. 12, pp. 2493–2537, Aug 2011. [Online]. Available: http://leon.bottou.org/papers/collobert-2011

[14] D. Klein, "The unsupervised learning of natural language structure," Ph.D. dissertation, Stanford University, 2005.

[15] Y. Wang, L. Deng, and A. Acero, "Semantic frame-based spoken language understanding," in *Spoken Language Understanding: Systems for Extracting Semantic Information from Speech*, G. Tur and R. D. Mori, Eds. West-Sussex, UK: Wiley, 2011, ch. 3, pp. 41–91.

[16] J. van de Loo, G. De Pauw, J. Gemmeke, P. Karsmakers, B. Van Den Broeck, W. Daelemans, and H. Van hamme, "Towards shallow grammar induction for an adaptive assistive vocal interface: a concept tagging approach," in *Proceedings NLP4ITA*, 2012, pp. 27–34.

[17] F. Class, A. Kaltenmeir, P. Regal-Brietzmann, and K. Trottler, "Fast speaker adaptation combined with soft vector quantization in an hmm speech recognition system," in *Acoustics, Speech, and Signal Processing, 1992. ICASSP-92., 1992 IEEE International Conference on*, vol. 1, 1992, pp. 461–464 vol.1.

[18] J. Driesen and H. Van hamme, "Fast word acquisition in an NMF-based learning framework," in *Proceedings of the 36th International Conference on Acoustics, Speech and Signal Processing*, Kyoto, Japan, 2012.

[19] H. Van hamme, "Hac-models: a novel approach to continuous speech recognition," in *Proceedings INTERSPEECH*, 2008, pp. 2554–2557.

[20] D. Lee and H. Seung, "Learning the parts of objects by nonnegative matrix factorization," *Nature*, vol. 401, pp. 788–791, 1999.

[21] J. Eggert and E. Korner, "Sparse coding and nmf," in *Neural Networks, 2004. Proceedings. 2004 IEEE International Joint Conference on*, vol. 4, 2004, pp. 2529–2533 vol.4.

[22] Y.-X. Wang and Y.-J. Zhang, "Nonnegative matrix factorization: A comprehensive review," *Knowledge and Data Engineering, IEEE Transactions on*, vol. 25, no. 6, pp. 1336–1353, 2013.

[23] H. Lee, J. Yoo, and S. Choi, "Semi-supervised nonnegative matrix factorization," *Signal Processing Letters, IEEE*, vol. 17, no. 1, pp. 4–7, 2010.

[24] L. Boves, L. ten Bosch, and R. Moore, "Acorns-towards computational modeling of communication and recognition skills," in *Proc. IEEE int. Conf. On Cognitive informatics*, California, USA, 2007, pp. 349–355.

[25] J. F. Gemmeke, J. van de Loo, G. De Pauw, J. Driesen, H. Van hamme, and W. Daelemans, "A self-learning assistive vocal interface based on vocabulary learning and grammar induction," in *Proc. INTERSPEECH*, 2012, pp. 1–4.

[26] B. Ons, J. F. Gemmeke, and H. Van hamme, "Label noise robustness and learning speed in a self-learning vocal user interface," in *Proc. of the International Workshop on Spoken Dialog Systems (IWSDS)*, Ermenonville, France, 2012.

[27] L. Rabiner, "A tutorial on hidden markov models and selected applications in speech recognition," *Proceedings of the IEEE*, vol. 77, no. 2, pp. 257–286, 1989.

[28] N. Tessema, B. Ons, J. Gemmeke, and H. Van hamme, "Technical report (aladin-tr01)," KULeuven ESAT-PSI, Tech. Rep., 2013.

[29] C. Middag, "Automatic analysis of pathological speech," Ph.D. dissertation, Ghent University, Belgium, 2012.

The dramatic piece reader for the blind and visually impaired

Milan Rusko[1], *Marian Trnka*[1], *Sakhia Darjaa*[1], *Juraj Hamar*[2]

[1] Institute of Informatics of the Slovak Academy of Sciences, Bratislava, Slovakia
[2] Department of Aesthetics, Comenius University, Bratislava, Slovakia

milan.rusko@savba.sk, trnka@savba.sk, utrrsach@savba.sk, juraj.hamar@sluk.sk

Abstract

The paper presents the concept and realization of the intelligent audio-book reader for the visually impaired. The system is capable of presenting personalities of different characters. The synthesizer mimics the way how a puppeteer portrays different characters. A traditional puppeteer generally uses up to a dozen different marionettes in one piece. Each of them impersonates a character with its own typical voice manifestation. We studied the techniques the puppeteer uses to change his voice and the acoustical correlates of these changes. The results are used to predict appropriate settings of the parameters of the voice for every character of the piece. The information on the personality features of every particular character is inserted manually by a human operator. Similarly to the puppeteer's show only one speaker's voice is used in this concept and all the modifications are made using speech synthesis methods.

Index Terms: audio-book, speech synthesis, personality

1. Audio-books for the blind in Slovakia

The first audio-book in Slovakia was published 50 years ago. The first studio specialized to audio-book recording was founded in 1962 and the first four audio-books were published. The Slovak Library for the Blind – SLB (Slovenská knižnica pre nevidiacich Mateja Hrebendu v Levoči) has now about 37 thousands of library units, from which about 5 000 are audio-books. These books have been read by professional actors - readers. Some of these readers are working for SLB for more than 30 years and some have recorded more than 865 titles [1].

2. Text-to-speech reading eBooks

Reading the book by an actor is time consuming and costly. It takes about two weeks for a professional audio-book narrator to record a novel of a length of about 85.000 words. To fully produce it takes another 2-3 weeks. [2] Moreover the actors and recording studio are not always available. Therefore, the authors of this paper started to cooperate with the SLB library in order to make much more books available – via reading by advanced expressive speech synthesis system.

Text-to-speech (TTS) uses speech synthesizer to read out the given text. TTS in English and some other languages is built into the Windows and Macintosh computer operating systems, phones, tablets and other devices. (The choice of synthetic voices for Slovak was very limited until recently, and there was practically only one producer of professional quality Slovak speech synthesizers in Slovakia – The Institute of Informatics of the Slovak Academy of Sciences.)

The main advantages of eBooks with text to speech over performed audio books is the availability, ease of access and new titles becoming available much quicker. [3]

Several authors have checked the possibilities of expressive speech synthesis for storytelling (e.g. [4] [5]). So did the authors in this study, but their aim was to design a system capable of creating a unique voice for each character.

The Slovak Library for the Blind has made first two synthesized audio-books available for informal evaluation on their web site and presented them also on the international conference Accessibility of audiovisual works to visually impaired people.[6] Two versions were published - one synthesized by unit selection synthesizer Kempelen 2.1 [7] and the second one by statistical parametric synthesizer Kempelen 3.0 [8]. As it was referred in [6] it can be seen from the e-mail reactions of the visually impaired that the quality of both synthesizers was assessed as acceptable with a slight favoring of the unit selection synthesizer. This one was rated as a voice that sometimes sounds almost indistinguishable from human.

The problem with synthesized speech is that it has smaller variability than the natural speech and it becomes tedious after a short while. Therefore the authors decided to prepare and verify a new concept of semi-automatic synthetic audio-books generation, a concept that they called DRAPER - the virtual dramatic piece reader. The idea is that the synthetic or virtual reader should not only read the text of the dramatic piece, but that it should change its voice according to the character being depicted. This concept stems from the former research on the presentation of the personality of the dramatic characters by puppeteers.[9][10] The authors think that the approach of deriving all the synthetic voices from the original voice of one voice-talent has an advance to fulfill the requirement of consistency of chosen voices for audio-book reading, that: " ... the voice for each character has to not only be distinctive and appropriate for the character in isolation, but it must also make sense in an ensemble of various characters." [11].

A traditional Slovak puppeteer generally used up to a dozen different marionettes in one piece. Each of them impersonated a character with its own typical voice manifestation. The authors have therefore studied the techniques used by the puppeteers to change their voice and the acoustical correlates of these changes. The prototypical characters (archetypes) were identified. The psychological and aesthetic aspects of their personalities were studied and acoustic-phonetic means of their vocal presentation by the actor were identified [10].

3. Speech synthesizers

The modern speech synthesis system development is dependent on speech databases that serve as a source of synthesis units or a source of data needed to train the models. In the current work we use some of our earlier results, such as neutral speech database [12] and unit-selection synthesizer [7]. On the other hand the expressive databases and expressive HTK voices belong to the most recent results of our research.

3.1. Speech databases

The set of speech databases containing the voice of our voice talent consists of:

1. Neutral database (Level 0) – 2000 sentences
2. Expressive speech database with higher levels of voice effort
    a. Base level (Level 1) – 300 sentences
    b. Increased level (Level 2) -300 sentences
    c. Highly increased level (Level 3) - 300 sentences
3. Expressive speech database with lower levels of vocal effort
    a. Base level (Level -1) - 150 sentences
    b. decreased level (Level -2) 150 sentences
    c. Highly decreased level (Level -3) 150 sentences
4. Whispered speech database - 150 sentences

The Neutral database, VoiceDat-SK, serves for creating the neutral voice with good coverage of synthesis elements.

The method of development of smaller expressive databases that serve for adaptation to voices with higher and lower expressive load (limited to the dimension of emphasis and insistence) was published in [13]. One of the features that are known to be correlated with the level of arousal and vocal effort is the average F0. Figure 1 shows the histograms of F0 for our three databases with one reference-neutral and two increased levels of vocal effort. Histograms of F0 for the expressive databases with one reference-neutral and two lower levels of arousal are presented in Figure 2.

A Gaussian approximation is added to each of the histograms.

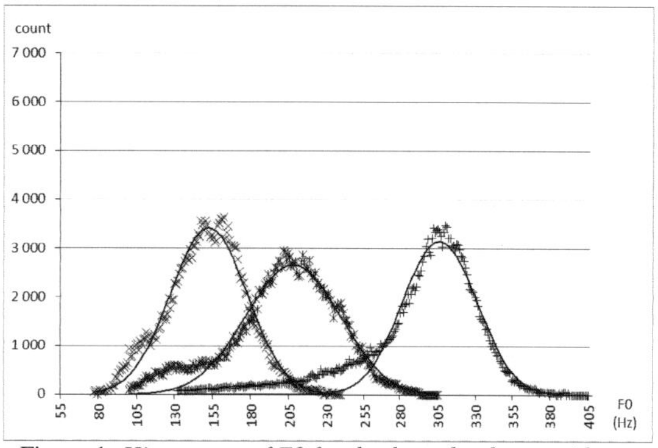

Figure 1: *Histograms of F0 for the three databases with increased vocal effort (from left to right: Level 1, 2, 3).*

In the databases with increasing expressive load the second and third levels of expressivity are clearly distinguishable from the base (reference) level 1. In addition to the neutral voice it is therefore possible to train two more significantly different expressive voices - one with higher and the second one with very high emphasis and insistence.

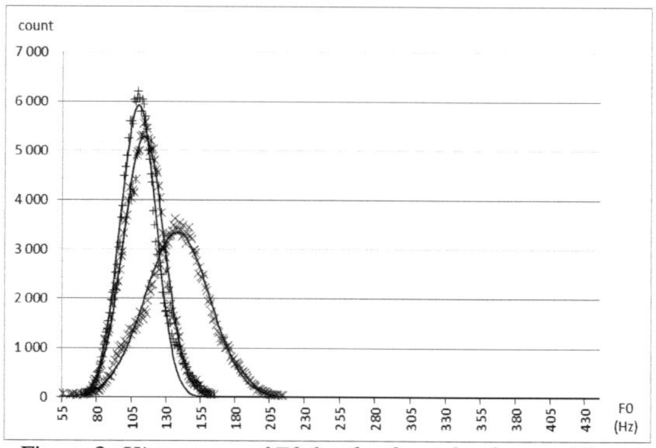

Figure 2: *Histograms of F0 for the three databases with decreased vocal effort (from left to right: Level -3, -2, -1).*

In the databases with decreasing expressive load it was very hard for the speaker to make the second and third levels distinguishable one from another. The differences in vocal intensity and timbre were small and the average F0 was nearly the same for these two databases (level -2 and -3 of expressive load – soothing and very soothing speech). This was probably due to a physiological limit - the lowest frequency of oscillation of the glottal chords. We therefore decided to train only one voice with low expressive load. So we at last came to the choice of speech modes which is identical to the modes examined by Zhang and Hansen from the point of view of vocal effort in their work on classification of speech modes [14] (i.e.: whispered, soft, neutral, loud and shouted in Zhang's description).

A special database of whispered voice was created by the same speaker whispering the same set of 150 phonetically rich sentences as was used in the preceding expressive databases. As it turned out this volume was sufficient to achieve a good quality of synthesized whisper by direct training the HMM voice on this database, without using the neutral voice and adaptation. This is probably due to the absence of voiced parts, which are critical in HMM synthesis because of the problems with pitch tracking. In contrast to voiced parts of the other HMM voices the vocoder buzz is nearly unobservable in the synthesized whisper.

3.2. Synthesizer voices

The authors have several types of synthesizers available derived from the voice of the same voice talent [15]. Two of the used synthesis methods provide sufficient quality for the audio-books reading – the Unit-selection [16] and Statistical-parametric synthesis [17].

Kempelen 2.0 unit-selection synthesizer utilizes the Neutral database with a CART [18] [19] prosody model consisting of F0 model and segmental lengths model. It offers possibilities to change average F0 (AvgF0), to linearly change average speech rate (AvgSr) and to change the depth of application of the prosody model (PDepth). Figure 3 shows the interface for setting these parameters and checking the resulting voice.

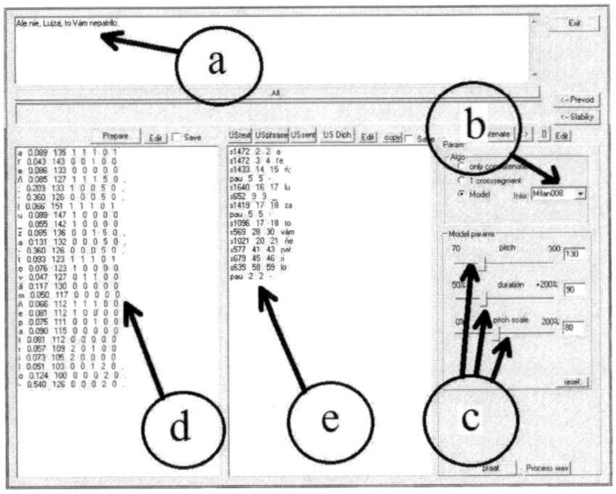

Figure 3: *The graphical interface of the unit selection synthesizer: a) text, b) prosody model selection, c) sliders for setting the AvgF0, AvgSr and PDepth, d) needed phonemes e) best syllable candidates found in the database from which the utterance is concatenated.*

Only neutral voice Unit-selection is available in the actual version of DRAPER as the volume of expressive databases is too small to create good quality expressive Unit-selection voices from them. However certain changes in expression and fitting the voice to different characters can be obtained by changes in average pitch, average speech rate and the weight of prosody model, which influences the depth of the prosody modulation. The last one can change the intonation from monotonous to exaggerative intonation obtained by extrapolation of the model values up to 200%.

Other voices are based on Statistic-parametric speech synthesis [17]. We created the neutral voice in the HTS [20] system and adopted it to three other voices using smaller expressive databases. The statistical parametric synthesis uses Hidden Markov Modeling, and therefore this method is often denoted as HMM synthesis.

The brand name of our synthesizers is Kempelen. The full set of synthesizer voices available in the current version of DRAPER is the following:

- Kempelen 2.1 neutral Unit-selection voice
- Kempelen 3.0 neutral HMM voice
- Kempelen 3.1 HMM voice with higher expressive load
- Kempelen 3.2 HMM voice with very high expressive load
- Kempelen 3.3 HMM voice with lower expressive load
- Kempelen 3.4 HMM whispering voice

4. Personality and voice

In this chapter we shortly introduce our previous research on the relationship between personality and voice.

4.1. Individuality and its components / the notion of personality

In our work, individuality is understood as a psychological entity, a unit consisting of three components [21]. First, personality, is a rather stable component that remains practically unchanged during the life. Second, mood, may change in time, but its changes are rather slow. Third, emotions, are the most dynamical and can change rapidly. In this paper we focus mainly on the first component, personality, and leave the other two components for subsequent studies.

4.2. Traditional psychological classification of personality dimensions

Personality is most commonly described using the formal psychological model called the Five Factor Model [22], [23] with factors representing the basis of the personality space. We have adopted a very simple annotation convention. Each of the personality dimensions - Neuroticism, Extraversion, Openness to experience, Agreeableness and Conscientiousness - will be assigned only one of three values: 1, 0 or -1. For instance, N1 denotes that the character is neurotic, N0 means that this dimension is not applicable, i.e. not important for expressing the character's personality, and N-1 denotes the absence of neuroticism, i.e. that the character comes across as secure and confident, which is opposite to neurotic (see Table 1.).

4.3. Semantic dimension – taxonomy of characters based on elementary semantic oppositions

Personal characteristic of the theatre characters is a complex of three interconnected levels: semantic, visual and acoustical. The semantic level characterizes the character as to its function in the play. The visual layer represents all components of visual representation of a puppet (face, costume, material and animation). The acoustical layer includes speech, music and all the sounds generated by actor and his puppets.

The description of personalities encoded in the speech and acting of puppet characters requires at least a three dimensional space consisting of semantic, visual and auditory dimensions. In the semantic domain the character is best described following its functions in the play. Table 2 gives classification of functions of the characters (the concept) on the basis of elementary semantic oppositions, proposed by us for aesthetic and semantic description on of characters for the purposes of this study.

The classification includes eight dimensions. Some of them are binary, e.g. Sex or Anthropological view, some are coarsely continuous, e.g. Social Status or Ethnicity, and some represent a fine-grained continuum, e.g. Age, Morality, or Intelligence. We will initially code all dimensions as binary since even Age, Morality, or Intelligence are considered archetypal and thus extremely polar for the purposes of the plays.

Table 1. *Five Factor Model of personality with description and examples*

Personality dimension	Code value	Description	High level [1] (example adjectives)	Low level [-1] (example adjectives)
Neuroticism	N 1,0,-1	Tendency to experience negative thoughts	Sensitive Nervous Insecure Emotionally distressed	Secure Confident
Extraversion	E 1,0,-1	Preference for and behaviour in social situations	Outgoing Energetic Talkative Social	Shy With-drawn
Openness to experience	O 1,0,-1	Open minded-ness, interest in culture	Inventive Curious Imaginative Creative Explorative	Cautious Conserva-tive
Agree-ableness	A 1,0,-1	Interactions with others	Friendly Compassio-nate Trusting Cooperative	Competitive
Conscien-tiousness	C 1,0,-1	Organized, persistent in achieving goals	Efficient Methodical Well organized Dutiful	Easy-going Careless

Table 2. C*lassification of the characters based on several elementary semantic oppositions.*

Criteria	One pole	code	Second pole	code
Sex	Male	XM	Female	XF
Anthropological view	human	HH	Non-human	HN
Age	Old	AO	Young	AY
Morality	Positive	MP	Negative	MN
Aesthetics	Tragical	ET	Comical	EC
Reflexion of ethnic	Our	RO	Foreign	RF
Intelligence	Clever	IH	Stupid	IL
Social status	Noble	SN	Low	SL

For deeper understanding of the actor's notion of personality of his characters, we asked a puppeteer, Anton Anderle, to characterize the personality and to explain the changes of his voice he uses to present them. The actor based the description on both psychological features of the character and the acoustic-phonetic means to express them.

He presented us a set of archetypical characters and their typical features:

I. NEGATIVE MALE TYPE - Intriguer, bad knight

- High volume, hyper-articulation

II. POSITIVE MALE TYPE -Leading man - Royal type dignified, deliberate, wise - *Low pitch, monotonous*

IV. BAD MAN - hoarse, low pitch

V. SWAGGERER Convivial, bold farmer, folk type, straight man, unshuffling, not cunning, frank - *Pharyngeal resonance, great pitch range*

VI. LEAD WOMAN - young, *soft modal*

VII. OLD WOMAN – *lower voice*

VIII. BAD OLD WOMAN Cunning, sarcastic - *Increased* hoarseness, articulator setting as for smile

IX. GOOD OLD WOMAN - Low falsetto, medium pitch range

This actor's classification scheme in fact assigns personality features and semantic features to the acoustical features of the character's voice.

4.4. Voice quality and settings of the articulators

A common way of describing voice settings uses the notion of a reference or neutral setting. This reference corresponds to a normal position relative to possible adjustments [24]. Discrete or continuous variation in voice settings is then depicted as deviations from the reference/neutral setting.

Following the basic pattern outlined in Laver's work [24], one can then attempt to classify voice qualities primarily in terms of description of the position of the articulators. For annotation we used a simple set of labels derived from Laver's terminology e.g. Labial protrusion = LP, Laryngopharyngealized = LPH, Denasal = DN, Harsh whispery creaky falsetto = HWCF, etc. Laver´s classification scheme is considered to be carefully worked-out, and it is being used widely. Despite this, however, some speech qualities are not covered, e.g. smiling or weepy speech. In producing these types of speech, complex positioning of the articulators (wide high/top and wide and low/bottom mouth corner positioning) along with special phonation modes (vibrato etc.) are used, and these are not included in the scheme. Pathological phenomena occurring in spoken utterances, whether acted or natural, such as lisping, stammering, muttering are not included in the scheme either; we have added the PAT (Pathological) annotation mark for them.

Considering prosodic features, we denote slow speech as SRL (Speech rate low), fast speech as SRH (Speech rate high), large pitch range as PRH (Pitch range high), small pitch range as PRL (Pitch range low), and low voice pitch is denoted as LOW.

A complex feature covering both voice quality and prosody is vocal effort. We denote high vocal effort as VEH (Vocal effort high) and low vocal effort as VEL (Vocal effort low).

4.5. Relationship between personalities and acoustic characteristics

We have analyzed 24 voices (the actor's own voice and 23 characters) presented by a puppeteer and we summarize the results in Tables 3 and 4. The numbers representing the highest observed correlation are written in Bold and highlighted. These data can be used for a first analysis of mutual links among personality factors, semantic and articulatory-acoustic features.

As expected, the 2D analysis performed on a relatively limited number of data – does not provide clear answers to the queries related to coding of personality characters by aesthetic-semantic and acoustic speech means. However, the results in Table 3 still suggest some dependencies. For example, negative moral features (MN) can be observed with neurotic (N1), extrovert (E1) and competitive (A-1) characters. Comical characters (EC) are often neurotic (N1). High social position (SH) is connected with calmness (N-1), extroversion

(E), openness to new impressions (O) and strong-mindedness (C). Similar personality characteristics also tend to correlate with wisdom (IH). Results in Table 4 suggest that actors use mostly pitch changes in their voice (LOW+F+CF=22.95%) to express diversity of characters. While female voices (F+CF=12.57% of the total of assigned acoustic marks) are naturally expressed by falsetto, low voices (LOW=10.38% acoustic marks) correlate robustly with the N-1 factor, i.e. with calm and self-assured nature, and obviously with orderliness and resolution (C1).

Additionally, most often used acoustic means include speech rate (SRH+SRL=12.57%) and voice effort intensity (VEH+VEL=12.57%). High speech rate is usually related to neuroticism (N1), extroversion (E1), but also to competitiveness and assertiveness (A-1). On the other hand, slow speech (SRL) tends to be linked to reliability (C1). Considerable range of frequencies of the basic tone in melodic structures (PRH) and high voice effort (VEH), have also been used several times to express neurotic and extrovert nature. More data would be necessary for us to be able to evaluate the function of additional voice properties.

5. Texts of dramatic pieces

DRAPER is meant for reading pieces from various areas of dramatic art in future. However it is still under development and it was decided to prove the concept first on the set of traditional puppet plays. Therefore we use for our first experiments a collection of the texts of puppet shows covering most of the repertoire of the traditional folk Slovak puppeteer Bohuslav Anderle (father of Anton Anderle who presented the puppeteer art to us). The pieces were recorded by Bohuslav Anderle himself in nineteen-seventies and reconstructed, transcribed, edited and published recently by one of the authors of this study, Juraj Hamar [21]. The collection consists of 28 complete puppet plays.

One could reasonably argue that there is no need to create synthesized versions of the games if there are recordings of the text spoken by the puppeteer. The sound quality of the original recordings is very low and is therefore not suitable for publication. On the other hand it can serve as a good study material and reference in evaluation of the quality of our first synthesized dramatizations.

6. Dramatic Piece Reader DRAPER

We have developed a software system for reading texts of dramatic works of art and called it "Dramatic Piece Reader - DRAPER". It makes use of available set of synthesizers with different expressive load and with wide possibilities to change the characteristics of voices. The schematic diagram of DRAPER is shown in Figure 4.

6.1. DRAPER architecture

With a help of human expert, the Operator, who controls, checks and fine-tunes the text pre-processing and voice assignment, the system creates sound-files of dramatic pieces where every character have a special voice with default acoustical characteristics automatically predicted according to the simple Operator's description. Illustrative sounds can be added wherever it is appropriate (see the following chapter).

After the operator has chosen the text of the dramatic piece to be read the automatic text preprocessing is done. It automatically identifies the characters and shows the list of the characters to the operator. For every character the operator has to manually choose the type of every character (see Table 5).

Table 3. *Counts and mutual occurrences of personality dimensions and semantic characteristics.*

***	XM	XF	HH	HN	AO	AY	MP	MN	ET	EC	RO	RF	SH	SL	IH	IL	*SUMA*	%
Neurotic	3	**4**	**4**	2	2	1	2	**4**		**4**	3		1	**4**		3	**37**	**13,41**
Confident	**4**	2	**4**	1	2	1	3	1	1	1		1	3	1	3		**28**	**10,14**
Extravert	**7**	2	**7**	1	3		2	4		3	2	2	2	5		2	**42**	**15,22**
With-drawn	2	1	**3**		1		1	1		2	1	1		**3**		1	**17**	**6,159**
Open	**3**	2	**3**		1	1	2		1	1	1		2	1	**3**		**21**	**7,609**
Conservative	2	2	**4**		1	1	3	1		2	1	1		3			**21**	**7,609**
Agreeable	**5**	4	**5**	3	2	1	**5**	2		2	1		2	3	3	2	**40**	**14,49**
Competitive	2	3	3	2	2			**5**	1				2			1	**21**	**7,609**
Conscientious	**8**	3	6	4	2		4	3	1	1		1	4	1	2		**40**	**14,49**
Careless	1		**2**		1					1		**2**		**2**			**9**	**3,261**
SUM	**37**	**23**	**41**	**13**	**17**	**5**	**22**	**21**	**4**	**17**	**9**	**8**	**16**	**23**	**11**	**9**	**276**	**100**
%	13,4	8,3	14,9	4,7	6,2	1,8	8,0	7,6	1,4	6,2	3,3	2,9	5,8	8,3	4,0	3,3	100	***

Table 4. *Counts and mutual occurrences of personality dimensions and voice characteristics.*

***	PAT	SRH	SRL	PRH	PRL	VEH	VEL	LOW	WV	F	CF	HV	RL	TV	MV	LV	LS	CR	LP	LL	N	BV	DN	*SUMA*	%
Neurotic	**3**	**4**		2		3				3	1		2	1			2				2			**23**	**12,57**
Confident			3		2		2	**5**	1	2		1				2		2	1	2		1		**24**	**13,11**
Extravert	**2**	**4**		2		3		2		2		1	1	1	1		2				1	2	2	**26**	**14,21**
With-drawn	**1**		**2**		1		1					1									1			**7**	**3,825**
Open	**1**			1			**2**			**2**			1	1	**2**									**10**	**5,464**
Conservative		1	**2**		1		1	**2**		1		1	1			1		1		1				**13**	**7,104**
Agreeable	**2**	1		1		2	**3**	2		**5**				1	1	1	2	1	1		2			**25**	**13,66**
Competitive		**3**		1		**3**		1		2	1	1					2			1				**15**	**8,197**
Conscientious			3	1	2	2	1	**5**	1	3	1	2		1	1	2	2	2	1	3		1		**34**	**18,58**
Careless								**2**														**2**	**2**	**6**	**3,279**
SUM	**9**	**13**	**10**	**8**	**6**	**13**	**10**	**19**	**2**	**20**	**3**	**7**	**5**	**5**	**5**	**6**	**10**	**6**	**3**	**7**	**6**	**6**	**4**	**183**	**100**
%	4,9	7,1	5,5	4,4	3,3	7,1	5,5	10,4	1,1	10,9	1,6	3,8	2,7	2,7	2,7	3,3	5,5	3,3	1,6	3,8	3,3	3,3	2,2	100	***

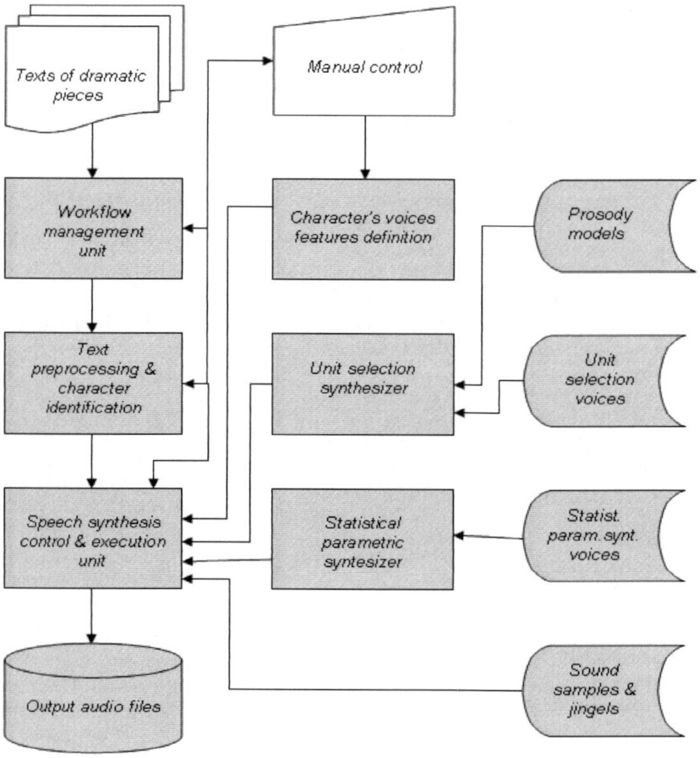

Figure 4: *Schematic diagram of the virtual Dramatic Piece Reader.*

The system then offers a default voice for every character. One arrow means a shift approximately 30 Hz in AvgF0, 15% in AvgSr and 30% in PDepth. The operator can then open the Synthesizer settings window, try the voice with the offered parameter setting and eventually fine-tune the settings for every particular voice. Fine-tuning of the voice can be done also for a smaller part of the text (e.g. whispering or crying only several words).

The sentences ending with exclamation mark are automatically labeled with a tag causing they will be read with expressivity increased by one level (if available).

One of the most important tasks of the operator is to check the text for the words with unusual pronunciation (e.g. names or foreign words) and use the find-replace function of the text editor to replace their written form for the text representation of their pronunciation in Slovak ("write it the way you hear it").

All the preparation of the text for synthesis is technically done by adding tags to the source text. The basic text to be processed is the pure text of the utterances of the characters and the text of director notes, descriptions of the stage and other comments.

Special tags designating the changes of voices and voice parameters are automatically inserted at the appropriate places in the text under the control of Operator.

6.2. A comment on speech temporal dynamics

At various emotions, the same character can have different dynamics of speech. Sometimes he speaks quickly, sometimes slowly, but most often he speaks in a quasi neutral manner. This speed can be set in the Synthesizer settings.

But this is only a so called linear (or horizontal) dynamics applied to the utterance of one character. It is followed (in a vertical direction downwards in the text) by an utterance of another character. The vertical dynamics reflects the dynamics of the dialogue, dynamics of taking the ground, of the speed of changing the characters. If they are speaking calmly, there is a "normal" more or less short pause between the utterances of the characters. However, if the dialogue is expressive (argument, hassle, fear, threats, etc..) the cadence of rotation of the characters in the dialogue is much faster, almost without pause.

Table 5. *The basic set of default voices that the Operator has available.*

Character archetype	Characteristics	Synt. Voice	Avg F0	AvgSr	Pros. Depth
Neutral male	father, comment reader	Unit-sel.	135 Hz = male refe-rence	standard	100%
Leading man	royal type	Unit-sel.	↓	↓	↓
coy	weak	HMM level-2	↑	↓	↓
bigmouth	convivial, folksy	HMM level+2	↑	↑	↑
Negative male	intriguer	HMM level+2	-	-	↑
Very bad man	malicious	HMM level+2	↓↓	↓	↓
Neutral female	mother, comment reader	Unit-sel.	240 Hz = female Refe-rence	standard	100%
Leading woman	royal type	Unit-sel.	↓	↓	↓
Timid woman	shy, un-experienced	HMM level-2	↑	↓	↓
Jovial woman	convivial, folksy	HMM level+2	↑	↑	↑
Negative female	intriguer	HMM level+2	-	-	↑
Very bad woman	malicious	HMM level+2	↓↓	↓	↓
Ghost	Whispering	HMM whisper	-	-	-
Comment reader	neutral to less expressive	HMM level 0	-	-	-

Special marks can be inserted in the text in DRAPER to shorten or lengthen the pauses between replicas of two characters.

7. Commentary reading and Illustrative sounds - Acousticons

One voice has to be dedicated to the Commentary reader, which reads the comments of the theater script, e.g.: "He arrives on the scene; She hits the robber with a stick; He falls to the ground; She catches Kuranto's hand; She hides behind the statue; There is a small cabin near the forest.; etc ...". This voice should be neutral or with a slightly lower expressivity, but distinguishable from the voices of the characters.

Some actions and phenomena mentioned in the text, for example knocking, ringing, strike, whistle, snoring etc... could be expressed in the acoustic form. Similarly there are different changes of voice qualities, mood, presence of emotions, or speaker non-lexical sounds identified in the text, e.g.: "tearfully, for himself, in a whisper, seriously, screams, angry ...". Finally, from time to time it is marked in the comment or it is obvious from the text itself, that the character sings the text as a song. Other situations, where the insertion of sounds can be suitable are interjections "Br, brrr" that are usually used when the devil comes. This is also often accompanied by a sound of thundering.

To get an idea of what sounds and what kind of emotionally colored voices are required by the comments, we have analyzed several hundred pages of scenarios of puppet plays.
The examples are from the collection of all 28 games. We list the sounds, emotions or voice modulations that we found in [25].

Sounds: knocking on the door (15 times) , ringing the bell (5 times), whizzing (2 times), striking clocks (4 times), whistling (6 times), snoring (2 times).

Voices: angry (2 times), shouting (4 times), parodying (11 times), crying (13 times), moaning, sobbing (15 times), to himself (13 times), whispering (9 times).

We have therefore included a possibility in DRAPER to insert illustrative sounds in the synthesized speech.

The 256 sounds (acoustic emoticons) are organized in a system of 16 thematically oriented subsets (Transporticons, Zooticons, Sporticons, Eroticons, Partycons, etc.) and are inserted using an easy to remember code. This set of sounds, called SOUNDI we have developed earlier for SMS to Voice service in telecommunications [26].

The Operator can decide which of the instructions (comments) should be read and which should be performed. Some of them can be done by changing the settings of voices and some by insertion of the illustrative sounds.

The letter in the code designates the class and every sound in the class has its own number.

The second way of inserting the sounds is to remember the names of the sound file, which is listed in the full definition of SOUNDI specification (e.g. kiss1 = E1, or gallop = S2).

In further versions of DRAPER the SOUNDI sound database will be enriched and changed substantially including the possibility to use user defined sound samples.

8. Conclusions and future work

Expectations that speech synthesis will be widely used for reading text aloud by readers of electronic books failed to become truth. The reason is that the readers have greater experience from their own reading than listening to synthetic speech, which is often unnatural and is unable to credibly convey the personality of the characters, their moods and emotions.

The possibilities of visually impaired readers are more limited. If the book is not available in Braille, or if their computer is not equipped with Braille display, they would probably like to use to the audio-books. Unfortunately, these are produced in quite a small amount. For this group of people we offer speech synthesis software, which is capable of presenting various characters and their personality.

Similar activities of other researchers in this area [27] [28] indicate that this is a well-grounded approach that will hopefully bring even better effectiveness in producing naturally sounding audio-books in future.

One of the goals of our research was to improve our understanding of the acoustic and auditory correlates of personality dimensions. We introduced a novel approach to the analysis of functional variation, i.e. the need to express personalities of particular characters, in the speech and vocal features of a puppeteer.

Table 6. *The descriprtion of SOUNDI database of sound samples.*

Code	Class	Description	Examples
A1-A16	Acoustic emoticons	sounds reflecting human feelings, moods and attitude to the text	short giggling, laughter, devil laughter, Oooops..., Wow!, Yeees!, sad groan ... Sounds suitable for acoustic interpretation of the graphical emoticons.
B1 - B16	Babycons	Acoustic displays of children	children giggling, cry, etc.
E1 - E16	Eroticons	Sounds of love, passion, sex, yearning	kisses, hard beating, sniff, screams, orgasm etc.
V1 - V16	Vulgaricons	Indecent sounds, "dirty sounds" or sounds on the boundary of social acceptability	Fart, belch, spittle, vomit, squelch, hiccup, snore... Whether You like it or not, these sounds belong to the most marketable.
Z1 - Z16	Zooicons	Acoustic displays of animals	Roaster, dog, cat, horse, lion, hen, pig, goat, donkey, mouse, snake, gadfly...
I1 - I16	Symbolicons	Illustrative and symbolical sounds	Church bell, clocks, gun shot, circular saw, glass crack, doors, toilet, etc.
T1 - T16	Transporticons	Sounds of transport means and vehicles	Human steps, horse gallop, car alarm, car crash, car brakes, locomotive, firemen car, ambulance, etc.
P1 - P16	Partycons	Sounds of party and having fun with friends	Filling a glass with a drink, pinging with glasses, opening a bottle of vine, opening a bottle of champagne, sipping, step dancing, Cheers, drunk singing, etc.
S1 - S16	Sportikons	Sports	Table tennis, tennis, judge's whistle, gong, mountaineer falling from a rock, stadium atmosphere, etc.
J1 - J16	Instrumenticons	Jingles or sounds played by musical instruments	Jaw harp, cymbal, church organ, drums, ethnic instruments, etc.
M1-M16	Melodicons	Fragments of the well known melodies with a symbolical meaning	Jingle bells, Happy birthday, Wedding march, etc.

We argued that the system of stylized personality expressions by a puppeteer provides an excellent source of information both for understanding cognitive aspects of social communicative signals in human-human interactions as well as for utilization of observed patterns of human behavior in applications based on interactive voice systems in human machine interactions.

Most important feature of the DRAPER system is, that with a help of human operator it can convert high volume of books into audio form and make them accessible to the blind. The sound-files that will be distributed by the Slovak library for the blind in a form of copy protected files without a violation of the copyright law.

We presented our virtual dramatic piece reader at the conference Accessibility of audiovisual works to the visually impaired - a means of social inclusion and awareness, Bratislava 2012, organized by Blind and Partially Sighted Union of Slovakia. The quality of the generated speech was evaluated as a surprisingly good and acceptable also for longer texts.

At present DRAPER is still under development, but it is already capable of generating sound-files. The formal subjective evaluation tests have not been carried out yet, as we want to further improve our HMM voices through improvements in the vocoder. More work is still needed to make the system less dependent on human operator and to match the automatic text preprocessing to the requirements of this special task.

Our further work will be aimed at adapting the Manual control interface so that it can be operated by a blind person. We also plan experiments with the development of over-articulated highly expressive voice, as the intelligibility of the highest level of expressive speech synthesis is often a bit lower than needed.

Regardless of how 'natural' text to speech can sound, it does not compare to the emotion and performance that an actor can bring to a performed audio book. [3] However the authors of this work try to take steps towards automatic reading of dramatic works in a quality acceptable for the blind and partially sighted people.

Demo sound-files generated by DRAPER can be downloaded from http://speech.savba.sk /DRAPER.

9. Acknowledgements

This publication is the result of the project implementation: Technology research for the management of business processes in heterogeneous distributed systems in real time with the support of multimodal communication, RPKOM, ITMS 26240220064 supported by the Research & Development Operational Programme funded by the ERDF.

10. References

[1] http://unss.sk/sk/aktuality/2012-zvukova-kniha.php, accessed on 19 March 2013.

[2] http://thewritersguidetoepublishing.com/how-does-audio-book-narration-work-heres-the-scoop-from-d-d-scotts-a-mazing-narrator-christine-padovan

[3] http://www.rnib.org.uk/livingwithsightloss/reading/how/ebooks/accessibility/Pages/text-to-speech.aspx accessed on 19 March 2013.

[4] Raimundo, G., Cabral, J., Melo, C., Oliveira, L. C., Paiva, A., Trancoso, I.: Telling Stories with a Synthetic Character: Understanding Inter-modalities Relations, In: Verbal and Nonverbal Communication Behaviours Lecture Notes in Computer Science Volume 4775, 2007, pp 310-323.

[5] Buurman H.A.: Virtual Storytelling: Emotions for the narrator, Master's thesis, University of Twente, August 2007, 113 pages.

[6] Vegh, N.: Commented movies and audio book first realized artificial voice on the website SKN, Accessibility of audiovisual works of art to the visually impaired - a means of social inclusion and awareness organized by Blind and Partially Sighted Union of Slovakia, Bratislava 2012.

[7] Darjaa, S., Trnka, M.: Corpus Based Synthesis in Slovak with Simplified Unit Cost and Concatenation Cost Computation. Proceedings of the 33rd International Acoustical Conference - EAA Symposium ACOUSTICS, High Tatras 2006, Štrbské Pleso, Slovakia. ISBN 80-228-1673-6, pp. 316-319.

[8] Darjaa, S., Trnka, M., Cerňak, M., Rusko, M., Sabo, R., Hluchý, L.: HMM speech synthesizer in Slovak. In GCCP 2011 : 7th International Workshop on Grid Computing for Complex Problems. - Bratislava : Institute of Informatics SAS, 2011, p. 212-221.

[9] Rusko, M., Hamar, J.: Character Identity Expression in Vocal Performance of Traditional Puppeteers. In: Text, Speech and Dialogue, 9th International Conference, TSD 2006, Brno, Czech Republic. LNAI 4188, pp. 509-516.

[10] Rusko, M., Hamar, J., Benus, S.: Acoustic, semantic and personality dimensions in the speech of traditional puppeteers, Proceedings Coginfocom 2012, Košice, Slovakia, 2012, pp.83-88.

[11] Greene, E., Mishra, T., Haffner, P., Conkie, A.: Predicting Character-Appropriate Voices for a TTS-based Storyteller System, INTERSPEECH 2012.

[12] Rusko, M., Daržágín, S., Trnka, M., Cerňak, M.: Slovak Speech Database for Experiments and Application Building in Unit-Selection Speech Synthesis. In: Proceedings of Text, Speech and Dialogue, TSD 2004, Brno, Czech Republic, pp. 457 – 464.

[13] Rusko, M. Darjaa, S., Trnka, M., Cerňak, M.: Expressive speech synthesis database for emergent messages and warnings generation in critical situations. In Language Resources for Public Security Workshop (LRPS 2012) at LREC 2012 Proceedings, Istambul, 2012, p. 50-53.

[14] Zhang, Ch., Hansen , J., H., L.: Analysis and classification of speech mode: whispered through shouted., Interspeech 2007, 8th Annual Conference of the International Speech Communication Association, Antwerp, Belgium, 2007, pp. 2289-2292.

[15] Rusko, M., Trnka, M., Daržágín, S.: Three Generations of Speech Synthesis Systems in Slovakia. In: Proceedings of XI International Conference Speech and Computer, SPECOM 2006, Sankt Peterburg, Russia, 2006, pp. 297-302.

[16] Hunt, A.J. Black, A.W.: Unit selection in a concatenative speech synthesis system using a large speech database, ICASSP-96. Conference Proceedings., 1996 IEEE International Conference on Acoustics, Speech, and Signal Processing, 1996, pp. 373–376.

[17] Zen, H., Tokuda, K., & Black, A. W. (2009). Statistical parametric speech synthesis. Speech Communication, 51(11), 1039-1064.

[18] Breiman, Friedman, Stone, Ohlsen: Classification and Regression Trees. Chapman Hall, New York, USA, 1984.

[19] Rusko M., Trnka M., Darjaa S., Kováč R.: Modelling acoustic parameters of prosody in Slovak using Classification and Regression Trees. In: Human Language Technologies as a Challenge for Computer Science and Linguistics - Proceedings. Poznań, Poland, 2007. ISBN 978-83-7177-407-2, pp. 231-235.

[20] http://hts.sp.nitech.ac.jp, accessed on 13 Dec 2012.

[21] Egges, A., Kshirsagar, S., Magnenat-Thalmann, N.: Imparting Individuality to Virtual Humans. First International Workshop on Virtual Reality Rehabilitation, pp. 201-108, 2002.

[22] Digman, J. M., Personality structure: Emergence of the five factor model, Annual Revue of Psychology, 41, pp. 417-440, 1990.

[23] McRae, R.R., John, O.P.: An introduction to the five-factor model and its applications, Journal of Personality 60, pp.175-215, 1992.

[24] Laver, J., The gift of speech, Edinburgh, UK: Edinburgh University Press, 1991.

[25] Hamar, J. , Puppet Plays of the Traditional Puppeteers, (in Slovak) Slovak Center for Traditional Culture, 2010, 655 pages.

[26] Rusko M., Daržagín S., Trnka M.: "Multilinguality, Singing Synthesis, Acoustic Emoticons and Other Extensions of the Slovak Speech Synthesizer for SMS Reading", ICA 2004, Kyoto, Japan, 2004, pp. IV.3345-IV.3348.

[27] Doukhan, D., Rosset S., Rilliard, A., d'Alessandro, Ch., Adda-Decker, M.: Designing French Tale Corpora for Entertaining Text To Speech Synthesis. LREC 2012: 1003-1010.

[28] Székely, É., Kane J., Scherer S., Gobl Ch., Carson-Berndsen J.: Detecting a targeted voice style in an audiobook using voice quality features. ICASSP 2012: 4593-4596.

Sub-lexical Dialogue Act Classification in a Spoken Dialogue System Support for the Elderly with Cognitive Disabilities

Ken Sadohara[1], Hiroaki Kojima[1], Takuya Narita[2], Misato Nihei[2], Minoru Kamata[2], Shinichi Onaka[3], Yoshihiro Fujita[3], Takenobu Inoue[4]

[1]National Institute of Advanced Industrial Science and Technology (AIST), Japan
[2]The University of Tokyo, Japan
[3]NEC Corporation, Japan
[4]Research Institute of National Rehabilitation Center for Persons with Disabilities, Japan

ken.sadohara@aist.go.jp

Abstract

This paper presents a dialogue act classification for a spoken dialogue system that delivers necessary information to elderly subjects with mild dementia. Lexical features have been shown to be effective for classification, but the automatic transcription of spontaneous speech demands expensive language modeling. Therefore, this paper proposes a classifier that does not require language modeling and that uses sub-lexical features instead of lexical features. This classifier operates on sequences of phonemes obtained by a phoneme recognizer and exhaustively analyzes the saliency of all possible sub-sequences using a support vector machine with a string kernel. An empirical study of a dialogue corpus containing elderly speech showed that the sub-lexical classifier was robust against the poor modeling of language and it performed better than a lexical classifier that used hidden Markov models of words.

Index Terms: dialogue acts, support vector machines, string kernels, spontaneous speech, elderly speech, dementia

1. Introduction

This paper presents an information support system for elderly subjects with cognitive disabilities. The target users have difficulties maintaining their attention and absorbing new information, so this system tries to maintain conversations with them to deliver information necessary for their independent and autonomous life in a similar way to their caregivers. Thus, this system needs to recognize colloquial speech and to understand the intentions of utterances so that it can respond sufficiently correctly to sustain conversations. The assignment of an utterance with a predefined functional tag that represents the communicative intentions behind the utterance is referred to as dialogue acts (DAs) classification, which is considered to be a useful first step in dialogue processing. This paper proposes a DA classification method for the colloquial utterances made by the elderly to facilitate the production of an appropriate correct response.

Many studies of DA classification have shown that word n-grams are effective features for determining DAs [1, 2, 3, 4]. To obtain the lexical feature, the automatic transcription of colloquial speech is required. However, some difficulties of the speech recognition have been discussed in previous studies of spontaneous speech recognition [5, 6]. Spontaneous speech includes disfluencies (e.g., filled pauses, repairs, hesitations, repetitions, false starts, or partial words) [7], pronunciation variation [8, 9], and speaking rate variation [10, 9]. For the colloquial speech considered in this paper, its casual style of speech, the speech characteristics of the elderly subjects and the noisy room environment create additional difficulties in terms of the acoustics and language modeling. Among these difficulties, this paper focuses on the difficulty of language modeling.

As pointed out before in many studies, individuals differ not only in their acoustics but also in their lexical patterns. The difference is particularly great in spontaneous speech, so speaker-dependent language modeling has been considered a potential approach to cope with the variation. For example, the quantity of disfluencies varies depending on the speaker, so different models of different classes of speakers are effective for removing disfluencies [7]. Disfluency removal is useful because disfluencies cause problems during subsequent higher-level natural language processing such as DA classification. Another study [8, 9] showed that the lexical pattern used during lecture speech is quite variable among speakers, so language model adaptation to a specific speaker is effective for lecture speech recognition. This can be achieved provided a relatively long speech is available for each lecturer. Unfortunately, the cost of speaker-dependent language modeling is prohibitive in our application because it is difficult to obtain sufficient data to build speaker-dependent language models.

The limitation of the lexicon itself has also been noted. During spontaneous speech, the actual pronunciation of a word can vary greatly from its canonical pronunciation because of sloppy pronunciation, word contractions, or co-articulation between words. To address this variation, a previous study [11] proposed a data-driven dictionary adaptation that adds new entries for words that correspond to the actual pronunciations appearing in given corpora that are obtained using a phoneme recognizer. Another study [9, 12] also found that the use of multiple surface forms for each word baseform is effective for reducing the word error rate during the recognition of spontaneous Japanese speech. In the Japanese language, the different surface forms can be represented as different words, which ensures that they are faithful to the actual pronunciation. Thus, these words can be included as different baseforms in a dictionary. The existence of different representations of a single morpheme can have a harmful effect on DA classification, so it is necessary to normalize the recognized text by replacing the different representations with the corresponding baseform. Unfortunately, the normalization process is not straightforward, unlike word stemming.

Elaborate language modeling is required to transcribe spontaneous speech faithfully but faithful transcription without normalization is not necessarily useful for our immediate goal of DA classification. To explore the utilization of lexical features in a more cost-efficient manner, this paper proposes a sub-lexical DA classifier that does not require language modeling and that operates on the sequences of phonemes obtained using a phoneme recognizer. The central hypothesis of this study is that if word n-grams are effective indicators for determining DAs, then sub-sequences of phonemes, which are fragments of words in a sense, should also be effective indicators. If this hypothesis is true, then even when effective language modeling is impossible and some salient words are misrecognized, it is expected that their fragments should be preserved, so a more robust form of DA classification based on fragments is possible. Furthermore, the use of phonemes facilitates the analysis of the saliency of the fragments based on the actual pronunciation while considering the patterns of misrecognition for each speaker. Other features such as prosodic features have been investigated [13] to compensate for inherently useful but unreliable and costly lexical features in colloquial speech, but this paper investigates the utilization of lexical features in a more robust and computationally inexpensive manner.

This paper is organized as follows. After describing our information support system and the DAs used in our elderly speech corpus in the next section, Section 3 presents the sub-lexical DA classifier. Section 4 presents an empirical study of the effectiveness of the classifier.

2. DAs used by our assistive system

People with mild dementia, who exhibit memory impairment, disorientation, and an impaired executive function, may use assistive devices [14, 15, 16] to compensate for their problems with absorbing or retaining new information, which have been shown to be effective in their independent and autonomous life. Our information support system is another general-purpose assistive device that was designed to provide information about schedules, times, or dates during conversations [17, 18]. The target users have difficulties maintaining their attention and absorbing information, so the system tries to maintain a conversation with a user based on the following protocol: (1) *attention-seeking* captures the user's attention, which is diminished by dementia; (2) *pre-sequence* prepares the user's mind for absorbing new information; (3) *distributing information* delivers the necessary information; and (4) *end of interaction* closes the conversation. During each stage of the conversation, the system can ask whether the user is following the conversation and can go back to a previous stage if necessary.

To facilitate the computational modeling of the transition of dialogue states, we designed the 12 dialogue acts (DAs) described in Table 1. DAs, which are representations of the communicative intention of each utterance, have been considered integral to the understanding and production of natural dialogue, and they are useful for various forms of speech and language processing, such as speech retrieval, summarization, resolution of ambiguous communication, or the improvement of speech recognition. This paper defines the specific set of DAs used by our application, although efforts to develop domain-independent sets of DAs exist such as DAMSL [19]. Each user utterance is classified as one of the 12 DAs and the system produces an appropriate response based on the classification.

Thanks to the cooperation of 20 single people who were living in nursing homes, we built a dialogue corpus between

Table 1: *Dialogue acts and their frequency of occurrence (percentages). The inter-labeler agreement was* 81.9% *and* $\kappa = 0.782$.

Tag	Example	%
Question	What did you eat for dinner?	0.2
Confirmation	Can you understand?	8.2
Request Action	Would you like to go to the bathroom?	4.3
Request Attention	May I ask a question?	15.1
Request Repeat	Pardon?	2.1
Affirmative Answer	Yes, I can.	26.9
Negative Answer	No, I can't.	0.2
Statement	I ate fish.	60.0
Greeting	How are you?	15.1
Affirmative Backchannel	Sure it is.	19.9
Negative Backchannel	Really?	0.2
Other	`Laughter, Filler`	5.4

the system and the users. The details of the participants are as follows: 3 were male and the other 17 were female, the average age was 82.9 ± 7.2 (ranging from 67 to 97), and the average MMSE score [20] was 21.4 ± 5.8 (from 9 to 30). In total, 7,123 utterances were transcribed and annotated, of which 4,080 were user utterances. The total length of user utterances was about 115 hours and the average length of them is about 1.7 ± 1.6 seconds (from 0.2 seconds to 14.8 seconds). The DAs were annotated by two labelers and the inter-labeler agreement was 81.9%, while κ was 0.782.

3. Classification of DAs

The automatic classification of DAs comprises two important components: features and modeling methods. The features investigated previously used various types of knowledge, e.g., lexical [21, 1, 2, 3, 22, 4, 23], syntactic [22, 24], prosodic [13, 1, 3, 22, 23], and discourse structural [25, 1]. In this study, sub-lexical features, i.e., sequences of phonemes, were considered together with the DA of the preceding utterance as contextual knowledge. To examine the effectiveness of the sub-lexical feature, typical lexical features, i.e., word n-grams, were also considered together with the contextual knowledge.

These features are used by various modeling methods, e.g., decision trees [13], transformation-based learning [26], hidden Markov models (HMMs) [1], maximum entropy models [22], conditional random fields [27], and support vector machines (SVMs) [3, 4]. To facilitate an exhaustive analysis of all the sub-sequences of phonemes, an SVM with a string kernel based on phonemes was used in this study. Before describing the sub-lexical classifier, we describe a typical classifier based on HMMs of words using a simpler formalization that was obtained by restricting the formalization in [1] to our problem.

3.1. Lexical DA classifiers with HMMs

In a previous study [1], based on the assumption that each observation E_i is emitted from an unobservable DA U_i and the prior distribution of U is Markovian, the optimal sequences U^* of DAs were obtained as follows:

$$U^* = \operatorname*{argmax}_U \prod_{i=1}^{n} P(U_i|U_{i-1})P(E|U_i). \qquad (1)$$

In our application, the preceding DA U_{i-1} is observable because the corresponding utterance is given by the system. Therefore, given an utterance of the system with a DA U_R, it is sufficient to maximize the following equation to obtain the optimal DA U^* of the subsequent utterances E of users,

$$U^* = \operatorname*{argmax}_U P(U|U_R)P(E|U). \quad (2)$$

When the observation E is a text, i.e., a sequence $W_1, \ldots, W_n$ of words and W_j is i.i.d.,

$$U^* = \operatorname*{argmax}_U P(U|U_R) \prod_{j=1}^{n} P(W_j|U). \quad (3)$$

When the observation E is a speech signal A represented in spectral features and is conditioned on the N-best texts $W^{(1)}, \ldots, W^{(n)}$ hypothesized by a speech recognizer, U^* is obtained as follows.

$$U^* = \operatorname*{argmax}_U P(U|U_R)P(A|U) \quad (4)$$

$$= \operatorname*{argmax}_U P(U|U_R) \sum_n^N P(A|U, W^{(n)})P(W^{(n)}|U) \quad (5)$$

$$= \operatorname*{argmax}_U P(U|U_R) \sum_n^N P(A|W^{(n)})P(W^{(n)}|U), \quad (6)$$

where the last equality holds under the assumption that $P(A)$ depends only on the words $W^{(n)}$, although this is not true in general because U affects the pronunciation of $W^{(n)}$. Although $P(A|W^{(n)})$ can be computed based on the acoustic likelihood of the speech recognizer, it tends to be a very small value. To avoid underflow, the maximization is computed using the maximum acoustic likelihood $M = \max_n P(A|W^{(n)})$ as follows.

$$U^* = \operatorname*{argmax}_U \frac{P(U|U_R)}{M} \sum_n^N P(A|W^{(n)})P(W^{(n)}|U) \quad (7)$$

$$= \operatorname*{argmax}_U P(U|U_R) \sum_n^N \exp(L(n)) \quad (8)$$

$$L(n) = \ln(P(A|W^{(n)})) - \ln(M) + \ln(P(W^{(n)}|U)) \quad (9)$$

In the rest of the paper, N is set as 10.

3.2. Sub-lexical DA classifiers with SVMs

The DA classifier presented in this paper operates on sequences of phonemes obtained using a phoneme recognizer. For any sequence of phonemes, the DA classifier analyzes whether any noncontiguous sub-sequence is salient to the discrimination of a particular class. The analysis is performed using an SVM [28, 29] by computing the optimal hyperplane that separates positive samples from negative samples in the feature space spanned by all possible sub-sequences of phonemes. Although the dimension of the feature space is exponential in terms of the length of sub-sequences, the analysis can be performed efficiently using string kernels [30].

A string kernel modified for the analysis of sequences of phonemes was investigated in a previous study [31] for topic segmentation. Given two sequences of phonemes, s and t, the string kernel computes the similarity between s and t efficiently in $O(p|s||t|)$, where p is the maximum length of sub-sequences. The similarity is computed based on the number of occurrences of any non-contiguous sub-sequence, where the occurrence count is decayed according to λ^g $(0 \leq \lambda \leq 1)$ for the number g of gaps in each sub-sequence. In the occurrence count, a soft-matching method is used between phonemes, which assigns 1 if they are identical and a value between 0 and 1 otherwise. Based on this definition of the similarity, the classifier is expected to be robust against insertion, deletion, and substitution errors of phonemes.

The kernel function is normalized and extended to consider the contextual DA of the preceding utterance as follows:

$$K_\ell(s,t) \stackrel{\text{def}}{=} \delta_{c(s),c(t)} \frac{\kappa_\ell(s,t)}{\sqrt{\kappa_\ell(s,s)}\sqrt{\kappa_\ell(t,t)}} \quad (10)$$

where κ_ℓ is the kernel function with the length ℓ of sub-sequences, as defined in [31], $c(s)$ is the DA of the preceding utterance of s, and $\delta_{c(s),c(t)} = 1$ if $c(s) = c(t)$, but 0 otherwise.

The string kernel is extended further to consider the weighted contributions of different lengths ℓ of sub-sequences as follows.

$$K^{\leq p}(s,t) \stackrel{\text{def}}{=} \sum_{\ell=1}^{p} \gamma_\ell K_\ell(s,t). \quad (11)$$

We can see that the kernel function satisfies the Mercer condition [29] required for SVM optimization because it is actually the inner-product of the feature space spanned by the sub-sequences of phonemes, although it is computed implicitly. In the rest of the paper, we assume $\gamma_k = 1$, $\lambda = 0.7$, and $p = 4$.

Using the string kernel, an SVM is trained to discriminate a particular class. Because an SVM is fundamentally a binary classifier, various methods have been considered for extending multiple SVMs to a multi-class classifier. In this study, the simple one-versus-the-rest approach is adopted, i.e., for each DA U, an SVM f_U is trained that discriminates U from the other DAs, and the optimal DA U^* for any sequence s of phonemes is obtained as $U^* = \operatorname{argmax}_U f_U(s)$.

In the same way as the previous section, the N-best hypotheses of a phoneme recognizer are considered as follows

$$U^* = \operatorname*{argmax}_U \sum_n^N P(A|s_n)f_U(s_n) \quad (12)$$

$$= \operatorname*{argmax}_U \sum_n^N \exp(\ln(P(A|s_n)) - \ln(M))f_U(s_n) \quad (13)$$

where M is the maximum acoustic likelihood $M = \max_n P(A|s_n)$.

4. Empirical study

The aim of the empirical study was to verify the effectiveness of the sub-lexical DA classifier. In the experiments described below, several classifiers were trained for 4,080 user utterances and DAs of the utterances were predicted. For each user, the utterances from the first several days were used for training while the rest were used for testing. As a result, 1,920 utterances were used for training and 2,160 utterances were used for testing. Because the training data contain a small number of samples with the following four tags: *Request Action*, *Request Attention*, *Negative Answer*, and *Negative Backchannel*, for the remaining eight tags, eight classifiers were trained and tested.

The transcriptions were obtained manually and automatically, where the latter was conducted using a large-vocabulary continuous speech recognizer, Julius [32]. Its dictionary and

Table 2: *Accuracy and F-measure of a lexical classifier using HMMs and a sub-lexical classifier using SVMs for manual (MT) and automatic (ASR) transcription.*

	word-HMM		phone-SVM	
	Accuracy	F1	Accuracy	F1
MT	0.800	0.521	0.817	0.624
ASR	0.758	0.521	0.789	0.563

word trigram model were built from the training data. The number of entries in the dictionary was 1,008, the test set perplexity of the language model was 17.97, and the OOV rate was 6.37%. Its acoustic model was a gender-independent PTM triphone model of elderly speech [33] distributed by CSRC [34], which was adapted to each speaker using the MLLR method [35]. The word error rate in the test data were 58%. Phonetic transcriptions were obtained using the same decoder, except a phoneme trigram model was trained and used where the phoneme error rate was 46%.

During the training of classifiers for manual transcriptions, transcribed texts or sequences of phonemes converted from the texts were used. On the other hand, during the training of classifiers for automatic transcriptions, the five best hypotheses of the output of the speech recognizers for the training data were used as well as the texts or the sequences of phonemes obtained from the manual transcriptions. For the parameters of SVMs, we used $\lambda = 0.7$, $\gamma = 1.0$, $C = 10.0$, and p was set as $p = 4$ because the average lengths of the words were 4.8 phonemes.

During the evalution of the classifiers, texts or sequences of phonemes obtained form manual or automatic transcriptions for the test data were used. Especially for automatic transcriptions, the 10 best hypotheses of the output of the speech recognizers with the acoustic likelihood of them are used.

Table 2 summarizes the results of the experiments where the accuracy indicates the ratio of correct predictions and F1 indicates the average harmonic mean of the precision and recall, i.e., the F-measure averaged across DAs. We can see that the phone-SVM, i.e., the sub-lexical DA classifier with SVMs, performed better than the word-HMM, i.e., the lexical DA classifier with HMMs in both the manual and automatic transcriptions. The difference in the manual transcription was significant ($p < 0.05$) according to McNemar's test and the difference in the automatic transcription was also significant ($p < 0.01$). In the following section, these results are discussed in more detail.

4.1. Robustness of the sub-lexical DA classifier

Figure 1 depicts the accuracy of the two classifiers during manual and automatic transcription for the convenience of the reader. It also shows the result of the word-HMM for another automatic transcription, which was obtained using a cheating language model built from all of the data including the test data. The number of entries in the dictionary for the cheating model was 1,587, the test set perplexity was 4.70, and the word error rate was 32.6%. There was no significant difference between ASR and ASR(CHEAT), which suggests that the accuracy would not be improved even if a better language model could be obtained from a larger amount of training data. Thus, it is unlikely that that the accuracy of the word-HMM would improve without an elaborate language modeling and text normalization for spontaneous speech. Furthermore, the accuracy of word-HMM would become worse as the mismatches between

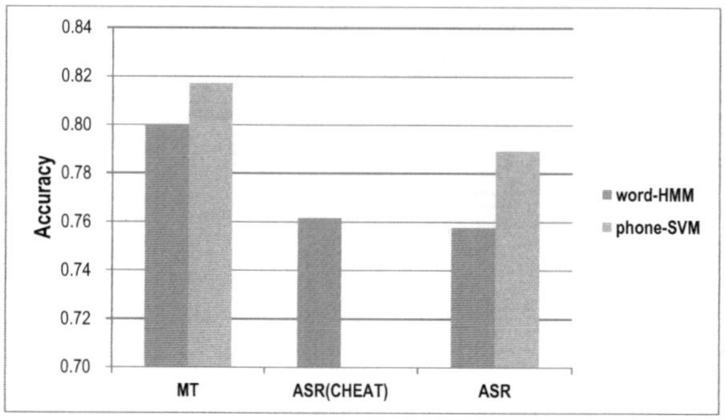

Figure 1: *The lexical classifier vs. the sub-lexical classifier.*

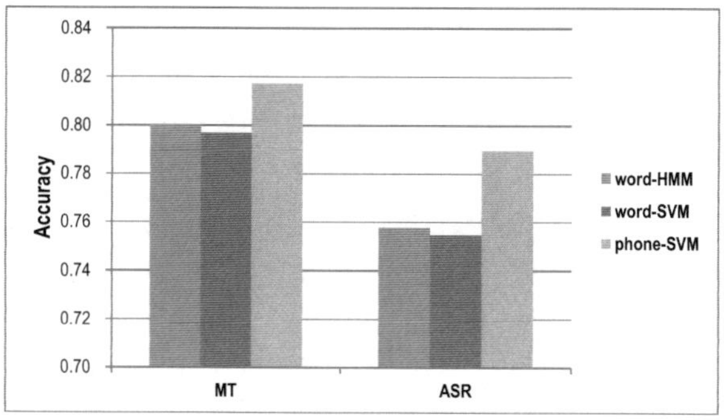

Figure 2: *Lexical features vs. sub-lexical features.*

the language model and the corpus increased. On the other hand, the accuracy of the phone-SVM would not decline because the sub-lexical classifier does not depend on the language model.

4.2. Effectiveness of the sub-lexical features

Figure 2 shows another result of a SVM (word-SVM) using the bag-of-words feature that operates on the feature spaces spanned by the frequency of each word appearing in the training data. The performance of word-SVM was worse than that of phone-SVM, and its performance was not significantly different from that of word-HMM. This suggests that the superior performance of phone-SVM was not attributable to the SVM-based modeling method, but instead it was due to the sub-lexical features.

In particular, the difference between the word-SVM and phone-SVM results with manual transcription was due only to the difference between the lexical feature and the sub-lexical feature. A possible explanation for this difference is that the existence of multiple surface forms of a baseform degraded the performance of word-SVM. Using phone-SVM, however, the common fragments of the different surface forms allowed us to capture salient properties for DA classification.

Furthermore, the difference between word-SVM and phone-SVM in ASR was larger than in MT. The results for both classifiers were obtained using the same decoder and the same acoustic model, so the bigger difference may have been because some salient word features were lost by the poor modeling of language, whereas some fragments of the salient features were still preserved with phone-SVM.

5. Conclusion and future work

This paper proposed a sub-lexical DA classifier for use as a dialogue management module in a spoken dialogue system that provides necessary information to elderly users with cognitive disabilities. To avoid costly and difficult language modeling when transcribing the colloquial utterances of the elderly users in a faithful manner, the classifier determines the DAs based on the sequences of phonemes obtained using a phoneme recognizer. Instead of searching for salient word features used by many lexical classifiers, the sub-lexical classifier searches for salient sub-sequences of phonemes while considering possible misrecognitions, i.e., insertion, deletion, and substitution errors. To search the space spanned by the exponentially many features efficiently, the proposed method uses an SVM with a string kernel based on sequences of phonemes. An empirical study was conducted using a dialogue speech corpus collected from elderly subjects with mild dementia. The sub-lexical classifier was found to be robust against the poor modeling of language, while it performed better than a lexical classifier using HMMs.

These results are now limited to our small and simple dialogue corpus, which contains only four thousands short (1.7 seconds on average) user utterances, and only 8 of 12 DA tags have been tested. The effectiveness of the sub-lexical DA classifier should be investigated for larger and well-studied corpora. The DA classification itself does not essentially need any faithful transcription of spontaneous speech. We believe the analysis of the frequency of sub-sequences of phonemes instead of the frequency of words is effective especially when the faithful transcription is hard to obtain. Furthermore, the robust and cost-efficient use of the sub-lexical feature without language modeling could be more effective when it is used together with other non-lexical features, e.g., prosody.

6. Acknowledgements

We would like to thank Seikatsu Kagaku Un-Ei Co. Ltd. This work was supported partially by the Japan Science and Technology Agency, JST, as part of the Strategic Promotion of Innovative Research and Development Program.

7. References

[1] A. Stolcke, K. Ries, N. Coccaro, E. Shriberg, R. Bates, D. Jurafsky, P. Taylor, R. Martin, C. V. Ess-Dykema, and M. Meteer, "Dialogue act modeling for automatic tagging and recognition of conversational speech," *Computational Linguistics*, vol. 26, no. 3, pp. 1–34, 2000.

[2] N. Webb, M. Hepple, and Y. Wilks, "Dialogue act classification based on intra-utterance features," in *Proceedings of the AAAI Workshop on Spoken Language Understanding*, 2005.

[3] D. Surendran and G. A. Levow, "Dialog act tagging with support vector machines and hidden Markov models," in *Proceedings of the Annual Conference of the International Speech Communication Association*, 2006.

[4] B. Gambäck, F. Olsson, and O. Täckström, "Active learning for dialogue act classification," in *Proceedings of the Annual Conference of the International Speech Communication Association*, 2011.

[5] S. Furui, "Spontaneous speech recognition and summarization," in *Proceedings of the Baltic Conference on Human Language Technologies*, pp. 39–50, 2005.

[6] E. Shriberg, "Spontaneous speech: how people really talk and why engineers should care," in *Proceedings of the European Conference on Speech Communication and Technology*, 2005.

[7] M. Honal and T. Schultz, "Automatic disfluency removal on recognized spontaneous speech - rapid adaptation to speaker-dependent disfluencies," in *Proceedings of the IEEE International Conference on Acoustics, Speech, and Signal Processing*, 2005.

[8] H. Nanjo and T. Kawahara, "Unsupervised language model adaptation for lecture speech recognition," in *Proceedings of the ISCA & IEEE Workshop on Spontaneous Speech Processing and Recognition*, 2003.

[9] H. Nanjo and T. Kawahara, "Language model and speaking rate adaptation for spontaneous presentation speech recognition," *IEEE Transactions on Speech and Audio Processing*, vol. 12, no. 4, pp. 391–400, 2004.

[10] H. Nanjo and T. Kawahara, "Speaking-rate dependent decoding and adaptation for spontaneous lecture speech recognition," in *Proceedings of the IEEE International Conference on Acoustics, Speech, and Signal Processing*, pp. 725–728, 2002.

[11] T. Sloboda and A. Waibel, "Dictionary learning for spontaneous speech recognition," in *Proceedings of the International Conference on Spoken Language Processing*, pp. 2328–2331, 1996.

[12] Y. Akita and T. Kawahara, "Statistical transformation of language and pronunciation models for spontaneous speech recognition," *IEEE Transactions on Audio, Speech, and Language Processing*, vol. 18, no. 6, pp.1539–1549, 2010.

[13] E. Shriberg, A. Stolcke, D. Jurafsky, N. Coccaro, M. Meteer, R. Bates, P. Taylor, K. Ries, R. Martin, and C. V. Ess-Dykema, "Can prosody aid the automatic classification of dialog acts in conversational speech?," in *Language and speech*, vol. 41, no. 3-4, pp. 443–492, 1998.

[14] T. Inoue, R. Ishiwata, R. Suzuki, T. Narita, M. Kamata, M. Shino, and M. Yaoita, "Development by a field-based method of a daily-plan indicator for persons with dementia," in *Assistive Technology from Adapted Equipment to Inclusive Environments: AATE 2009*, pp. 364–368, IOS Press, 2009.

[15] "Cognitive aids", Online: http://www.abilia.org.uk, accessed on 24 Mar 2013.

[16] "Automatic pill dispenser", Online: http://www.pivotell.co.uk/, accessed on 24 Mar 2013.

[17] M. Nihei, T. Narita, R. Ishiwata, M. Onoda, M. Shino, H. Kojima, S. Ohnaka, Y. Fujita, M. Kamata, and T. Inoue, "Development of an interactive information support system for persons with dementia," in *Proceedings of the International Technology and Persons with Disabilities Conference*, 2011.

[18] T. Inoue, M. Nihei, T. Narita, M. Onoda, R. Ishiwata, I. Mamiya, M. Shino, H. Kojima, S. Ohnaka, Y. Fujita, and M. Kamata, "Field-based development of an information support robot for persons with dementia," *Technology and Disability*, vol. 24, no. 4, pp.263–271, 2012.

[19] M. Core and J. Allen, "Dialogs with the DAMSL annotation scheme," in *Working Notes of the AAAI Fall Symposium on Communicative Action in Humans and Machines*, pp. 28–35, 1997.

[20] M. F. Folstein, S. E. Folstein, and P. R. McHugh, *Mini-mental state: a practical method for grading the cognitive state of patients for the clinician*, Pergamon Press, 1975.

[21] D. Jurafsky, E. Shriberg, B. Fox, and T. Curl, "Lexical, prosodic, and syntactic cues for dialog acts," in *Proceedings of the Workshop on Discourse Relations and Discourse Markers*, pp. 114–120, 1998.

[22] V. K. R. Sridhar, S. Bangalore, and S. Narayanan, "Combining lexical, syntactic and prosodic cues for improved online dialog act tagging," *Computer Speech & Language*, vol. 23, no. 4, pp. 407–422, 2009.

[23] N. G. Ward and A. Vega, "Towards empirical dialog-state modeling and its use in language modeling," in *Proceedings of the Annual Conference of the International Speech Communication Association*, 2012.

[24] J. O'Shea, Z. Bandar, and K. Crockett, "A multi-classifier approach to dialogue act classification using function words," *Transactions on Computational Collective Intelligence VII*, pp. 119–143, 2012.

[25] D. Jurafsky, R. Bates, N. Coccaro, R. Martin, M. Meteer, K. Ries, E. Shriberg, A. Stolcke, P. Taylor, and C. V. Ess-Dykema, "Automatic detection of discourse structure for speech recognition and understanding, " in *Proceedings of the IEEE Workshop on Automatic Speech Recognition and Understanding*, pp. 88–95, 1997.

[26] K. Samuel, Sandra. Carberry, and K. Vijay-Shanker, "Dialogue act tagging with transformation-based learning," in *Proceedings of the International Conference on Computational Linguistics*, pp. 1150–1156, 1998.

[27] S. Quarteroni, A. V. Ivanov, and G. Riccardi, "Simultaneous dialog act segmentation and classification from human-human spoken conversations," in *Proceedings of the IEEE International Conference on Acoustics, Speech and Signal Processing*, pp. 5596–5599, 2011.

[28] V. Vapnik, *The Nature of Statistical Learning Theory*. Springer-Verlag, 1995.

[29] N. Cristianini and J. Shawe-Taylor, *An Introduction to Support Vector Machines*. Cambridge Press, 2000.

[30] H. Lodhi, C. Saunders, J. Shawe-Taylor, N. Cristianini, and C. Watkins, "Text classification using string kernels," *Journal of Machine Learning Research*, vol. 2, pp. 419–444, 2002.

[31] K. Sadohara, "Kernel topic segmentation for informal multi-party meetings and performance degradation caused by insufficient lexicon," in *Proceedings of the IEEE Workshop on Spoken Language Technology*, pp. 430–435, 2010.

[32] A. Lee, T. Kawahara, and K. Shikano, "Julius — an open source real-time large vocabulary recognition engine," in *Proceedings of the European Conference on Speech Communication and Technology*, pp.1691–1694, 2001.

[33] A. Baba, S. Yoshizawa, M. Yamada, A. Lee, and K. Shikano, "Elderly acoustic model for large vocabulary continuous speech recognition," in *Proceedings of the European Conference on Speech Communication and Technology*, pp.1657–1660, 2001.

[34] A. Lee, T. Kawahara, K. Takeda, M. Mimura, A. Yamada, A. Ito, K. Itou, and K. Shikano, "Continuous speech recognition consortium: an open repository for CSR tools and models," in *Proceedings of the International Conference on Language Resources and Evaluation*, pp. 1438–1441, 2002.

[35] C. Leggetter and P. Woodland, "Maximum likelihood linear regression for speaker adaptation of continuous density hidden Markov models," *Computer Speech and Language*, vol. 9, pp. 171–185, 1995.

Experimental Evaluation of Speech Recognition Technologies for Voice-based Home Automation Control in a Smart Home

Michel Vacher[1], *Benjamin Lecouteux*[1], *Dan Istrate*[2], *Thierry Joubert*[3], *François Portet*[1], *Mohamed Sehili*[2], *Pedro Chahuara*[1]

[1]LIG, UMR5217 UJF/CNRS/Grenoble-INP/UPMF, 38041 Grenoble, France
[2]ESIGETEL, 77210 Avon - France
[3]THEORIS, 75000 Paris - France

{Michel.Vacher,Benjamin.Lecouteux,Pedro.Chahuara, Francois.Portet}@imag.fr
dan.istrate@esigetel.fr, mohamed.sehili@esigetel.fr, thierry.joubert@theoris.fr

Abstract

This paper presents an audio-based interaction technology that lets the user have full control over her home environment and at detecting distress situations for the elderly and frail population. We introduce the PATSH framework which performs real-time recognition of voice commands anywhere in the home and detail its architecture and the state-of-the-art processing technologies it employs. This system was evaluated in a realistic Smart Home with three user groups: seniors, visually impaired people and people with no special needs. Results showed the validity of the PATSH approach and shed light on its usability for people with special needs.

Index Terms: Real-time audio analysis, experimental in-situ evaluation, Smart Home, Ambient Assisted Living

1. Introduction

Due to the demographic change and ageing in developed countries, the number of older persons is steadily increasing. In this situation, the society must find solutions to allow these people to live in their home as comfortably and safely as possible by assisting them in their daily life. This concept, known as Ambient Assisted Living (AAL) aims at anticipating and responding to the special needs of these persons. In this domain, the development of Smart homes and intelligent companions is seen as a promising way of achieving in-home daily assistance [1]. However, given the diverse profiles of the senior population (e.g., low/high technical skill, disabilities, etc.), complex interfaces should be avoided. Nowadays, one of the best interfaces seems to be the speech interface, that makes possible interaction using natural language so that the user does not have to learn complex computing procedures or jargon. Moreover, it is well adapted to people with reduced mobility and to some emergency situations because the user doesn't need to be close to a switch ("hands free" system). Despite all this, very few Smart Home projects have seriously considered speech recognition in their design [2, 3, 4, 5, 6, 7, 8]. Part of this can be attributed to the complexity of setting up this technology in a real environment and to important challenges that still need to be overcome [9].

In order to make in home voice control a success and a benefit for people with special needs, we argue that a complete framework for audio analysis in Smart Home must be designed. This framework should be able to provide real-time response, to analyse concurrently several audio channels, to detect audio events, to filter out noise and to perform robust distant speech recognition. Furthermore, in contrast with current triggered-by-button ASR systems commonly found in smart phone, this voice control should be able to work in an "hand free" manner in case the person is not able to move. Another important aspect is the respect for privacy: the system should not disseminate any raw personal data outside the home without the user's consent. Our approach, called PATSH is a step toward these goals. The originality of the approach is to consider these problems together while they have mostly been studied separately.

To the best of our knowledge, the main trends in audio technology in Smart Homes are related to augmented human machine interaction (e.g., voice command, conversation) and security (mainly fall detection and distress situation recognition). Regarding security, the main application is the fall detection using the signal of a wearable microphone which is often fused with other modalities (e.g., accelerometer) [4, 3]. However, the person is constrained to wear these sensors at all times. To address this constraint, the dialogue system developed by [6] was proposed to replace traditional emergency systems that requires too much change in the lifestyle of the elders. However, the prototype had a limited vocabulary (yes/no dialogue), was not tested with aged users and there is no mention about how the noise was taken into account. Most of the speech related research or industrial projects in AAL are actual highly focused on dialogue to build communicative agent (e.g., see the EU funded Companions or CompanionAble projects or the Semvox system [1]). These systems are often composed of ASR, NLU, Dialogue management and TTS parts supplying the user the ability to communicate with the system in an interactive fashion. However, it is generally the dialogue module (management, modelling, architecture, personalization, etc.) that is the main focus of these projects (e.g., see Companions, OwlSpeak or Jaspis). Moreover, this setting is different from the Smart Home one as the user must be close to the avatar to speak (i.e., not a distant speech setting). In [7], a communicative avatar was designed to interact with a person in a smart office. In this research, enhanced speech recognition is performed using beamforming and a geometric area of recording. But this promising research is still to be tested in a multiroom and multisource realistic home.

Designing and applying speech interfaces in Smart Home to provide *security reassurance* and *natural man-machine interaction* is the aim of the SWEET-HOME[2] project. With respect

[1]http://www.semvox.de
[2]http://sweet-home.imag.fr

to this short state-of-the-art, the project addresses the important issues of distant voice command recognition and sound source identification. The outcomes of this research are of high importance to improve the robustness of the systems mentioned above. In this paper, we introduce the PATSH system which perform the real-time identification of the voice command anywhere in the home. Its architecture and the state-of-the-art processing technologies employed are detailed in Section 2. This system was evaluated in a realistic Smart Home with three user groups: people with no special needs, seniors and, visually impaired people. These experiments are summarised in Section 3. PATSH was used on-line (vs. off-line) during the experiment, these results are analysed in Section 4. The paper finishes with a short outlook of future work.

2. The Audio Analysis System

The SWEET-HOME system is composed of an Intelligent Controller which analyses the streams of data and makes decision based on these. This framework acquires data from sensors and interprets them, by means of IA techniques, to provide contextual information for decision making. The description of this intelligent controller is out of the scope of the paper, the reader is thus referred to [12] for further details. This system uses a two-level ontology to represent the different concepts handled during the processing which also contains SWRL instances to automatise some of the reasoning. An important aspect is the relationship between the knowledge representation and the decision process which uses a dedicated Markov Logic Network approach to benefit from the formal logical definition of decision rules as well as the ability to handle uncertain facts inferred from real data. The location of the inhabitant was determined by the intelligent controller that analysed continuously the data stream of the smart-home (not only audio) and made decisions based on the recognized voice commands and this contextual information.

Therefore, the streams of data are composed of all the usual home automation data sensors (switches, lights, blinds, etc.), multimedia control (uPnP), and the audio events processed in real-time by the multi-channel audio analysis system: PATSH. Indeed, this section describes the overall architecture of PATSH, details the sound/speech discrimination and the ASR part.

2.1. PATSH framework

The global architecture of PATSH is illustrated in Figure 1. The PATSH framework is developed with the .Net cross platform technology. The main data structure is the **Sound object**, which contains a segment of the multidimensional audio signal whose interpretation is continuously refined during the processing pipeline. PATSH deals with the distribution of the data among the several plugins that perform the processing to interpret the audio events. The execution can be done, in parallel, synchronously or asynchronously, depending on the settings stored in a simple configuration file. In SWEET-HOME, the plugins were actually developed in C or C++ and PATSH includes the mechanism to transfer sound events from the plugins to the PATSH framework and vice-versa.

In the SWEET-HOME configuration, PATSH runs plugins that perform the following tasks:

1. Multichannel data Acquisition through the NI-DAQ6220E card. Seven channels are acquired at 16kHz (16 bits quantification);
2. Sound Detection and Extraction, detecting the start and end of sound events on each channel in parallel;
3. Sound/Speech Discrimination, discriminating speech from other sounds to extract voice commands;
4. Sound Classification, recognizing daily living sounds (not developed in this paper, see [13] for details);
5. Automatic Speech Recognition (ASR), applying speech recognition to events classified as speech and extracting vocal orders; and
6. Presentation, communicating the sound event to the Intelligent Controller. If a vocal order is detected and according to the context (activity and localisation of the user in the flat), a home automation command is generated to make the light up, close the curtains or emit a warning message thanks to a voice synthesizer.

The PATSH framework was developed to process on-line sound objects continuously detected on the 7 audio channels. However, it exists a bottleneck between the acquisition task and the event processing task. Given that one sound event can be simultaneously detected by several channels, the amount of the sound events in the queue can quickly rise.

2.2. Sound Event Detection

The detection of the occurrence of an audio event is based on the change of energy level of the 3 highest frequency coefficients of the Discrete Wavelet Transform (DWT) in a sliding window frame (last 2048 samples without overlapping). Each time the energy on a channel goes beyond a self-adaptive threshold, an audio event is detected until the energy decrease below this level for at least an imposed duration [2]. At the end of the detection, the Signal to Noise Ratio (SNR) is computed by dividing the energy in the event interval and the previous energy in a window outside this interval. This process is operated on each channel independently.

2.3. Sound/Speech Discrimination

Once sound occurrences are detected, the most important task is to distinguish speech from other sounds. In everyday life, there is a large number of different sounds, modelling all of them is irrelevant. For the SWEET-HOME project, distant voice command and distress situation detection, speech is the most important sound class. The method used for speech/sound discrimination is a GMM (Gaussian Mixture Models) classification.

The Sound/Speech Discrimination stage has a very important role: firstly, vocal orders must not be missed, secondly, daily living sounds must not be sent to the ASR because undesirable sentences could be recognized. To recognize only vocal orders and not all sentences uttered in the flat, all sound events shorter than 150 ms and longer than 2.2 seconds were ignored as well as those whose SNR is below 0 dB. These values were chosen after a statistical study on our data bases.

2.4. Voice order recognition

In a Smart Home, the microphones are generally set in the ceiling and on the wall. This places the study in a distant-speech context where microphones may be far from the speaker and may record different noise sources. Moreover, the application calls for quick decoding so that voice commands are sent as soon as possible to the intelligent controller. This is why we used the Speeral tool-kit [10] developed by the LIA

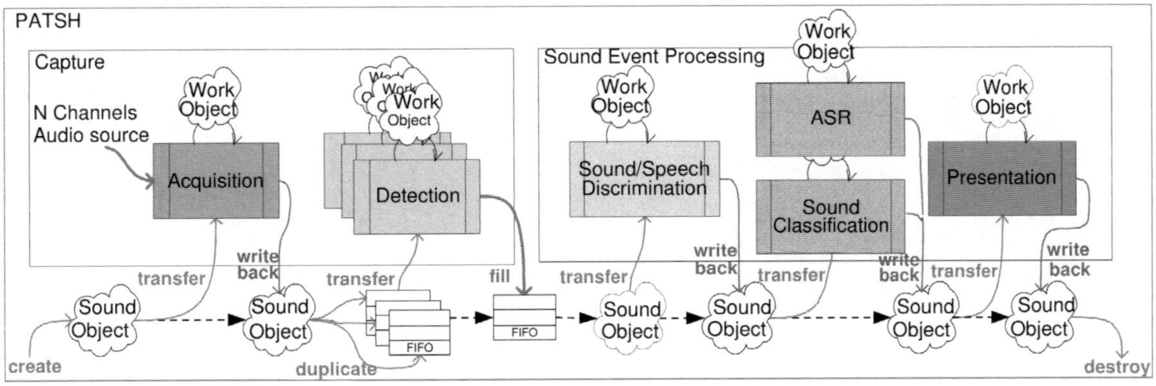

Figure 1: The PATSH architecture.

(Laboratoire d'Informatique d'Avignon). Indeed, its 1xRT configuration allows a decoding time similar to the signal duration. Speeral relies on an A^* decoder with HMM-based context-dependent acoustic models and trigram language models. HMMs are classical three-state left-right models and state tying is achieved by using decision trees. Acoustic vectors are composed of 12 PLP (Perceptual Linear Predictive) coefficients, the energy, and the first and second order derivatives of these 13 parameters.

The acoustic models of the ASR system were trained on about 80 hours of annotated speech. Furthermore, acoustic models were adapted to the speech of 23 speakers recorded in the same flat during previous experiments by using Maximum Likelihood Linear Regression (MLLR) [8]. A 3-gram Language Model (LM) with a 10K lexicon was used. It results from the interpolation of a *generic* LM (weight 10%) and a *domain* LM (weight 90%). The *generic* LM was estimated on about 1000M of words from the French newspapers *Le Monde* and *Gigaword*. The *domain* LM was trained on the sentences generated using the grammar of the application (see Fig. 3). The LM combination biases the decoding towards the *domain* LM but still allows decoding of out-of-domain sentences. A probabilistic model was preferred over using strictly the grammar because it makes it possible to use uncertain hypotheses in a fusion process for more robustness.

3. Experiments in real conditions

3.1. Experimental flat

Experiments were run in the DOMUS smart home. Figure 2 shows the details of the flat. It is a thirty square meters suite flat including a bathroom, a kitchen, a bedroom and a study, all equipped with 150 (konnex) KNX sensors and actuators. The flat has been equipped with 7 radio microphones set in the ceiling for audio analysis. A specialized communication device, *e-lio*, from the *Technosens* company was used to initiate a communication between the user and a relative.

3.2. Voice orders

Possible voice orders were defined using a very simple grammar as shown on Figure 3. Each order belongs to one of three categories: initiate command, stop command and emergency call. Except for the emergency call, every command starts with a unique key-word that permits to know whether the person is

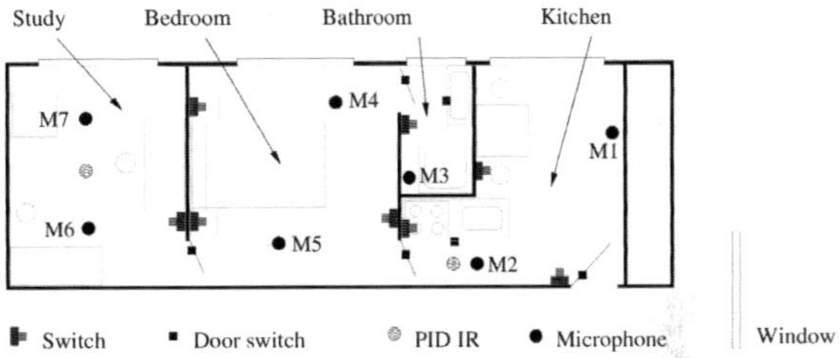

Figure 2: Position of the microphones and other sensors inside the DOMUS smart home.

talking to the smart home or not. In the following, we will use *'Nestor'* as key-word:

set an actuator on:	(e.g. `Nestor ferme fenêtre`) `key initiateCommand object`
stop an actuator:	(e.g. `Nestor arrête`) `key stopCommand [object]`
emergency call:	(e.g. `Nestor au secours`)

The grammar was built after a user study that showed that targeted users would prefer precise short sentences over more natural long sentences [11]. In this study, although most of the older people spontaneously controlled the home by uttering sentences, the majority said they wanted to control the home using keywords. They believe that this mode of interaction would be the quickest and the most efficient. This study also showed that they also had tendency to prefer or to accept the 'tu' form (informal in French) to communicate with the system given this system would be their property.

3.3. Scenarios and experiments

To validate the system in realistic conditions, we built scenarios in which every participant was asked to perform the following activities: (1) Sleeping; (2) Resting: listening to the radio; (3) Feeding: preparing and having a meal; and (4) Communicating: having a talk with a remote person thanks to *e-lio*. Therefore, this experiment allowed us to process realistic and representative audio events in conditions which are directly linked to usual daily living activities. Moreover, to evaluate the decision making, some specific situations were planned in the scenarios. For instance, for the decision regarding the activation of the light,

```
basicCmd          = key initiateCommand object |
                    key stopCommand [object] |
                    key emergencyCommand
key               = "Nestor" | "maison"
stopCommand       = "stop" | "arrête"
initiateCommand   = "ouvre" | "ferme" | "baisse" | "éteins" | "monte" | "allume" | "descend" |
                    "appelle" " | "donne"
emergencyCommand  = "au secours" | "à l'aide"
object            = [determiner] ( device | person | organisation)
determiner        = "mon" | "ma" | "l'" | "le" | "la" | "les" | "un" | "des" | du"
device            =  "lumière" | "store" | "rideau" | "télé" | "télévision" |
                     "radio" | "heure" | "température"
person            = "fille" | "fils" | "femme" | "mari" | "infirmière" | "médecin" | "docteur"
organisation      = "samu" | "secours" | "pompiers" | "supérette" | "supermarché"
```

Figure 3: Excerpt of the grammar of the voice orders (terminal symbols are in French)

given that the bedroom had two lights (the ceiling and the bedside one) as well as the kitchen (above the dinning table and above the sink), the four following situations were planed:

1. **Situation 1**. The person is having a meal on the kitchen table. The most appropriate light is the one above the table.
2. **Situation 2**. The person is cleaning up the bedroom. The most appropriate light is the ceiling one.
3. **Situation 3**. The person is cleaning the sink and doing the dishes. The most appropriate light is the one above the sink.
4. **Situation 4**. The person has just finished a nap. The most appropriate light is the bedside one.

Each participant had to use vocal orders to make the light on or off, open or close blinds, ask about temperature and ask to call his or her relative. The instruction was given to the participant to repeat the order up to 3 times in case of failure. In case of, a wizard of Oz was used in case of persistent problem.

Sixteen participants (including 7 women) without special needs were asked to perform the scenarios without condition on the duration. A visit, before the experiment, was organized to ensure that the participants will find all the items necessary to perform the scenarios. It was necessary to explain the right way to utter vocal orders and to use the *e-lio* system. Before the experiment, the participant was asked to read a text of 25 short sentences in order to adapt the acoustic models of the ASR for future experiments. The average age of the participants was 38 years (19-62, min-max) and the experiment lasted between 23min and 48min. The scenario includes at least 15 vocal orders for each participant but more sentences were uttered because of repetitions.

3.4. Acquired Corpus

During the experiment, audio data were recorded and saved in two ways. Firstly, the 7-channel raw audio signal was stored for each participant to make subsequent analysis possible. In total, 8h 52min 36s of data was recorded for the 16 participants. Secondly, the individual sound events automatically detected by PATSH were recorded to study the performances of this framework.

Apart from daily living sounds and sentences uttered in the flat by the participant, PATSH also detected the system messages (vocal synthesizer) and the *e-lio* communications. Overall, 4595 audio events were detected whose 993 were speech and 3503 were other noise occurrences. The number of events corresponding to each category –speech or everyday living sound– is displayed Table 1.

Table 1: *Number of audio events (speech and sound).*

Speaker ID	Speech and sound	Sound	Speech	Mis classified speech	Mis classified sound
S01	213	184	29	8	1
S02	285	212	73	10	6
S03	211	150	61	8	6
S04	302	211	91	10	11
S05	247	100	48	11	4
S06	234	189	45	17	6
S07	289	216	72	21	6
S08	249	190	59	25	3
S09	374	283	91	19	7
S10	216	163	53	10	4
S11	211	155	56	18	2
S12	401	346	55	13	13
S13	225	184	41	4	7
S14	235	173	62	9	10
S15	641	531	111	39	17
S16	262	216	46	10	5
ALL	4595	3503	993	232	108

In this study, we are only interested in recognizing vocal orders or distress sentences. All other spontaneous sentences and system messages are not irrelevant. Therefore, the global audio records were annotated using Transcriber in order to extract the syntactically correct vocal orders, results are shown in Table 2. The average SNR and duration are 15.8dB and 1s, this SNR value is low compared to studio conditions (SNR$\geq$35dB). As the home automation system needs only one correct sentence to interact, only the less noisy channel was kept. The number of vocal orders is different for each speaker because if a vocal order was not correctly recognized, the requested action was not operated by the intelligent controller (light on or off, curtains up or down...) and thus the speaker often uttered the order two or three times. Thanks to this annotation, an oracle corpus was extracted. The comparison between experimental real-time results with thus obtained with the same ASR on the oracle corpus will allow to analyse the performance of the PATSH system.

Table 2: *Number of syntactically correct vocal orders*

Speaker ID	Number	SNR (dB)	Speaker ID	Number	SNR (dB)
S01	20	17	S02	32	17
S03	22	19	S04	26	18
S05	26	12	S06	24	15
S07	19	25	S08	33	12
S09	40	20	S10	40	11
S11	37	14	S12	26	17
S13	21	14	S14	27	12
S15	28	14	S16	22	14
All	443	15.8			

Table 3: *Home automation order error rate (DER)*

Speaker ID	Expe. (%)	Oracle (%)	Speaker ID	Expe. (%)	Oracle (%)
S01	35	20	S02	12.5	6.2
S03	22.7	22.7	S04	23	7.7
S05	15	3.8	S06	21	8.3
S07	79	52.6	S08	30	33.3
S09	40	22.5	S10	67	47.5
S11	46	27	S12	21	7.7
S13	43	19	S14	48	29.6
S15	71	55.5	S16	18	13.6
Average	38%	23.9%			

4. Results

4.1. Discrimination between speech and sounds

The detection part of the system is not specifically evaluated because of the lack of time to label all the sound events on the 7 channels. However, all the results presented take into account the performances of the detection because the signals are extracted automatically by the system. The sound/speech discrimination misclassified 108 sound and 232 speech occurrences which gives a total error rate of about 7.4% which is in line with other results of the literature [13]. 23.4% of speech occurrences were classified as sound. Theses poor performances are explained by the fact that PATSH was not successful in selecting the best audio event among the set of simultaneous events and thus the events with low SNR introduced errors and were not properly discriminated. For the sounds, 3.1% of sound occurencies are classified as speech. Sounds such as dishes, water flow or electric motor were often confused with speech. For instance, when certain persons stirred the coffee and chocked the spoon on the cup or when they chocked plates and cutlery, the emitted sounds had resonant frequencies very close to the speech one. This is emphasizing the difficulty of the task and models must be improved to handle these problematic samples.

4.2. Home automation order recognition

The global performance of the system is directly related to vocal order recognition. The DER (Domotic Error Rate) is shown in Table 3, the 2nd and 5th columns "Expe." indicates the results for the real-time experiment. This error rate is evaluated after filtering at the input of the intelligent controller and includes the global effects of all stages: detection, discrimination between speech and sound, ASR. When the uttered voice orders were not respecting the grammar, for example when a sentence such as “Nestor heure” is uttered instead of the command “Nestor donne l’heure”, these utterances were discarded. Moreover, some speakers’ utterances exceeded the 2.2s duration threshold because of their hesitation, therefore corresponding vocal orders were not analysed and considered as missed. In case of music in the room, vocal orders were often longer because of the mixing between speech and music. Consequently future experiments will need to set the threshold to 2.5s and to include a short training step to allow the participant to become familiar with this technology.

The ASR system used generic acoustic models without adaptation to the speaker and then regional or foreigner accent may have an influence: it’s in particular the case for S10 (Arabic) and S14 (Alsatian). The participants S07 and S15 show low performance because they were not able to follow the given instructions, the presence of large part of silence mixed with noise between the words is analysed as phoneme and therefore increases the error rate.

Part of the errors was due to the way PATSH managed simultaneous detections of one sound event. At this time of the process, the SNR is not known with a sufficient precision and the choice is not perfect. Then, in some cases, a part of the speech signal is missed (beginning or end of the order) and this introduces a bad recognition. Moreover, very often the detection is not perfectly simultaneous and more than one channel is analysed by the ASR. Therefore, some improvement were introduced in PATSH for future experiments: that consisted in making the decision after the end of detection on the 7 threads (each thread corresponding to one channel) thanks to a filtering window of 500ms. The disadvantage is that the system is slowed down with a delay of 500ms but this will avoid the recognition of bad extracted sentences and this is compensated by the analysis of only the signal of the best channel.

An important aspect is the decoding time because the device must be activated with a delay as short as possible. In this experiment, the decoding times reached up to 4 seconds which was a clear obstacle for usage in real condition. Hopeful, this has been reduced.

5. Preliminary Results from experiments with the aged and visually impaired population

The method has also been applied in the same context but with aged and visually impaired people. The aim was both to validate the technology with this specific population and to perform a user study to assess the adequacy of this technology with the targeted users and to compare with the other user studies of the literature [14, 11].

Between the two experiments, several corrections were applied to PATSH so that the sound/speech discrimination was greatly improved as well as the speech decoding time. The measured decoding time was 1.47 times the sentence duration; as the average duration of a vocal order was 1.048s, the delay between the end of the utterance and the execution of the order was 1.55s. This is still not a satisfactory delay but this does not prevent usage in real conditions.

5.1. Experimental set up

In this experiment, eleven participants either aged (6 women) or visually impaired (2 women, 3 men) were recruited. The average age was 72 years (49-91, min-max). The aged persons were fully autonomous but were living alone. The participants were asked to perform 4 scenarios involving daily living activities and distress or risky situations.

1. The participant is eating her breakfast and is preparing to go out. She asked the house to turn on the light, close the blinds or ask for the temperature while doing these activities.
2. The participant is coming back from shopping and is going to have a nap. She asked the same kind of commands but in this case, a warning situation alerts about the front door not being locked.
3. The participant is going to the study to communicate with one relative through the dedicated e-lio system. After the communication, the participant simulates a sudden weakness and call for help.
4. The participant is waiting in the study for friends going to visit her. She tests various voice orders with the radio, lights and blinds.

During this experiment, 4 hours and 39 minutes of data was collected including the same sensors as the one previously described in Section 3.4.

5.2. First feedbacks

All the participants went through a questionnaire and a debriefing after the experiment. We are still in the process of analysing the results but overall, none of the aged or visually impaired persons had any difficulty in performing the experiment. They all appreciated to control the house by voice.

It is worth emphasizing that aged people preferred the manual interaction because this was quicker. However, they liked the voice warning in case of risky situations. Regarding the visually impaired participants, they found that the voice command would be more adequate if it could enable performing more complex or dangerous tasks than controlling blinds or radio. For instance, by enabling them to use the household appliances. Overall, half of the participants found the system adapted for their use.

6. Discussion

Overall, the performance of the system was still low but the results showed there is room for improvement. Sound/Speech discrimination has been improved since the beginning of the experiment and continue to be improved. The biggest problems were the response time which was unsatisfactory (for 6 participants out of 16) and the mis-understanding of the system which implied to repeat the order (8/16). These technical limitations were reduced when we improved the ASR memory management and reduced the search space. After this improvement, only one participant with special needs complained about the response time. None of the encountered problem challenged the PATSH architecture. That is why we are studying the possibility of releasing the code publicly.

The grammar was not the focus of the project but it has been built to be easily adaptable at the word level (for instance, if someone wants to change "Nestor" for another word). All the 16 participants found the grammar easy to learn. Only four of them found the keyword "Nestor" unnatural while the others found it natural and funny. However, this approach suffers a lack of natural adaptivity to the user's preferences, capacities and culture as any change would require technical intervention. For instance, [15] emphasized that elder Germans tend to utter longer and politer commands than their fellow countrymen which contrast with our findings. Despite longitudinal studies are require to understand human preferences regarding voice orders, methods to adapt on-line the grammar to the user must be developed.

The acquired corpus made it possible to evaluate the performance of the audio analysis software. But interest goes far beyond this experiment because it constitutes a precious resource for future work. Indeed, one of the main problems that impede researches in this domain is the need for a large amount of annotated data (for analysis, machine learning and reference for comparison). The acquisition of such datasets is highly expensive both in terms of material and of human resources. For instance, in a previous experiment involving 21 participants in the DOMUS smart home, the acquisition and the annotation of a 33-hour corpus has cost approximatively 70k€. Thus, making these datasets available to the research community is highly desirable. This is why we are studying the possibility of making part of it available to the society as we did in our previous project [16].

7. Conclusion

This paper presents the PATSH system, the audio processing module of the voice controlled SWEET-HOME system which performs real-time identification of voice commands in the home for assisted living. In this system, the identified sound events are sent to an intelligent controller for final context-aware decision about the action to make on the house [17]. The experiments made in the Smart Home to evaluate the system showed promising results and validate the approach. This technology can benefit both the disabled and the elderly population that have difficulties in moving or seeing and want security reassurance.

Our application of this technology within a realistic Smart Home, showed that one of the most sensible tasks is the speech/noise discrimination [9]. According to the SNR level, the performance can be quite poor, which has side effects on both the ASR and the sound classification (and then on the decision making). Another issue is linked to the lack of handling of simultaneous sound event records. These fill the sound object queue, which is the system bottleneck, and thus slow down the processing while real-time performances are required. To increase the performance and free this bottleneck, we had implemented a filtering strategy to remove low SNR audio events as well as too delayed events. The preliminary results showed a significant increase in performance. In a second step, PATSH will be modified to allow in real-time a multisource ASR thanks to the Driven Decoding Algorithm [18].

Although the participants had to repeat, sometimes up to three times, the voice command, they were overall very excited about commanding their own home by voice. We are still in the process of analysing the results of the experiment which included seniors and visually impaired people to get essential feedback from this targeted population. Future work will include improvements of the speech recognition in noisy environment and customisation of the grammar as well as experiments using specialised communication devices to enhance user's communication capacity.

8. Acknowledgements

This work is part of the SWEET-HOME project founded by the French National Research Agency (Agence Nationale de la Recherche / ANR-09-VERS-011). The authors would like to thank the participants who accepted to perform the experiments. Thanks are extended to B. Meillon, N. Bonnefond, D. Guerin, C. Fontaine and S. Pons for their support.

9. References

[1] M. Chan, D. Estève, C. Escriba, and E. Campo, "A review of smart homes- present state and future challenges," *Computer Methods and Programs in Biomedicine*, vol. 91, no. 1, pp. 55–81, 2008.

[2] D. Istrate, E. Castelli, M. Vacher, L. Besacier, and J.-F. Serignat, "Information extraction from sound for medical telemonitoring," *IEEE Transactions on Information Technology in Biomedicine*, vol. 10, pp. 264–274, April 2006.

[3] D. Charalampos and I. Maglogiannis, "Enabling human status awareness in assistive environments based on advanced sound and motion data classification," in *Proceedings of the 1st international conference on PErvasive Technologies Related to Assistive Environments*, 2008, pp. 1:1–1:8.

[4] M. Popescu, Y. Li, M. Skubic, and M. Rantz, "An acoustic fall detector system that uses sound height information to reduce the false alarm rate," in *Proc. 30th Annual Int. Conference of the IEEE-EMBS 2008*, 20–25 Aug. 2008, pp. 4628–4631.

[5] A. Badii and J. Boudy, "CompanionAble - integrated cognitive assistive & domotic companion robotic systems for ability & security," in *1st Congres of the Société Française des Technologies pour l'Autonomie et de Gérontechnologie (SFTAG'09)*, Troyes, 2009, pp. 18–20.

[6] M. Hamill, V. Young, J. Boger, and A. Mihailidis, "Development of an automated speech recognition interface for personal emergency response systems," *Journal of NeuroEngineering and Rehabilitation*, vol. 6, no. 1, p. 26, 2009.

[7] G. Filho and T. Moir, "From science fiction to science fact: a smart-house interface using speech technology and a photorealistic avatar," *International Journal of Computer Applications in Technology*, vol. 39, no. 8, pp. 32–39, 2010.

[8] B. Lecouteux, M. Vacher, and F. Portet, "Distant Speech Recognition in a Smart Home: Comparison of Several Multisource ASRs in Realistic Conditions," in *Interspeech 2011*, Florence, Italy, 2011, pp. 2273–2276.

[9] M. Vacher, F. Portet, A. Fleury, and N. Noury, "Development of Audio Sensing Technology for Ambient Assisted Living: Applications and Challenges," *International Journal of E-Health and Medical Communications*, vol. 2, no. 1, pp. 35–54, 2011.

[10] G. Linarès, P. Nocéra, D. Massonié, and D. Matrouf, "The LIA speech recognition system: from 10xRT to 1xRT," in *Proc. TSD'07*, 2007, pp. 302–308.

[11] F. Portet, M. Vacher, C. Golanski, C. Roux, and B. Meillon, "Design and evaluation of a smart home voice interface for the elderly: acceptability and objection aspects," *Personal and Ubiquitous Computing*, vol. 17, no. 1, pp. 127–144, 2013.

[12] P. Chahuara, F. Portet, and M. Vacher, "Context aware decision system in a smart home : knowledge representation and decision making using uncertain contextual information," in *The 4th International Workshop on Acquisition, Representation and Reasoning with Contextualized Knowledge (ARCOE-12)*, Montpellier, France, 2012, pp. 52–64.

[13] M. Sehili, B. Lecouteux, M. Vacher, F. Portet, D. Istrate, B. Dorizzi, and J. Boudy, "Sound Environnment Analysis in Smart Home," in *Ambient Intelligence*, Pisa, Italy, 2012, pp. 208–223.

[14] R. López-Cózar and Z. Callejas, "Multimodal dialogue for ambient intelligence and smart environments," in *Handbook of Ambient Intelligence and Smart Environments*, H. Nakashima, H. Aghajan, and J. C. Augusto, Eds. Springer US, 2010, pp. 559–579.

[15] F. Gödde, S. Möller, K.-P. Engelbrecht, C. Kühnel, R. Schleicher, A. Naumann, and M. Wolters, "Study of a speech-based smart home system with older users," in *International Workshop on Intelligent User Interfaces for Ambient Assisted Living*, 2008, pp. 17–22.

[16] A. Fleury, M. Vacher, F. Portet, P. Chahuara, and N. Noury, "A french corpus of audio and multimodal interactions in a health smart home," *Journal on Multimodal User Interfaces*, vol. 7, no. 1, pp. 93–109, 2013.

[17] M. Vacher, P. Chahuara, B. Lecouteux, D. Istrate, F. Portet, T. Joubert, M. Sehili, B. Meillon, N. Bonnefond, S. Fabre, C. Roux, and S. Caffiau, "The SWEET-HOME project: Audio processing and decision making in smart home to improve well-being and reliance," in *34th Annual International Conference of the IEEE Engineering in Medicine and Biology Society (EMBC'13)*, 2013.

[18] M. Vacher, B. Lecouteux, and F. Portet, "Recognition of voice commands by multisource ASR and noise cancellation in a smart home environment," in *EUSIPCO (European Signal Processing Conference)*, Bucarest, Romania, August 27-31 2012, pp. 1663–1667.

Towards Personalized Synthesized Voices for Individuals with Vocal Disabilities: Voice Banking and Reconstruction

Christophe Veaux, Junichi Yamagishi, Simon King

Centre for Speech Technology Research (CSTR), University of Edinburgh, UK
{cveaux, jyamagis}@inf.ed.ac.uk, Simon.King@ed.ac.uk

Abstract

When individuals lose the ability to produce their own speech, due to degenerative diseases such as motor neurone disease (MND) or Parkinson's, they lose not only a functional means of communication but also a display of their individual and group identity. In order to build personalized synthetic voices, attempts have been made to capture the voice before it is lost, using a process known as voice banking. But, for some patients, the speech deterioration frequently coincides or quickly follows diagnosis. Using HMM-based speech synthesis, it is now possible to build personalized synthetic voices with minimal data recordings and even disordered speech. The power of this approach is that it is possible to use the patient's recordings to adapt existing voice models pre-trained on many speakers. When the speech has begun to deteriorate, the adapted voice model can be further modified in order to compensate for the disordered characteristics found in the patient's speech. The University of Edinburgh has initiated a project for voice banking and reconstruction based on this speech synthesis technology. At the current stage of the project, more than fifteen patients with MND have already been recorded and five of them have been delivered a reconstructed voice. In this paper, we present an overview of the project as well as subjective assessments of the reconstructed voices and feedback from patients and their families.

Index Terms: HTS, Speech Synthesis, Voice Banking, Voice Reconstruction, Voice Output Communication Aids, MND.

1. Introduction

Degenerative speech disorders have a variety of causes that include Multiple Sclerosis, Parkinson's, and Motor Neurone Disease (MND) also known in the USA as Amyotrophic Lateral Sclerosis (ALS). MND primarily affects the motor neurones in the brain and spinal cord. This causes a worsening muscle weakness that leads to a loss of mobility and difficulties with swallowing, breathing and speech production. Initial symptoms may be limited to a reduction in speaking rate, an increase of the voice's hoarseness, or an imprecise articulation. However, at some point in the disease progression, 80 to 95% of patients are unable to meet their daily communication needs using their speech; and most are unable to speak by the time of their death [1]. As speech becomes difficult to understand, these individuals may use a voice output communication aid (VOCA). These devices consist of a text entry interface such as a keyboard, a touch screen or an eye-tracker, and a text-to-speech synthesizer that generates the corresponding speech. However, when individuals lose the ability to produce their own speech, they lose not only a functional means of communication but also a display of their individual and social identity through their vocal characteristics.

Current VOCAs are not ideal as they are often restricted to a limited set of impersonal voices that are not matched to the age or accent of each individual. Feedback from patients, careers and patient societies has indicated that there is a great unmet need for personalized VOCAs as the provision of personalized voice is associated with greater dignity and improved self-identity for the individual and their family [2].

In order to build personalized VOCAs, several attempts have been made to capture the voice before it is lost, using a process known as voice banking. One example of this approach is ModelTalker [3], a free voice building service that can be used from any home computer in order to build a synthetic voice based on diphone concatenation, a technology developed in the 1980s. The user of this service has to record around 1800 utterances in order to fully cover the set of diphones and the naturalness of the synthetic speech is rather low. Cereproc [4] has provided a voice building service for individuals, at a relatively high cost, which uses unit selection synthesis, and is able to generate synthetic speech of increased naturalness. Wants Inc. in Japan also provides a commercial voice building service for individuals called "Polluxstar". This is based on a hybrid speech synthesis system [5] using both unit selection and statistical parametric speech synthesis [6] to achieve a natural speech quality. However, all these speech synthesis techniques require a large amount of recorded speech in order to build a good quality voice. Moreover the recorded speech data must be as intelligible as possible, since the data recorded is either used directly or partly as the voice output. This requirement makes such techniques more problematic for those patients whose voices have started to deteriorate. Therefore, there is a strong motivation to reduce the complexity and to increase the flexibility of the voice building process so that patients can have their own synthetic voices build from limited recordings and even deteriorating speech.

Recently, a new voice building process using the hidden Markov model (HMM)-based speech synthesis technique has been investigated to create personalized VOCAs [7-8]. This approach has been shown to produce high quality output and offers two major advantages over existing methods for voice banking and voice building. First, it is possible to use existing speaker-independent voice models pre-trained over a number of speakers and to adapt them towards a target speaker. This process known as speaker adaptation [9] requires only a very small amount of speech data. The second advantage of this approach is that we can control and modify various components of the adapted voice model in order to compensate for the disorders found in the patient's speech. We call this process "voice reconstruction". Based on this new approach, the University of Edinburgh, the Euan MacDonald Center for MND and the Anne Rowling Regenerative Neurology Clinic have started a collaborative project for voice banking and voice reconstruction [10-11]. At the current stage of the project, more than 15 patients with MND have already been recorded and 5 of them have been delivered a reconstructed voice. We present here the technical concepts behind this project as well as a subjective assessment of the reconstructed voices.

2. HMM-Based Speech Synthesis

Our voice building process is based on the state-of-the-art HMM-based speech synthesizer, known as HTS [6]. As opposed to diphone or unit-selection synthesis, the HMM-based speech synthesizer does not use the recorded speech data directly as the voice output. Instead it is based on a vocoder model of the speech and the acoustic parameters required to drive this vocoder are represented by a set of statistical models. The vocoder used in HTS is STRAIGHT and the statistical models are context-dependent hidden semi-Markov models (HSMMs), which are HMMs with explicit state duration distributions. The state output distributions of the HSMMs represent three separate streams of acoustic parameters that correspond respectively to the fundamental frequency (logF0), the band aperiodicities and the mel-cepstrum, including their dynamics. For each stream, additional information is added to further describe the temporal trajectories of the acoustic parameters, such as their global variances over the learning data. Finally, separate decision trees are used to cluster the state durations probabilities and the state output probabilities using symbolic context information at the phoneme, syllable, word, and utterance level. In order to synthesize a sentence, a linguistic analyser is used to convert the sequence of words into a sequence of symbolic contexts and the trained HSMMs are invoked for each context. A parameter-generation algorithm is then used to estimate the most likely trajectory of each acoustic parameter given the sequence of models. Finally the speech is generated by the STRAIGHT vocoder driven by the estimated acoustic parameters.

3. Speaker Adaptation

One advantage of the HMM-based speech synthesis for voice building is that the statistical models can be estimated from a very limited amount of speech data thanks to speaker adaptation. This method [9] starts with a speaker-independent model, or **"average voice model"**, learned over multiple speakers and uses model adaptation techniques drawn from speech recognition such as maximum likelihood linear regression (MLLR), to adapt the speaker independent model to a new speaker. It has been shown that using 100 sentences or approximately 6-7 minutes of speech data is sufficient to generate a **speaker-adapted voice** that sounds similar to the target speech [7]. This provides a much more practical way to build a personalized voices for patients. For instance, it is now possible to construct a synthetic voice for a patient prior to a laryngectomy operation, by quickly recording samples of their speech [8]. A similar approach can also be used for patients with degenerative diseases before the diseases affect their speech. The speaker adaptation process is most successful when the average voice model is already close to the voice characteristics of the target speaker. Therefore, one goal of the voice-bank project is to record a large catalogue of healthy voices from which we can derive a set of average voice models corresponding to different age, gender and regional accents combinations. This will be presented in Section 5.

4. Voice Reconstruction

Some individuals with neurodegenerative disease may already have speech symptoms at the time of the recording. In that case, the speaker adaptation process will also replicate these symptoms in the speaker-adapted voice. Therefore we need to remove speech disorders from the synthetic voice, so that it sounds more natural and more intelligible. However since the HTS is based on a vocoder model of the speech, we can now exploit the acoustic models learned during the training and the adaptation processes in order to control and modify various speech features. This is the second major advantage of using HMM-based speech synthesis. In particular, HTS has statistically independent models for duration, log-F0, band aperiodicity and mel-cepstrum. This allows the substitution of some models in the patient's speaker-adapted voice by that of a well-matched healthy voice or an average of multiple healthy voices, as illustrated in Figure 1. Although disordered speech perceptually deviates considerably from normal speech in many ways, it is known that its articulatory errors are consistent [12] and hence relatively predictable [13]. Therefore we can pre-define a substitution strategy for a given condition, to some extent.

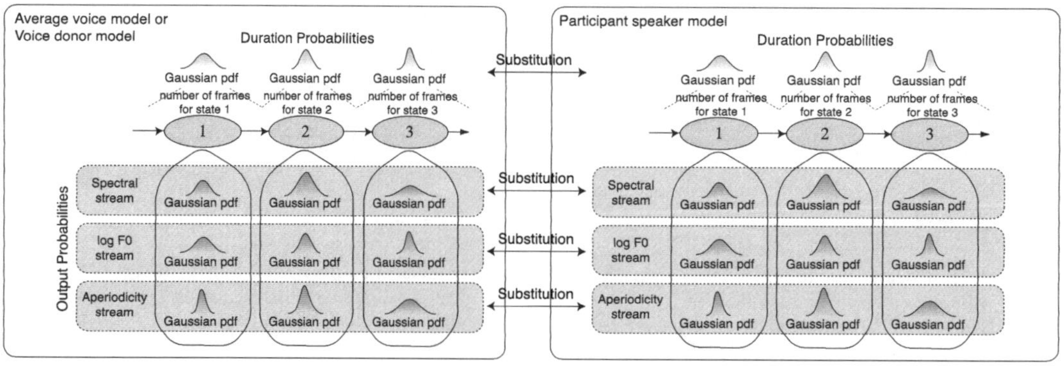

Figure 1: *The structure of the acoustic models in HTS means that there can be a substitution of state output or state duration models between an healthy voice model and the patient voice model in order to compensate for any deterioration in the patient's speech.*

For example, patients with MND often have a disordered speaking rate, contributing to a loss of the speech intelligibility. The substitution of the state duration models enables the timing disruptions to be regulated at the phoneme, word, and utterance levels. Furthermore, MND speakers often have breathy or hoarse speech, in which excessive breath through the glottis produces unwanted turbulent noise. In such cases, we can substitute the band aperiodicity models to produce a less breathy or hoarse output. In the following part of this section, we present different levels of model substitution. All these levels are combined in the final voice reconstruction process.

4.1. Baseline model substitution

In a first approach [7], the following models and information are substituted:

- Duration and aperiodicity models
- Global variances of log-F0, aperiodicity and mel-cepstrum

These parameters are the less correlated with the speaker identity and their substitution can fix some disorders such as slow speaking rate and excessive hoarseness. However, this substitution strategy cannot correct articulation disorders.

4.2. Component-wise model substitution

This is an extension of the baseline model substitution. Since the state output distributions have diagonal covariance matrix, we can substitute a component independently from the others. This component-wise substitution strategy allows to substitute the parts of the mel-cepstrum and log-F0 streams that are the less correlated with the speaker identity. In this way, we can further reduce some disorders without altering the voice identity. In particular, we substitute the mean and variance for the following components:

- 1st coefficient of the mel-cepstrum (energy)
- High-order coefficients of the mel-cepstrum
- Dynamics coefficients of the mel-cepstrum and log-F0
- Voiced/Unvoiced weights

The substitution of the high order static coefficients and the dynamics coefficients of the mel-cepstrum will help to reduce the articulation disorders without altering the timbre. In our implementation, we replace all static coefficients of order N>40. The substitution of the dynamics coefficients of the log-F0 will help to regulate the prosodic disorders such as monotonic F0. Finally the replacement of the voiced/unvoiced weights will fix the breathiness disorders. The duration models, aperiodicity models, and global variances are also substituted as in the baseline strategy. We will refer to this method as the **component-wise strategy**.

4.3. Context-dependent model substitution

In the two previous strategies, the model substitutions are independent of the context. However, in HTS, the acoustic models are clustered after their contexts by separate decisions trees. We can use this contextual information to further refine the model substitution. For example, some MND patients cannot pronounce correctly the plosives, the approximants and the diphthongs. In these contexts, it is preferable to substitute all the mel-cepstrum coefficients in order to enhance the intelligibility of the speech. Therefore, we have defined a **context-dependent strategy**, in which the mel-cepstrum models are entirely substituted for some specific contexts. Since these contexts may vary from one patient to the other, we have designed a screening procedure in which the patients have to read out a set of 50 sentences covering most of the phonetic contexts. Their speech is then assessed by a speech therapist in order to define the contexts for which the models are to be substituted. Finally, the context-dependent and the component-wise model substitutions are combined in order to get the final version of the repaired voice. Ideally the voice donors used for the voice reconstruction should share the gender, age range and regional accent of the patient since these factors are likely to contribute to the characteristics of the voice. This is why we need to record a large number of healthy voice donors with a variety of age and regional accents, as presented in the next section.

5. Database of Voice Donors

One of the key elements of the voice-banking project is the creation of a catalogue of healthy voices with a wide variety of accents and voice identities. This voice catalogue is used to create the average voice models for the speaker adaptation and to select the voice donors for the voice reconstruction. So far we have recorded about 500 healthy voice donors with various accents (Scottish, Irish, Other UK). This database is already the largest UK speech research database. An illustration of the geographical distribution of the speakers' birthplaces is shown on Figure 2. Each speaker has been recorded in a semi-anechoic chamber for about one hour using at each time a different script in order to get the best phonetic coverage on average. The database of healthy voices is first used to create the average voice models used for speaker adaptation. Ideally, the average voice model should be close to the vocal identity of the patient and it has been shown that gender and regional accent are the most influent factors in speaker similarity perception [14]. Therefore, the speakers are clustered according to their gender and their regional accent in order to train specific average voice models. A minimum of 10 speakers is required in order to get robust average voice models.

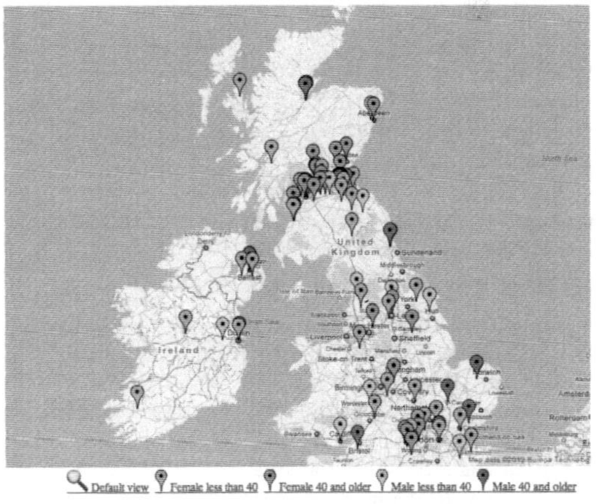

Figure 2: UK-wide speech database.

The healthy voice database is also used to select the voice donors for the model substitution process described in section 4. The voice donors are chosen among the speakers used to build the average voice model matched to the patient's gender and accent.

We first build a speaker-adapted voice for each of these speakers using the same average voice model. The acoustic models used in HTS represent each stream of parameters separately. Therefore, a set of acoustic distances between speaker-adapted voices can be defined for each of these streams (duration, log-F0, band aperiodicity, mel-cepstrum). These distances are defined as the average Karhunen-Loeve (KL) distances [15] between the acoustics models associated to the same stream of parameters. Finally, a voice donor is selected for each stream separately, as the one that minimizes the average acoustic distance for this stream.

6. Clinical Trial

As part of the voice-banking project, we are conducting a clinical trial in order to assess and further refine the voice building process for patients with degenerative speech disorders. So far, more than 15 patients with MND have already been recorded and 5 of them have been delivered a reconstructed voice. We present in the following sections a subjective assessment of the voice repair as well as the feedbacks from patients and their families.

4.3. Subjective evaluation of the voice repair

The substitution strategy presented in Section 4 was evaluated for the case of a MND patient. This patient was a 45 years old Scottish male that we recorded twice. A first recording of one hour (500 sentences) has been made just after diagnosis when he was at the very onset of the disease. At that time, his voice did not show any disorders and could still be considered as "healthy". A second recording of 15 minutes (50 sentences) has been made 10 months later. He has then acquired some speech disorders typically associated with MND, such as excessive hoarseness and breathiness, disruption of speech fluency, reduced articulation and monotonic prosody. The synthetic voices used in this experiment are shown in Table 1. The same male-Scottish average voice model, denoted as AV, was used to create all the synthetic voices. This average voice was trained on 17 male Scottish speakers using 400 sentences each giving a total of 6800 sentences. The synthetic voice created from the first recording of the patient ("healthy" speech) was used as the reference voice for the subjective evaluations. This reference voice is referred to as HC. This choice of a synthetic voice as reference instead of the natural recordings was done to avoid any bias due to the loss of quality inherent to the synthesis. The reconstructed voice IR was obtained by applying the combination of the **component-wise** and **context-dependent** substitution strategies to the speaker-adapted voice IC build from the second recording of the patient ("impaired" speech).

Voice	*Description*
AV	Average voice used for speaker adaptation
HC	Speaker adapted voice of the "**healthy**" speech
IC	Speaker adapted voice of the "**impaired**" speech
IR	Reconstructed voice using the **component-wise** and **context-dependent** model substitutions

Table 1: Voices compared in the evaluation tests

In order to evaluate the effectiveness of the voice reconstruction, two subjective tests were conducted. The first one assesses the intelligibility of the synthesized voice and the second, the speaker similarity. The same 40 semantically unpredictable sentences [16] were synthesized for each of the 3 voices created from the patient's recordings (see Table 1). The resulting synthesized samples were divided into 4 groups such that each voice is represented by 10 samples in a group. A total of 40 native English participants were asked to transcribe the synthesized samples, with 10 participants for each group. Within each group, the samples were presented in random order for each participant. The participants performed the test with headphones. The transcriptions were evaluated by measuring the word error rate (WER).

Voice	*Mean WER (%)*	*std*
HC	26	12
IC	53	18
IR	36	16

Table 2: Word Error Rate (mean, standard deviation)

The same test sentence "People look, but no one ever finds it." was synthesized for each of the 4 voices in Table 1. Participants were asked to listen alternatively to the reference voice HC and to the same sentence synthesized with the reconstructed voice IR and the average voice model AV. The presentation order of the voices being tested was randomized. Participants should rate the similarity between the tested voice and the reference HC on a 5-point scale (1: Very dissimilar, 2: Dissimilar, 3: Quite Similar, 4: Very similar; and 5: Identical). However, the participants were not given further instruction in order to avoid biasing towards rating any specific form of similarity. A total of 40 native English speakers performed the test using headphones.

Voice	*Mean Opinion Score*	*std*
AV	2.05	1.05
IC	2.61	1.21
IR	3.09	1.34

Table 3: Similarity to the reference voice HC on a MOS-scale (mean, standard deviation)

The resulting average WERs for the intelligibility test are shown in Table 2. We are not interested here in the absolute values of the WER but in their relative values compared to the reference voice HC. As expected, the synthetic voice IC created from the "impaired" speech has a high WER, which means that the articulation disorders from the patient's speech have degraded the intelligibility. The important result here is that the model substitution improves the speech intelligibility of the reconstructed voice IR. The results of the similarity test are shown in Table 3. A first interesting result is that the voice clone IC created by speaker adaptation from the "impaired" speech is more similar to the healthy clone HC that the average voice AV. In the case of this patient, this validates an implicit assumption of the voice reconstruction process: some valuable information about the original vocal identity should remain in the impaired speech. The other important result is the improvement of the average similarity scores when the model substitution strategies are applied. Between IR and AV, there is a mean improvement of 1 MOS (with a p-value << 1.e-5) and more surprisingly, there is also a significant improvement of 0.5 MOS (p-value << 1.e-3) between IC and IR. One explanation of this last result could be that the similarity of vocal identity is better perceived once the disorders have been regulated.

4.3. Feedback from patients and families

The results presented in the previous section are relative to the only patient whose 'healthy' voice was available to establish a reference. However, it remains to be demonstrated that similar results could be achieved with different patients. It is also important to assess the usability of the reconstructed voice in real conditions of use. Therefore, we have conducted an experimental trial with 5 patients whose voices have been reconstructed and made available through an on-line server. These patients can use their reconstructed voices from any computer, tablet or mobile phone as long as an Internet connection is available. A simple web interface allows them to enter a text and a synthesis request is sent to a remote server. Once the synthesis is done on the server, the synthesized speech is sent to the device and played through its loudspeakers. The patients and their families were asked to give their feedback on the quality of the reconstructed voice after a few weeks of use. In particular, they were asked to assess the intelligibility of the voice and its similarity to the user's voice before the start of the disease. We get 15 feedback in total corresponding to the 5 patients, their husbands/wives or their parents. The table 4 shows the mean opinion scores on a 5-point scale (1 being the worst and 5 the best). These results are consistent with the subjective test presented in the previous section. It shows that the voice reconstruction process manages to remove most of the speech artifacts while retaining some of the voice characteristics of the patient. Most importantly, all the patients said they would rather choose their reconstructed voices over any commercially available synthetized voice.

Question	*Mean Opinion Score*	*std*
Similarity	3.5	0.7
Intelligibility	4	1.1

Table 4: Feedback from patients and families (mean, standard deviation)

7. Conclusions

For VOCA users, speech synthesis is not an optional extra for reading out text, but a critical function for social communication and identity display. Therefore, there is a great need for personalized VOCAs as the provision of personalized voice is associated with greater dignity and improved self-identity for the individual and their family. In order to build personalized synthetic voices, attempts have been made to capture the voice before it is lost, but for some patients, the speech deterioration frequently coincides or quickly follows diagnosis. In such cases, HMM-based speech synthesis has two clear advantages: speaker adaptation and improved control. Speaker adaptation allows the creation of a synthetic voice with a limited amount of data. Then the structure of the acoustic models can be modified to repair the synthetic speech. In this paper, we have presented the results of an on-going clinical trial based on this new approach. The subjective evaluations and the feedback from the patients show that it is possible to build a synthesized voice that retains the vocal identity of the patient while removing most of the speech disorders. Although these results are presented for MND patients, the principle of the voice building and reconstruction process could be easily generalized to any other degenerative or acquired speech disorder.

8. References

[1] Doyle, M. and Phillips, B. (2001), "Trends in augmentative and alternative communication use by individuals with amyotrophic lateral sclerosis," *Augmentative and Alternative Communication* 17 (3): pp.167–178.

[2] Murphy, J. (2004), "I prefer this close': Perceptions of AAC by people with motor neurone disease and their communication partners. *Augmentative and Alternative Communication*, 20, 259-271.

[3] Yarrington, D., Pennington, C., Gray, J., & Bunnell, H. T. (2005), "A system for creating personalized synthetic voices," *Proc. of ASSETS.*

[4] http://www.cereproc.com/

[5] Kawai, H., Toda, T., Yamagishi, J., Hirai, T., Ni, J., Nishizawa, N., Tsuzaki, M., and Tokuda, K. (2006) "XIMERA: a concatenative speech synthesis system with large-scale corpora," IEICE Trans. Information and Systems, J89-D-II (12), pp.2688–2698.

[6] Zen, H., Tokuda, K., & Black, A. (2009) "Statistical parametric speech synthesis, Speech Communication," 51, pp.1039-1064.

[7] Creer, S., Green, P., Cunningham, S., & Yamagishi, J. (2010) "Building personalized synthesized voices for individuals with dysarthia using the HTS toolkit," IGI Global Press, Jan. 2010.

[8] Khan, Z. A., Green P., Creer, S., & Cunningham, S. (2011) "Reconstructing the Voice of an Individual Following Laryngectomy," Augmentative and Alternative Communication.

[9] Yamagishi, J., Kobayashi, T., Nakano, Y., Ogata, K. & Isogai, J. 2009. Analysis of speaker adaptation algorithms for HMM-based speech synthesis and a constrained SMAPLR adaptation algorithm. IEEE Trans. on ASL, 17, 66-83.

[10] Veaux, C., Yamagishi, J., King, S. (2011) "Voice Banking and Voice Reconstruction for MND patients," *Proceedings of ASSETS.*

[11] Veaux, C., Yamagishi, J., King, S. (2012) "Using HMM-based Speech Synthesis to Reconstruct the Voice of Individuals with Degenerative Speech Disorders," *Interspeech*, Portland, USA.

[12] Yorkston, K. M., Beukelman, D. R. and Bell, K. R. (1998) "Clinical management of dysarthric speakers," College-Hill Press.

[13] Mengistu, K.T. and Rudzicz, F., (2011) "Adapting acoustic and lexical models to dysarthric speech," Proc. ICASSP 2011.

[14] Dall, R., Veaux, C., Yamagishi, J. & King, S. (2012) "Analysis of speaker clustering strategies for HMM-based speech synthesis," *Proc. Interspeech*, Portland, USA.

[15] Trung Hieu Nguyen, Haizhou Li, and Eng Siong Chng. (2009) "Cluster criterion functions in spectral subspace and their application in speaker clustering," In *Proceedings of ICASSP.*

[16] Benoît C., Grice M., & Hazan, V. (1996) "The SUS test: A method for the assessment of text-to-speech synthesis intelligibility using Semantically Unpredictable Sentences," Speech Communication.

Automatic Monitoring of Activities of Daily Living based on Real-life Acoustic Sensor Data: a preliminary study

Lode Vuegen[1,2,3], *Bert Van Den Broeck*[1,2,4], *Peter Karsmakers*[1,2,4], *Hugo Van hamme*[3], *Bart Vanrumste*[1,2,4]

[1]MOBILAB, TM Kempen, Kleinhoefstraat 4, 2440, Geel, Belgium
[2]iMinds, Future Health Department, Kasteelpark Arenberg 10, 3001, Leuven, Belgium
[3]ESAT-PSI, KU Leuven, Kasteelpark Arenberg 10, 3001, Leuven, Belgium
[4]ESAT-SISTA, KU Leuven, Kasteelpark Arenberg 10, 3001, Leuven, Belgium

Lode.Vuegen@kuleuven.be

Abstract

This work examines the use of a low-power Wireless Acoustic Sensor Network (WASN) for the observation of clinically relevant activities of daily living (ADL) (e.g. eating, personal hygiene, toilet usage, etc.) from elderly. The sensors used in the WASN are both audio and ultrasound receivers. To the best of our knowledge, the combination of audio and ultrasound as a basis for ADL monitoring has not been investigated yet. This paper describes a baseline approach for ADL classification based on Gaussian mixture models. Preliminary results in this work indicate that classification accuracies up to 85.0 % $\pm$ 14.6 for audio and 61.7% $\pm$ 11.3 for ultrasound are already achievable on realistic real-life recorded data.

Index Terms: acoustic scene analysis, audio, ultrasound, acoustic scene classification, activities of daily living, automatic monitoring

1. Introduction

Because of the retirement of the baby-boom generation and the increasing life expectation, the ratio of dependent elderly to working people is rising sharply. Research predicts that in 2020, 19% (extrapolated to 26% in 2060) of the Belgian population will be older than 65 years [1, 2]. This aging brings important challenges for our society. One of these challenges is to facilitate a safe functioning of elderly people in their own home environment. Even solutions which only allow a small additional fraction of care-requiring elderly to live longer safely at home, for a reasonable investment, make economical sense.

The functioning of elderly at home is often limited by underlying physical or cognitive dysfunctions, which are often the cause of diseases. Nowadays, these changes in functioning are often unrecognized, or recognized too late. One of the reasons for under-detecting these changes is that they are often minimal and not noticed or ignored by the patient or family. Still, early detection could lead to early intervention and prolong the possibility to live safely at home. As technological support, a monitoring system aims to detect and analyze relevant changes and create a safe environment to the elderly at home. More specifically, the aim of this research is to provide the caregiver objective information, compiled in a summary report, concerning the daily activities of the elderly.

The present solutions found in the literature can be split into two main categories based on the type of sensors used. A first category requires the use of sensors that make contact with the human body such as Radio Frequency Identification (RFID) readers [3, 4, 5], accelerometers [6, 7, 8, 9, 10] and gyroscopes [11]. A second category uses contact-less sensors. These have the advantages over wearable sensor systems in that they do not affect the normal behavior of the users, do not require human interaction (e.g. such as a push button system), and cannot be forgotten to wear. In [12] a survey of different approaches to detect human activities using video images is discussed. Aside video cameras also other contact-less sensors were explored in this context such as infra-red sensors [13], door contacts [13], radars [14], sensors for monitoring the use of domestic utilities [13, 15, 16] and microphones [17, 18, 19, 20, 21]. Compared to the other modalities, acoustic (specifically audio) technology has received little attention. Few research groups have considered using daily living acoustics in their systems.

Our research investigates the use of a wireless acoustic sensor network (WASN) that extracts information from both the audio and ultrasound frequency range. Such networks contain multiple so-called nodes each holding one or more acoustic sensors. These WASNs have advantages over other kinds of setups. For instance, the nodes can be small while maintaining large spatial sampling [22]. The nodes can be placed in a room without inconvenient cables, which is a desirable property in a home environment. Additionally, the workload (which can be significant) can be distributed among nodes so that cheaper hardware can be selected [22]. A WASN allows to estimate the source position from the acoustic signal and increase the quality of the recorded signals through spatial filtering [22, 23]. To our knowledge such a WASN setup that extracts acoustic information from audio and ultrasound signals for the purpose of home monitoring has not yet been reported in the literature. Aside the clinically relevant information that is present in the audio frequency range it is also investigated which useful information could be extracted from the ultrasonic frequency range. More in detail, it will be examined if typical ADLs (e.g. eating, personal hygiene, walking, etc.) can be detected and recognized in the ultrasound spectrum. The combination of audio and ultrasound might have the following advantages over existing contact-less alternatives: a) occlusions might have less impact compared to a video-based system, b) less processing power might be needed compared to video-based approaches, c) ultrasound and audio signals might provide complementary information, d) is expected to be easily integrated with dialog systems (notably for virtual assistants or robots), with emergency and security systems (mainly fall detection and distress situation recognition), is expected to be augmented with human machine interaction (e.g. voice commands, conversational systems), e) can be extended with ultrasound transmitters which allows to estimate object distances to detect changes in the living environment.

This paper describes a baseline architecture for daily activity observation via audio and ultrasonic measurements and discusses the preliminary results obtained on realistic real-life recorded data. The work will serve as a starting point for further improvements of the classification accuracy and required annotation efforts for model estimation.

In section 2 we will briefly discuss the used experimental setup. Topics such as hardware configuration, living environment, and the performed Activity of Daily Living (ADL) scenarios will be clarified. Section 3 describes the baseline system architecture and clarifies a functional block diagram of the proposed solution. Section 4 discusses the feature extraction process and how these features are implemented in a classifier. The conducted experiments and obtained results are presented and clarified in section 5. In Section 6 the findings will be discussed and is followed by the conclusions in Section 7.

2. Experimental setup

2.1. Hardware

The acoustic sensor network used during the recordings consisted of two different types of nodes, i.e. audio and ultrasound, and are briefly explained in the following two paragraphs.

Each audio node was equipped with three linearly spaced electret microphones with an inter-sensor distance of 6.8 cm. The microphone signals are sent to preamplifiers with a cut-off frequency of 20 kHz to improve the signal level.

The ultrasound node consisted of three 40 kHz centered ultrasound receivers with an inter-sensor distance of 10 cm. Next, the captured ultrasound spectrum is downshifted to the audible frequency range to make it recordable with standard audio hardware. The latter is done by analog mixing the ultrasound signal with a square block wave of 31.5 kHz which results into a transformed center frequency of 8.5 kHz. Next, the downshifted signal is filtered by a 10 kHz low pass filter to cancel out the higher order harmonic product terms. The motivation for downshifting to a center frequency of 8.5 kHz instead of direct to DC (and using a square wave of 40 kHz) is merely because it is expected that the lower ultrasound frequencies (range from 31.5 till 40 kHz) also contain valuable information.

All captured acoustic signals were recorded using a 4 channel 24-bit soundcard sampling at 32 kHz. Each soundcard additionally recorded a reference signal that was received from a single transmitter through a RF channel. These reference signals were used for the purpose of off-line synchronization of the different inter node channels as described in [24].

2.2. Living environment

The domestic environment used in this work was a room of size 6 m by 4 m with a combined kitchen and living space as shown in Figure 1. Each of the 4 corners was equipped with an audio node to ensure full coverage of the acoustic sensor network. Additionally, the use of multiple node reduces the maximum possible distance between source and node and thereby increasing the SNR of the received signals as well. In contrast with the audio nodes, only a single ultrasound node was available for installation in the domestic environment. The most suitable position for this node with respect to the maximum possible

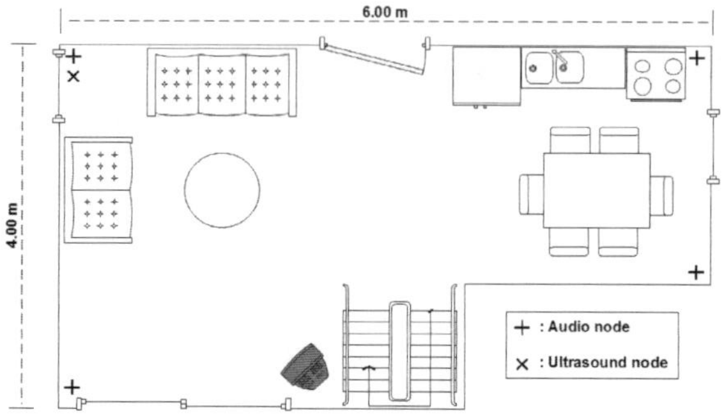

Figure 1: Floor plan of the domestic environment.

coverage was the the corner in the living room.

2.3. Recording scenario and data

The collection of audio and passive ultrasound data from clinically relevant domestic events is required to analyze and explore the proposed observation system. Therefore, during this data collection session eight different people performed some typical ADLs over a time span of three days in the domestic environment. Table 1 gives an detailed overview of the collected data in terms of both audio and ultrasound.

Table 1: *A detailed overview of the collected audio and ultrasound data.*

Activity class	**Number of examples**	**Recording Duration** (minutes)
Cooking and eating	7	287.01
Reading	2	22.04
Using laptop	2	21.16
Vacuum cleaning	4	34.15
Walking around	6	59.12
Watching TV	3	73.44

3. System architecture

The proposed system architecture is shown in Figure 2. Each node first estimates whether or not the input contains acoustic information by using a sound activity detector (SAD). Since a wide range of acoustics can be useful in recognizing an activity it is difficult to select a certain model-based sound activity detector. Therefore, a simple energy based threshold is implemented as SAD. First each sample is squared and thresholded. Then a hangover scheme labels each sample within 25 ms of a sample which passed the threshold as a positive detection. If acoustic information is detected, the raw waveform data will be further processed into acoustic and position features (as described in 4.1 and 4.2). Both acoustic and position features are calculated on 25 ms blocks of data with a time shift of 10 ms. The SAD is also used to estimate the signal-to-noise ratio (SNR) at which the acoustic information is received. Only this low dimensional information (SNR, acoustic and position features) is sent to a central processor. This strategy reduces the necessary bandwidth and power consumption.

The central processor combines the position features of all nodes and only selects the acoustic features from the micro-

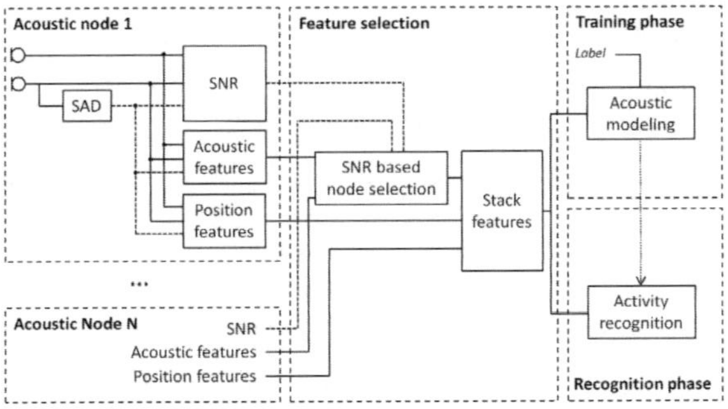

Figure 2: Block schematic of system architecture.

phone that receives the acoustic signal with the highest SNR. Once the features are combined, these will form the basis for the training and testing phase. It is worth mentioning that Figure 2 depicts a simplified architecture. In practice the block node selection will notify each node whether or not its acoustic features are needed such that no unnecessary CPU time nor bandwidth will be wasted.

4. Feature extraction and modeling

As discussed in previous sections, this work aims to reveal ADLs from the associated acoustic information. In order to optimize the classification objective, the raw stream of acoustic data is transformed into more consistent features. Therefore, two types of features will be extracted from collected sensor data, i.e. acoustic source localization features and acoustic features. It is expected that these two feature sets contain complementary information which will boost the classification performance. For instance, running water detected in the bathroom is more associated to personal hygiene than to cooking.

4.1. Acoustic features

Most of the presently available acoustic feature extraction approaches find their origin in speech applications and are often based on the properties of human speech production and perception. A well-known and often used feature extraction approach in the domain of speech- and speaker recognition applications are the so-called Mel-Frequency Cepstral Coefficients (MFCCs) [25]. Despite the fact that MFCCs are initially developed for speech applications, research indicates that MFCCs are also a successful choice for processing non-speech acoustic signals as well [26, 27]. Therefore, this work will use the MFCC approach as a baseline for computing the acoustic features from the collected audio data. The feature extraction process for the downshifted ultrasound signals is slightly different. Here, linearly spaced filter banks make more sense since there is no reason to assume that the frequency resolution should be significantly different at the low versus the high end of the spectrum. This changes the Mel-Frequency Cepstral Coefficients into a linear alternative which is denoted as Linear-Frequency Cepstral Coefficients (LFCCs) [28].

Both the MFCC- and LFCC-features will be extracted using the same parameter setting. Literature indicates that window sizes of 25 ms with an overlap of 10 ms are typically used [25]. The number of filterbanks is set to 40. The filtering operation is followed by a 13th order Discrete Cosine Transform. Finally, the Δ and $\Delta\Delta$ are computed and added as acoustic features. This leads into a 42-*dimensional* acoustic feature vector for both audio and the downshifted ultrasound. Finally, each feature dimension is normalized by applying a standard mean and variance normalization algorithm.

4.2. Position features

Since sound travels at a finite speed, information about the direction of arrival (DOA) can be found in the time differences of arrival (TDOA) between different microphones in a node. The most simple way of measuring a TDOA is by a cross correlation, but this approach has a time resolution of a single sampling period. This problem can be resolved by using the so-called steered response power (SRP) algorithm [29]. SRP is based on a delay and sum beamformer, which is steered in multiple directions at once (ranging from -90°to +90°with a resolution of 2°) for one block of data and measures the retrieved energy in each direction. In this work, an enhancement on SRP is used, namely SRP phase transform (SRP-PHAT). PHAT basically pre-transforms the microphone frames to have an unity spectral density. This operation decorrelates the different microphone signals over time, making the directional energy peaks corresponding to a source narrower. The SRP-PHAT algorithm is described further in [29].

SRP-PHAT finally produces 91 points of the directional energy curve per node. These points were not directly used as features for the classification model. Since only a limited amount of training data was available it is desirable to keep the feature space low dimensional. Therefore, it was chosen to split-up the directional energy curve into two regions with broadside as the boundary. The energy in each region was integrated and the resulting two measures were combined into a single feature per node by taking the logarithmic ratio. The logarithm is taken to reshape the ratio intervals from $]0,1]$ and $[1,\infty[$ to $]-\infty,0]$ and $[0,\infty[$ to equalize the importance of both sides. Despite the resulting low resolution, using a combination of nodes allows to partition the living environment into several areas. Therefore, the position feature vectors used for the classification model are formed by concatenating the node specific position features. This differs from the acoustic features where only features from a single node are selected.

4.3. Gaussian Mixture Models

ADLs are classified by training a GMM with diagonal covariance per class. A sequence of feature vectors, possibly originating from multiple nodes and from both modalities, is assigned to the class that produces the maximal log-likelihood. In earlier work on similar problems [30], it was found that classification accuracy did not depend critically on the number of mixture components in the range from 5 to 20. For parsimony, five mixture components were used.

5. Experiments and results

Due to the limited amount of training data, a 10-fold cross-validation approach was used to evaluate the classification performance of the proposed system. The data was not first permuted before partitioning to leave the acoustic variation between training and validation partition as realistic as possible. In order to preserve the class balance in training- and validation set, each activity class was first partitioned into 10 folds followed by the combination of corresponding class specific folds.

5.1. Audio based ADL classification

The first conducted experiment in this work analyzes the audio based classification performance of the sensor network. In order to examine the additional value of the position information in terms of classification accuracy this experiment is carried out twice, i.e. once without and once including the position features. The corresponding confusion matrices are shown in Table 2 and Table 3 respectively. As one can see, promising results are obtained. The obtained average accuracy is 81.7 % $\pm$ 14.6 when only the acoustic features are taken into account. This value increases by 3.3 % to an average accuracy of 85.0 % $\pm$ 14.6 when the position information is added as a feature. The following observations can be made by analyzing the corresponding confusion matrices more in detail:

1. The ADL *Cooking and eating*, *Vacuum cleaning*, and *Watching TV* have the best classification results. This is easy to comprehend because: 1) these activities are characterized by their own typical recurring characteristic acoustic information and 2) the energy of the acoustic sounds in these events is sufficiently high which results into higher SNRs.
2. The increase in accuracy by adding position information is due to the higher classification results obtained at *Reading* and *Walking around*. For these activities, the energy in the acoustic waves is low (e.g. page turn or a footstep) making the acoustic features unreliable.

Table 2: *Confusion matrix of the obtained audio classification results without the position information.*

True label: / Classified label:	Cooking and eating	Reading	Vacuum cleaning	Walking around	Watching TV	Working laptop
Cooking and eating	**9**	-	-	1	-	-
Reading	1	**5**	-	3	-	1
Vacuum cleaning	-	-	**10**	-	-	-
Walking around	2	-	-	**7**	-	1
Watching TV	-	-	-	-	**10**	-
Working laptop	-	1	-	1	-	**8**

5.2. Complementarity of audio and ultrasound

This experiment examines the complementarity of the audio and ultrasound signals. As discussed in section 2, only 1 ultrasound node was placed in the domestic environment. Therefore, in order to have a fair comparison between both modalities only the audio data from the corresponding audio node is used in this experiment. This differs from 5.1 where the node selection depends on the node's SNR.

Table 4 and 5 represent the obtained audio and ultrasound results. The average accuracy of the audio classification drops to 81.7% $\pm$ 12.3, as expected. The average score of ultrasound is 61.7% $\pm$ 11.3 which is lower than that when using audio but still very promising. By analyzing the results more in detail the following conclusions can be made:

Table 3: *Confusion matrix of the obtained audio classification results when the position features are included.*

True label: / Classified label:	Cooking and eating	Reading	Vacuum cleaning	Walking around	Watching TV	Working laptop
Cooking and eating	**9**	-	-	1	-	-
Reading	1	**6**	-	3	-	-
Vacuum cleaning	-	-	**10**	-	-	-
Walking around	1	1	-	**8**	-	-
Watching TV	-	-	-	-	**10**	-
Working laptop	-	-	-	2	-	**8**

1. Also in the ultrasound modality, the ADLs *Cooking and eating*, *Vacuum cleaning*, and *Watching TV* have the best accuracy. For these, the same explanation as in 5.1 is valid.
2. The classification accuracy of the activities *Reading* and *Working laptop* with the down-shifted ultrasound signals is inferior to the performance when using the audio data. Listening to the recording confirms that these activities are harder to recognize from the ultrasound recordings than from the audio recordings.
3. Ultrasound signals will be more attenuated than audio over a same distance since the attenuation of acoustic waves depends on the frequency [29]. This in combination with a sub-optimal ultrasound node (i.e. analog downshifting introduces a significant amount of noise) makes the ultrasound part of the sensor network less sensitive compared to audio and thereby also affecting the results.

Table 4: *Confusion matrix of the obtained audio classification accuracies (only the acoustic and position features from the audio node corresponding to the ultrasound node position is used).*

True label: / Classified label:	Cooking and eating	Reading	Vacuum cleaning	Walking around	Watching TV	Working laptop
Cooking and eating	**9**	-	-	1	-	-
Reading	1	**5**	-	3	-	1
Vacuum cleaning	-	-	**10**	-	-	-
Walking around	1	1	-	**8**	-	-
Watching TV	-	-	-	-	**10**	-
Working laptop	-	-	-	3	-	**7**

Table 5: *Confusion matrix of the obtained ultrasound classification results (position features included).*

True label: / Classified label:	Cooking and eating	Reading	Vacuum cleaning	Walking around	Watching TV	Working laptop
Cooking and eating	**10**	-	-	-	-	-
Reading	-	**0**	-	2	8	-
Vacuum cleaning	-	-	**10**	-	-	-
Walking around	-	-	-	**6**	4	-
Watching TV	-	-	-	1	**9**	-
Working laptop	-	-	-	3	5	**2**

Table 6 shows the confusion matrix of the classification results when audio and ultrasound are combined. The latter is done by summing the audio an ultrasound class posteriors together. The obtained average classification score is 80.0% $\pm$ 10.5 which is slightly less accurate compared to the audio results from Table 4 but nevertheless still promising.

Table 6: *Confusion matrix of the combination audio and ultrasound.*

True label: / Classified label:	Cooking and eating	Reading	Vacuum cleaning	Walking around	Watching TV	Working laptop
Cooking and eating	**10**	-	-	-	-	-
Reading	-	**4**	1	3	1	1
Vacuum cleaning	-	-	**10**	-	-	-
Walking around	-	1	1	**6**	-	2
Watching TV	-	-	-	-	**10**	-
Working laptop	-	-	-	2	-	**8**

6. Discussion

The preliminary results in Section 5 indicate promising ADL classification results for both the audio and ultrasound modalities. Although the ultrasound based classification results were inferior to those obtained using audio data, one must be careful before drawing conclusions.

1. The SNR of the ultrasound signals was significantly lower than that of the audio signals. Further investigation is required to check which hardware improvements can be used to increase the SNR.
2. Although a simple combination of both the audio and ultrasound modalities resulted in a decrease of overall performance, other types of combination, such as a class-dependent weighted combination of both outcomes, might be more successful.

Therefore, future work will focus on the development of more sensitive and less-noisy ultrasound nodes and the optimal integration of both modalities with respect to the classification performance of the WASN. Moreover, the added value of active observation will be investigated as well by extending the sensor network with ultrasound transmitters. This can lead to a better observation of dynamic ADLs (e.g. walking around) and thereby can also lead to an improved overall classification accuracy.

Furthermore, real-life data collection sessions over a longer time span in homes of elderly living alone are also planned in the near future. This allows the creation of larger acoustic datasets which will improve the estimation of acoustic models.

7. Conclusions

This work presents a distributed acoustic sensor network for the observation of activities of daily living from elderly on the basis of the corresponding audio and ultrasound data. The baseline system that is proposed was validated on realistic real-life data that was recorded in a domestic environment equipped with a prototype of the sensor network. The conducted classification experiments on the acquired data revealed promising preliminary classification accuracies, i.e. 85.0 % $\pm$ 14.6 and 61.7% $\pm$ 11.3 for audio and ultrasound respectively. Combining both modalities by posterior summation did not yield an improvement over the audio-only modality. Other classifier combination methods will be studied in the near future. Despite these promising preliminary results, further work on a larger scaled dataset collected with multiple and more sensitive ultrasound nodes is required to increase the significance of the obtained results.

8. Acknowledgements

This work was performed in the context of following projects: ALADIN (IWT-SBO project contract 100049) and IWT doctoral scholarships (contract 111433 and 121565).

9. References

[1] N. Consortium. (2010) The business of aging: Commercial challenges and opportunities in ambient assisted living. [Online]. Available: http://www.netcarity.org

[2] F. planbureau: Economische analyses en vooruitzichten. (2011) Bevolkingsvooruitzichten 2010-2060. [Online]. Available: http://www.plan.be

[3] D. J. Patterson, D. Fox, H. Kautz, and M. Philipose, "Fine-grained activity recognition by aggregating abstract object usage," in *Proceedings of the Ninth IEEE International Symposium on Wearable Computers*, ser. ISWC '05. Washington, DC, USA: IEEE Computer Society, 2005, pp. 44–51. [Online]. Available: http://dx.doi.org/10.1109/ISWC.2005.22

[4] J. Wu, A. Osuntogun, T. Choudhury, M. Philipose, and J. M. Rehg, "A scalable approach to activity recognition based on object use," in *In Proceedings of the International Conference on Computer Vision (ICCV), Rio de*, 2007.

[5] M. Stikic, T. Huynh, K. Van Laerhoven, and B. Schiele, "Adl recognition based on the combination of rfid and accelerometer sensing," in *Proceedings of the 2nd International Conference on Pervasive Computing Technologies for Healthcare (Pervasive Health 2008)*, IEEE Xplore. Tampere, Finland: IEEE Xplore, January 2008, pp. 258–263.

[6] X. Long, B. Yin, and R. M. Aarts, "Single-accelerometer-based daily physical activity classification," in *2009 Annual International Conference of the IEEE Engineering in Medicine and Biology Society*. IEEE, Sep. 2009, pp. 6107–6110. [Online]. Available: http://dx.doi.org/10.1109/iembs.2009.5334925

[7] O. Amft, H. Junker, and G. Troster, "Detection of eating and drinking arm gestures using inertial body-worn sensors," in *Proceedings of the Ninth IEEE International Symposium on Wearable Computers*, ser. ISWC '05. Washington, DC, USA: IEEE Computer Society, 2005, pp. 160–163. [Online]. Available: http://dx.doi.org/10.1109/ISWC.2005.17

[8] W.-Y. C. Amit Purwar, Young-Dong Lee, "Triaxial mems accelerometer for activity monitoring of elderly person," *Sensor Letters*, vol. 6, no. 6, pp. 1054–1058, 2008.

[9] A. Jin, B. Yin, G. Morren, H. Duric, and R. M. Aarts, "Performance evaluation of a tri-axial accelerometry-based respiration monitoring for ambient assisted living." *Conf Proc IEEE Eng Med Biol Soc*, vol. 1, pp. 5677–80, 2009. [Online]. Available: http://www.biomedsearch.com/nih/Performance-evaluation-tri-axial-accelerometry/19964139.html

[10] C. Zhu and W. Sheng, "Multi-sensor fusion for human daily activity recognition in robot-assisted living," in *HRI*, 2009, pp. 303–304.

[11] A. K. Bourke and G. M. Lyons, "A threshold-based fall-detection algorithm using a bi-axial gyroscope sensor," *Medical Engineering and Physics*, vol. 30, no. 1, pp. 84–90, 2008. [Online]. Available: http://dx.doi.org/10.1016/j.medengphy.2006.12.001

[12] P. Turaga, R. Chellappa, V. S. Subrahmanian, and O. Udrea, "Machine recognition of human activities: A survey," *Circuits and Systems for Video Technology, IEEE Transactions on*, vol. 18, no. 11, pp. 1473–1488, nov 2008. [Online]. Available: http://dx.doi.org/10.1109/tcsvt.2008.2005594

[13] A. Fleury, N. Noury, and M. Vacher, "Supervised classification of activities of daily living in health smart homes using svm," in *31th Annual International Conference of the IEEE Engineering in Medicine and Biology Society (EMBC09)*, Minnesota, USA, 2009, pp. 6099–6102.

[14] P. Karsmakers, T. Croonenborghs, M. Mercuri, D. Schreurs, and P. Leroux, "Automatic in-door fall detection based on microwave radar measurements," in *Proceedings of the 9th European Radar Conference,*, B. Arbesser-Rastburg, Ed. ESA-ESTEC, TEC-EE, Oct. 2012, pp. 202–205. [Online]. Available: https://lirias.kuleuven.be/handle/123456789/353333

[15] F. G.-B. M. Berenguer, M. Giordani and N. Noury, "Automatic detection of activities of daily living from detecting and classifying electrical events on the residential power line," in *10th IEEE Int. Conf. e-Health Netw., Appl. Serv. HealthCom*, ser. -, 2008, pp. pp. 29–32.

[16] S. Tsukamoto, H. Hoshino, and T. Tamura, "Study on indoor activity monitoring by using electric field sensor," *Gerontechnology*, vol. 7, no. 2, 2008. [Online]. Available: http://www.gerontechnology.info/index.php/journal/article/view/gt.2008.07.02.163.00

[17] D. Istrate, M. Vacher, and J.-F. Serignat, "Embedded implementation of distress situation identification through sound analysis," in *the 5th ICICTH International Conference on Information Communication Technologies in Health*, Greece, Jul. 5-7 2007, pp. 226–231. [Online]. Available: "http://www.ineag.gr/docs/Scientific_Programme_of_5th_ICicth_Samos_2007.pdf"

[18] M. Sehili, B. Lecouteux, M. Vacher, F. Portet, D. Istrate, B. Dorizzi, and J. Boudy, "Sound Environnment Analysis in Smart Home," in *Ambient Intelligence*, ser. Lecture Notes in Computer Science, F. Paternò, B. de Ruyter, P. Markopoulos, C. Santoro, E. van Loenen, and K. Luyten, Eds., vol. 7683. Pisa, Italy: Springer, nov 2012, pp. 208–223.

[19] A. Temko, C. Nadeu, D. Macho, R. Malkin, C. Zieger, and M. Omologo, "Acoustic event detection and classification," in *Computers in the Human Interaction Loop*, 2009, pp. 61–73.

[20] H. Lozano, I. Hernáez, A. Picón, J. Camarena, and E. Navas, "Audio classification techniques in home environments for elderly/dependant people," in *Proceedings of the 12th international conference on Computers helping people with special needs: Part I*, ser. ICCHP'10. Berlin, Heidelberg: Springer-Verlag, 2010, pp. 320–323. [Online]. Available: http://dl.acm.org/citation.cfm?id=1886667.1886725

[21] H. Kun-Yi, H. a Chi-Chun, T.Ming-shih, and Y. G.-L. C.Yu-Hsien, "Activity recognition by detecting acoustic events for eldercare," in *6th World Congress of Biomechanics*, ser. WCB 2010, 2010, pp. 1522–1525.

[22] A. Bertrand, "Applications and trends in wireless acoustic sensor networks: a signal processing perspective," in *Proc. IEEE Symposium on Communications and Vehicular Technology (SCVT)*, November 2011. [Online]. Available: ftp://ftp.esat.kuleuven.be/pub/sista/abertran/papers_website/11-197.html

[23] A. Brutti, M. Omologo, and P. Svaizer, "Oriented global coherence field for the estimation of the head orientation in smart rooms equipped with distributed microphone arrays," in *INTERSPEECH'05*, 2005, pp. 2337–2340.

[24] I. K. R. Lienhart and S. Wehr, "Universal synchronization scheme for distributed audio-video capture on heterogeneous computing platforms," in *eleventh ACM international conference on Multimedia*, ser. -, 2003, pp. pp. 263–266.

[25] H. Beigi, *Fundamentals of Speaker Recognition*. Springer, 2011.

[26] X. Zhuang, X. Zhou, T. Huang, and M. Hasegawa-Johnson, "Feature analysis and selection for acoustic event detection," in *Acoustics, Speech and Signal Processing, 2008. ICASSP 2008. IEEE International Conference on*, 2008, pp. 17–20.

[27] S. Ntalampiras, I. Potamitis, and N. Fakotakis, "Automatic recognition of urban soundscenes," in *New Directions in Intelligent Interactive Multimedia*, 2008, pp. 147–153.

[28] X. Zhou, D. Garcia-Romero, R. Duraiswami, C. Espy-Wilson, and S. Shamma, "Linear versus mel frequency cepstral coefficients for speaker recognition," in *Automatic Speech Recognition and Understanding (ASRU), 2011 IEEE Workshop on*, 2011, pp. 559–564.

[29] I. J. Tashev, *Sound Capture and Processing: Practical Approaches*. Wiley Publishing, 2009.

[30] L. Vuegen, B. Van Den Broeck, P. Karsmakers, J. Gemmeke, B. Vanrumste, and H. Van hamme, "An mfcc-gmm approach for event detection and classification," in *AASP Challange: Detection and Classification of Acoustic Scenes and Events*, 2013.

Word Recognition from Continuous Articulatory Movement Time-Series Data using Symbolic Representations

Jun Wang [1], *Arvind Balasubramanian* [2], *Luis Mojica de la Vega* [2], *Jordan R. Green* [3]
Ashok Samal [4], *Balakrishnan Prabhakaran* [2]

[1] Callier Center for Communication Disorders
[2] Department of Computer Science
University of Texas at Dallas, Dallas, Texas, United States
[3] MGH Institute of Health Professions, Boston, Massachusetts, United States
[4] Department of Computer Science & Engineering
University of Nebraska-Lincoln, Lincoln, Nebraska, United States
{wangjun, arvind, luis.mojica, prabha}@utdallas.edu
jgreen2@mghihp.edu, samal@cse.unl.edu

Abstract

Although still in experimental stage, articulation-based silent speech interfaces may have significant potential for facilitating oral communication in persons with voice and speech problems. An articulation-based silent speech interface converts articulatory movement information to audible words. The complexity of speech production mechanism (e.g., co-articulation) makes the conversion a formidable problem. In this paper, we reported a novel, real-time algorithm for recognizing words from continuous articulatory movements. This approach differed from prior work in that (1) it focused on word-level, rather than phoneme-level; (2) online segmentation and recognition were conducted at the same time; and (3) a symbolic representation (SAX) was used for data reduction in the original articulatory movement time-series. A data set of 5,900 isolated word samples of tongue and lip movements was collected using electromagnetic articulograph from eleven English speakers. The average speaker-dependent recognition accuracy was up to 80.00%, with an average latency of 302 miliseconds for each word prediction. The results demonstrated the effectiveness of our approach and its potential for building a real-time articulation-based silent speech interface for clinical applications. The across-speaker variation of the recognition accuracy was discussed.

Index Terms: silent speech recognition, laryngectomy, support vector machine, SAX, time-series

1. Introduction

Persons who lose their voice after laryngectomy (a surgical removal of the larynx due to the treatment of cancer) or who have speech impairment struggle with daily communication [1]. In 2012, more than 52,000 new cases of head and neck cancers (including larynx, pharynx, etc.) were estimated in the United States [2]. Currently, there are only limited treatment options for these individuals, which include (1) "esophageal speech", which involves oscillation of the esophagus and can be difficult to learn; (2) electrolarynx, which is a mechanical device resulting in a robotic-like voice; and (3) augmented and alternative communication (AAC) devices (e.g., text-to-speech synthesizers operated with keyboards), which are limited by slow manual text input [1]. New assistive technologies are needed to provide a more efficient oral communication mode with natural voice for those individuals.

Silent speech interfaces (SSIs), although still in early development stages [3] (e.g., speaker-dependent recognition, small-vocabulary, devices are not ready for clinical use), may provide an alternative interaction modality for persons with voice and speech problems. The common purpose of SSIs is to convert non-audio articulatory data to text that drives a text-to-speech (TTS) synthesizer (e.g., [4]) (see Figure 1 for a schematic of our SSI design). Potential articulatory data transduction methods for SSIs include ultrasound [5, 6], surface electromyography electrodes [7, 8], and electromagnetic articulograph (EMA) [9, 10, 11]. The current project used EMA, which registers the 3D motion of sensors adhered to the tongue and lips.

One major challenge for building effective SSIs is developing accurate and fast algorithms that recognize words or sentences based on articulatory data (i.e., without audio information). Articulatory data have been successfully used to improve the accuracy of voiced speech recognition from both healthy talkers [12, 13] and neurologically impaired individuals [14]. This typically involves the use of *articulatory features* (AFs), which include lip rounding, tongue tip position, and manner of production, for example. Phoneme-level AF-based approaches have typically obtained word recognition accuracies less than 50% [13] because articulation can vary significantly within those categorical features depending on the surrounding sounds and the speaking context [15].

These challenges in phoneme-level recognition motivate a higher unit level of articulatory recognition, for example, word-level or sentence-level. Although sentence-level recognition accuracy is high [9], it lacks the scalability of phoneme- and word-level recognition because all sentences are required to be known prior to prediction. Word-level recognition may have better scalability than sentence-level recognition and the potential for higher accuracy than phoneme-level recognition. Word-level recognition from acoustic data has outperformed monophone recognition by approximately 25% [16, 17]. However, whole-word recognition has rarely been investigated in articulatory data probably due to logistic difficulty of collecting articulatory data [10, 11].

Online word recognition from continuous articulatory movements can be extremely challenging because word

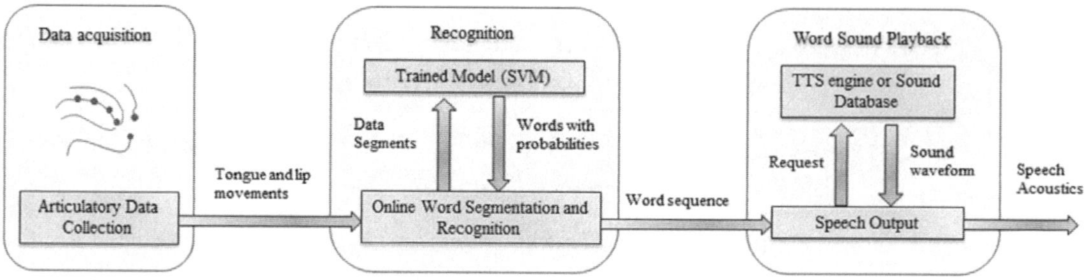

Figure 1. *Three-component design of the articulatory movement-based silent speech interface.*

boundaries (onset and offset) are difficult to identify. Recent works have shown offline word classification (word boundaries are known) accuracy can be greater than 90% for a small vocabulary [10, 11]. However, because of word segmentation issues, online recognition accuracy can be significantly lower than offline classification accuracy. Online word segmentation based on articulatory movements has rarely been attempted [18]. A threshold (e.g., 2 SD) of the articulatory movements has been successfully used for isolated word datasets [19, 20]. Such amplitude-based segmentation may not be well suited for words produced in a continuous sequence because of co-articulation (illustrated in Figure 1) or for words within sentences (connected speech). Co-articulation is an effect characterized by a sound is affected by its adjacent sounds [21, 22].

Figure 2 illustrates the articulatory movements for a word sequence with co-articulation produced by one of the participants. The top panel shows the continuous motion of sensors (y and z coordinates, where y is vertical and z is front-back) attached on the tongue and lips. T1, T2, T3, and T4 are four sensors attached on the midsaggital line of the tongue, from tip to back; UL is upper lip; LL is lower lip. Details of the coordinate system and the labels of the sensors are provided in Section 4. The bottom panel shows the synchronously recorded audio.

The goal of this project was to investigate word recognition from continuous articulatory movements. A novel, real-time algorithm for word recognition from continuous stream of articulatory movements has been recently proposed [10]. The algorithm was designed to solve the online segmentation and recognition problems simultaneously. The algorithm is characterized by the following: recognition is at the word level rather than the phoneme- or sentence-level; recognition employs a dynamic thresholding technique based on patterns in the probability change returned by a classifier; and the algorithm is extensible (i.e., it can be embedded with a variety of classifiers). The algorithm has been tested on the minimally processed articulatory movements [10]. Although the results were promising (missing only 1.93 words on a sequence with twenty-five words), false positives caused a relatively low overall accuracy.

The current project implemented the following three strategies for improving word recognition accuracy: (1) using symbolic aggregation approximation (SAX) representation to reduce the local variation in the original articulatory movement time-series data, (2) adding a look-back strategy to handle a situation in which two words are so close that the onset of the second word may not be accurately identified, and (3) using speaker-dependent thresholds to determine the word candidates during online recognition. A phonetically-balanced and isolated word dataset of tongue and lip movements was collected using electromagnetic articulograph and used to evaluate the effectiveness and efficiency of the improved algorithm.

2. Design & Method

The design of our articulation-based silent speech interface is illustrated in Figure 1, which contains three major components [9, 10]: (a) data acquisition, (b) online (word) recognition, and (c) sound playback or synthesis. Data acquisition is performed using an electromagnetic articulograph that tracks the motion of sensors attached on a speaker's tongue and lips.

The focus of this paper is the second component, online word recognition, whose goal is to recognize a set of isolated words from continuous articulatory data (without using audio data). The core recognition problems are to (1) convert a time-series of spatial configurations of multiple articulators to time-delimited words, and (2) identify the onset of those recognized words. Here, a spatial configuration is an ordered set of 3D locations of the sensors. In this whole-word recognition algorithm, segmentation and identification are conducted together in a variable-size sliding window. The algorithm is based on the premise that a word has its highest matching probability given an observation window with an appropriate starting point and width. A trained machine learning classifier that derives these matching probabilities is embedded into the algorithm, as described in the rest of this section. In the future, this algorithm will serve as the recognition component of our articulation-based SSI.

2.1. Symbolic representation of articulatory time-series data

SAX is a symbolic representation technique [23] that has been widely used in time-series data pattern analysis (e.g., [24, 25, 26]). The main idea of SAX is to represent the original time-series amplitude using discrete symbols that can still capture the patterns. The potential benefits of SAX are (i) efficient dimensionality reduction while retaining essential features; and (ii) lower bounding of the distance measure on the original series. To our best knowledge, however, SAX has not been used for articulatory movement time-series data analysis.

The underlying contention behind representing the tongue motion data in the form of symbols is to capture the motion pattern for a particular word and to reduce the local variation. If the motion trajectory can be captured in terms of symbols that represent different regions in the motion distribution space, then the symbolic representation should reduce the amount of data required while overcoming local variations and scaling effects, thus may enable efficient comparison of the

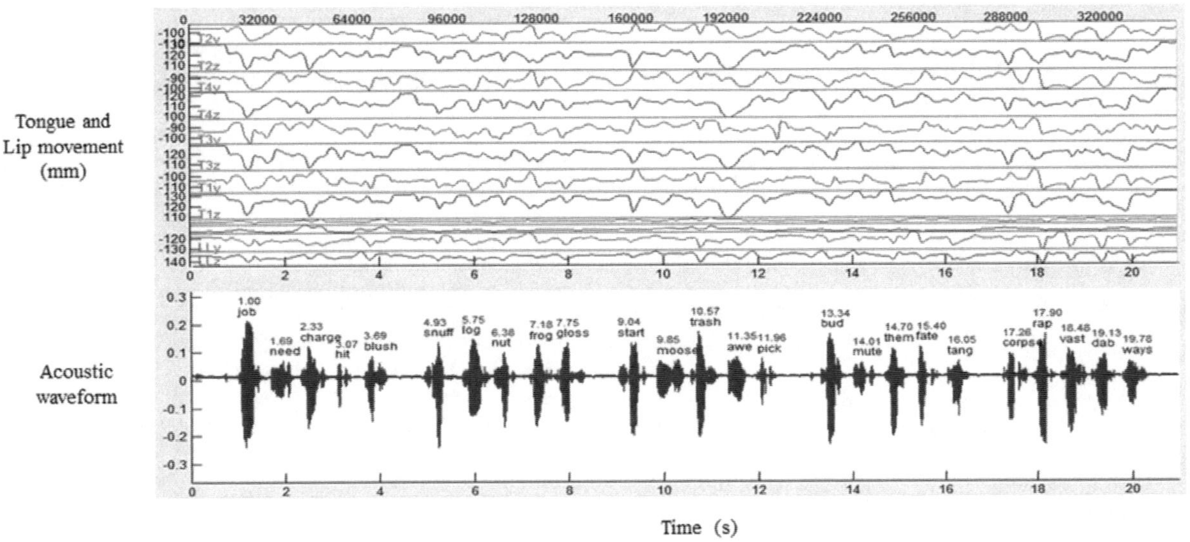

Figure 2. *Example of a sequence of tongue and lip movements (top panel) of twenty five words and synchronously recorded sounds (bottom panel). Labels of the tongue and lip sensors are described in text. The articulatory movement data was low-pass filtered (20 Hz). In the acoustic waveform panel, the numbers in blue above words are the actually occurrence time of that word.*

motion data of different words with a higher accuracy.

In this study, SAX symbolic representation was used to discretize the tongue and lip motion time series data. In SAX, each time sequence is z-normalized (mean = 0 and SD = 1), and split into w equal segments. For each segment, the mean is calculated and a symbol is assigned based on a set of breakpoints that divide the distribution space into α equiprobable regions, where α is the alphabet size. When α is given, the breakpoints (that separate the space to α regions) are definite. For the definition of breakpoints, please refer to [23]. Thus, each time subsequence is converted into a string of length w, formed by symbols from an alphabet of size α. Both the length w and the alphabet size α are pre-specified. Theoretically, an optimal combination of the two parameters – w and α – should be able to efficiently represent the variation in the sequences of any given time series data. Figure 3 illustrates how a time-series is converted to string of symbols (using $w = 5$, and $\alpha = 6$).

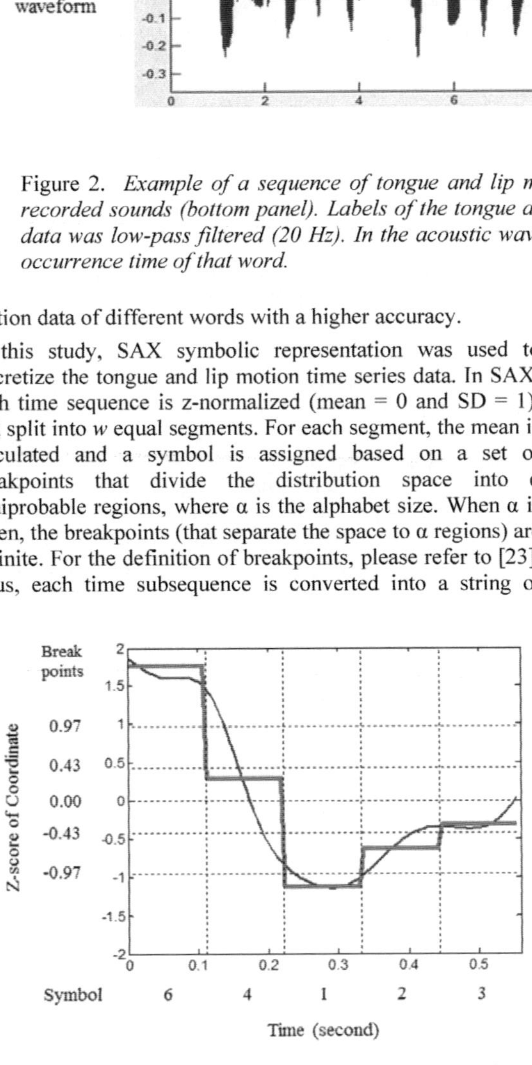

Figure 3. *Example of a symbolic representation of articulatory movement time-series data using SAX; the blue curve is the z-scored vertical coordinate of tongue tip producing a word "job"; the red segments are the discretized results. The original articulatory time-series data are finally converted into a string of symbols "64123".*

In this project, however, a word sample contains multiple time sequences, multi-dimensional coordinates (y and z) from multiple sensors. The following procedure was used to convert a data sample of original articulatory movement data to a string of symbols. The original data captured from all sensors was first time-normalized and amplitude shifted to have a mean of zero. These data arrays were then combined into a single-dimension data vector (with sequences of multi-dimension data from multiple sensors). The data vector was then converted into a single SAX vector. The reason for using concatenation of all sensor data (rather than converting on each sensor separately) to generate a single SAX vector is to preserve the relative variation in amplitude across sensors. Conversion to SAX reduced the data by a constant factor (number of data points for each sensor / w). The SAX vectors were served as input to the training and testing phases of the recognition module.

The optimal SAX parameters (w and α) needed to be determined before word recognition experiment could be conducted. Most of the words in our dataset were of the phonetic structure CVC (consonant-vowel-consonant) or CCVCC, thus, $w = 5$ was chosen as the length of symbol string for capturing the motion characteristics. A preliminary experiment was conducted to determine the best α value. Figure 4 gives the average word off-line classification accuracy across speakers for different α values (from 3 to 15), and $w = 5$. $\alpha = 6$ resulted in the highest classification accuracy, and was thus used in the online recognition experiment, which will be described in the next two sub-sections.

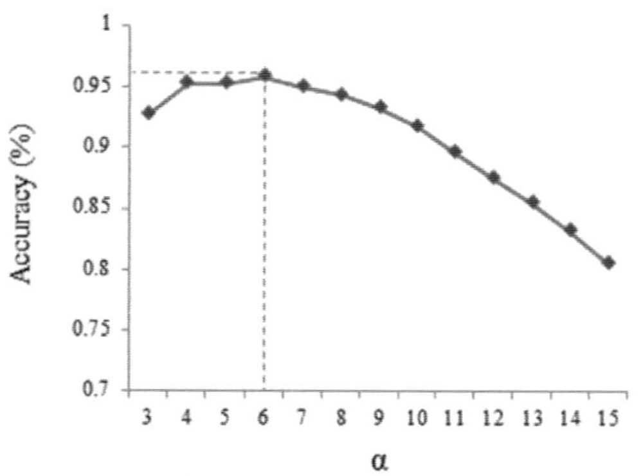

Figure 4. *Average offline classification accuracy across speakers using different* α *values.*

2.2. Model training

Support vector machine (SVM) [27], a widely used machine learning classifier, was used to recognize words in this project. SVMs are soft margin classifiers that find separating hyperplanes with maximal margins between classes in high dimensional space [28]. Model training was conducted by training a SVM using pre-segmented multi-dimension articulatory movement data from multiple sensors associated with known words. A kernel function is used to describe the distance between two data points (i.e., *u* and *v* in Equation 1). A radial basis function (RBF) was used as the kernel function in this experiment, where λ is an empirical parameter:

$$K_{RBF}(u,v) = \exp(1 - \lambda \| u - v \|) \quad (1)$$

Details of the implementation of SVM used in this experiment were described in [28].

The training component was developed off-line before the SSI was deployed in a real-time application. Therefore, the time required to build the model is not a relevant problem. Rather, the time taken for a trained model to predict words is an important measure for evaluating real-time applications. To obtain a high speed in prediction, input data was minimally processed and converted to SAX symbols before being fed into the SVM. The sampled motion paths of all articulator were time-normalized to a fixed-width (SVMs require samples to have a fixed number of values) and concatenated as one vector of attributes. The vector was then converted to SAX symbols, which formed a word sample. To understand the improvement of using SAX itself, we compared the offline classification accuracy using SAX and using the minimally processed original time-series data (used in [10]).

2.3. Online recognition

A prediction window with variable boundaries was used to traverse the sequence of tongue and lip movement data to recognize words and their locations (onset) within the window based on the probabilities returned by LIBSVM, which extends the generic SVM by providing probability estimates transformed from SVM decision values [28]. The SVM was trained offline using pre-segmented articulatory movement data. Pseudo-code of the original whole-unit recognition algorithm is provided in [9].

The major steps of the *improved* word recognition algorithm are described as below. Steps 1 to 3 are for finding word candidates; Steps 4 to 6 are to verify those candidates; Step 7 is sound playback of recognized words.

In Step 1 to 3 (Figure 5), word candidates are identified within the prediction window based on the probabilities returned from the trained SVM. At each time point *t*, all possible word lengths (within the length range of training words with a step size Δt) are considered and the maximum probability is returned as the probability for time point *t*. The word length in our list ranges from 370 to 885 ms. The offset of the probability function varied considerably across words, which made it difficult to identify a sensitive candidate threshold. Therefore, the probability associated with each word was baseline-corrected by subtracting the average probability derived from the first 600 ms of the test sequence. Candidates are identified in a prediction window (represented by its left and right boundaries, w_l and w_r) when probability values exceed a candidate threshold ($thres_c$). The candidate threshold was obtained empirically from training data. In the current experiment, a single constant threshold was used for all words (but varies for different subjects). In the future, each word will have its own threshold for each subject. In this speaking-dependent recognition experiment, the threshold varied slightly for different subjects (ranged from 0.30 to 0.40).

If no candidates are found in the current prediction window, w_r moves forward (to get more data), and the process goes back to step 1, until $w_r \leq w_l + l_{max}$, where l_{max} is the maximum word length in this data set.

In Step 4, a candidate is verified based on probability change trend. If the probabilities for that word are decreasing in a time span of half of the minimum word length, implying ongoing decreases, the candidate is confirmed; otherwise, the decision-making is delayed. This strategy is to confirm a word right after the peak probability of the word happens, while the peak probability is unknown in online recognition.

Look-back strategy. When the currently recognized word is very close to the next word, the location of w_l may be erroneously located after the actual beginning of the next

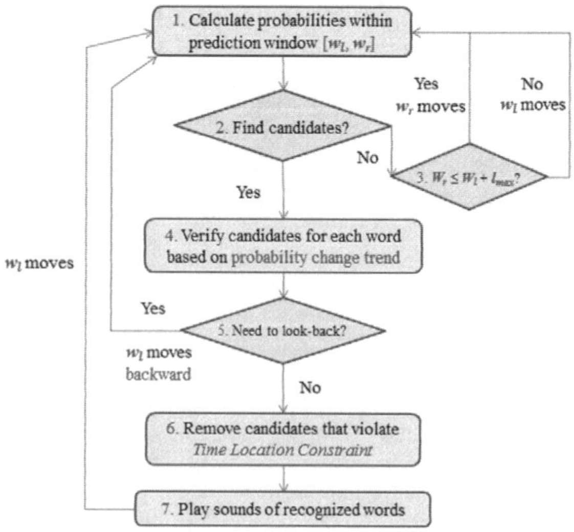

Figure 5. *Schematic of the improved word recognition algorithm from continuous articulatory movement data.*

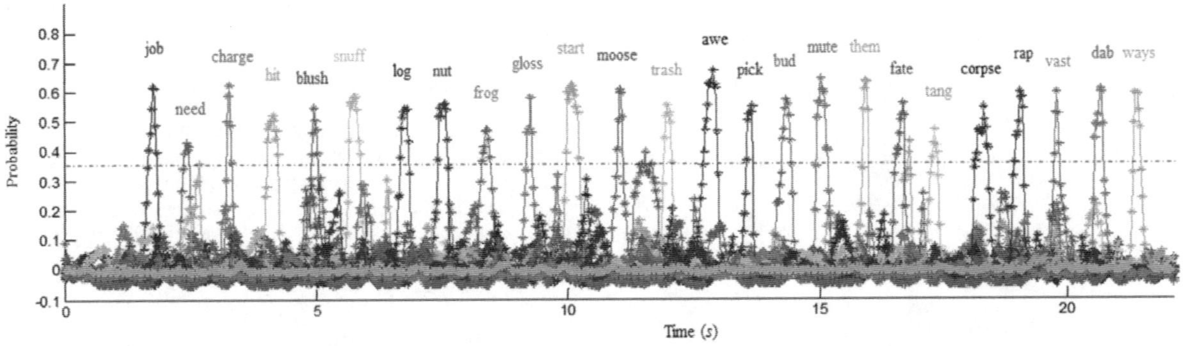

Figure 6. *Example of probabilities (baseline removed) of twenty-five words on a test sequence. The dashed horizontal line is the probability threshold for word candidates.*

word. This situation may cause error predictions, which was not considered in [10]. A look-back strategy was introduced to address this problem in this experiment (Step 5). A threshold $thres_{look\text{-}back}$ (> candidate threshold $thres_c$) is defined first. When a word candidate was found at time t_c with probability p_c, if $p_c \leq thres_{look\text{-}back}$, the window location before t_c was saved as the candidate predicted time location, which means $w_l = w_l - \Delta t$. In the current setting, w_l takes at most one step back because two or more step size back is unlikely to happen in real articulatory movement data (otherwise the two words may have overlap). Also to avoid dead loop of the execution, this procedure executes at most once in the implementation of the algorithm.

Time Location Constraint allows only one word to occur within each time span (Step 6). A time span must not be less than the minimum word length in the training data (i.e., 370 ms). If more than one word candidate is found within a time span, only the one with the highest probability is retained in the recognized word list.

In Step 7, after playing prerecorded audio samples of recognized words, the left boundary of the prediction window (w_l) moves to w_r. The whole procedure (Step 1 to 7) is repeated until the rightmost boundary of the prediction window (w_r) reaches the end of the input sequence.

2.4. Evaluation

Recognition accuracy and processing time were used to evaluate the performance of the word recognition algorithm.

A word prediction is correct if the expected word is identified within half a second of its actual occurrence time. That is, both missing values and wrongly predicted occurrence times are considered as errors. A false positive is a word that is recognized at a time point where there is actually no word. Figure 6 illustrates the word probability distribution on a selected sequence. In this example, all twenty-five words were correctly recognized.

Two measures were used to evaluate the efficiency of this algorithm: *prediction location offset* (machine-independent) and *prediction processing time*, or *latency* (machine-dependent). Prediction location offset was defined as the difference in location on a sequence between where a word is actually spoken and where it is recognized [29]. The prediction location offset provides an estimate of how much information is needed for predicting a word. Latency is the actual CPU time needed for predicting a word.

3. Data Collection

3.1. Participants and stimuli

Eleven healthy native English speakers participated in data collection. Each speaker participated in one session in which he/she repeated a sequence of twenty-five words (i.e., one of the four phonetically-balanced word lists in [30]) multiple times.

Subjects, who were blinded to the specific purpose of the research, were asked to pronounce the target words in their habitual speaking rate and loudness. Thus, the production contained co-articulation between adjacent words, although the co-articulation might not be similar to that in connected speech.

3.2. Tongue motion tracking devices

The electromagnetic articulograph (EMA) AG500 (Carstens Medizinelektronik GmbH, Bovenden, Germany) was used to collect the 3-D movement time-series data of the tongue, lips, and jaw for ten of the eleven participants. Wave Speech Research System (Northern Digital Inc., Waterloo, Canada) was used for the other participant. The two devices are based on the same electromagnetic tracking technologies [31, 32]. Both devices record tongue movements by establishing a calibrated electromagnetic field in a cube that induces electric current into tiny sensor coils that are attached to the surface of the articulators, and they have similar data collection procedure [33]. Thus, only the data collection procedure using EMA will be described in this paper (in Section 3.3). The spatial precision of motion tracking using EMA (AG500) and Wave are both approximately 0.5 mm [34, 35]. The sampling rate of the original data is 200 Hz for EMA AG500 and 100 Hz for Wave, respectively.

3.3. Procedure

Participants were seated with their head within the calibrated magnetic field. Then sensors (pellets) were attached to the surface of each articulator using dental glue (PeriAcryl Oral Tissue Adhesive). The participants were then asked to produce the word sequences at their habitually comfortable speaking rate and loudness. Before the beginning of actually data recording, a two-minute training and practice helped the participants to adapt to the wired sensors. Previous studies have shown these sensors do not significantly affect their

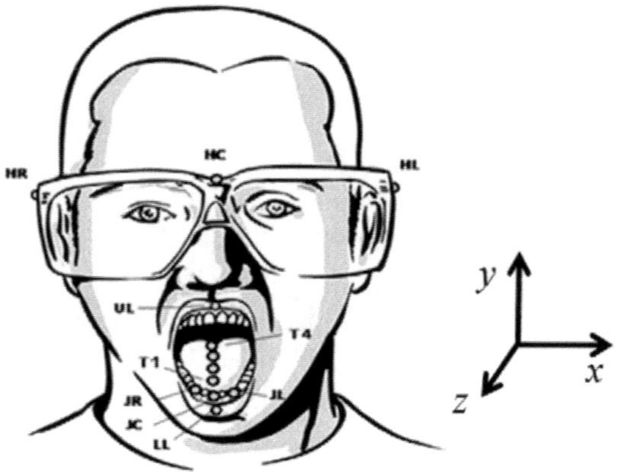

Figure 7. *Positions of sensors attached on the subject's head, tongue, lips, and jaw in data collection.*

speech output [36].

Figure 7 (picture adapted from [37]) shows the positions of 12 sensors attached to a participant's head, face, and tongue [38, 39]. Three of the sensors were attached to a pair of glasses. HC (Head Center) was on the bridge of the glasses; HL (Head Left) and HR (Head Right) were on the left and right outside edge of each lens, respectively. The movements of HC, HL, and HR sensors were used to calculate the movements of other articulators independent of the head. Four sensors - T1 (Tongue Tip), T2 (Tongue Blade), T3 (Tongue Body Front) and T4 (Tongue Body Back) - were attached approximately 10 *mm* from each other at the midline of the tongue [38, 39, 40]. Lip movements were captured by attaching two sensors to the vermilion borders of the upper (UL) and lower (LL) lips at midline.

Data from the four tongue sensors and the two lip sensors were used for this word recognition experiment. The movements of three jaw sensors, JL (Jaw Left), JR (Jaw Right), and JC (Jaw Center), were recorded for future use.

3.4. Data preprocessing

The time-series data of sensor locations recorded using EMA went through a sequence of preprocessing steps prior to analysis. First, the head movements and orientations were subtracted from the tongue and lip locations to give head-independent measurements of the analysis variables. The orientation of the derived 3-D Cartesian coordinate system is displayed in Figure 7. Second, a zero phase lag low pass filter (i.e., 20 Hz) [10, 40] was applied for removing noise. Third, all sequences were manually segmented based on synchronously recorded audio data and annotated with words using a Matlab-based software called SMASH [33].

Only y (vertical) and z (front-back) coordinates (see Figure 7) of the six tongue and lip sensors (i.e., T1, T2, T3, T4, UL, LL) were used for this word recognition experiment because the movement along the x axis (left-right) is not significant in normal speech production [38, 41]. In the future, however, x dimension will be used for predicting speech articulated by individuals with laryngectomy or other speech disorders. The center of the magnetic field is the origin (zero point) of the EMA coordinate system.

Error samples (e.g., mispronunciation or sensor falling off during the production) were rare and were excluded from the experiment. In all, 5,900 word samples (in 236 sequences) were obtained and used in this experiment.

4. Results & Discussion

Cross validation is a standard procedure to evaluate the performance of classification algorithms, where training data and test data are separate. Leave-one-out cross validation was conducted on the dataset from each subject in both training and online recognition, where one sequence (with twenty-five words) was used for testing and the rest of the sequences were used for training.

4.1. Training accuracy

The average training (offline classification) accuracy was 94.01% using minimally processed articulatory data (used in [10]) and 96.90% using SAX transformed data in the current experiment. A paired *t*-test showed that the 2.89% improvement in accuracy was statistically significant ($p < 0.001$).

The experimental results demonstrated that SAX is effective in retaining the articulatory movement patterns while reducing the local variation. SAX may have potential for a greater improvement in classification accuracy for a larger vocabulary.

4.2. Online recognition accuracy and processing time

The average online recognition accuracy across all subjects was 80.00% (SD = 10.95%). More specifically, our algorithm failed to recognize 1.96 words (SD = 0.88) and generated 3.04 (SD = 1.95) false positives in a sequence of twenty-five words. The average difference of correctly predicted word locations and their actual locations was 48 ms (SD = 9). The online word accuracy was improved up to 20%, compared with the performance of the original algorithm [10].

The average prediction location offset and latency were 150 ms (SD = 68) and 302 ms (SD = 11) for a word prediction, respectively. Latency was measured on a PC with 2.6 GHz dual-core CPU and 4GB memory.

Table 1 summarizes the performance findings of the original and current algorithm [10]. During offline classification, the only difference between the original

Table 1. *Summary of the performances of current and the original algorithm.*

Measure	The Original Algorithm	The Current Algorithm	Statistical Significance
Offline Classification Accuracy	94.01%	96.90%	$p < 0.001$
Online Missing Words	1.93	1.96	
Online False Positives	8.08	3.04	$p < 0.001$
Online Recognition Accuracy	60.00%	80.00%	$p < 0.001$

algorithm and the current algorithm was the use of SAX and only a modest improvement in recognition was achieved. For online recognition, the current algorithm implemented not only SAX, but also a look-back strategy, and speaker-dependent thresholds. This implementation improved overall accuracy by primarily reducing the number of false positives. Additional work, however, is needed to determine the individual benefit of each newly-added component (i.e., SAX, look-back strategy, and speaker-dependent thresholds).

The high accuracy showed the effectiveness of our proposed algorithm to address the challenge in word recognition caused by co-articulation. The low prediction location offset and latency demonstrated the potential of our approach for real-time applications. The low standard deviations of the accuracy and other measures across subjects indicate that our approach can be applied generally with multiple subjects.

4.3. Across-talker accuracy variation

Although speech articulation is thought to vary across talkers [21], reports on this variability have been limited because most silent speech recognition or relevant studies have involved less than five participants.

As reported previously, the standard deviation of the online word recognition accuracy across eleven subjects was 10.95%, which is not surprising. To examine across taker differences in our study, the eleven subjects were grouped into four groups according to their word recognition accuracy, < 70%, 70-80%, 80-90%, and ≥ 90%. Figure 8 shows the distribution of the subjects with regard to the word recognition accuracy. 18.18% of the subjects obtained an accuracy equivalent or greater than 90%; 36.36% obtained an accuracy greater than 80% but less than 90%; 27.27% obtained an accuracy between 70% and 80%; 18.18% obtained an accuracy less than 70%. In other words, 81.82% of the subjects obtained accuracy greater than 70%. It is notable that two of the participants had significantly lower recognition accuracies than the other nine participants, while the two participants had similarly high offline classification accuracies. Future work is required to determine the factors that account for across participant differences in recognition accuracy.

4.4. Adaptability for real online recognition

Our word recognition algorithm was designed for online recognition. In this experiment, the algorithm was tested using pre-recorded sequences of continuous articulatory movement data. That is, the algorithm was not tested in a real online recognition experimental setup. However, our experiment, to some extent, simulated online recognition. During the recognition, at time t, only data before ($t + l_{max}$) can be reached (l_{max} = 885 ms), which can be considered as an approximation of a real online recognition setting. Therefore, the word recognition algorithm used in this study should be well suited for real-time applications. Testing the algorithm in a real online recognition experimental setting is a next step.

4.5. Limitations

Although the results are very promising, there are a number of limitations of the current algorithm. First, quite a few parameters (e.g., candidate threshold, threshold for look-back, step size of the sliding window) need to be determined before

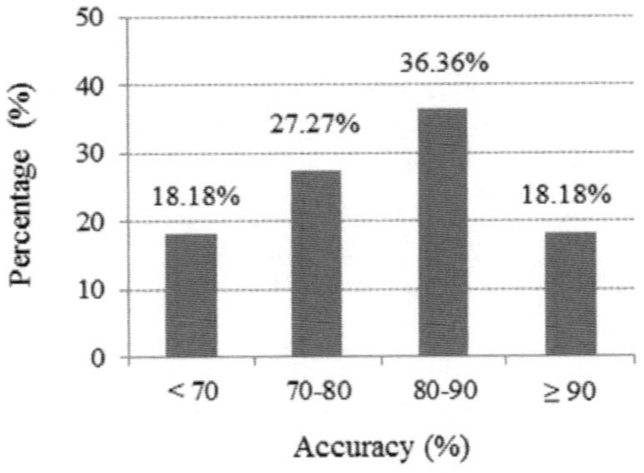

Figure 8. *Distribution of talkers regarding to online recognition accuracy.*

online prediction, although they can be manually adjusted at the beginning (for example, candidate threshold). An automatic approach for determining the optimal parameters is needed before the silent speech recognition algorithm can be used in practice.

Although the EMA and Wave are able to register 3D tongue motion accurately in real-time, and Wave is lightweight enough to be installed on a wheelchair, they may be still cumbersome in clinical use. An ideal or practical silent speech interface could be a handheld or a wearable device. Fortunately, the electromagnetic motion tracking technology is advancing rapidly. For example, devices that are wearable, and even with wireless sensors are being investigated (e.g., [11, 42, 43]). Our algorithm that uses the sensor coordinates will be seamlessly embedded with those portable systems when they are ready for clinical use.

5. Conclusions & Future Work

Experimental results showed the potential of our word recognition algorithm for building an articulation-based silent speech interface, which can be used in command-and-control systems using silent speech and may even enable voiceless patients to produce synthetic speech using their tongue and lips.

Although the current results are encouraging, future work is required to determine the optimal parameters (e.g., candidate thresholds) automatically for online recognition. In addition, the efficacy of alternative classifiers should be explored such as Hidden Markov Models [44, 45, 46], Fast DTW [47], Dynamic Bayesian Network [48], Random Forest [14]; the current design is easily adapted to classifiers that generate estimated probabilities associated with candidates.

6. Acknowledgments

This work was in part funded by Excellence in Education Fund, University of Texas at Dallas, Barkley Trust, University of Nebraska-Lincoln, and a grant awarded by the National Institutes of Health (R01 DC009890/DC/NIDCD NIH HHS/United States). We would like to thank Dr. Tom Carrell, Dr. Lori Synhorst, Dr. Mili Kuruvilla, Cynthia Didion, Rebecca Hoesing, Kate Lippincott, Kayanne Hamling, Kelly Veys, Toni Hoffer, and Taylor Boney for their contribution to subject recruitment, data collection, data management, and data processing.

7. References

[1] Bailey, B. J., Johnson, J. T., and Newlands, S. D., *Head and Neck Surgery – Otolaryngology*, Lippincot, Williams & Wilkins, Philadelphia, PA, USA, 4th Ed., 1779-1780, 2006.

[2] American Cancer Society, "Cancer Facts and Figures 2012", Atlanta, GA*: American Cancer Society*. Retrieved on December 26, 2012.

[3] Denby, B., Schultz, T., Honda, K., Hueber, T., Gilbert, J. M., and Brumberg, J. S. "Silent speech interface", *Speech Communication*, 52:270-287, 2010.

[4] Sproat, R. (Ed.), "Multilingual text-to-speech synthesis : The Bell Labs approach", in *Computational Linguistics* (1st ed.), vol. 24, p. 328. 1998: Springer.

[5] Hueber, T., Benaroya, E.-L., Chollet, G., Denby, B., Dreyfus, G., Stone, M., "Development of a silent speech interface driven by ultrasound and optical images of the tongue and lips", *Speech Communication*, 52:288–300, 2010.

[6] Denby, B., Cai, J., Roussel, P., Dreyfus, G., Crevier-Buchman, L., Pillot-Loiseau, C., Hueber, and T., Chollet, G., "Tests of an interactive, phrasebook-style post-laryngectomy voice-replacement system", *the 17th International Congress on Phonetic Sciences*, Hong Kong, China, 572-575, 2011.

[7] Jorgensen, C. and Dusan, S., "Speech interfaces based upon surface electromyography", *Speech Communication*, 52:354–366, 2010.

[8] Heaton, J. T., Robertson, M., and Griffin, C., "Development of a wireless electromyographically controlled electrolarynx voice prosthesis", *Proc. of the 33rd Annual Intl. Conf. of the IEEE Engineering in Medicine & Biology Society*, Boston, MA, 5352-5355, 2011.

[9] Wang, J., Samal, A., Green, J. R., and Rudzicz, F., "Sentence recognition from articulatory movements for silent speech interfaces", *Proc. IEEE Intl. Conf. on Acoustics, Speech, and Signal Processing*, 4985-4988, 2012.

[10] Wang, J., Samal, A., Green, J. R., and Rudzicz, F., "Whole-word recognition from articulatory movements for silent speech interfaces", *Proc. Interspeech*, Portland, OR, 1327-30, 2012.

[11] Fagan, M. J., Ell, S. R., Gilbert, J. M., Sarrazin, E., and Chapman, P. M., "Development of a (silent) speech recognition system for patients following laryngectomy", *Medical Engineering & Physics*, 30(4):419-425, 2008.

[12] King, S., Frankel, J., Livescu, K., McDermott, E., Richmond, K., and Wester, M., "Speech production knowledge in automatic speech recognition", *Journal of Acoustical Society of America*, 121(2):723-742, 2007.

[13] Livescu, K., Cetin, O., Hasegawa-Johnson, M., King, S., Bartels, C., Borges, N., Kantor, Lal, P., Yung, L., Bezman, A., Dawson-Haggerty, S., Woods, B., "Articulatory feature-based methods for acoustic and audio-visual speech recognition: Summary from the 2006 JHU Summer Workshop", *Proc. Intl. Conf. on Acoustics, Speech, and Signal Processing*, 621-624, 2007.

[14] Rudzicz, F., "Articulatory knowledge in the recognition of dysarthric speech", *IEEE Trans. on Audio, Speech, and Language Processing*, 19(4):947-960, 2011.

[15] Uraga, E. and Hain, T., "Automatic speech recognition experiments with articulatory data", *Proc. Inerspeech*, 353-356, 2006.

[16] Sharma H. V., Hasegawa-Johnson, M., Gunderson, J., and Perlman A., "Universal access: Speech recognition for talkers with spastic dysarthria", *Proc. Interspeech*, 1451-1454, 2009.

[17] Kantor, A., "Pronunciation modeling for large vocabulary speech recognition", PhD Dissertation, Dept. Comput. Sci., University of Illinois, Urbana, 2011.

[18] Akdemir, E., and Ciloglu, T., "The use of articulator motion information in automatic speech segmentation", *Speech Communication*, 50(7):594-604, 2008.

[19] Gilbert, J. M., Rybchenko, S. I., Hofe, R., Ell, S. R., Fagan, M. J., Moore, R.K., and Green, P., "Isolated word recognition of silent speech using magnetic implants and sensors", *Medical Engineering & Physics*, 32(10):1189-1197, 2011.

[20] Green, J.R., Beukelman, D.R., and Ball, L. J., "Algorithmic estimation of pauses in extended speech samples", *Journal of Medical Speech-Language Pathology*, 12, 149-154, 2004.

[21] Kent, R. D., Adams, S. G., and Tuner, G. S. *Models of speech production*. Lass, N. J. : Principles of experimental Phonetics. Mosby, 1996.

[22] Kent, R. D., and Minifie, F. D., "Coarticulation in recent speech production models", *Journal of Phonetics*, 5(2):115–133, 1977.

[23] Lin, J., Keogh, E., Lonardi, S., and Chiu, B. "A symbolic representation of time series, with implications for streaming algorithms", *Proc. of the 8th ACM SIGMOD Workshop on Research Issues in Data Mining and Knowledge Discovery*. San Diego, CA, 2003.

[24] Mueen, A., Keogh, E., "Online discovery and maintenance of time series motifs", *Proc. 16th ACM SIGKDD Intl. Conf. on Knowledge Discovery and Data Mining*, Washington, DC, 1089-98, 2010.

[25] Wei, L., Kumar, N., Lolla, V. N., Keogh, E., Lonardi, S., and Ratanamahatana, C. A., "Assumption-free anomaly detection in time series", *Proc. 17th International Scientific and Statistical Database Management Conference*, Santa Barbara, CA, 237-240, 2005.

[26] Lin, J., Keogh, E., and Lonard, S. "Visualizing and discovering non-trivial patterns in large time series databases", *Information Visualization*, 4(2):61-82, 2005.

[27] Boser, B., Guyon, I., Vapnik, V., "A training algorithm for optimal margin classifiers", *Conf. on Learning Theory (COLT)*, 144–152, 1992.

[28] Chang, C. -C., and Lin. C. -J., "LIBSVM: a library for support vector machines", *ACM Trans. on Intelligent Systems and Technology*, 2(27):1-27, 2011.

[29] Wang, J., "Silent speech recognition from articulatory motion", Ph.D. dissertation, Dept. Comput. Sci., Univ. of Nebraska-Lincoln, 2011.

[30] Shutts, R. E., Burke, K. S., and Creston, J. E., "Derivation of twenty-five-word PB Lists", *Journal of Speech Hearing Disorders*, 29:442-447, 1964.

[31] Perkell, J. S., Cohen, M. H., Svirsky, M. A., Matthies, M. L., Garabieta, I., and Jackson, M. T. T., "Electromagnetic midsagittal articulometer systems for transducing speech articulatory movements", *Journal of Acoustical Society of America*, 92(6):3078–3096, 1992.

[32] Hoole, P., and Zierdt, A., "Five-dimensional articulography", in *Speech Motor Control: New Developments in Basic and Applied Research*, B. Maassen and P. van Lieshout, Eds. Oxford University Press, ch. 20, pp. 331–349, 2010.

[33] Green, J. R., Wang, J., and Wilson, D. L., "SMASH: A tool for articulatory data processing and analysis", *Proc. Interspeech*, 2013 (In press).

[34] Yunusova, Y., Green, J. R., and Mefferd, A., "Accuracy assessment for AG500 electromagnetic articulograph", *Journal of Speech, Language, and Hearing Research*, 52(2):547-555, 2009.

[35] Berry, J. "Accuracy of the NDI wave speech research system", *Journal of Speech, Language, and Hearing Research*, 54:1295-1301, 2011.

[36] Katz, W., Bharadwaj, S., Rush, M., and Stettler, M., "Influences of EMA receiver coils on speech production by normal and aphasic/apraxic talkers", *Journal of Speech, Language, and Hearing Research*, 49:645-659, 2006.

[37] Wang, J., Green, J. R., & Samal, A., "Individual articulator's contribution to phoneme production", *Proc. IEEE Intl. Conf. on Acoustics, Speech, and Signal Processing*, Vancouver, Canada, 7795-89, 2013.

[38] Wang, J., Green, J. R., Samal, A. and Yunusova, Y. "Articulatory distinctiveness of vowels and consonants: A data-driven approach", *Journal of Speech, Language, and Hearing Research*, 2013 (In press).

[39] Wang, J., Green, J. R., Samal, A., and Marx, D. B. "Quantifying articulatory distinctiveness of vowels", *Proc. Interspeech*, Florence, Italy, 277-280, 2011.

[40] Green, J. R. and Wang, Y., "Tongue-surface movement patterns during speech and swallowing", *Journal of Acoustical Society of America*, 113:2820-2833, 2003.

[41] Westbury, J. *X-ray microbeam speech production database user's handbook*. University of Wisconsin, 1994.

[42] Chen, W.-H., Loke, W.-F., Thompson, G., and Jung, B., "A 0.5V, 440uW frequency synthesizer for implantable medical devices", *IEEE Journal of Solid-State Circuits*, 47:1896-1907, 2012.

[43] Park, H, Kiani, M., Lee, H. M., Kim, J., Block, J., Gosselin, B., and Ghovanloo, M., "A wireless magnetoresistive sensing system for an intraoral tongue-computer interface", *IEEE Transactions on Biomedical Circuits and Systems*, 6(6):571-585, 2012.

[44] Cai, J., Denby, B., Roussel, P., Dreyfus, G., and Crevier-Buchman, L., "Recognition and real time performances of a lightweight ultrasound based silent speech interface employing a language model", *Proc. Interspeech*, Florence, Italy, 1005-08, 2011.

[45] Heracleous, P., and Hagita, N., "Automatic recognition of speech without any audio information", *Proc. IEEE Intl. Conf. on Acoustics, Speech, and Signal Processing*, pp. 2392-2395, 2011.

[46] Hofe, R., Ell, S. R., Fagan, M. J., Gilbert, J. M., Green, P. D., Moore, R. K., and Rybchenko, S. I., "Small-vocabulary speech recognition using a silent speech interface based on magnetic sensing", *Speech Communication*, 55(1):22-32, 2013.

[47] Salvador, S., and Chan, P., "Toward accurate dynamic time warping in linear time and space", *Intelligent Data Analysis*, 11(5):561-580, 2007.

[48] Frankel, J., Wester, M., and King, S., "Articulatory feature recognition using dynamic bayesian networks", *Computer Speech Language*, 21(4):620-640, 2006.

Robust Feature Extraction to Utterance Fluctuation of Articulation Disorders Based on Random Projection

Toshiya Yoshioka, Tetsuya Takiguchi, Yasuo Ariki

Graduate School of System Informatics, Kobe University, Japan

yoshioka@me.cs.scitec.kobe-u.ac.jp, takigu@kobe-u.ac.jp, ariki@kobe-u.ac.jp

Abstract

We investigated the speech recognition of a person with an articulation disorder resulting from the athetoid type of cerebral palsy. The articulation of the first speech tends to become unstable due to strain on speech-related muscles, and that causes degradation of speech recognition. In this paper, we introduce a robust feature extraction method based on PCA (Principal Component Analysis) and RP (Random Projection) for dysarthric speech recognition. PCA-based feature extraction performs reducing the influence of the unstable speaking style caused by the athetoid symptoms. Moreover, we investigate the feasibility of random projection for feature transformation in order to gain more performance in dysarthric speech recognition task. Its effectiveness is confirmed by word recognition experiments.

Index Terms: articulation disorders, speech recognition, PCA, random projection, ROVER

1. Introduction

Recently, the importance of information technology in the welfare-related fields has increased. For example, sign language recognition using image recognition technology [1][2][3], text-reading systems from natural scene images [4][5][6], and the design of wearable speech synthesizers for voice disorders [7] [8] have been studied.

There are 34,000 people with speech impediments associated with articulation disorders in Japan alone, and it is hoped that speech recognition systems will one day be able to recognize their voices. One of the causes of speech impediments is cerebral palsy. Cerebral palsy results from damage to the central nervous system, and the damage causes movement disorders. Three general times are given for the onset of the disorder: before birth, at the time of delivery, and after birth. Cerebral palsy is classified as follows: 1) spastic type 2) athetoid type 3) ataxic type 4) atonic type 5) rigid type, and a mixture of types [9].

In this paper, we focused on a person with an articulation disorder resulting from the athetoid type of cerebral palsy. Athetoid symptoms develop in about 10-15% of cerebral palsy sufferers. In the case of a person with this type of articulation disorder, the first movements are sometimes more unstable than usual. That means, in the case of speaking-related movements, the first utterance is often unstable or unclear due to the athetoid symptoms, and that causes degradation of speech recognition. Therefore, we recorded speech data for a person with an articulation disorder who uttered each of the words five times, and investigated the influence of the unstable speaking style caused by the athetoid symptoms.

The goal of front-end speech processing in ASR is to obtain a projection of the speech signal to a compact parameter space where the information related to speech content can be extracted. In current speech recognition technology, MFCC (Mel-Frequency Cepstrum Coefficient) is being widely used. The feature is uniquely derived from the mel-scale filter-bank output by DCT (Discrete Cosine Transform). The low-order MFCCs account for the slowly changing spectral envelope, while the high-order ones describe the fast variations of the spectrum. Therefore, a large number of MFCCs is not used for speech recognition because we are only interested in the spectral envelope, not in the fine structure. In [10], PCA-based feature extraction has been studied. Also, [11] proposed a robust feature extraction method based on PCA instead of DCT in a dysarthric speech recognition task, where the main stable utterance element is projected onto low-order features while fluctuation elements of speech style are projected onto high-order ones. Therefore, the PCA-based filter will be able to extract stable utterance features only (Fig. 1). The proposed method improved the recognition accuracy, but the performance was not sufficient when compared to that of persons with no disability.

Random projection has been suggested as a means of space mapping, where a projection matrix is composed of the columns defined by the random values chosen from a probability distribution. In addition, the Euclidean distance of any two points is approximately preserved through the projection. Therefore, random projection has also been suggested as a means of dimensionality reduction [12]. In contrast to conventional techniques such as PCA, which find a subspace by optimizing certain criteria, random projection does not use such criteria; therefore, it is data independent. Moreover, it represents a computationally simple and efficient method that preserves the structure of the data without introducing significant distortion [13]. Goel et al [13] have reported that random projection has been applied to various types of problems, including information retrieval (e.g., [14]), image processing (e.g., [15][16]), machine learning (e.g., [17][18][19]), and so on. Although it is based on a simple idea, random projection has demonstrated good performance in a number of applications, yielding results comparable to conventional dimensionality reduction techniques, such as PCA.

The main contributions of this paper are the following. Firstly, we introduce a PCA-based feature extraction approach to extract stable utterance features only. Secondly, PCA-based features are projected using various random matrices. Then, we use the same number of dimensions for the projected space as that of the original space. There may be some possibility of finding a random matrix that gives better speech recognition accuracy among random matrices, since we are able to produce various RP-based features (using various random matrices). Therefore, a vote-based combination method is introduced in order to obtain an optimal result from many (infinite) random matrices, where ROVER combination [20] is applied to the results from the ASR systems created from each RP-based feature.

The rest of this paper is organized as follows. Section 2 describes a PCA-based feature extraction method. In Section 3, the proposed feature projection method using random orthogonal matrices, and, a vote-based combination method are explained. Results and discussion for the experiments on a dysarthric speech recognition task are given in Section 4. Section 5, concludes the paper with a summary of our proposed method, contribution, and future work.

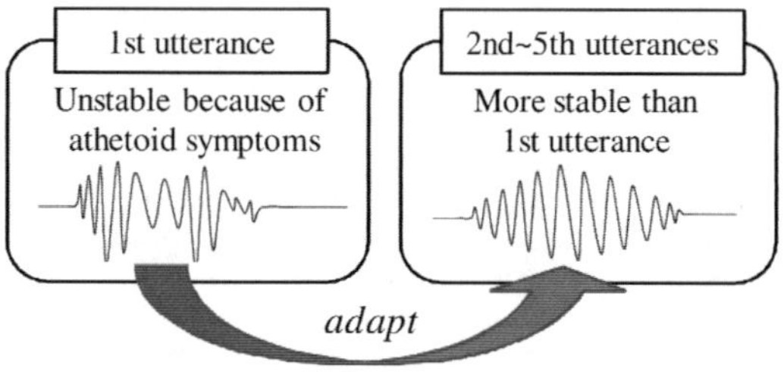

Figure 1: Corrective strategy for articulation disorders.

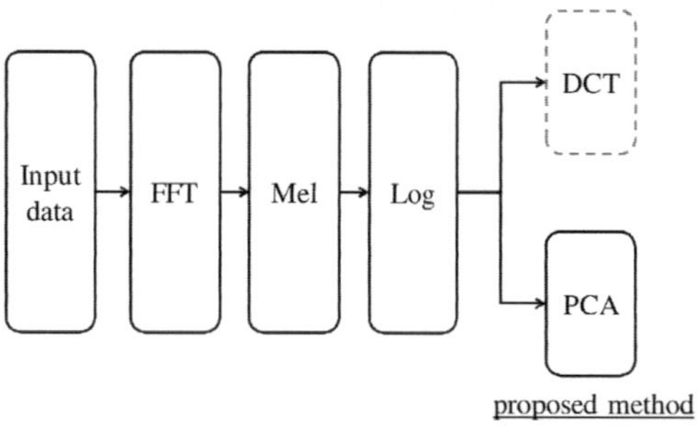

Figure 2: Feature extraction using PCA.

2. Feature extraction using PCA

Robust feature extraction was proposed based on PCA with the more stable utterance data instead of DCT (Fig. 2), where PCA is applied to the mel-scale filter bank output [11].

In this paper, we computed the filter (eigenvector matrix) using the more stable utterance. Then we applied the filtering operation to the first utterance (unstably articulated utterance) in the log-spectral domain. Given the frame of short-time analysis t and frequency ω, we represent the first utterance $\mathbf{Y}_t(\omega)$ as the multiplication of the stable speech $\mathbf{X}_t(\omega)$ and the fluctuation element of speaking style $\mathbf{H}(\omega)$ in the linear-spectral domain:

$$\mathbf{Y}_t(\omega) = \mathbf{X}_t(\omega) \cdot \mathbf{H}(\omega) \quad (1)$$

The multiplication can be converted to addition in the log-spectral domain as follows:

$$\log \mathbf{Y}_t(\omega) = \log \mathbf{X}_t(\omega) + \log \mathbf{H}(\omega) \quad (2)$$

Next, we use the following filtering based on PCA in order to extract the feature of stable speech only:

$$\hat{\mathbf{X}} = \mathbf{V}^T \mathbf{Y}_{log} \quad (3)$$

For the filter (eigenvector matrix), $\mathbf{V}$ is derived by the eigenvalue decomposition of the centered covariance matrix of a stable speech data set, in which the filter consists of the eigenvectors corresponding to the D dominant eigenvalues.

3. Proposed method

3.1. RP-based feature projection method

This section presents a feature projection method using random orthogonal matrices. The main idea of random projection arises from the Johnson-Lindenstrauss lemma [21]; namely, if original data are projected onto a randomly selected subspace using a random matrix, then the distances between the data are approximately preserved.

Random projection is a simple yet powerful technique, and it has another benefit. Dasgupta [17] has reported that even if distributions of original data are highly skewed (have ellipsoidal contours of high eccentricity); their transformed counterparts will be more spherical.

First, we choose an n-dimensional random vector, $\mathbf{p}$, and let $\mathbf{P}^{(l)}$ be the l-th $n \times d$ matrix whose columns are vectors, $\mathbf{p}_1^{(l)}$, $\mathbf{p}_2^{(l)}$, ..., $\mathbf{p}_d^{(l)}$. Then, an original n-dimensional vector, $\mathbf{x}$, is projected onto a d-dimensional subspace using the l-th random matrix, $\mathbf{P}^{(l)}$, where we compute a d-dimensional vector, $\mathbf{x}'$, whose coordinates are the inner products $\mathbf{x}'_1 = \mathbf{p}_1^{(l)} \cdot \mathbf{x}$, ..., $\mathbf{x}'_d = \mathbf{p}_d^{(l)} \cdot \mathbf{x}$.

$$\mathbf{x}' = \mathbf{P}^{(l)^T} \mathbf{x} \quad (4)$$

In this paper, we investigate the feasibility of random projection for speech feature transformation. As described above, a random projection from n dimensions to d $(= n)$ dimensions is represented by an $n \times d$ matrix, $\mathbf{P}$. It has been shown that if the random matrix $\mathbf{P}$ is chosen from the standard normal distribution (with mean 0 and variance 1, referred to as $N(0, 1)$), then the projection preserves the structure of the data [21]. In this paper, we use $N(0, 1)$ for the distribution of the coordinates. The random matrix, $\mathbf{P}$, can be calculated using the following algorithm [13][17].

- Choose each entry of the matrix from an independent and identically distributed (i.i.d.) $N(0, 1)$ value.
- Make the orthogonal matrix using the Gram-Schmidt algorithm, and then normalize it to unit length.

Orthogonality is effective for feature extraction because the HMMs used in speech recognition experiments consist of diagonal covariance matrices. Fig. 3 shows examples of random matrices from $N(0, 1)$.

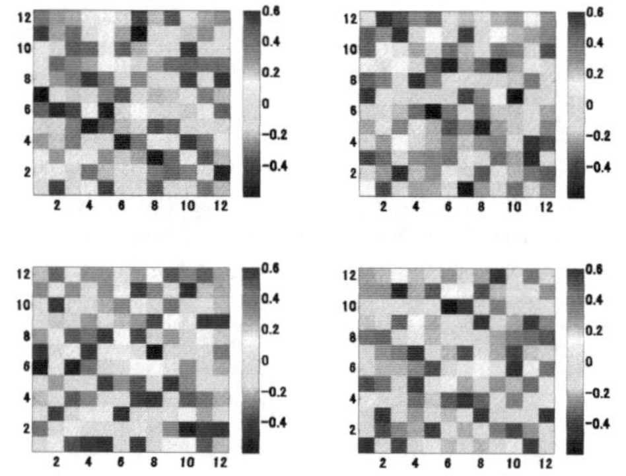

Figure 3: Examples of random matrices 12 dim (12 × 12).

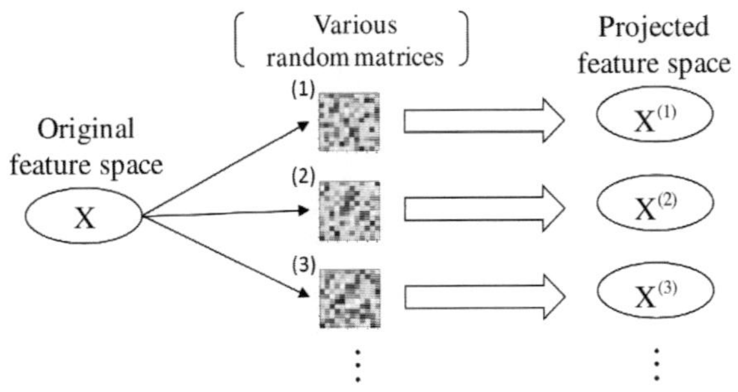

Figure 4: Random projection on the feature domain. An original feature is transformed to various features using various random matrices. (Eq. 4)

3.2. Vote-based combination

As mentioned in the previous section, we can make many (infinite) random matrices from $N(0, 1)$ (Fig. 4). Since there may be some possibility of finding a random matrix that gives better performance, we will have to select the optimal matrix or the optimal recognition result from them. To obtain the optimal result, a majority vote-based combination is introduced in this paper, where ROVER combination is applied to the results from the ASR systems created from each RP-based feature.

Fig. 5 shows an overview of the vote-based combination. First, random matrices, $\mathbf{P}^{(l)}$ (l = 1, ..., L), are chosen from the standard normal distribution, with mean 0 and variance 1. Speech features are projected using each random matrix. An acoustic model corresponding to each random matrix is also trained. For the test utterance, using each acoustic model, an ASR system outputs the best scoring word by itself. To obtain an optimal result from among all the results for random projection, voting is performed by counting the number of occurrences of the best word for each RP-based feature.

For example, in the case of L = 20, 20 kinds of new feature vectors are calculated using 20 kinds of random matrices. Then, we train the 20 kinds of acoustic models using 20 kinds of new feature vectors. In the test process, 20 kinds of recognition results are obtained using 20 kinds of acoustic models. To obtain a single hypothesis from among 20 kinds of recognition results, voting is performed.

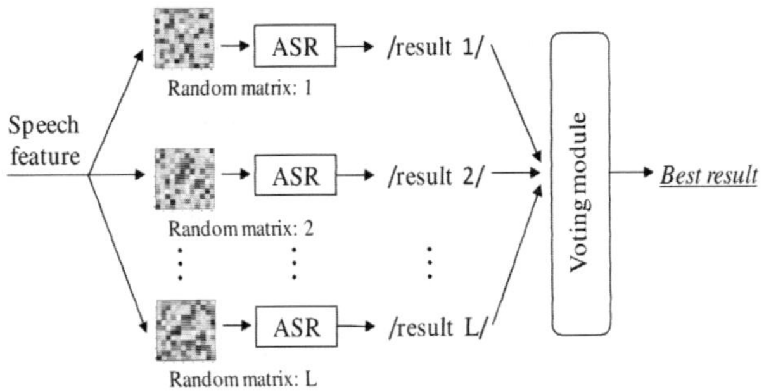

Figure 5: Overview of the vote-based combination.

4. Evaluation

4.1. Experimental conditions

The proposed method was evaluated on a word recognition task for one male with an articulation disorder. For the conducted experiments, we recorded 210 words included in the ATR Japanese speech database. Each of the 210 words was repeated five times (Fig. 6). The speech signal was sampled at 16 kHz and windowed with a 25-msec Hamming window every 10 msec.

It was difficult to recognize an utterance of an articulation disorder using an acoustic model trained by utterances of physically unimpaired persons. Therefore, in this paper, we trained the acoustic model using the utterances of a person with an articulation disorder. When we recognized the 1st utterance, the 2nd through 5th utterances were used for training. We iterated this process for each utterance. The acoustic models consist of a HMM set with 54 context-independent phonemes and 8 mixture components for each state. Each HMM has three states and three self-loops.

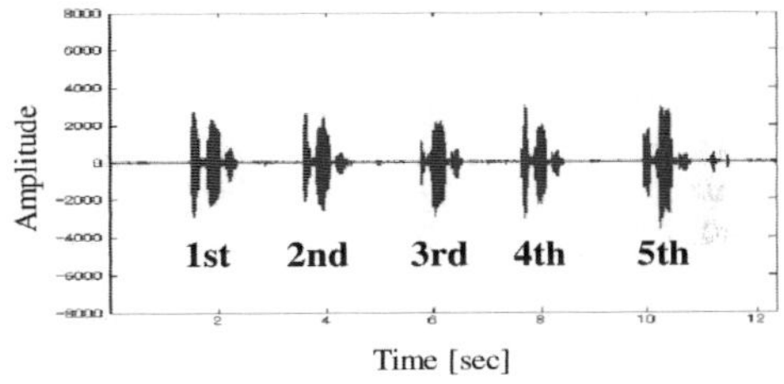

Figure 6: Example of recorded speech data.

4.2. Experiment 1

In Experiment1, recognition results were obtained for each utterance of a person with an articulation disorder using speaker-dependent model.

The system was trained using 24-dimensional feature vectors consisting of 12-dimensional MFCC parameters, along with their delta parameters.

Table 1: Recognition results [%] for each utterance in Experiment 1

1st	2nd	3rd	4th	5th
75.7	86.7	92.9	90.5	88.6

Table 1 shows the results obtained in Experiment 1. In a person with an articulation disorder, the recognition rate for the 1st utterance was 75.7%. As can be seen in Table 1, it was significantly lower than other utterances. It is considered that the speaker experiences a more strained state during the first utterance compared to subsequent utterances because the first utterance is the first intentional movement. Therefore, athetoid symptoms occur and articulation becomes difficult. It is believed that this difficulty causes fluctuations in speaking style and degradation of the recognition rates.

4.3. Experiment 2

The aim of Experiment 2 is to evaluate the improvement introduced by the use of a PCA-based feature extraction method. For Experiment 2, PCA was applied to 24 mel-scale filter bank output. Then, we computed the filter $\mathbf{V}$ using the 2nd through 5th utterances (the more stable utterances). We experimented on the number of principal components, using 11, 13, 15, 17, and 19 dimensions. Then, the delta coefficients were also computed. Comparison results between the baseline method (MFCC) and the PCA-based feature extraction method for the 1st utterance were shown in Fig. 7.

As can be seen in Fig. 7, the use of PCA instead of DCT improved the recognition rate for the 1st utterance from 76.7% (15-dimensional MFCC and their delta) to 80.5% (17-principal components and their delta). This results gives the evidence of the improvement introduced by the use of PCA instead of DCT when dealing with the 1st utterance. In addition, the recognition rates of the other utterances were equal to those of MFCC.

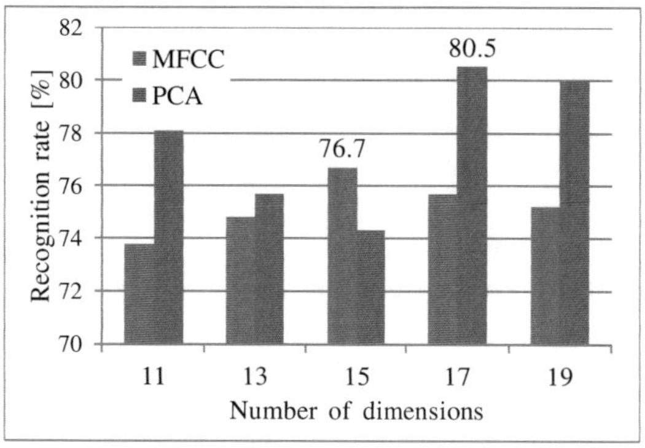

Figure 7: Comparison of DCT and PCA for the 1st utterance in Experiment 2.

4.4. Experiment 3

In order to test the effectiveness of a RP-based feature projection method, in Experiment 3, two RP-based features were evaluated. Each feature description was found below:

1. PCA[17]→RP[17] + ΔRP[17]:
   Random projection is applied to PCA-based features at the t-th frame, $\mathbf{x}(t) \in \mathrm{R}^{17}$, and the new feature, $\mathbf{y}(t) \in \mathrm{R}^{17}$, is obtained.

$$\mathbf{y}(t) = \mathbf{P}^{(l)^T}\mathbf{x}(t) \qquad (5)$$

   Then, the new feature also has the delta parameter of projected feature, $\mathbf{y}(t)$. The final system feature dimensionality is 34.

2. PCA[17]→RP[17] + ΔPCA[17]:
   Random projection is applied to PCA-based features, $\mathbf{x}(t) \in \mathrm{R}^{17}$, and the new feature, $\mathbf{y}(t) \in \mathrm{R}^{17}$, is obtained. Then, the new feature also has the delta coefficient of original feature, $\mathbf{x}(t)$. The final system feature dimensionality is 34.

We investigated the performance of random projections for various random matrices (l = 20, 40, 60, 80, and 100) sampled from $N(0, 1)$. Tables 2 and 3 show the recognition rate versus the number of random matrices for each feature. The results of "RP w/o combination" show the maximums, means, and minimums obtained from each random projection without ROVER-based combination.

Table 2: Word recognition rate (%) for the 1st utterances using feature 1 in various random matrices. (The recognition rate of PCA-based features is 80.5%)

Number of random matrices	RP combination based on ROVER	RP w/o combination		
		Max.	Mean	Min.
20	79.5%	80.5%	76.5 %	72.9%
40	80.0%	81.0%	76.8%	72.9%
60	80.5%	**83.3%**	76.8%	72.9%
80	80.5%	**83.3%**	76.8%	72.4%
100	80.5%	**83.3%**	76.8%	72.4%

Table 3: Word recognition rate (%) for the 1st utterances using feature 2 in various random matrices. (The recognition rate of PCA-based features is 80.5%)

Number of random matrices	RP combination based on ROVER	RP w/o combination		
		Max.	Mean	Min.
20	83.3%	81.9%	79.5%	76.7%
40	**85.2%**	83.8%	79.6%	71.9%
60	**85.2%**	83.8%	79.5%	71.9%
80	84.8%	83.8%	79.5%	71.9%
100	84.8%	83.8%	79.5%	71.9%

Table 2 shows the performance results obtained using feature 1 in Experiment 3. As can be seen in Table 2, the maximums of random projections without ROVER-based combination for 60, 80, and 100 random matrices were higher than the recognition rate of PCA-based features. However, even if ROVER-based combination is applied, we could not show further performance increases in our experiments using feature 1.

The recognition results obtained using feature 2 are shown in Table 3. As can be seen in Table 3, the results for feature 2 indicated that the vote-based random-projection combination improved the recognition rate from 80.5% (17-dimentional PCA and their delta) to 85.2% using the combination of 40 or 60 random matrices, although the means of random projections without combination for some random matrices was lower than the recognition rate of the original features.

We can see that the combination of random projection and ROVER outperforms both the baseline method (MFCCs) and the PCA-based feature extraction method. This result gives the evidence of the improvement introduced by the feature transformation based on random projection and the use of ROVER to obtain an optimal result. One of the possible reasons the random projection improves the recognition rates may be that if distributions of original data are skewed (have ellipsoidal contours of high eccentricity), their transformed counterparts will become more spherical [17]. However, there were 'bad' projections that cause degradation of speech recognition accuracy compared with the recognition of original features. Therefore, more research will be needed to investigate the effectiveness of the random projection methid for speech features.

5. Conclusions

As a result of this work, a method for recognizing dysarthric speech using a robust PCA-based feature extraction and transformation based on random projection has been developed. In the feature extraction, PCA is applied to the mel-scale filter bank output. It can be expected that PCA will project the main stable utterance elements onto low-order features, while elements associated with fluctuations in speaking style will be projected onto high-order features. Moreover, the proposed method transforms the PCA-based features using various random matrices. It also introduces a vote-based combination method to obtain an optimal result from the ASR systems created from each RP-based feature. Word recognition experiments were conducted to evaluate the proposed method for one male with an articulation disorder. The results of the experments showed that a method based on random projection outperformed both a baseline method (using MFCC) and a PCA-based feature extraction method.

As future work, we will continue to investigate how to select the optimal basis vector from a random matrix.

6. References

[1] T. Starner, J. Weaver, and A. Pentland, "Real-Time American Sign Language Recognition Using Desk and Wearable Computer Based Video," IEEE Transactions on Pattern Analysis and Machine Intelligence, 20(12), pp. 1371–1375, 1998.

[2] J. Lin, W. Ying, and T.S. Huang, "Capturing human hand motion in image sequences," IEEE Workshop on Motion and Video Computing, pp. 99–104, 2002.

[3] G. Fang, W. Gao, and D. Zhao, "Large vocabulary sign language recognition based on hierarchical decision trees," International Conference on Multimodal Interaction, pp. 125–131, 2003.

[4] V. Wu, R. Manmatha, and E. M. Riseman, "Textfinder: an automatic system to detect and recognize text images," IEEE Transactions on Pattern Analysis and Machine Inteligence, 21(11), pp. 1224–1229, 1999.

[5] M.K. Bashar, T. Matsumoto, Y. Takeuchi, H. Kudo, and N. Ohnishi, "Unsupervised Texture Segmentation via Wavelet-based Locally Orderless Images (WLOIs) and SOM," International Conference on Computer Graphics and Imaging, pp. 279–284, 2003.

[6] N. Ezaki, M. Bulacu, and L. Schomaker, "Text Detection from Natural Scene Images: Towards a System for Visually Impaired Persons," International Conference on Pattern Recognition, pp. 683–686, 2004.

[7] T. Ohsuga, Y. Horiuchi, and A. Ichikawa, "Estimating Syntactic Structure from Prosody in Japanese Speech," IEICE Transactions on Information and Systems, 86(3), pp. 558–564, 2003.

[8] K. Nakamura, T. Toda, H. Saruwatari, and K. Shikano, "Speaking Aid System for Total Laryngectomees Using Voice Conversion of Body Transmitted Artificial Speech," Annual Conference of the International Speech Communication Association, pp. 1395–1398, 2006.

[9] S.T. Canale, and W.C. Campbell, "Campbell's Operative Orthopaedics," Mosby-Year Book, 2002.

[10] S-M. Lee, S-H. Fang, J-W. Hung, and L-S. Lee, "Improved MFCC Feature Extraction by PCA-Optimized Filter Bank for Speech Recognition," IEEE Workshop on Automatic Speech Recognition and Understanding, pp. 49–52, 2001.

[11] H. Matsumasa, T. Takiguchi, Y. Ariki, I. LI, and T. Nakabayashi, "PCA-Based Feature Extraction for Fluctuation in Speaking Style of Articulation Disorders," Annual Conference of the International Speech Communication Association, pp. 1150–1153, 2007.

[12] Ella Bingham, and Heikki Mannila, "Random projection in dimensionality reduction: applications to image and text data," Knowledge Discovery and Data Mining, pp. 245–250, 2001.

[13] N. Goel, G. Bebis, and A. Nefian, "Face recognition experiments with random projection," Storage and Retrieval for Image and Video Databases, pp. 426–437, 2005.

[14] P. Thaper, S. Guha, and N. Koudas, "Dynamic multidimensional histograms," International Conference on Management of Data, pp. 428–439, 2002.

[15] L. Liu, P. Fieguth, G. Kuang, and H. Zha, "Sorted Random Projections for robust texture classification," IEEE International Conference on Computer Vision, pp. 391–398, 2011.

[16] H. T. Ho, and R. Chellappa, "Automatic head pose estimation using randomly projected dense SIFT descriptors," IEEE International Conference on Image Processing, pp. 153–156, 2012.

[17] S. Dasgupta, "Experiments with random projection," Uncertainty in Artificial Intelligence, pp. 143–151, 2000.

[18] X.Z. Fern, and C.E. Brodley, "Random projection for high dimensional data clustering: A cluster ensemble approach," International Conference on Machine Learning, pp. 186–193, 2003.

[19] S. Lee, and A. Nedic, "Distributed Random Projection Algo-rithm for Convex Optimization," IEEE Journal of Selected Topics in Signal Processing, 7(2), pp. 221–229, 2013.

[20] J.G. Fiscus, "A post-processing system to yield reduced word error rates: Recogniser output voting error reduction (rover)," IEEE Workshop on Automatic Speech Recognition and Understanding, pp. 347–352, 1997.

[21] R.I. Arriaga, and S. Vempala, "An algorithmic theory of learning: robust concepts and random projection," IEEE Symposium on Foundations of Computer Science, pp. 616–623, 1999.

Author index